THE DIPLOMATS

THE DIPLOMATS
The Foreign Office Today

Geoffrey Moorhouse

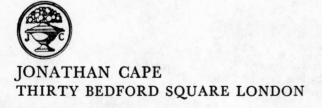

JONATHAN CAPE
THIRTY BEDFORD SQUARE LONDON

First published 1977
© 1977 By Geoffrey Moorhouse

Jonathan Cape Ltd
30 Bedford Square, London WC1

British Library Cataloguing in Publication Data

Moorhouse, Geoffrey
  The diplomats.
  Bibl.–Index.
  ISBN 0–224–01323–8
  1. Title
  341.3'3 DA592
  Great Britain – Diplomatic and consular
service

Printed in Great Britain by The Anchor Press Ltd
and bound by Wm Brendon & Son Ltd
both of Tiptree, Essex

To the best of them

Contents

Tables and Figures

Acknowledgments

I would like to thank the Longman Group Ltd for permission to reproduce figure 2, which is taken from Sir Ernest Satow, *Guide to Diplomatic Practice*, 4th edn, revised by Sir Nevile Bland (1957), p. 321; and Her Majesty's Stationery Office for permission to quote from Sir Val Duncan, *Report of the Review Committee on Overseas Representation, 1968–1969*, Cmnd 4107.

Preface

This is a peculiar book, in that it has been written with a great deal of help from the Foreign and Commonwealth Office without in any sense having been sponsored by it. I would not, indeed, have accepted my publisher's invitation to tackle the subject on any other terms. I was informed by the FCO, when I began my research in 1974, that I would be subject to the provisions of the thirty-years rule like anybody else, but that otherwise I was free to conduct whatever investigation I wanted, and that as much assistance as possible would be given. The FCO was true to its word. This is not to say that everybody I talked to in the next couple of years (and the number approached 400 by the time I had done) was equally helpful. Some diplomats were evasive, and a comparative handful made it plain that they thought I was poking my nose where it had no business to be. When I asked one Ambassador if I might see his diary of engagements for a typical week, he declined the request. 'In our sort of life', he wrote, 'every day is different and no one is "typical" except in its variety and interest.' But the majority of people spoke as freely as they could have been expected to, and some were very much more open than I had dared hope for. Most of the research was done in London, but I made three expeditions abroad to study the diplomats in their natural habitats. I visited fourteen British missions on four continents, all of my own choice, and I think they reasonably represented the range of the FCO's work overseas. At all these stops, diplomats took me into their homes, in three places they invited me to stay with them as their guest, and I am particularly grateful to all who offered me their hospitality. The list of those, inside and outside the Diplomatic Service, who helped me in my researches is a very long one. They must remain anonymous, but I should like to thank them all here. One other piece of aid should be mentioned. The British Council met half the cost of one air ticket, which enabled me to visit some of the Council's offices overseas; my thanks for that, too. It was the only subsidy I received.

For myself, I came to the task inquisitively, in much ignorance, and with my fair share of prejudices. I found out as much as I could, I sought to report it accurately, and I felt free to make whatever judgments and comments I liked. Some diplomats will doubtless think I have been unjust in some of the things I have said; I would like to believe they are in a minority. The warts on their profession would not always have been detected had diplomats themselves not drawn my attention to them. Laymen should remember that, before their derision becomes uncontrolled. In the civil service as a whole, I believe, there is now a greater readiness than ever before to open themselves to the rest of us – in spite of loud, defensive noises in the past couple of years, when the civil servants have been under very heavy public attack. Some of the most senior men today may be heard lecturing their juniors about their concern to abolish the image of a secretive civil service. This book is some evidence that such concern is as strong among senior diplomats as it is anywhere in Whitehall. One of the top men in the Foreign Office told me: 'This is a service I'm very proud to belong to, justifiably, I think. At the same time, it's got quite a lot of shortcomings.' That has seemed to me a more balanced assessment than what diplomats have usually written about themselves in memoirs, or what outsiders generally say about diplomats.

It will be noticed that I have already referred to the FCO as the Foreign Office, and I do so at least as often as not in the main text. The Foreign Office has not been its proper title for the best part of ten years, though it is the name by which the institution is still best known to most of us. And, in any case, the proper title is too cumbersome to bear much repetition on the printed page, and diplomacy contains quite enough unavoidable abbreviations already, without adding to them with 'FCO' at every other turn. Though some retired gentlemen will wish to chastise me for it, I have rejected 'diplomatist', because usage has now just about seen it off, even among diplomats themselves.

GEOFFREY MOORHOUSE

PART ONE

1 The Palazzo

In 1868, which was the year Basutoland was annexed to the British Crown, Mr Disraeli performed the official opening ceremony for a magnificent new building at the sacred end of Whitehall. This contained a set of government offices from which, henceforth, Britain's foreign affairs would be conducted. Opening them was an act of necessity, much more than a celebration of imperial heyday. The Crown had enjoyed many years of annexation with its Foreign Office situated just round the corner in Downing Street: but one day the ceiling of the Foreign Secretary's room had gently subsided on to his table while Lord Malmesbury was sitting there reading a dispatch, and it was decided that a general move was called for before the entire edifice collapsed about the diplomatic presence.

This was only the latest of many shifting arrangements, most of which had been dictated by administrative convenience rather than structural weakness. The origins of a secretariat for the monarch's foreign affairs can be traced to the Middle Ages, when John Maunsell was put in charge of the seal for Henry III's personal correspondence, and entitled '*secretarius noster*'. By the time of the Stuarts the office had been divided: a Southern Secretary supervised royal communications with Spain, Flanders, Italy and Ireland; while a Northern Secretary tended the correspondence with Holland, the Baltic States, France, Germany and Turkey. When James Burke, Paymaster to the Forces in Lord Rockingham's administration, reformed the business of government in 1782, the Southern Department was renamed the Home Office, but still controlled His Majesty's affairs with the Irish and with the Colonies. The Northern Department became the Foreign Office and kept watch over the rest of the world. Charles James Fox became the first Foreign Secretary, and Richard Brinsley Sheridan, the playwright, was appointed the first Under Secretary for Foreign Affairs – in modern terms, the first civil servant to supervise the work of the Office. When the change took place, the Foreign Office found itself at premises in Cleveland Row, but in 1786 was moved to part of the old Tennis Courts in Whitehall. Seven years later it was transferred to a building owned by Lord Sheffield in Downing Street, which one occupant was to describe as 'dingy and shabby to a degree, made up of dark offices and labyrinthine passages – four houses at least tumbled into one, with floors at uneven levels and wearying corkscrew stairs that men cursed as they climbed – a thorough picture of disorder, penury and meanness'.[1] There it stayed until the roof fell in.

Had there been any divine sense of propriety, the new government offices would have been opened in 1868 by Lord Palmerston, but he was lately dead. The building had been his creation, almost as much as that of the architect, Sir Gilbert Scott, who may be thought exceedingly fortunate to have obtained the final commission. A competition had been held, with two alternative schemes to be submitted for final adjudication. The best No 1 Scheme sent forward was that of a Frenchman, M. Crepinet; and Scott's plan was only third choice for the No 2 Scheme. Yet this was the one which Sir John Manners, the First Commissioner, recommended to the Prime Minister for adoption. Obsessed with the apexes and angles of the medieval building period, Scott was proposing a wildly Gothic fantasy and Palmerston would have none of it. He told the architect that he required something designed in the Italian manner, and Scott in due course reappeared with a vaguely Byzantine creation, which Palmerston thought 'a regular mongrel affair'. The story goes that Scott then 'bought some costly books on Italian architecture and set vigorously to work to rub up' his limited expertise, finally emerging with a scheme which passed muster with the uncommonly patient Pam. A thrifty fellow as well as a dogged one, Scott subsequently used his first idea, with suitable modifications, for a new Midland Hotel at the other end of town; a monument to perseverance which

---

[1] Rumbold, vol. 1, p. 109.

still stands, adored by the preservationists, as the unlikely preamble to St Pancras Station.

His other monument, the one Lord Palmerston was pleased to accept and which Disraeli opened, was designed for a nation with a self-confidence not often seen before in all history. It was planned to provide an ample base for administrators whose inheritance was an already substantial Empire which was still marvellously expanding. These men could not have conceived of a time to come when their country would not have a mighty influence in the affairs of the world, however majestic, however trifling. Being as civilized as anyone in Europe, which was very nearly their definition of the civilized world, they eschewed warfare whenever possible by carefully manipulating an unsteady device called the balance of power; though a little musketry in the cause of annexations farther afield, an occasional cannonade to subdue savages, were hardly to be counted as warfare. For three-quarters of a century, their suppositions held together just as firmly as their Empire, until their successors emerged from a second world war which had cost one quarter of the nation's wealth, and inspired notions of freedom and independence among once-subject peoples. In 1943, the British government was informed by its chief economic adviser, John Maynard Keynes, that the country was running out of money; and by the end of the conflict it had been reduced to the level of a pauper. Nothing could be the same again, though few of the British—inside or outside the Foreign Office—showed signs of recognizing this immediately.

Ever since the dissolution of the British Empire, a large slice of which was painstakingly and fairly generously conducted from within the pedimented walls of Scott's building, a number of revolutionary souls have suggested that British foreign policy ought in future to be ordered from some place less outrageously reminiscent of a mighty imperialism. More cogently, a whole generation of Foreign Office officials themselves—from senior Ambassadors, dropping in on HQ between one debilitating bout of negotiation and the next, down to Grade 10 Registry Clerks, at their wits' ends with far-flung filing systems—have complained of its inadequacy as a diplomatic workshop even in the reduced circumstances of the post-imperial years. A Foreign Secretary, George Brown, has called it 'downright

B

inconvenient, ugly and shabby inside'.[1] Outspoken officials refer to it briskly as a Dickensian slum. The Duncan Committee of 1969 said that it was 'manifestly unbusinesslike for the conduct of a great Ministry of State' and calculated that its replacement would save the taxpayer £1 million a year.[2] None of the epithets seems at all probable to the casual passer-by. Seen at a distance from the bridge across the lake in St James's Park, its tower poking above the willows, the pelicans and the fountains, the Foreign Office offers one of the most blessedly soothing sights in London. The close-up view from Horse Guards, say, or King Charles Street, particularly since the stone washers squirted off much soot, is of something as elegant as a Venetian or a Genoan palace; which, indeed, served as Scott's models.

But downright inconvenient it certainly has become, if only because Scott's palazzo is no longer big enough to contain British foreign policy and all its works: not to mention the machinations of the Home Office which, although it long ago shed its responsibilities for the Colonies and has even managed to detach itself from the Irish, still occupies the southern end of the building, with the only doorway leading into Whitehall. When Scott planned his new government headquarters, he placed the Foreign Office at the park end and gave it two mighty entrances for carriages, which would rattle under archways into a large courtyard, not unlike a college quadrangle in the universities of Oxford and Cambridge. One of these entrances, directly opposite No 10 Downing Street, is now permanently closed by great iron gates. The other is in King Charles Street; and through this, after inspection by the security men under the arch, motor vehicles now lurch on to the cobblestoned expanse of the quadrangle, which serves for most of the time as a diplomatic parking lot.

It is a curious and risible fact of administrative history that far more men have been needed to conduct the nation's affairs abroad in its declining years than were ever required in its age of grandeur. In 1914, the Foreign Office managed with 176 people in London (and that included the cleaners), with another 450 on diplomatic service overseas. By 1974, there were some 6,000 officials in the Diplomatic Service and several

[1] Brown, p. 128.
[2] Duncan, p. 158.

thousand dogsbodies to help them.[1] So much greater is this representative army than even Palmerston could have envisaged in his most grandiose Victorian dreams, that Foreign Office business in London is scarcely contained in nine different premises, which are scattered widely around the capital. The tight-lipped fellows who puzzle over security matters are posted not far away in what looks like the carefully chosen cul-de-sac of Matthew Parker Street. The India Office Library is located beyond the Old Vic Theatre on the South Bank of the river. The Finance Department is in Lower Regent Street. The Chief Clerk of the Foreign Office, who supervises its administration, is quartered across Whitehall from the main building and has to hop, skip and jump through the metropolitan traffic at least once every day in order to confer with the Permanent Under Secretary, the commander of the Diplomatic Service. This is undignified, even in these chapfallen times. Sir Douglas Busk, who had a similar problem some years ago, has said all he saw fit to print about the Foreign Office in one appropriately wandering sentence:[2]

Anyone familiar with its remoter rooms, anyone who has had to try and grope his way from Room 134 in the Great George Street building (which is inexplicably next to Room 67E), via Room 366 in what used to be the India Office, to the Commonwealth Relations Office on the other side of the quadrangle with no passage under cover, and then on again to visit eleven other departments housed in Queen Anne's Mansions, Lower Regent Street or across the Thames, will be staggered by the inefficiency, even though it maintains lightness of foot and a mile-devouring stride in all weathers.

Inefficiency, however, is by no means the most striking thing about the interior of the Foreign Office, which is where Matthew

---

[1] The 'dogsbodies' include the 7,800 locally-engaged staff working at posts overseas. The full FCO muster, at home and abroad, amounts to just over 6,400 people – though this figure should be treated cautiously. It includes 1,500 people who work within the diplomatic organization – from messengers in London to Attachés abroad—who are members of the Home Civil Service.

[2] Busk, p. 248.

Digby Wyatt's imagination took over from Gilbert Scott's. Instantly, it suggests something of a Victorian museum, something of a stately home whose occupants have long been fighting a losing battle against death duties and general dilapidations. The latter seems the stronger bet at first in the entrance hall, where gloomy portraits of Lord Salisbury and Lord Lansdowne eye all-comers marching up the steps from the quadrangle. Behind a rampart of mahogany, a lady of great presence commands the messengers upon their lawful occasions: she is by rank a fairly junior civil servant, but she attends to the world at Reception as splendidly as (one hopes) the grandest Ambassador's wife abroad. Adjacent doors, massively panelled, seem to have been built to be handled by flunkeys in periwigs; but when they open, they disclose only composed-looking gents in dark suits, bearing papers which minute the latest state of play in some arcane corner of the Common Market, or the diplomatic response to a complaint of riot by Glasgow football fans in the fastnesses of Barcelona. Fifty paces along the mosaic corridor, it is possible to see in startling detail how far Great Britain has come since their predecessors were around. For there is the Grand Staircase, flanked at its foot by alabaster statues of George Villiers, Earl of Clarendon, and (yet again) Robert Cecil, Marquess of Salisbury. With its plum-coloured carpet, this is not at all unlike the main stairway that finally fetched up at St Pancras. The walls and ceilings of this one, however, are decorated with frescoes, and they are an afternoon's entertainment on their own.

They were inspired (according to Sir Sigismund Goetze, who painted them at his own expense)[1] by a speech from the Archbishop of Canterbury in 1912. The mind blinks at what His Grace's text could have been, for the pictures include a swirling harem of over-ripe beauties and at least one apparent rape, a variety of excitements which the artist made some effort to subdue by clothing the different panels in titular Latin. They are meant to show the origin, education, development, expansion and triumph of the British Empire, leading up to the Covenant of the League of Nations — for some seven years passed between the archiepiscopal blessing and the final touch

[1] Goetze (1866–1939) had exhibited at the Royal Academy in 1888. He became an Associate of the Royal Institute of British Architects in 1930 and a gold medallist of the Royal Society of Sculptors in 1938.

of cobalt. Starting with *Britannia Sponsa*, they revolve through *Britannia Nutrix* to *Britannia Pacificatrix* by way of *Britannia Bellatrix* and *Britannia Colonorum Mater*, a sequence which is capped by an exhortation wound round the rotunda above: 'Let the nations rejoice and be glad, for thou shalt judge the folk righteously ... '

It would be quite unfair to Sir Sigismund and his public to paraphrase his descriptions, for they have a flair and flavour that no man writing in the 1970s could possibly hope to match. *Britannia Sponsa* 'represents the seafarers or successive waves of oversea tribes landing to obtain possession of Britannia, conceived as a wild, fair-haired shepherd girl, and the withdrawal of an earlier and ruder race'. In *Nutrix* 'the Bride becomes the Mother, and, in the Springtime of the race, ... the rearing of a sturdy race of children and the mother's devotion are emphasised—Britain the Motherland'. In *Bellatrix* 'Britannia is teaching her sons those bodily exercises and manly sports which will fit them to take their part in war should it come. It is not "Warfare" but the "Art of War" which is being inculcated ... '. By the time we reach *Colonorum Mater* we have 'the spirit of the expansion of the race overseas. The mother of the colonists holds the trident aloft; she has won it fairly, and she sends forth her sons to seek their fortunes. The ruling passion holds even the little ones, who in the foreground launch their tiny boat upon the waves'. *Pacificatrix* is where the League of Nations gets a look-in and where Sir Sigismund is to be seen and read at his most vivid:[1]

> The original conception of this picture was inspired by Great Britain being the first Great Power to propose and carry through a general Arbitration Treaty. The grasping of the 'hands across the sea' of the two great English-speaking races, Great Britain and the United States of America, seemed, in the artist's imagination, to be the fittest conclusion of his whole theme, and the other panels were severally designed to lead up to this ... Emerging from the horrors of war, which the allied nations are trampling underfoot, Belgium, a Psyche-like figure of pure girlhood,

[1] *Mural Decorations at the Foreign Office*; descriptive account by the artist. Foreign Office leaflet.

personification of the small nation with a great soul, appeals to Britannia. She has lost everything but her honour is safe! She holds aloft her broken sword (she has fought heroically); she grasps her flag unsullied, without a rent (her honour is untouched); she wears the crown of thorns (her sufferings have been her Calvary) ... America, wearing the cap of Liberty, as the greatest of Republics, holds the scales of Justice ... Italy, clad in white, carries the 'fasces', emblem of the Roman Law, which she has given to the world. France, with her Tricolour garlanded with laurels, points her sword to the 'Scrap of Paper' and the broken Crucifix, and to the debris of Despotism and Militarism which she has been fighting to destroy ... Roumania's natural resources are hinted at by a Figure carrying an oil jar on her head; Portugal is represented with a basket of grapes; and Russia, in mourning, hiding her face in sorrow, gropes her way forward on the extreme left ... India, who took such a conspicuous part in the War, is represented as a martial figure in old armour. Behind India stands Prince Feisul, representing the Epic of Arabia; and in front a little Swaheli boy, bearing tropical fruits, reminds us of our obligations and possibilities in the dark Continent.

The First World War, having happened between conception and completion, caused Sir Sigismund to revise somewhat the final deployment of his national figures. 'Happily,' he remarks, 'the diplomatic regrouping of the nations did not cause serious artistic difficulties.'

Anyone proceeding past that staircase and venturing further into the interior may need to remind himself how much times have changed since Sir Sigismund put pigment to panel. For straight away he finds himself in that sector of the building once occupied by the India Office, which retains even now much more than a whiff of the Raj. There is an air of dusty celebration lingering here, and one or two quite remarkable relics. The India Office was set around the Durbar Court, which was built and decorated just ten years after Victoria had been proclaimed Queen Empress in Calcutta. Scott cribbed the basic design of the courtyard from something Bramante had created in Rome 250 years earlier. A Wedgwood blue frieze runs round its sides and beneath this are busts of twenty-eight old India hands like

Admiral Watson, Lord Macartney and Charles Grant. Below them, snugly perched in their separate niches, are almost as many statues of the Governors-General and the Viceroys — Warren Hastings, Lord Minto and the rest. The courtyard was covered by a curving glass roof to keep out the weather, but one or two panes have since been broken, so that the memorial figures suffer a little from the pigeons. For three-quarters of a century, after an opening ball for the Sultan of Turkey, this space was reserved for tea parties and other diplomatic con-vivialities. The Life Guards band would be summoned to make background music, while the gentlemen who administered a large portion of the globe gossiped with each other's ladies and sipped Lapsang or best Assam, as they considered the latest inflammations of Bengal, or how most adroitly to muffle that irritating beggar Gandhi; and then pleasantly passed the seed cake to the visiting Indian princelings at their elbows. It is possible that the last time the Durbar Court fulfilled its original purpose was in April 1939, when the King and Queen played hosts at the Foreign Office to President Lebrun, M. Daladier and M. Bonnet. Having given them a state banquet elsewhere in the building, the royal couple entertained their guests here, in a small theatre specially rigged for the occasion by Sir Edwin Lutyens, to a programme devised by the Permanent Under Secretary and Seymour Hicks, which ranged through snatches of *Romeo and Juliet* to songs and dances by Cicely Courtneidge. There would be no room for such an entertainment today, for the floor of the court is almost wholly occupied by a large hut, which looks as if it might be where the maintenance men keep their tools. It is, in fact, the communications centre of the Foreign Office and the first stop for any homing message emitted by the embassies abroad.

India may have owed its allegiance to Buckingham Palace, but its affairs were ordered from a room close by the Durbar Court. Here sat a full Secretary of State, a distinction shared by no other single country in the Empire; but, then, no other country contained one-fifth of the world's population, as India did by the start of the twentieth century. Mr Secretary inhabi-ted quite the most engaging office in the entire building, a neat not a gaudy place, whose oak-panelled walls were hung with delicate Persian miniatures which had been filched from the Mogul Emperor's palace in the Red Fort at Delhi, and whose furniture was dragooned from old East India Company properties. It was part of this politician's duties to receive the more substantial and more complaisant Indians, when they had travelled (poshly, by P & O) to the heart of Empire in order to make their humblest submissions to the sovereign – and afterwards, perhaps, to watch a little cricket at Lord's. Receiving them was not always the straightforward matter it could have been and necessitated some adjustment to the structure. Along one curving wall of this office, two identical doorways were set, side by side, their surrounds heavily swagged in the manner of Grinling Gibbons. This was so that when a brace of Maharajahs arrived – as happened from time to time – they could effect their entrances simultaneously, neither being forced to yield one inch of his highly cherished precedence. British rule could be very obliging.

The miniatures and the furniture are still there. So are the doorways, with 'IO' still highly polished upon brass plates outside. One of them, however, has been sealed to keep the draught off the Minister of State within, who is probably trying to comprehend a departmental submission on the intricacies of MBFR, IBRD, UNCTAD (which are enough to put the wind up anybody) before legging it down the road to the Commons, to defend his policies at Question Time. When, in 1935, Sir Samuel Hoare ceased to be Secretary of State for India and became Foreign Secretary instead, he was not at once gratified by his promotion. For one thing, he would have preferred the Prime Minister to send him to New Delhi, to be the King Emperor's Viceroy. For another, he much regretted leaving that stylish little room behind. He thought his new base on the first floor had the atmosphere of a pretentious hotel lounge, and it certainly has something of the same scale.

The Foreign Secretary is approached through an anteroom, which itself is as large as almost any other office in the building, with space for a switchboard as well as for the Private Secretaries, with a high desk on which the morning papers may be read standing up, and with pictures of previous Foreign Secretaries crowding round the walls. Lord Halifax used to dump his gumboots in here on winter mornings, after loping into work across the park as though he were coming in from his Yorkshire estates; having replaced them with more seemly shoes and socks, he would then pass into his own room and reluctantly make another concession to Herr Hitler. The wonder is that he didn't get equally lost among the furniture. To say that there is one enormous desk, one smaller desk, two tables, four arm-chairs and a sofa is to give the impression that it is a cluttered room. It is not, for considerable distances separate each piece. It must be the best part of twenty yards from the doorway to the windows overlooking Horse Guards Parade opposite. There is an even better view through the windows running down the left-hand wall; though when Sir Edward Grey stood by them one day in 1914 he saw, not the willows round the lake in St James's Park, but the lamps going out all over Europe. At the massive desk, where Lord Curzon plotted British domination of the Middle East, there are two telephones, a printed list of the Foreign Secretary's engagements for the day, and not much else. There is another telephone on the desk by the fireplace, together with a cheap-looking globe which might have been picked up at Hamley's. A rather fine pottery lamp stands on the table by the St James's windows. A bookcase almost covers one wall and is crammed with Hansards and State Papers in calf bindings. All this lies beneath a ceiling which is gilded when it isn't cream and green, which just about harmonizes with the green flock wallpaper, the heavy brown satin curtains, and the dun armchairs. This is a setting which goes with that ponderous figure who appears in the copperplate prologue to our passports as 'Her Britannic Majesty's Principal Secretary of State for Foreign Affairs', who still swaggeringly Requests and requires all those it may concern to allow law-abiding Britons to pass freely without let or hindrance. One can well imagine Salisbury scheming his next bout with Bismarck in this room, which will scarcely have changed since he was here, although successive Foreign Secretaries have been known to make minor adjustments to suit their own tastes. The fireplace, another trophy from the East India Company, burned with coal until Sir Alec Douglas-Home banished the filthy stuff in favour of the gas fire. George Brown took one look at the painting of George III on the wall above and had a portrait of Palmerston put in its place. Someone else summoned the bust of William Pitt to the table between the Horse Guards windows, but omitted to remove a sticky label from the back which says 'Ministry of Works'. James Callaghan, when he was here, seemed to have contributed nothing but three bottles of pills and a blue plastic shoehorn, which doubtless gave rise to the rumour that British diplomacy now trod the world in its stockinged feet.

There are other landmarks in the Foreign Office. There is the Ambassadors' Waiting Room just round the corner from where the Permanent Under Secretary is based, an elegant chamber that would grace Chatsworth or any other superior stately home, and quite large enough to contain all the Queen's representatives overseas, or most of the diplomatic corps in London. Thomas Wentworth, 3rd Earl of Strafford, surveys it sadly from one wall and an Indian prince enigmatically from another. There is the Locarno Suite where a butler, after a feast for the King and Queen of Portugal in Lord Curzon's time, set fire to Her Majesty's hat and veil while attempting to light her cigarette. The suite is still splendid, though some time has passed since the Life Guards last stood to attention amidst swathes of gladioli, while distinguished guests moved into the banquet. Even with the best of navigational aids – one of the motherly messengers who will have been provided by the re-doubtable Miss Shaw at her command post in the entrance hall – one has need of all these landmarks in this great rambling palazzo, for there is a similarity about most of the corridors that defies orientation. One is perpetually going round in rectangles.

What were once corridors of great power tend for the most part now to be bleakly institutional. They are pedestrian thoroughfares whose high Victorian ceilings do not go naturally with neon strip lights. Sometimes they are decorated with oil paintings of imperial grandees, not all of them priceless. In one conspicuous spot there is a bust of Ernest Bevin, which may be the only piece of contemporary art in the whole building apart from the pair of Pipers which the head of the Cultural Relations Department has bagged to hang opposite his desk. Formidable batteries of pneumatic tubes convey heaven knows what state secrets from one floor to another, but in doing so suggest only the comfy workings of a rather old-fashioned department store. Sofas, visible a hundred yards away, apparently parked against a wall in the middle of nowhere, announce the proximity of some fairly senior person's room: an Under Secretary lurks within or, at least, a head of department. If it is the former, then the room will possibly be spacious, with another sofa and arm-chairs inside; and it will be original to the building plan with no alteration to it since. If it is the latter, it may have space for little but its occupant and his desk, a tin cupboard and a tubular office chair for a visitor; and, considering that a good many such rooms have been created out of hardboard partitionings, it is surprising how infrequently one can hear a conversation going on next door. The only privilege offered heads of department seems to be that they do not have to find their way up to the topmost floors, where the corridors are laid with brown linoleum and are so devoid of anything as to be verging on the penitentiary.

There are, moreover, so many corridors in the Foreign Office and so many identical doors that more than one state secret may have been mislaid round here through the inability of some poor fellow to retrace his steps accurately. You can certainly open some doors and walk into something that seems to have been forgotten by diplomats and supporting staff alike. High up under the roof there is a startling display of bric-à-brac, such a collection of firedogs and mantelpieces and coat racks and rolltop desks and chairs as will have the antique dealers slavering if they are ever put up for auction; Victorian administrative furniture stored away for an expansive moment that never came. Elsewhere there is something between a room and a right of way, a corner where documents in Sanskrit, Pali and other Oriental languages used to be filed. The drawers and the shelves banked up to the ceiling still bear these old titles but the original contents have long since disappeared, to be replaced by the makings of a Russian research collection – handouts from Tass, Novosti and other low-grade sources – which is strewn about in such a half-hearted fashion, accumulating dust, that it looks as if someone got bored with the idea early on and dropped it. This is one of the minor bewilderments of the Foreign Office, but it fits into a generally haphazard form. Even the way out is baffling more often than not. There must be half a dozen exits and, except for the one by the main lobby, it is almost impossible to predict until the last moment whether one is going to emerge somewhere round the quadrangle, at the top of the Clive Steps, or half-way up Downing Street.

The institution whose labours are centred upon this building is nowadays, of course, properly called the Foreign and Commonwealth Office, which its members wisely reduce to its conversational limit of 'FCO'. The full title at least serves to

remind connoisseurs of governmental evolution that it represents the latest stage of a long and organic process of growth
since Burke's reform in the eighteenth century. For almost 150
years after that, strictly foreign (as distinct from imperial)
affairs were conducted by two bodies which, while working in
tandem, nevertheless managed to retain largely separate identi-
ties and personnel. To call the Foreign Office of that period a
collection of gentlemanly scribes is to oversimplify as much as
if one were to regard the Diplomatic Service as no more than
a collection of affluent dilettantes acting in their country's
interests abroad. There is, however, truth in both these summaries. The men of the Foreign Office worked in London at
the business of drafting submissions and copying messages from
abroad for the benefit of their political masters. People who
joined the Diplomatic Service expected to spend their careers
abroad as the monarch's envoys, under the direction of the
political Ministers. While both groups were recruited totally
from the ranks of the upper and upper-middle classes, a leaning
towards the aristocracy was rather more marked in the Diplomatic Service, and certainly no man could hope to become a
diplomat without a private income. The Foreign Office clerk
was paid a salary from the outset, but Attachés abroad were paid
nothing for the first two years of their service. Occasionally
there was a transfusion of blood from one to the other, but that
rarely happened below the highest levels. This was so even in
the early twentieth century when, for example, after long
careers abroad in the Diplomatic Service, two successive British
Ambassadors at St Petersburg, Charles Hardinge and Arthur
Nicolson, became Permanent Under Secretaries at the Foreign
Office, one after the other. This curiously divided arrangement
was made to work until 1920, when the staffs of the Foreign
Office at home and the Diplomatic Service abroad were amalgamated into one unit.

There have been other conjunctions. The early years of the
twentieth century also saw a separate Consular Service; and a
Commercial Diplomatic Service, whose members were intended
to stimulate British trade in foreign parts, being under the
general supervision of an independent Department of Overseas
Trade which, however, issued instructions to these particular
officers in the name of the Foreign Secretary. This was con-
fusing. It remained so until 1943, when clerks and diplomats,

Consuls and Commercial Officers, were united in the logic of
the Foreign Service. Four years later there was a rearrangement
of other overseas duties. The staff of the India Office and members of the Indian Civil Service, who had also enjoyed separate
existences, suddenly found themselves bereft of work on the
declaration of Indian independence. They were promptly
reincarnated as the Commonwealth Relations Office, together
with the manpower of the Dominions Office, which had been
established in 1928 to attend to Britain's links with the white
nations of the Empire. By 1947, therefore, a great deal of
Britain's involvement in the world beyond the English Channel
was in the hands of two bodies which officialdom conveniently
identified by their initials: the FO (alias the Foreign Service)
and the CRO. Remaining portions of the globe were administered by a third body, which had not nearly come to the end of
a very long and undisturbed run.

This was the Colonial Office, which from 1875 onwards had
been situated at the south-east corner of Gilbert Scott's palazzo,
where Downing Street turns into Whitehall. Here was the administrative headquarters of all British possessions in Black
Africa and Asia, with the exception of India, as it was of all
those scores of red dots elsewhere splattering the pre-war atlases
so fondly produced by John Bartholomew & Co. The Colonial
Secretary and his officials sent abroad not Ambassadors or
High Commissioners, but Governors, and between them they
were responsible for the fortunes of 65 million people in 1946.
Thereafter, Colonial Office power began to leak rather steadily
as other subjects followed where Indians had led. It invariably
ran in a diluted form across Scott's quadrangle to where the
CRO was freshly based, willing and eager to shoulder all available responsibility for the exciting new concept of Commonwealth. The poor Colonialists, indeed, very soon found themselves ejected by this cuckoo in the imperial nest. So great
became the accommodation problem in the palazzo at this time
that, fortified with the promise of a brand new building to themselves in due course, they were sent wandering from one billet
to another in the passing of the next few years. The brand new
building eventually turned out to be Westminster Hospital, and
what ultimately happened to the Colonial Office was that it
expired, through an insufficiency of colonies, at premises in
Great Smith Street. Officially, its death in 1966 was presented

to the world as a merger with the CRO under the new title of the Commonwealth Office. Even that proved to be a short-lived arrangement. On October 17th, 1968, all was combined into the Foreign and Commonwealth Office, which has so far managed to remain more or less intact. But the title of Diplomatic Service has been revived, on the suggestion of the Plowden Committee which reported in 1964, to cover all who work for the FCO at home and overseas: when these people refer to 'the FCO' they mean the apparatus which functions in London, and the Scott palazzo.

It is a convoluted history, but some things apart from the fabric of the building have survived all the institutional changes that have taken place over the years, one of them being the word 'clerk'. Not only is the FCO's head of administration called the Chief Clerk, but there is a nocturnal species of diplomat called the Resident Clerk. There are, in fact, six of them at any one time. These are bright young men and women who have generally reached the rank of First Secretary and who are always, without exception, unmarried. They inhabit a range of flats high up in the eaves of the building, with spectacular views across the park or overlooking Horse Guards Parade. A writer of thrillers, presumably stimulated by Frederick Forsyth's success, is said to have been so captivated by these vantage points after visiting a friend up there that he instantly devised a new plot, in which the Prime Minister was assassinated in the garden of Downing Street by a bullet fired from the duty Clerk's window. The purpose of these officials is to take it in turns, once a week, to keep watch through the night in the belief that the sun never sets on what used to be the British Empire – and even on some other parts of the globe. This is what each Resident Clerk does after a day spent in whatever is his normal working department, clocking on in his flat at 6 p.m., with a small battery of telephones in his sitting room and, down the corridor, his special safe for the day's swatch of telegrams and any other classified documents he may need before 10 a.m. the next day. A stimulating sensation it must be when it is your night or your weekend on duty for, once the shop downstairs has shut, the Resident Clerk is all the authority that immediately stands between the British government and crisis overseas. If the Foreign Secretary at 1 a.m. needs a comforting chat with the US Secretary of State (or vice versa), it is the

Clerk who must do the transatlantic fixing. If revolution breaks out Somewhere at four in the morning, with dire threats to British interests, it is he who must press the first buttons in response. 'It's a nice thing,' says one, 'because you really can feel your power when you have to ring the Ministry of Defence, say, after conferring with your Under Secretary and tell them —no, ask them—to take some course of action.' Power is something that a First Secretary, in the normal course of events, is rarely allowed to enjoy, being more accustomed to a fairly anonymous position midstream in an endless flow of paper. It is not by any means an everyday occurrence even when a man puts in a two-year stint as Resident Clerk, and collects a special allowance for his weekly turn on the night shift. But it is not really worth his while going to bed before half-past midnight, if only because British missions on the other side of the Atlantic —the Embassy in Washington or the High Commission in Ottawa—have a wearisome habit of ringing up just before their tea-times (which is about 11 p.m. in London) to save themselves the labour of drafting a telegram. On the whole, however, British diplomats abroad are sympathetically inclined towards the night watchmen in Whitehall. They are very good, say the Resident Clerks, at not sending Flash telegrams in the middle of your night unless their part of the world is beginning to fall about their ears. A Flash message is something that might justify awakening the Foreign Secretary himself. When the night duty messengers bring up a cable which is merely marked Immediate, it is understood that the Clerk need not take action immediately; he may leave it in his in-tray till eight o'clock in the morning. Not often does he enjoy a night of unbroken slumber, though, for something usually crops up in the hours of darkness which causes him prudently to consult an Under Secretary who is blissfully abed in the peaceful purlieus of Banstead or Esher. When one has to do this, say the Clerks, it is curious how almost always it is the senior man's wife who answers the telephone first.

There can be little doubt that the diplomatic watchman will still be called Resident Clerk when this building is less spooky with imperial ghosts than it is now, for someone who has to go padding down a corridor in his dressing-gown to fetch a code book or instructions from the safe. But a taste for tradition has its limits, and these were long ago reached as far as general

working conditions in Gilbert Scott's building are concerned.
Plans to make a new Foreign Office were drafted in the early
1950s, and for the next ten years it was believed that our
diplomacy would soon be based on the other side of the park,
behind the façade of John Nash's Carlton House Terrace. The
idea was finally dropped for indistinct reasons which were
officially camouflaged as impracticability 'after feasibility
studies'. In 1963, however, a Conservative government decided
that Scott's building should be demolished and replaced with
a new one on the same site: within twelve months a Labour
government had ratified this notion. That this plan never came
to pass can be attributed to a variety of reasons. Government in
the late 1960s became committed to a restriction on office
accommodation in Central London and it dodged the Martin–
Buchanan proposals for a general redevelopment of Whitehall.
It pleaded economic difficulties, though these were paltry compared with those that were to send the nation sprawling within
a few years. As much as anything, however, Scott's palazzo has
never vanished beneath a cloud of bulldozers because the preservationists, mettled by two campaigns to save the railway
stations of Euston and St Pancras from destruction (one of
which was lost, the other won), put enough pressure on the
government to save it; or, at least, to delay the fatal starting
signal. By 1971, so persistent had been the efforts of the
Victorian Society and its allies, that the decision to demolish was
finally reversed.

The outcome has been a willingness to compromise in what
all hands would like to believe is the best British and diplomatic
tradition; and governments of both parties have in turn agreed
to it. All that remains to be settled is the finance, the Chancellor
of the Exchequer's Catch 22. But the plan is that the Home
Office should move out of Whitehall in 1978 and take up a new
position in the building Sir Basil Spence has designed opposite
St James's Park Underground station. Subsequently, the staff
of the FCO will be transferred to the new Caxton House in
Westminster, where they will remain for the next few years. By
the time that move has been accomplished, some genius will
have worked out how to leave the walls of Gilbert Scott's
creation standing and how to leave what are called the 'fine
features' inside untouched, then how to insert into the otherwise empty cavern the most superb office accommodation in

Europe, equipped with every relevant device of an electronic age. In less complicated circles, this operation would be known as having your cake and eating it. It seems to call for nothing less than a combination of Michelangelo, Buckminster Fuller and Wernher von Braun in one mortal man, and the authorities do not doubt that he is waiting there unrecognized somewhere near the FCO's doorstep. Should he get his headsplitting sums right and should any construction company be found that can translate them into pre-stressed concrete, the diplomats alone will eventually troop back into a set of offices that will doubtless strike them as Paradise Regained. The Foreign Secretary will return to his pretentious hotel lounge, which will be just as he left it. His Minister of State will still be in a position to admit Maharajahs simultaneously, should a pair happen to turn up. Sir Sigismund Goetze's frescoes will still be intact and thrilling. Ambassadors will still have room to wait *en masse* beneath Strafford's mournful gaze. The Life Guards band will probably be recalled to the floor of the Durbar Court.

But throughout the rest of the British Foreign and Commonwealth Office, things will have changed. There will, for a start, be room for 3,000 people instead of the 1,300 who now find themselves crammed (in a diplomatic manner of speaking) into its outdated enclosures, less than half of whose theoretical space is really usable, because the Victorian ceilings are so high. There will be an ingathering of stray officials from outposts all over London. The Chief Clerk will no longer be dangerously exposed to the Whitehall traffic in office hours, for the Curtis Green administrative block will have been handed over to the police, who used to live in New Scotland Yard next door until the Members of Parliament cast covetous eyes upon it and commandeered it for a set of study-suites. In this new FCO (or whatever it may be called by then), ceilings will have been lowered to within visibility and corridors will no longer be embellished with pneumatic tubes. Senior diplomats will be able to lunch on the spot instead of tramping over to the Travellers' Club, and junior diplomats will be able to keep fit in squash courts. Ladies of the Diplomatic Service will be able to have their hair dressed *in situ*. Even babies, mysteriously, will be provided for in crèches. The Nizam of Hyderabad, the Maharaj Krishnaraj of Mysore, and several other worthies who stayed loyal to the Raj during the Indian Mutiny, will still be

C

securely placed upon their pedestals around the great quadrangle. But their begetter, Sir Gilbert Scott, were he to return,
would have a job recognizing the old place inside, once the
mutation has been completed. The authorities even have a date
in mind by which all these things shall have come to pass. It is,
God bless 'em, 1984.[1]

---

[1] Since this was written in 1976, the Chancellor has indeed invoked his
Catch 22 and the rebuilding plans have been indefinitely shelved.

2 The Worldly View

At the end of a career that had seen him as the Queen's representative in Addis Ababa, Helsinki and Caracas, Sir Douglas Busk allowed himself, in the manner of many ex-Ambassadors, a public reflection on his old profession. 'About once every 20 years,' he wrote, 'owing to wars or domestic failure to realize the magnitude of its task, the British Diplomatic Service almost grinds to a halt.'[1] This modest hyperbole seemed to be Sir Douglas's way of explaining the government's regular habit of taking a considered look at the diplomats, to a degree not experienced by any other department of state. Three times since the Second World War broke out has this occurred, and that does not include the Drogheda Committee's report on British information work overseas in 1954, the Fulton Committee's look at the civil service as a whole in 1968, or an examination of the FCO alone by the Central Policy Review Staff of the Cabinet Office, which began early in 1976.[2] Sir Douglas went on to claim that 'the Service was saved' by one of the other investigations – conducted by the Plowden Committee in 1964 – but that 'this new charter was at once insidiously eroded, in a fashion all too familiar, by unpublished directives that rendered the task of constructive planners infinitely more difficult'. The inference to be drawn from the ex-Ambassador's remarks was that the diplomats themselves are no more than other people's tools, incapable of fashioning their own role over a period when nothing has changed more swiftly or profoundly

[1]Busk, p. xii.

[2]This was announced by the Foreign Secretary after much public criticism of the Foreign Office in the preceding twelve months. Within a few weeks, the Foreign Office had set up a special unit of its own to liaise with the CPRS, under the direction of Sir Andrew Stark, who had just been British Ambassador in Copenhagen.

than the shape and the texture of the world beyond the English Channel. As we shall see in the course of this book, this is very far from being the case.

The first of the three diplomatic examinations was initiated by Anthony Eden in 1941, in one of those wartime waves of optimistic planning for a brave new world after hostilities had ceased. When it was published as a White Paper two years later,[1] this subsequently became known as the Eden–Bevin reforms for the two Foreign Secretaries who finally had a hand in them. They were almost entirely concerned with reorganizing the internal structure of the Foreign Service. Recruitment was generally liberalized, women were henceforth to be considered for diplomacy proper instead of being confined to its secretarial drudgery, and Consuls, Commercial Officers and other hitherto lesser breeds were admitted to the same corps as the purely political specialists serving in the chanceries abroad. Given the traditions of the profession up to then, the 1943 White Paper can still be seen as a blueprint for the most radical change that British diplomacy has undergone since Burke took a hand in it in 1782. The tone was bound to change now, whatever else was unaltered. As for the role these people were expected to play in future, the reforming mind of 1943 could scarcely be expected to have had a clear vision of that.

By 1964, however, a great number of worldly things had been made manifest and the Plowden Committee tried to come to terms with them. It pointed out at the start that the world our overseas services had to work in was no longer the world of 1943, or even one which could have been foreseen twenty years before. The balance and nature of military power had changed and was dominated by the United States and the Soviet Union. International problems, great heavens, had acquired an ideological content and 'this has greatly complicated the handling of our overseas relations'. Britain had not only lost an Empire (a word which, however, even when the Committee looked back on what was past, did not appear once in its report), but had almost lost any residuary maternal role in the Commonwealth as well. This did not mean that Lord Plowden and his assistants had mentally consigned Great Britain to the back row of the international stalls. The British at home, after all, were

---

[1] *Proposals for the Reform of the Foreign Service* (Cmd 6420), 1943.

generally rejoicing in what they were pleased to think of as the swinging sixties, and this mood was possibly responsible for a spasm of what might otherwise have been construed as plain old-fashioned nostalgia.[1]

> There are, however, other measurements than those of physical strength alone. Britain retains many wide responsibilities and a high degree of world-wide influence. We believe that the British people wish to sustain that influence and share Sir Winston Churchill's view that Britain should not be content to be 'relegated to a tame and minor role in the world'. If our influence is not felt, not only national but international interests and objectives will suffer. It is in the general interest that Britain's voice should continue to be heard and to carry weight in the world ... What we can no longer ensure by power alone, we must secure by other means.

Plowden, however, was too realistic to tarry overlong on that tack. It quickly went on to point out that not only had the balance of military power swung heavily away from the British; the problem of earning a living had also become much harder. It was seen to be our major preoccupation: 'The survival of Britain, let alone her influence, depends on trade.' Lord Palmerston could have said as much, of course; but not, perhaps, with quite the anxious undertones in Plowden's first look at the world it lived in. The view from 1964 was that economic and commercial work had become fundamentally important in British diplomacy: 'It must be regarded as a first charge on the resources of the overseas services.' Having sounded this distant early-warning signal, the authors of a report running to more than 600 paragraphs then spent no more than 22 paragraphs in closer examination of economic and commercial diplomacy. For the most part, they were working out problems of structure which post-war history and imperial dissolution had bequeathed to the various overseas services.

Five years later came the Duncan Committee's report, which was really inspired by Treasury pressure for cuts in expenditure. This had apparently been no concern of Lord Plowden's

[1] Plowden, pp. 2-3.

Committee, which had concluded that, if anything, overseas representation was likely to increase rather than dwindle, and had allowed for the topping up of existing manpower by 10 per cent. Duncan was not only obliged by its terms of reference to take a glum look at that assumption; it was emotionally more able to concentrate with some realism on Britain's international role because of political events since Plowden had sat. The Duncan Committee was appointed just as a major change in British policy was announced: to withdraw military forces from East of Suez. As one of the report's authors later remarked, what Duncan really did was 'to spell out, belatedly, the logic of the end of Empire'.[1] More than this, it specifically projected its recommendations upon the world it believed Britain would be inhabiting by the middle of the following decade: where we are now.

It came up with a novel appraisal of the diplomatic universe in the mid-1970s. It divided it into two halves: 'One is the category of advanced industrial countries with which we are likely to be increasingly involved to the point where none of us will be able to conduct our domestic policies efficiently without constant reference to each other ... The other category of countries comprises the rest of the world.'[2] The first group of nations was grandly capitalized as the Area of Concentration, consisting of a dozen or so places in Western Europe plus North America. The Committee allowed that there were a few industrially advanced nations outside this block—like Australia and Japan—with whom Britain would maintain close and important relations for different reasons. But basically the Area of Concentration was to be exactly that. The twelve Europeans (plus North America) were selected for the diplomatic corral because

their social structures, ways of living, methods of conducting political and economic business are sufficiently similar to make it possible for them to conduct their external relations with one another in a style different from the traditional one. Because their domestic affairs are increasingly interrelated and impinge on each other at so many points, it

[1] Quoted by Boardman and Groom, p. 3.
[2] Duncan, p. 12.

is likely that the range of topics in the diplomacy of the future will be much wider, with an emphasis on economic and social issues. These countries will also be even more closely enmeshed with one another commercially and in other fields of activity, eg tourism, than they are today.

All these forms of interrelationship would be reinforced if Britain and others in the membership queue actually joined the Common Market but they were not, in the Committee's tactful view, dependent upon such an event. Whatever the ultimate composition of the Common Market, Britain's foreign policy henceforth must be based on commitments to an increasingly integrated Western Europe and a North Atlantic alliance under American leadership. In this context negotiations would be conducted, ideas exchanged, proposals floated, arguments heard and treaties (hopefully) concluded not only by traditional methods of diplomacy. Tradition has always ordained that the professional envoys of two nations should meet secretively until they have reached agreement, compromise, rupture or declaration of war, while the rest of the world wonders what's going on, and no one ever thought to call this process bilateral until political science began to tamper with decent men's language. But henceforth, according to Duncan, amateur envoys from non-diplomatic professions would be increasingly enlisted to the aid of the professionals, forming joint teams of widespread accomplishments, colossal complexity and awesome size: thus represented, a dozen or more governments at a time might juggle with one another simultaneously in a truly bewildering display of activity known as multilateral negotiation. To this notion the Duncan Committee, with a bent towards its own resounding titles, applied the label New Diplomacy.

Duncan trod delicately across the rest of the world – as delicately as possible, that is, after consigning it to a so-called Outer Area of British diplomatic interest. 'There are issues outside Europe', the report said, 'which will continue to matter to the nation.' Britain would retain its concern for the welfare of the Commonwealth, would involve itself still in the economic struggles of the newer members. 'Thus our interest in the countries bordering the Indian Ocean and the Persian Gulf as well as Africa will not cease in the 1970s – nor is it likely even that it will be reduced to the low level of priority that it has had in the Foreign Ministries of most continental nations.' It was to be hoped that before too long a concerted Europe would return to more active diplomacy in these regions and others farther afield, in which case Britain's traditional expertise would be useful. Duncan was carefully not suggesting that Britain was eventually going to lead Europe on diplomatic expeditions abroad: she should not 'take it upon herself to act in some sense as the trustee of Western Europe's interest'. Instead,[1]

> Britain's connection with these distant places should be regarded as providing a valuable contribution to the instrument which, it is hoped, Western Europe will feel that it needs in the long run to express its common interests in the African continent and the areas bordering the Indian Ocean. These areas contain a high proportion of the world's population; their capacity to produce is growing fast; and their capacity for engendering problems for the rest of the world is unlikely to diminish. What we are suggesting is ... that in looking ahead to the kind of diplomatic instrument which Britain as a European power will need in the mid-1970s, we should not be guided entirely by the evidence of unconcern with extra-European problems which has been characteristic of most continental countries in recent years.

The attempts which have been made since 1941 to keep pace with the times cannot fairly be thought of as political efforts to change the diplomatic apparatus and its operation against massive diplomatic opposition. The Eden–Bevin reforms were widely supported in the Foreign Office. The seven members of Lord Plowden's team included Lord Inchyra (who, as Sir Frederick Hoyer Millar, had just ended his diplomatic career in the top Foreign Office job of Permanent Under Secretary) and Sir Percivale Liesching (who in the early 1950s had been PUS at the Commonwealth Relations Office). Sir Val Duncan's Committee consisted of himself, the economist Andrew Shonfield, and Sir Frank Roberts, who had been British Ambassador in both Bonn and Moscow. It would be silly to expect that the findings of any of these reformers tallied completely with

---

[1] Duncan, p. 15.

opinions that might have been canvassed at the time from top
to bottom of the Diplomatic Service. Anybody who has had
much to do with people in the FCO and the missions abroad
is soon struck by the fact that, although 'a Foreign Office view'
undoubtedly emerges in due course on any given topic, below
the level of its actual pronouncement there is an exceedingly
wide variety of opinion and argument about it. It is reasonable
to suppose that both Plowden and Duncan had their supporters
in the Foreign Office during their investigations. Lord Plowden's
quotation from Winston Churchill, certainly, would not have
gone down at all badly in the Travellers' Club at lunchtime in
1964. Duncan has proved much less acceptable, although some
of his concepts had been quietly brewing among the pneumatic
tubes and mosaic corridors of Gilbert Scott's palazzo before he
formulated them. His sub-Caesarean division of the world into
two parts was particularly objectionable to the diplomats,
however. Two years later the Chief Clerk declared:[1]

> We think the Duncan Committee described in black and
> white terms what really should be described in greyer
> terms ... the Duncan Committee definition has been useful
> in concentrating our minds on this problem, but the effect
> of it has been to reject it in its rigidity and to look at each
> country in the world and try to form an independent
> assessment of its value to the British interest.

Senior officials are still pained by Duncan's definition of so
many nations as an Outer Area of concern to this country. 'You
don't get much out of people', according to one Under Secretary, 'when you give them that sobriquet.'

Yet even the blunt realism of Duncan had its limits, and nothing is more fascinating in that report than the semantics employed to identify Britain's precise position in the world.
'Britain is nowadays', it decided, 'a major power of the second
order.'[2] Edward Heath, as Prime Minister, within a twelve-
month translated this into 'a medium power of the first rank'.
Whichever version one wished to cherish as the 1970s crossed
the calendar, both suggested a lingering reluctance to say a last

[1] Fifth Report from the Expenditure Committee, Session 1971-2, pp.
24-5.
[2] Duncan, p. 23.

goodbye to the idea of British power: depending on your sport-
ing temperament, you could think of yourself as half-way up the
First Division or at the top of the Second, but most emphatically
no lower in the league table. The way things have gone since
then, however, has been nothing less than a slide towards
relegation, and nowhere in Britain is this more starkly accepted
than by the diplomats. A distinguished ex-Ambassador, Lord
Trevelyan, wrote in 1973 that 'In the decade after the war the
British were still in the top class ... Now that time is over. We
are a European state, limited in size and power ... '[1] They can
be even more candid in his old office now. In August 1974, the
year's new intake of diplomats, young men and women fresh
from university, sat down to the customary fortnight of introductory lectures about the profession they were entering. At one
of the very first sessions they were told by a highly placed FCO
official: 'We're living in a Britain which is declining in the world
relatively, and maybe absolutely.' A couple of days later, in a
discussion centred upon the potential redundancy of all diplomatic work, another senior man told them: 'It's relevant that
we're not even a second-level power – like France and Germany
– any more ... ' And then, perhaps stirred by some deeply
instinctive loyalty to the past, ' ... though I don't want to say
we're a third-level power'.

Not many British diplomats today would reckon that an
intemperate observation, though plenty might baulk at pro-
claiming it in public. Possibly no one under the age of fifty
would disagree with it. Those in their thirties, who are entering
the middle stages of their career, can be caught sometimes in
attitudes bordering on dismay when they consider how far removed is their profession now from the days of British gunboat
diplomacy. A man who entered the FCO in 1962, since when
he has watched the country decline from the second richest in
the Area of Concentration to the second poorest, says: 'It's a
shattering experience to represent such a country; we here are
aware of our weak power base, the fact that we're left more and
more to our own resources ... ' When a couple of politicians
from Korea visited London in 1975, they were given lunch by
no less a person than the Permanent Under Secretary himself.
Had they come to town twenty years before, they might have

[1] Trevelyan, p. 9.

counted themselves lucky to be entertained by the head of the department handling Far Eastern affairs, an official standing three ranks lower in the London hierarchy. A small measurement of British decline, but a significant one. The best yardstick of our international stature in the mid-1970s was the British diplomatic response to nations which had once looked to London for a powerful protector. Nothing has been more enlightening than our reaction to events in Athens between the summer of 1974 and the spring of 1975.

At the beginning of July 1974, the *ci-devant* Colonels were almost finished as the government of Greece. In an attempt to buttress their tottering regime, they inspired the Samson coup in Cyprus, which deflected Greek attention from a long-suffering home front by inflaming the perennially smouldering furnace of relations with Turkey over the island question. With sovereign bases on Cyprus, and as one of the guarantor powers with a brief to guard the island's independent future, Britain could scarcely escape involvement in subsequent events, which culminated in the Turkish invasion of the northern beaches. We did little, in fact, apart from evacuating British holidaymakers by warship and offering sanctuary to refugees in the base camps. While all this was happening, however, a Greek mob marched on the British Embassy in Athens on what turned out to be the last day of the Colonels' rule. It smashed all the windows on the ground floor of the chancery building and busied itself inside long enough to cause £21,500 worth of damage.

Some six months later, the Karamanlis government having replaced that of the Colonels, another mob marched on the embassy and this time the riot was more serious. It was lunchtime on a Saturday in January and only a handful of staff were on duty. The ground-floor window openings had been bricked up since the previous episode, and the new wave of attackers approached the building through the churchyard next door. By pouring petrol under a garage door and stuffing oil rags inside the false ceiling of the entrance hall, they set the ground floor of the chancery alight. The blaze was eventually extinguished by members of the embassy, while crews of the Athens Fire Brigade engines drawn up in the street outside merely watched their efforts without so much as unhitching a hosepipe. Some onlookers believe they saw students scaling the churchyard wall on the shoulders of policemen. At any rate, the whole affair, which this time cost £31,000, looked to some people a bit like that scene in the film Z, where the coppers stood still and watched the anti-government politician being fatally beaten by thugs. No one seems sure what prompted the first attack on the embassy. The second is thought to have been the work of Greek-Cypriot students in Athens, who believed that the Royal Navy had helped the Turks in their invasion: and mainland Greeks, who have a weakness for blaming everyone but themselves for their own misfortunes, were ready enough to believe this, too.

The British diplomatic response was in the first place to present the repair bills to the Greek government, and to tell the Greek Ambassador in London that we didn't think much of these goings on. The July bill was paid promptly by the incoming Karamanlis government, the second more slowly by the same gentlemen. Beyond that, what we did was – as one diplomat put it – to look round for olive branches to offer the Greeks, to soothe their wounded feelings, which had been responsible for their offence to our property. The first olive branch, in 1974, was a suggestion to the Greeks that we were now prepared to restore British Ministerial visits to Athens, which had been suspended as a mark of disapproval against the Colonels. At the time this story was told to me, my informant turned to a colleague and said: 'We didn't manage to find a pro-Greek gesture after the embassy burning, did we?' We did, in fact, though he was not to know it at the time. In May 1975, a new round of Anglo-Greek cultural discussions was held in London, one of an annual series which takes place alternately in each of the two capitals. The outcome was a promise to mount an exhibition of British Old Masters in Athens as soon as possible. British officials taking part in the talks had no doubt that the offer would never have been made had it not been for what happened at the British Embassy and upon the hapless island of Cyprus: exhibitions like that are expensive, and it becomes increasingly difficult to persuade the owners of priceless paintings to denude their walls for several months yet again, merely to please some foreign audience. Americans, who have also been cast as bogeymen by simple Greek citizens, might not have reacted in quite this way; nor would Turks. Nothing is more symbolic in this Greek episode than the fact that, at the time of the British Embassy fire, a march of demonstrators on the

American Embassy was firmly deflected by a large cordon of police. Not one Greek, so far as is known, went within a mile of the Turkish Embassy. 'They know', sighed one of our men, 'that if they sack the British Embassy, no one will even be rude to a Greek Cypriot in Haringey. If they did it to the Turks, there'd be big reprisals.'

Britain's presence in Cyprus is seen by most of her diplomats as the last vestige of her old imperial status – and, generally speaking, the younger they are, the more thankful they are that this should be so. Yet, as is very often the case with diplomats, this response can be tempered by the immediate responsibilities of a man's own posting. The world view tends to be limited to the people at the top of the FCO: it is not easily accessible to the majority below, who are working in very clearly restricted compartments. 'Why, for God's sake, bases in Cyprus?' asked someone in the British mission to the United Nations in New York, shortly after the 1974 crisis broke in the island. He argued quite fiercely that our main concern should be to adjust our role in the world to our position in it. 'If you see a lot of FCO telegrams, you spot an awful lot of cases where we can be seen putting our oar into affairs where we've no place to be.' That mission has constantly been advising London to shed British bases wherever possible, in order to make our position within the United Nations even more that of a bystander on the international sidelines, no target at all for anyone still inclined to beat us with the anti-colonialist stick. But a diplomat whose work is directly concerned with affairs in the Eastern Mediterranean, will very quickly point out that Britain can't drop Cyprus like a hot potato. For one thing, he'll argue, we're a guarantor power. For another, the Americans would be much displeased if we abandoned a highly prized piece of strategic real estate, Cyprus being not only a vital staging post on the CENTO air route through the Middle East, but also a very useful intelligence base for NATO's concern in the same area. They see things in yet another light at the British Embassy in Washington. At the same time as his colleague in New York was despairing of Britain's presence in Cyprus, someone up Massachusetts Avenue was taking the view that 'in a sense, Cyprus has come as a blessing to us. We have a lead role in what goes on there. In terms of Callaghan's standing with Kissinger, it came as a godsend.'

The buddy boys act that gradually developed from early in 1974 between the new British Foreign Secretary and the American Secretary of State brought nothing but satisfaction to the hearts of those professionally most concerned with the transatlantic alliance. 'They have really got on wavelength very rapidly,' was the sort of remark one could hear from many British diplomats towards the end of that year. Some might not attempt to conceal the heretical thought that the public affability of the two men doubtless represented something of a flattery to one and a moral prop to the other in their variously difficult times. But splendid it certainly was for the professionals to see Dr Kissinger pausing regularly at Heathrow Airport, so that he might take Mr Callaghan into his confidence before flying on to Cairo or Tel Aviv or back to Washington; and most especially to witness that remarkably fraternal trip to Cardiff, to watch Mr Callaghan being given the freedom of the city which includes his Parliamentary constituency. Men at the United Nations mission may have taken a more jaundiced view of one by-product of this ostentatious friendship, when, in the spring of 1975, HMS *Lowestoft* went steaming close to the Vietnamese shoreline during the American evacuation; for it was hard to believe that the British would have allowed the frigate to be seen within a thousand miles of her actual cruising station if the Kissinger–Callaghan relationship had not matured so rapidly. If you weren't working on the sidelines in New York, however, it was a matter for applause. For it was clear evidence to the world that the alliance was in good repair, in better shape than it had been for a long time before James Callaghan became Foreign Secretary.

What the alliance really consists of, what it amounts to, is a matter for speculation among laymen and no very clear definition by diplomats. Lord Trevelyan has roundly declared that 'Our special relationship with the United States no longer exists ... The Americans nowadays look on the British like a cosy maiden aunt, whom they enjoy visiting as one of the family, but no longer regard as having a serious influence on international affairs'.[1] A tartly academic voice ten years ago brushed it aside as a relationship so special 'that it is inexplicable in terms of conventional alliance theory', which is usually based

[1] Trevelyan, pp. 10, 98.

upon a mutuality of interest and complementary strength.[1]
One man in Washington will say, 'I don't think any of us in the
embassy believes in the special relationship any more, if only
because of the economic and political disparity between us',
when, not half an hour earlier, a colleague just down the corridor has insisted that if it is not a special relationship still, then
it most certainly remains a 'natural relationship', a phrase he
has admittedly borrowed from Edward Heath. This is followed
by a third opinion in the same building that 'For some reason
the Yanks feel they need to have a special relationship with us':
and this is supported by the disclosure that 'The first thing
Ford did on mounting the White House was to have Kissinger
ring Wilson with the news "The President would like to speak
to you".' Meanwhile, at the Whitehall end of the link with
Washington, you may hear that 'Suez dispelled the Special
Relationship in capital letters, but something special remains'.

The general basis of the relationship, of course, is seen to be
the common heritage of language and history and the constant
traffic from one country to the other of academics, officials,
businessmen, holidaymakers and migrants; there is also a
touching faith that something called 'the English vote' still
exists among the American electorate a full generation after the
two peoples stood shoulder to shoulder in anything very much.
It is argued that the State Department finds it more natural to
talk to the FCO than anyone else abroad because American
officials know that from the direction of London they'll get an
honest answer, an intelligent and considered view. 'They think
we're the best of a tiresome bunch, not being gifted with strict
French Cartesian logic, which the Yanks don't follow.' While
conceding that the Germans have a pretty close relationship
with the Americans, too, our men are inclined to hint that,
being based upon purely economic and political considerations,
this leaves the Germans some way behind the British, whose
alliance with the United States is based upon Defence. We still
have greater representation than anyone else around the Persian
Gulf, they say; we're closer than anyone else to the Shah; we
still have those military bases and handy airstrips: all these are
instances of the German inability to compete with us in
American eyes. 'We are the one nation with whom it is quite

[1] R. Dawson and R. Rosencrance, *World Politics*, 19 (1966).

impossible that they will ever be at war'; a solemnity which is made to sound as if perhaps it is the biggest clincher of the lot.[1]

While emphasizing that the State Department talks freely to them on anything up to matters of the topmost secrecy, our men usually enter *caveats* that severely qualify this. Of course, they add, we wouldn't tell the Americans about a computer deal we might be making as part of a trade relationship with Eastern Europe. In London, the men on the American desk talk about scotching crises in the Anglo-American family before they can really happen. Dr Kissinger became very bad-tempered in February 1974, when he heard that the Europeans had started a dialogue with the Arab oil producers without so much as a by-your-leave to Washington, and London led in trying to soothe his wounded feelings. 'Our instinctive reaction in this building when Kissinger blows up is not to have a public row with our friends.' This demands the very subtlest diplomacy that Britain can muster, being as she is rather desperately concerned not to appear as some sort of linkman between Europe and the United States in the eyes of the European Community, while perhaps hoping that this may be the very job she's been looking for ever since that depressing day in 1962 when Dean Acheson thought, far too loudly for London's comfort, that Britain had lost an empire and not yet found another role. British diplomats will assert that the Americans actually need us as their window on Europe. This is, maybe, a way of comforting themselves in the stark knowledge that the Anglo-American relationship could dwindle to nothing but cool civility if the British aren't careful.

The British Embassy in Washington quakes at its foundations

---

[1] This has not always been so. In 1928 the Foreign Secretary, Austen Chamberlain, told the Committee of Imperial Defence that 'war with Germany, Italy and Japan is inconceivable', but that war with America was not. The Pentagon in Washington was then composing a *Joint Army and Navy Basic War Plan 1928–9*. This contemplated the possibility of a war causing 'the economic exhaustion of the United Kingdom' and included a memorandum by Brigadier General Simonds. In it he wondered about the strength of 'the irreconcilable elements in the Irish Free State' and asked, 'Could it be organised and would it be able to give active support to an American Expeditionary Force attempting to secure a base of operations on the Irish coast?' The State Department did not take the War Plan off the secret list until the end of 1975, because it was regarded as diplomatically embarrassing.

when the first telegram arrives from England, bearing rumour of more impending Defence cuts. When that happens 'you warn London of the disastrous consequences here of a cutback in Defence, and at the same time you put the best face possible on it when you see the Americans'. Life for a British diplomat in America can be very trying, what with Defence cuts and the unrelieved domestic gloom reported by the British press, which is usually remarked upon as though the newspapers were to blame for the nation's ills; or, at least, as if they were betraying a national confidence that were best kept to themselves. Just occasionally, British diplomacy in Washington can sound a trifle sad. They are very proud in the embassy of the fact that, for several years, the State Department preferred to make its assessment of London's thinking after picking their brains rather than those spread around the American embassy in London, because Dr Kissinger wasn't prepared to accept some of the appraisals passed back to the home plate by his Ambassador Walter Annenberg. The British wish that they could act as intellectual sparring partner in the alliance far beyond the mere supply of home thoughts from abroad. But 'we have difficulty in contributing ideas even when they invite us to'. When the question of peaceful nuclear explosions was first floated in the international atmosphere some years ago, the Americans, apparently in some doubt as to what would be their most advisable response, canvassed their British allies in Washington for some inspired thinking on the subject. 'After prodding London', according to someone who was around at the time, 'we produced a memo of some wetness.'

The alliance, however, is there and in some order. So is the one formed between Britain and the other eight member countries of the European Economic Community (a subject which demands, and will duly get, a chapter to itself). Between the two of them, Britain is to a limited degree trying to have something both ways. That is not a unique occurrence. The men who supervise our affairs with Africa make no bones about the fact that we are guilty of the same offence in our dealings with that continent. South Africa, they point out, is our twelfth biggest trading partner and it is vital that we should continue to hold at least our current share of the South African market. At the same time our trading balance with Black Africa has been growing in our favour since 1970, when it stood at 50/50.

D

Their intention – and it would take some highly dogmatic ministerial directives to deflect them from this course – is to continue having it both ways in future, whatever public opinion at home might think. Public opinion, they suggest, can be far too emotional on the subject, far too little aware of the facts of African life. After twelve years or more of independence, argues the FCO, Black African diplomacy recognizes that the facts of life are far more complicated than had been supposed when they became free nations. 'Simonstown, you see, really wasn't an issue to Black Africa.' When a British diplomat says something like that, he is ignoring African public opinion as much as British. He will freely admit that we have a love-hate relationship with the old colonial territories. It is commonplace, he says, for a Black African leader to make a public speech one morning in which the British are vilified as a breed of ineradicably colonialist monsters; and then, in the evening, to tell members of the British high commission, whose duty-free whisky he is slugging back quite affably, to take no notice of what he said earlier in the day, which was for domestic consumption only. The diplomats are not offended by this equivocal posture, for it is the way of the world they inhabit. They, and the African leader, understand these things together and jog along quite easily most of the time. The British, for their part, have seen no reason why they should not continue to do so unless they themselves were discovered making some false move in the tortuous preparations for a Black government in Rhodesia. Yet it would be quite unfair to conclude that their actions are wholly dominated by cynicism, for they frequently let slip a dispassionate regard for the future of the world between Cairo and Cape Town. They make worried noises about the seduction of African nationalism by Arab militancy, seeing little in common between the two aims. 'I'd hate to see Black Africa being deflected from its continental problems by the problems of the Middle East,' says a voice from the middle reaches of British diplomacy. One from very near the top remarks that 'The grand issue since decolonization ended is the transfer of wealth from the rich industrial countries to the rest of the world; *that* will be the big question for the rest of this century and well into the next.'

Anyone whose temperament insists that Britain must, by definition, have a leading role to play in some sphere, might well think that it could at least consist in heading the European alliance in its relationship with the Arab countries. Conditions now may seem to favour this idea. What James Callaghan said at the start of 1974, in his first Parliamentary debate as Foreign Secretary—namely, that the rise in oil prices, which had soared catastrophically in the previous few months, had completely altered the world in which British foreign policy had to be formulated—could have been repeated (and was) in every national assembly within the EEC. The singular thing about Britain's experience of the oil crisis was that it sprang from an area where her influence had once been a dominant factor in shaping local fortunes and destinies. Though it had never been part of her Empire, no other European country had ever had the same patronizing connection with the Arab countries of the Middle East. No one else's history had produced such a long string of figures to compare with Burton, Doughty, Stanhope, Lawrence, Thomas, Stark, Philby or Thesiger: men and women with a mystical and romantic feeling of kinship with the bedouin and the desert. None had thrown up a Glubb, to found an Arab Legion. No other diplomatic machine has ever contained a traditional elite like the Arabists of the British Foreign Office, whose skills and knowledge have accumulated over several generations of acquaintance with a specialized field. It was no chance that sent young Arab princes, like Faisal and Hussein, to English public schools, that has inclined most Arab sheikhs towards the medical attentions of the London Clinic. British diplomacy and a curious racial attraction have been responsible for such things, which, in their turn, for two or three generations had their own bonding effect on the relationship; until Arab rulers, who have an abiding respect for power won by force of arms, decided that the British Isles had become a land of enfeebled camp-followers.

To anyone pinning his hopes on tradition, it might seem a very natural thing for British expertise in Middle Eastern affairs to place her men at the forefront of any team concocted by the European alliance to negotiate with Arabs: what Duncan, with fastidious delicacy, called 'providing a valuable contribution to the instrument'. It is quite remarkable, however, that inside the FCO you hear Arabists and European specialists alike saying no such thing. Their view is that we are basically—in spite of the alliance—involved in hard and grinding competition with the other Europeans for Arab patronage, in which our traditions give us no head start at all. 'What, as an Arabist, I'd like to see, is the EEC speak with a stronger voice, but I'm not sure that we're going to develop a particular role in Europe vis-à-vis the Arabs; I think our Arabist background is a wasting asset. I don't think, for example, that in Egypt we're more acceptable interlocutors than the French, though we're in a good position still in Saudi Arabia, Kuwait, the Emirates and Iraq.' As for the notion that Britain might have some political role as an honest broker in the dispute between Arabs and Israel, it is regarded as comically naive – though it is still cherished by some politicians of the Left, who talk hopefully of the Foreign Office's Arabist tradition being fruitfully grafted on to the Labour party's old Zionist strain. As far as the FCO is concerned, the very most that a British Ambassador in Cairo could do independently would be to advise the Egyptians that, if they took a certain course of action, it would be Britain's belief, based upon past experience, that the Israelis would respond in a particular fashion. Substantially 'we just cheer Kissinger from the sidelines and it's very difficult to get any view across to him unless he comes and asks us for one, which happens only when things are going wrong for him'. Our policy in Arab countries, as defined by one man responsible for executing it on the spot, consists in 'treating the locals ostentatiously as equals and trying to get the most out of it'.

That will sound to some much more like the fawning of Uriah Heep than the embattled defiance of Winston Churchill. But it is at least consistent with a popular vision of Britain as the lame duck of Europe, in spite of its flickering assumption of fundamental superiority. It also conforms (although it may be an extreme and uncomfortable example) with a realism about relations with foreigners that is much more common among diplomats than their public image usually represents. What it does not at all tally with is the size, the shape and the deployment of Her Majesty's Diplomatic Service in the mid-1970s, which in most respects is grander now than ever it was when Britain was at the height of her power.

It is a truism of the diplomatic life in any country that a nation sends its most talented representatives to those places abroad which, for one reason or another, are of the most concern to it. It will not consign a senior Ambassador of proven skill to what it regards as an international backwater, except as a very rare and extreme form of discipline, in which, generally speaking, only those governments suffering from chronic instability and threatening revolution indulge. The most important British embassies up to 1914 were those in Berlin, Paris, Rome, Vienna, St Petersburg, Tokyo and Constantinople. Between the wars, Berlin and Paris outstripped all others for prestige and glamour on the 'inner circle' of diplomacy. After the immediate post-war confusions had died down, Washington became the embassy to which everyone aspired. It retained this primacy until the end of the 1960s, since when the most vital ambassadorial role has been that of leading the British Delegation to the EEC in Brussels. It was from this post that Sir Michael Palliser was recalled towards the end of 1975, to become PUS in London and Head of the Diplomatic Service.

The EEC job in Brussels is only one of fourteen posts to which the most senior and best-paid British Ambassadors can be assigned. These are the Grade 1 men, who have spent thirty-odd years climbing a career ladder with ten rungs to it. A diplomat can serve as an Ambassador somewhere in the world when he has reached only Grade 4, but in responsibility and prestige his post will be regarded as very small beer indeed compared with what awaits him when he has proved himself fit for Grades 1 and 2. At least, that is the theory of the grading structure. For the list of Grade 1 and 2 appointments reveals some very odd patches of assessment if they are meant to indicate – as logically they should – just where Britain sees her priorities today. In theory, the lists are revised every six months, though the correlation of foreign capitals and diplomatic gradings probably changes more from decade to decade than from year to year. At the middle of 1975, they stood as follows:

Grade 1 posts: Bonn, Brussels (EEC), Brussels (NATO), Cairo, Canberra, Lagos, Moscow, New Delhi, New York (United Nations), Ottawa, Paris, Rome, Tokyo, Washington.

Grade 2 posts: Ankara, Athens, Bangkok, Brasilia, Brussels, Buenos Aires, Cape Town, Copenhagen, Dublin, Geneva (United Nations), The Hague, Islamabad, Kuala Lumpur, Madrid, Nairobi, Stockholm, Teheran, Tel Aviv, Vienna,

Vienna (United Nations), Wellington – together with the No 2 jobs in New York and Washington.

The most striking thing about the lists is how much they are at variance with the world view taken by the Duncan Committee. If its report is read at face value, there are some sixteen capital cities throughout the world where British diplomacy ought to be concentrating its best efforts. When the five accreditations to the United Nations, the EEC and NATO have been subtracted from the Foreign Office lists, together with the two high gradings awarded to the diplomatic Ministers in New York and Washington, there seem to be thirty countries in the world regarded by the diplomats themselves as points of concentration. One may wonder why it is that, having relinquished our role of policeman in the Far East, Bangkok and Kuala Lumpur figure so highly in British calculations. Why, if our diplomats concede their insignificance in the political troubles of the Middle East, do they place such value on Tel Aviv? What is it about the Argentine and Brazil that engages so much of their attention? Is Austria, also bereft of its old empire but not, alas, a member of the EEC, of such importance in the concert of nations? Is it naughty to wonder, at the same time, why Italy is fractionally more alluring than Denmark, Holland or Belgium?

Such questions multiply rapidly when the rest of Britain's dispositions overseas are surveyed. Quite apart from the scores of British consulates, there were 88 full-blown embassies in foreign capitals in 1975, and 32 high commissions in Commonwealth countries.[1] There are the missions to international or regional organizations, like the United Nations, the EEC and NATO, about a dozen all told. There is a solitary legation, to

---

[1] These figures are deceptive. In some countries a string of subsidiary missions, much more substantial than the average consulate, stretches across the hinterland from the embassy or high commission itself. In West Germany, for instance, the embassy in Bonn oversees consulates-general in Düsseldorf, Frankfurt, Hamburg, Hanover, Munich, Stuttgart and Berlin, each of which includes an average of six London-based officials, three of whom are diplomats proper. There is also the British military government mission in Berlin, headed by a soldier but largely staffed by diplomats. This is quite separate from the British embassy in Berlin, which attends to relations with the German Democratic Republic. In India, apart from the high commission in New Delhi, there are large offices of Deputy High Commissioners in Bombay, Calcutta and Madras.

the Holy See in Rome.[1] And there are still nearly a score of
dependent territories scattered across the face of the earth,
which occasionally require a diplomatic presence. This network
of representation is bewildering in its complexity and very
formidable indeed in terms of the manpower required to sustain
it. So very nearly ubiquitous is it that sceptics may well wonder
why a handful of countries are not in a relationship thus hallmarked by the British. What has poor old Mauritania, for
example, done to deserve its lack of a British embassy or even
consulate? For it seems that, while Britannia may have shed
any of her former claims to rule the waves, she still insists on
having a finger in just about every pie going. She even keeps
in touch with places where nothing much, one would have
thought, can be cooking. What on earth can Our Man in
Mogadishu and his assistants be up to these days? Is it more
than a marvellous Mongolian fantasy that causes us to maintain an Ambassador and his staff (including, from time to time,
the Reverend Dr E. E. Staples, OBE, Honorary Chaplain and
normally resident in Helsinki) at 30 Peace Street, Ulan Bator?
Will historians in future immediately perceive the lustre of
Central America which, in 1975, occasioned an official flutter
of Union Jacks in every segment of the isthmus between
Guatemala and Panama, when the Canadians covered all six
countries from one mission in Costa Rica? Is the Anglo-French
Condominium such a weighty concern that it obliges us to
maintain a British residency in the New Hebrides?

The same imbalances are evident almost wherever you look,
although straightforward comparisons of embassy manpower
are not always trustworthy. French commercial diplomacy, for
example, is not reflected in their embassy roll calls, being conducted by officials who do not answer to the Quai D'Orsay in
Paris. The British figures invariably include such functionaries.
Nevertheless, only two nations have more men and women
working at their diplomacy than the British. They are the
United States and the Soviet Union. This is perplexing in a
country so enfeebled that its life is sustained partly by disburse-
ments of cash from a European Community chest in one direction, and a large loan from the Shah of Iran in another.

---

[1] The head of the legation is a Minister, not an Ambassador, and by
tradition he must always be a communicant member of the Church of
England.

Diplomacy is an expensive business, though it is perhaps not quite so expensive as most people may assume when certain diplomatic extravagances are made public. The Foreign Office cost the British taxpayer £144·7 million in 1976, of which £91·7 million was spent on the overseas establishment of diplomats. The larger figure was 0·32 per cent of government expenditure, which compares favourably with its French equivalent of 1·3 per cent. Generally speaking, British diplomacy in recent years has cost about one-fortieth of the Defence budget. Moreover, when diplomatic extravagance is discovered, it is well worth remembering that nothing in the Foreign Office and all its works ever reached the dizzying heights achieved by the Department of the Environment's motor-vehicle licensing centre at Swansea. This was expected, in 1965, to cost £95 million but, by 1976, had already cost £400 million – and even then wasn't working properly.

Nevertheless, our diplomatic representation abroad is faintly ridiculous in the context of a lecture to new diplomats, who are advised that they are about to serve a nation which can't even be called a second-rate power any more. Some might suggest that the British are merely suffering from a passing malaise; that Great Britain in the middle of the 1970s is in a critical state comparable to several she has emerged from in the past. British diplomacy in the chanceries of Europe must have seemed a very gaudy and irrelevant thing to men and women caught on the hopeless end of the slump in the 1930s. It is more plausible to argue that those unemployed were salvaged from their predicament only with the assistance of a world war which killed a lot of them off and that thereafter, for a couple of decades, the survivors lived in an illusion of plenty which was slipping away from them without many people paying attention. Only the perspectives of history will eventually show the British where they have really been all this time. But as an interim judgment there seems to have been nothing with a more truthful ring to it than something Sir Arnold Toynbee wrote in 1968.[1]

I think Britain today is in much the same position as Spain, the Netherlands and Sweden were at the turn of the seven-

[1] Quoted by Boardman and Groom, p. 2 (privately communicated to the authors).

teenth and eighteenth centuries. Spain has always looked
back, so she has never recovered from having ceased to be
a first-class power in the military and political sense.
Sweden and the Netherlands, after a spell in the doldrums,
turned their backs on their irrecoverable past, and looked
forward.

Much the same thing was said more directly by Professor
Alastair Buchan, founder and director of the Institute for
Strategic Studies, just before he died in 1976. 'We aren't
finished,' he told a friend. 'In fact, we can still give a lead if we
realize that we can only suggest, not command. Above all, we
must recognize that we must give our best intellectual attention
to finding our new proper role, not to shoring up our old un-
tenable positions.'[1]

Neither view obviously squares with running the third largest
diplomatic service in the world.

[1] *The Observer*, February 8th, 1976.

3 Selecting an Elite

There can be few sections of society so embalmed in mythology as the diplomats. The very nature of their job is partly responsible for this, holding them as it does at a physical distance from the rest of us for most of the time, so that we cannot actually see what they are like in the flesh. Very few of us will knowingly have clapped eyes on a diplomat unless he is a neighbour during one of his bouts of service in London. In spite of this, they themselves are sometimes directly responsible for their public image, for Ambassadors have a weakness in retirement for writing their memoirs, most of which are damnably dull, with a tendency towards self-inflation. But the mythology on the whole is passed to us secondhand, we do not construct it ourselves; and it is not, by and large, a felicitous one. Diplomats attract a remarkable degree of envy and disdain, which is occasionally sharpened to a point of venom. 'Caught with their striped pants down in Baghdad, in Paris and now in Havana, Britain's diplomatic representatives need a closer examination than they themselves are evidently able to give their surroundings.' That was *The Economist* fulminating in 1959, in a manner which is not uncommon, almost a reflex, among some journalists when things go ill for the nation abroad. Leisured writers between hard covers are apt to be more sidelong in their treatment; but they generally project their readers into a diplomatic world consisting of languid chaps who are limited in efficiency, living far too well off the public purse, blue with breeding, snobbish more often than not, and over-generously endowed with double-barrelled names. The diplomatic life may have been replete with such characters when Lawrence Durrell was a contract officer in the British Embassy in Belgrade. One can certainly try to roll off one's tongue a hyphenated litany of bygone ambassadorial names – Knatchbull-Hugessen and Millington-Drake, Ashton-Gwatkin and Stonehewer-Bird – without doubting for a moment that they were destined for something mighty impressive from birth.[1] But striped pants are infrequently worn in the FCO today, though it will still be a headstrong man who attempts anything less formal than a dark grey or blue suit. And, though hyphenated people are still to be found in the Diplomatic List (as well as two Lords and a baronet), it is nigh on twenty years since Britain was represented by an Ambassador rejoicing (we must hope) in the names of Herbert Reginald Dauphin Gybbon-Monypenny.

The people who know diplomats best, who work with them a great deal but are not of them, are sometimes astringently critical. A man from Overseas Development will say that 'The Diplomatic Service has an appalling influence on young people, who nervously go abroad as Third Secretaries, to be treated as skivvies by old-fashioned Ambassadors. They in their turn become pompous, wrapped up in the mystique of diplomacy.' To some extent, such a criticism seems to represent, as much as anything, an undercurrent of rivalry and interdepartmental jealousy that flows in varying strength throughout the course of British government, and which may be found within the Diplomatic Service itself. A diplomat is quite liable to say that someone with his origins in the old Colonial or Commonwealth Services is readily distinguishable by his pomposity from a colleague who has always been pure Foreign Office.

Touches of diplomatic arrogance do surface from time to time. A Home man when making sharp cracks about diplomats has possibly been told by some lofty FCO chap, whose department has exchanged memoranda with his own, that 'It takes you fellows two or three years to learn to draft.' New entrants to the FCO in 1974 were squarely informed by an Under Secretary that 'I regard this as an elitist job', before he went on about the need 'to resist pressures to make us like every other dreary little civil servant in Whitehall'. Some time later I asked a very senior man if I might sit as an observer at a particular meeting.

[1] Sir Hughe Knatchbull-Hugessen's greatest claim to fame, however, is an unfortunate one. He was Ambassador in Ankara during the war and his personal valet was the German spy code-named Cicero. Copies of all dispatches and instructions passed between Sir Hughe and London were sent straight off to Berlin by this man, including confidential reports on the Cairo and Teheran conference.

His immediate response was 'No', which was entirely reasonable on good security grounds. But then, after a perfectly timed pause, he could not resist adding 'and, in any case, I think you might find it all a bit cryptic', which is diplomatic language for 'above your head'. At one of our European embassies I tried to find out what our diplomats thought was the impression conveyed by British officials in that part of the world. 'I don't know what our image is as far as the locals or other embassies are concerned,' was the bland reply, 'because one doesn't ask; and, even if one did, one wouldn't accept it as true.'

Politicians who deal with diplomats never mention the arrogance, though Labour men are by no means uncritical of the way the FCO works. But even they are much more likely to applaud the intellectual calibre of diplomats. All politicians relish the diplomat's understanding of political ways and interest in political processes, which, they say, far exceeds that of the average Home civil servant. They may complain that diplomats are out of touch with ordinary people in Britain, but in the next breath they may boast that in the FCO there are probably half a dozen men who could be Permanent Secretaries elsewhere in Whitehall. Or else they say that 'The level up to and including Counsellors includes the most gifted men of their generation I've ever met. But there's something in the air of the FCO that too often turns such men into old deadbeats.' The most knowledgeable critics outside politics mark diplomats as, above all, experts in avoiding conflicts. 'They waffle endlessly because they're indecisive. They don't want to upset people. It springs from a professional fatalism which goes like this – "I'm only on this posting for three years with so and so (whom I don't much care for) so what the hell … let's not upset him." ' The waffling springs even more, perhaps, from a professional need to avoid all collision courses in dealing with foreigners; but it is very noticeable how the habit drifts into personal relationships. If a diplomat makes some critical or negative comment about anything at all, in the mildest form possible, he will almost always qualify it as though intent not to give offence; or maybe to construct the loophole that could assist subsequent argument in his favour.

Talleyrand used to advise his young men to avoid acting diplomatically with too much zeal. This eventually became a regular watchword among British diplomats – much more, to hear them talk, than among the French. It commended, after all, the cult of the gifted amateur; and, while the Diplomatic Service is unquestionably more professional today than in the past, the dilettante has not yet disappeared. There can be few embassies of medium size and above which do not contain at least one man who manages to convey that diplomacy is only one of several civilized aptitudes at his disposal, and that it was perhaps only the attractive emoluments which caused him to select it above the rest as his chief source of bread and butter. Not many professions, for example, have produced as many writers as diplomacy. Not many professions provide such a variety of stimulating experiences, or appear to leave a man with as much spare time and energy to write in. We are not talking here about retired diplomats, who write much but rarely produce anything as informative as Lord Gore-Booth's memoirs, or as close to literature as Lord Trevelyan's.[1] There is also a long tradition of publication by people still on active service. Notwithstanding Diplomatic Regulations which require severe caution of a man who wants to rush into print, some books emerge under the author's real name, while others don't. The Hon. John Wilson's biography of Campbell-Bannerman appeared as the undisguised work of the British Ambassador in Budapest. No attempt was made to conceal the fact that Alan Davidson's highly original book on Mediterranean seafood was researched while he was at the British embassies in Cairo and Tunis. ('He has also', said the blurb, 'published a study of snakes and scorpions in Tunisia and is working on other books. Otherwise he likes, as recreation, to do paintings of little-known saints, drawing his inspiration from the Sienese masters': none of which impeded his subsequent promotion to British Ambassador to Laos.) The British Ambassador to Costa Rica, on the other hand, publishes his books under the pseudonym of Peter Myllent, the head of an FCO department in London his using the pen-name Clement Fownes. Not all the bookish diplomats finally see themselves between hardbacks. The careful observer may notice that an illuminating piece of information about the Earl

[1] The anxiety of diplomats to publish memoirs is extraordinary. They are even known to do so at their own expense, when they cannot find a commercial house to take the risk. The latest example of a self-publishing diplomat is Sir Roderick Barclay, ex-Ambassador in Brussels, who appeared between his own hard covers in 1975.

of Bothwell's sixteenth-century remains has been submitted by the British Ambassador in Buenos Aires to the correspondence columns of *The Times Literary Supplement*. Nor is bookishness the only cultivation of diplomats. In the Cairo embassy not so long ago, both the Head of Chancery and the First Secretary (Information) were pillars of the Anglican Cathedral choir as well as enthusiastic amateur actors. The Counsellor's pleasure was to sing *lieder* by Schubert once a week, this being all the time that the only suitably talented accompanist in Cairo could spare him.

The origins of these men and how they are selected for their profession provokes much more debate than the qualifications of people in any other walk of life. The circumstances which have brought men into diplomacy tend to vary rather more than the stereotype suggests. A Deputy High Commissioner at an African post, who entered the FCO at the age of forty, after working for twenty years on railways at home and abroad, may indeed be a rarity, but it is not so very uncommon to come across men who have tasted other careers first.[1] In 1975 there was a First Secretary in Washington who had been employed by the *Financial Times* before abandoning journalism because, he said, he wasn't doing too well in it. There was a man of the same rank in London who had started life as a geographer in Edinburgh, who moved south in pursuit of his fiancée and who, having tired of the academic life anyway, killed two birds with one stone by submitting himself to the civil service examination. At one of our European embassies there was a former biologist who suffered a fall in salary on joining the Diplomatic Service, though he had almost certainly improved on it by reaching the level of Counsellor. The man in charge of Britain's economic diplomacy in another post was an ex-merchant banker and businessman whose first Foreign Office appointment was as Consul-General in Hanoi. Occasionally, diplomats have experienced life in the Home Civil Service first. One man, having read Classics for his first degree and economics for his second, joined the Scottish branch of the Ministry of Agriculture; seven years later he was sent to Copenhagen as an Agricultural Attaché, whereupon the Ambassador persuaded him

[1]On the other hand, plenty of people have aimed at the Foreign Office when young but instead have made their reputations in totally different professions. Mr Robin Day is one such.

to change services. People who have come straight to the FCO from university have, much more often than not, played with the idea of several different careers first, journalism, the BBC and merchant banking figuring very high on the list of possible alternatives. One woman was told by her Cambridge tutor that either journalism or the Foreign Office were the only possible avenues that someone with her talents should explore. What finally decides the toss-up for such people can be as infinitely varied as the reasons people in every other profession have for choosing which way they will go. This man takes to diplomacy for want of greater alternative enthusiasm and because it offers the prospect of variety and travel. That man says 'I always thought the Foreign Office would be an agreeable life, quite fun and all that sort of thing ... ' A number, who imply that they were always bent on diplomacy and nothing else, talk about their adolescent interest in the formulation of policy: 'a tactical interest – the cut and thrust of international interplay'. With a fractionally different cast of mind and enough driving power such men might clearly have ended up one day, like Harold Wilson, in No 10 Downing Street.

These, of course, are diplomats in the Administrative grades, who in 1976 numbered some 968 of the 6,400 or so Britons working at our diplomacy. These are the people who enter the Service with the most glittering academic qualifications, whose job prospects at the outset are brightest, whose work from the start is the most rewarding in every sense, and whose selection is most regularly questioned by outsiders. As we shall see later on, it is possible for men who have entered the Executive grades to switch into the Administrative stream when they have proved themselves, and reach moderately high rank. But it is the Administrative entrant, hot from university, who is much more likely to become an Ambassador abroad or an Under Secretary at home. He has joined an officer corps, whereas the Executives are among the other ranks. The critics know very well that the tradition of recruiting such men in the past was profoundly biased in favour of an elite securely nurtured on paternal wealth, with all its social and educational advantages.[1] The critics observe Lord Plowden's report that, in 1962, no less

---

[1] An old Etonian at one mission told me, 'There's always been an unconscious Foreign Office feeling that public school men are secure enough to speak their minds.'

than 70 per cent of such men came out of public schools; and they surmise that things have not yet changed so very much.

The case of Sir David Kelly, who was Ambassador in Moscow during the early years of the Cold War, exemplifies the old tradition. The son of a Classics professor, he was educated at St Paul's School and Oxford before entering the Diplomatic Service in 1919. The very first thing a potential candidate had to do in those days was to obtain the Foreign Secretary's nomination, which meant that he had to be recommended by 'some person who is known to the Foreign Secretary or one whose judgment the Secretary can rely on'.[1] If the recommendation was accepted, he then had to face a selection board at the Foreign Office. Only if he passed muster with those gentlemen as well, could he apply to the Civil Service Commission for the right to compete in the examination. That was never granted unless the candidate could demonstrate high proficiency in both French and German, and show that he could lay hands on a guaranteed private income of £400 a year. Thus armed, and carefully coached by the Reverend C. Dawson Clark, a famous diplomatic crammer, the young Kelly competed successfully with other highly educated and wealthy young hopefuls. 'I shall always be glad', he wrote much later, 'that my initiation into diplomacy was made under the auspices of Sir Reginald Tower, a complete representative of the old school … ' who was reckoned to have been the first British diplomat to manipulate a typewriter. Those were the days when the Diplomatic Service list ran to only three pages 'and it will easily be imagined that the Service conveyed the impression of a small family corporation and indeed regarded itself in that light'. A few months before Kelly joined the Diplomatic Service, officials were considering its union with the Foreign Office, which took place in 1920. A committee chaired by Lord Selborne was meeting periodically and, just before one of its sessions, the Diplomatic Secretary at the Foreign Office, the Hon. Theo Russell, wrote a note to the Chief Clerk, J. A. C. Tilley, about changes that might have to be made in recruiting procedures:[2]

[1] Kelly, p. 75.
[2] FO, 366/780 33A1 (b), June 14th, 1918.

Dear Jack,
　　We shall also have to decide:
　1　The composition of the Board of Selection ...
　4　How to exclude Jews, coloured men and infidels who
　　are British subjects.
　5　If a public school education is obligatory ...

There is no record of Tilley's reply and, when the committee
next met, Item 4 appeared on its agenda as 'Admission of
candidates of foreign origin'. Its decision was that current
Foreign Office regulations should continue to be observed.

A public school education was deemed to be very nearly
obligatory for a long time to come, though shortly thereafter the
private incomes rule was abolished. Consciences, however, did
not begin to prick too sharply until the Second World War, as
this passage from Anthony Eden's White Paper in 1943 shows:[1]

Among criticisms which have been brought against the
Diplomatic Service the view has been expressed that it is
recruited from too small a circle, that it tends to represent
the interests of certain sections of the nation rather than
those of the country as a whole, that its members lead too
sheltered a life, that they have insufficient understanding
of economic and social questions, that the extent of their
experience is too small to enable them properly to understand many of the problems with which they ought to deal,
and that the range of their contacts is too limited to allow
them to acquire more than a relatively narrow acquaintance
with the foreign people amongst whom they live.

The reforms which Eden planned and Ernest Bevin executed
had very far-reaching effects on the Foreign Service; most
notably they admitted women to diplomacy for the first time
and they closed the door for ever on the system of patronage
used by the young David Kelly as a general means of access to
the profession. How far they met the criticism that diplomats
were recruited from too small a circle, educated in the public
schools and at the universities of Oxford and Cambridge, may
to some extent be deduced from Table 1, for the men who form

---

[1] *Proposals for the Reform of the Foreign Service* (Cmd 6420), 1943, p. 2.
E

TABLE 1 *The Foreign Office Hierarchy, 1976*

	School	University	Club	Previous post
Permanent Under Secretary at the FCO and Head of the Diplomatic Service				
Sir Michael Palliser	Wellington	Merton College/Oxford	Guards	Ambassador to EEC, Brussels
Deputy Under Secretaries				
A. H. Campbell	Sherborne	Caius/Cambridge	Brooks's; United Oxford & Cambridge	Assistant Under Secretary, FCO
H. A. H. Cortazzi	Sedbergh	St Andrews; London	Travellers'	Minister (Commercial) Washington
Sir Antony Duff	Royal Naval College, Dartmouth		Royal Commonwealth Society	High Commissioner, Nairobi
N. Statham	Seymour Park Council School, Stretford; Manchester Grammar School	Caius/Cambridge	Travellers'	Minister (Commercial) Bonn
R. A. Sykes	Wellington	Christ Church/Oxford	Travellers'; Army & Navy	Minister, Washington
H. B. C. Keeble	Clacton County High School	London	Travellers'	Ambassador, Berlin
E. N. Larmour	Royal Belfast Academical Institution	Trinity/Dublin; Sydney NSW	MCC; Royal Commonwealth Society	High Commissioner, Kingston
Assistant Under Secretaries				
R. S. Faber	Westminster	Christ Church/Oxford	Travellers'	Counsellor, Cairo
R. A. Hibbert	Q. Elizabeth's School, Barnet	Worcester/Oxford	Reform	Minister, Bonn
M. D. Butler	Winchester	Trinity/Oxford	——	Head of European Integration Dept FCO

Name	School	College/University	Clubs	Position
R. S. Scrivener	Westminster	St Catherine's/Cambridge	White's; Travellers'	Ambassador, Prague
P. J. Male	Merchant Taylors'	Emmanuel/Cambridge	United Oxford & Cambridge	Minister, New Delhi
N. Aspin	Darwen Grammar School	Durham	Travellers'; Naval	Head of Personnel Policy Dept FCO
M. S. Weir*	Dunfermline High School	Balliol/Oxford	——	Head of Chancery, UN mission, New York
J. C. M. Mason	Manchester Grammar School	Peterhouse/Cambridge	Athenaeum	Head of European Integration Dept FCO
J. P. Hayes (Chief Economic Adviser)†	Cranleigh	Corpus Christi/Oxford	——	Director, Trade & Finance Division, Commonwealth Secretariat
A. J. Wilton*	Wanstead High School	St John's/Oxford	Athenaeum; Royal Automobile	Director, Middle East Centre for Arab Studies
J. A. Thomson	educated privately		Athenaeum	Head of UK delegation to MBFR negotiations, Vienna
R. H. G. Edmonds	Ampleforth	Brasenose/Oxford	Turf	High Commissioner, Nicosia (then year as Visiting Fellow, Glasgow University)
R. W. Houssemayne du Boulay	Winchester	New/Oxford	——	Resident Commissioner, Vila, New Hebrides
O. G. Forster	Hurstpierpoint	King's/Cambridge	——	Counsellor, New Delhi
D. F. Hawley	Radley	New/Oxford	Athenaeum; Travellers'	Ambassador, Muscat
P. H. Laurence	Radley	Christ Church/Oxford	United Oxford & Cambridge	Counsellor (Commercial) Paris
K. R. C. Pridham	Winchester	Oriel/Oxford	Travellers'	Counsellor FCO
H. S. H. C. Stanley	Eton	Balliol/Oxford	Travellers'	High Commissioner, Accra

*Trained at MECAS
†Not a member of the Diplomatic Service

the London hierarchy of the FCO today are among the most successful of those who joined just after the war, when the reforms were first practised.

Patronage did not vanish at once; it simply became a rapidly dwindling exception to the general rule of entry. In a most obvious way it still allowed a member of the royal family to serve as an Honorary Attaché in the 1960s. This was the late Prince William of Gloucester, who is remembered by contemporaries as an amiable young man who used to cause endless paperwork by a fad for flying himself home on leave in his own light aircraft, which required all manner of diplomatic clearances in order to cross foreign air space. Entrance for the overwhelming majority of aspirants to Branch A (the old term for the Administrative grades) of post-war diplomacy, however, was effected by processes identified as Methods I and II. Method I catered for those who, in Lord Plowden's kindly phrase, 'may have failed to do themselves justice in their degree examinations'.[1] They had to take a short qualifying examination in general subjects, followed by an interview and written papers in academic subjects up to honours level. Under Method II, candidates took the same qualifying tests but then embarked on a series of group tests and interviews at the Civil Service Selection Board, a process whose fundamental approach had originally been devised by the War Office Selection Board for the purpose of choosing officer material between 1939 and 1945. Having passed that hurdle, Method II candidates (like Method I candidates) went on to a Final Selection Board, whose approval ensured them a job, provided they had obtained a first- or second-class university degree.

This dual system, which offered candidates a choice of examining procedures, was practised until 1969, when Method I was abandoned, largely because comparatively few people made use of it. Something else (which is still deeply embedded in the diplomatic mythology) had disappeared much earlier. When Method II was launched just after the war, the CSSB examination and interviews took place in the semi-rural surroundings of Stoke D'Abernon in Surrey. This was the so-called 'country house party' at which, it has always been imagined (but strongly denied), the examiners spent as much time weigh-

---

[1] Plowden, p. 85.

ing up table manners as investigating intellect and character. Stoke D'Abernon was closed in 1949, mostly as an economy, but also with the thought that candidates might do themselves more justice if they felt they were not being scrutinized non-stop for a couple of days. Yet the kind of snobbery implicit in the popular myth of Stoke D'Abernon quite clearly outlived it by at least several years. A Head of Chancery in 1975 recalled his first days in the Foreign Office, which he entered as a Grade 9 recruit in 1955; that is to say, as someone whose inferior academic qualifications admitted him only to Branch B of the Service, or what is now called the Executive stream. 'Occasionally someone would ask "Which college were you at?" and there'd be an awful, deathly hush. One tended to steer conversations away from that topic afterwards.' The memory still hurt across twenty years, in spite of abilities which had carried him out of the Executive and into the Administrative stream, with the eventual self-confidence that he might yet end his career as an Ambassador.

The most enduring criticism is that far too many men have been to Oxford or Cambridge, far too few have been indoctrinated in the less rarefied atmosphere of the provincial universities. Lord Plowden's Committee said, 'We cannot regard the present situation as satisfactory either to the Foreign and Commonwealth Services or to the universities.'[1] Four years later, in 1968, there was a move to correct the imbalance. Michael Stewart, the Foreign Secretary, invited a group of university vice-chancellors from all over the country to spend a day at the Foreign Office to discuss with him and senior officials how to broaden the academic background of candidates. This gathering rather lamely came to the conclusion – which was actually proposed by an academic from a redbrick university – that the best brains obtained scholarships to Oxbridge, irrespective of their social backgrounds. It was a view that went down rather well among the senior diplomats. Another factor which Plowden adduced was the greater emphasis placed on various forms of public service at Oxbridge, home of the King and Country tradition. The Committee argued that students of provincial universities might generally find diplomacy a less attractive proposition because the tradition was missing from

[1] Plowden, p. 87.

their more recently founded campuses; in short, that they were less susceptible to the recruiting propaganda of the Foreign Office. Something that may well play a part in recruiting patterns was never mentioned by Plowden: the direct influence of provincial university teaching staffs, which is known in some cases to be hostile to what they think the Foreign Office represents. One provincial tutor, invited to supply an assessment of a candidate's potential on the man's application form, commented: 'He is not yet smooth enough to give lunch to an Arab oil sheikh.' That is not an isolated example of prejudice improperly aired. One young man was evidently undeterred by it; but who can tell how many others gave up the idea of a diplomatic career in the face of similarly cheap sneers from university teachers?

There is reason to suppose that Foreign Office recruiting propaganda at one stage was less beguiling than it might have been. Recruiting missions would be sent off on skirmishes round the provinces, but someone in a redbrick audience addressed by a diplomat in 1964 reckons that the talk seemed designed to put off any highly intelligent and ambitious young man, rather than to attract him: 'my clearest recollection at this distance is of a wearisome emphasis on serving my country, and I sometimes wonder what induced me to try for entrance after that'. It has probably improved a lot since then: the careers staff at the London School of Economics say that they have been impressed by the improvement in diplomatic performances there over the past ten years. There was certainly nothing wrong with the diplomatic overture made to the School in November 1974, when five civil servants descended on a roomful of students one evening. The solitary diplomat among them had a head start over her colleagues because she was the only woman, and an attractive one at that; she was also an LSE graduate. In total selling power, it soon became clear that she had only one real rival, a vastly experienced officer from the Inland Revenue who, against all the odds, made his job sound good fun. The diplomat made at least as fine an impression as he simply by being charming, jokey, distinctly non-patronizing and straightforward. She summarized the stages of her own career. She offered reasons for joining the FCO — travel, the fact that you worked with people at your own intellectual level, good pay. She spoke of the mandarin image of the Office and conceded that some such people were perhaps still to be found among the seniors but that most of the younger officers were quite ordinary, 'although I imagine that the bulk of my colleagues in the Diplomatic Service vote Conservative'. The three other civil servants in the room that night were halting in comparison.

The fact is, though, that in the decade after Plowden expressed its concern Oxbridge still heavily outweighed all the other universities in its supply of young diplomats. As Table 2 shows, however, the balance has been tilted appreciably since

TABLE 2   *The Backgrounds of Administrative Entrants*

Years	Sex		School		University	
	M	F	Private	LEA	Oxbridge	Others
1950–4	117	2	99	20	106	11
%	98·3	1·7	83·2	16·8	90·5	9·5
1955–9	85	4	78	11	80	9
%	95·5	4·5	87·6	12·4	89·9	10·1
1960–4	135	10	98	47	125	17
%	93·1	6·9	67·6	32·4	88	12
1965–9	150	18	111	57	122	42
%	89·3	10·7	66·1	33·9	74·3	25·7
1970–4	112	11	69	54	83	40
%	91·1	8·9	56·1	43·9	67·5	32·5

(*Source*: FCO.)

1964; while the balance between ex-public schoolboys and those from schools run by local education authorities has shifted enormously since the end of the 1950s.

No dramatic change has yet occurred in the expertise of young graduates entering diplomacy. Between 1970 and 1975, Administrative entrants brought the following university degrees into diplomacy with them:

History 35; PPE, Economics, Law, etc. 29; Modern Languages 22; English 11; Classics 9; Science 9; Psychology 2; Music 1; African Studies 1.

It has always been upon the historians, philosophers and modern linguists that the generalist tradition of the Diplomatic Service has been built, in the belief that if you took a good nonspecialist he would be good at anything he put his hand to, which a specialist implicitly would not be. Yet Plowden had argued for a wider range of qualifications, declaring that 'the Diplomatic Service will need to recruit a higher proportion of men trained in science; foreign affairs have an increasing scientific content'. The Service is rather apt to point proudly to its small crop of such entrants – the chemist, the geologist, the physicist and the mechanical engineer who joined in 1973, for example – while at the same time making noises to suggest that enough is quite enough. Sir Thomas Brimelow, Permanent Under Secretary from 1973 to 1975, said in a lecture to the Iranian Institute for International Affairs that 'while it is a fairly straightforward matter for us to take a geologist and teach him Arabic, we could not contemplate taking an Arabist and teaching him geology'. One wonders why not, given that (as the PUS pointed out in the same lecture) the Diplomatic Service is quite ready to shunt someone off the premises for a couple of years to be trained externally in Chinese or Japanese.

The diplomatic Establishment has never taken kindly to criticism, and the FCO can still be quite remarkably defensive about the origins of diplomats. In 1939 Knatchbull-Hugessen wrote about 'ancient and ill-formed criticisms' of diplomatic elitism and denounced them as 'entirely false', though Lord Plowden a quarter of a century later demonstrated them to be substantially right. In 1973, Sir William Hayter, sometime Ambassador in Moscow and by then Warden of New College, Oxford, could not resist taking a public swipe at the 'tired old phrases' of a Labour party document which also criticized diplomatic origins. He was challenged in a letter to *The Times* by Professor D. C.M . Platt, and this item in the correspondence column was very sharply noted at the FCO, being carefully filed for future reference with the marginal annotation, 'Prof. Platt was at Queen's, Cambridge, until last year. He is a Latin American specialist. He failed CSSB in 19——.' I myself ran up against the defensive posture in gathering material for this book. I had it in mind to produce tables which would show the education and father's occupation of successful candidates for the Diplomatic Service in selected years over the past quarter of a century, as a small indication of whatever shifting trends might have taken place. The argument about Oxbridge may very well be irrelevant, for the reasons given by the redbrick vice-chancellor at Michael Stewart's meeting; but the school

a child went to and what his father did for work are very sure
pointers to the section of British society he has come from—a
topic that has bothered the British audibly since 1943. A candidate is asked to state his father's occupation as well as his own
educational background on the forms he fills in when applying
to be examined by CSSB. The FCO's first response to my inquiry was to say that while the educational information could
be made available, the father's job was something that didn't
concern them; implicitly (though never actually stated), that
they really didn't know. When I pointed out that it could be
traced to the same source that would provide the educational
data, the ground of the argument swiftly changed. Well, now,
just supposing a chap who came in twenty years ago was a
miner's son; the public wouldn't be able to identify him, of
course, but his colleagues would soon be able to work out who
he was, and this might embarrass him ... still, leave it with us,
and we'll see what can be done. The information was not
forthcoming.

Other smokescreens drift across the horizon from time to
time. Whenever the subject of origins crops up, someone is sure
to point out that Lord Strang, who was PUS from 1949 to 1953,
started life as a Post Office messenger; and that the first job
Lord Greenhill (PUS from 1969 to 1973) ever had was as a
ticket collector on Leeds City Station. While both these facts
are sure evidence that two top Foreign Office officials had
mixed it with the plebs far more than public suspicions might
give them credit for, they conceal the equal truths that the first
was the son of an Essex farmer and came to the Foreign Office
as Captain Strang with a fine First World War record in his
valise, while Lord Greenhill's fledgling experiences on Platform
5 were culled as what would now be called a management
trainee, with the old London and North Eastern Railway,
shortly after his emergence from Christ Church, Oxford. It was
a distinguished war record which caused him to switch careers,
too.

Sensitivity to criticism in the mid-1970s is very curious in men
who must know that the selection processes of today are probably as impressive as any in the world, and rather more democratic than most. On the face of things, the French method of
picking diplomats seems to place a formidably greater weight
on sheer ability, with background completely discounted.

Virtually all entrants to the French equivalent of the Administrative grades have come from the École Nationale d'Administration; the isolated exceptions have passed on to the Quai D'Orsay from the École Nationale des Langues Orientales Vivantes. ENA is, in fact, the forcing house for the very best brains that the French civil service as a whole will absorb. There is very stiff competition to get into it in the first place, to admit a young man to the prestigious company of the meritocratic 'Énarques'; and it is said that there are ten or a dozen applicants for every place the school can offer. The course lasts for twenty-eight months, whatever branch of the civil service the entrant may privately be aiming for, and it is identical in every case. After a month of preliminary indoctrination in Paris, each student is packed off for a year to work and study on attachment at some préfecture in France or in some French government post overseas. A second year is spent studying at the school, followed by a two-month attachment to a private firm before a final four months at ENA and terminal examination. But the candidate is judged on an aggregate of marks acquired throughout the twenty-eight months, some of which are awarded for athletic skill. Only when these have been totted up can he know where his future will lie, for the top 20 per cent are creamed off by the French Treasury, the government audit bureau and the Conseil D'État, which is a tribunal of administrative law. The Quai D'Orsay and its diplomacy is rated fourth in the French bureaucratic hierarchy. Even so, it is acquiring extremely high-powered talent after twenty-eight months of treatment by ENA. Yet, in spite of superficial appearances, this cannot be divorced from the student's family background. A number of studies have shown that a clear majority of France's top civil servants have come from the grande bourgeoisie; it has been demonstrated that, in a twenty-year post-war period, almost a third began their education in one or other of three famous lycées located in expensive districts of Paris.

The British civil service recruiting system has one major thing in common with the French. There are separate schemes for the late entrants in the British system, and competitions for the very special requirements of the Inland Revenue Tax Inspectorate, the Government Economic Service and a few similar bodies. But, essentially, someone fresh from university

who wants to work for the British government at home or overseas at an Administrative level (which, in plainer language
than the civil service uses, means making and executing policy,
and *not* administering to the needs of the policy-making
machine) goes through exactly the same examining process
whether he is bent on diplomacy, the Treasury, the Home
Office or any of the other influential niches along Whitehall.
Once his academic achievements have been considered suitable, these consist of a written test to qualify for an appearance
before the Civil Service Selection Board, and a Final Selection
Board after a successful passage through the CSSB. This is, to
all intents and purposes, what happened to candidates in the
days of Method II.

In the 1950s, people had to stick thirty shillings' worth
(£1·50) of stamps on to their application forms for entry into
the civil service, which was intended to discourage the frivolous.
If they were aiming for the Diplomatic Service, however, they
were asked to subscribe £3, an indication perhaps that they were
expected to take this walk of life even more seriously. There is no
such division of spoils today. But there is one indication that the
Diplomatic Service regards itself as a cut above the rest.
Candidates for the Home Civil Service who seem likely to merit
accelerated promotion are marked as 'fast stream' men by the
CSSB adjudicators; and the Diplomatic Service makes it plain,
in its own instruction to CSSB, that it will have nothing to
do with anybody who would not qualify for the Home Services'
fast stream. It is more difficult for someone to get a job as a
diplomat than in any other branch of the civil service, in spite
of some deceptive figures, because the competition is much
fiercer. In 1974, for example, 2,570 civil service candidates sat
for the qualifying tests, of whom 1,072 were invited to attend
CSSB. Of these, 534 passed on to the Final Selection Board.
Only 333 were eventually offered posts in government service.
On the face of it, the most difficult branch to get into that year
was the Treasury, which took only 5 men; and it does, consistently, take the cream of those successful candidates who are
not bound for diplomacy. The Scottish Office (9), the Civil
Service Department (10), the Home Office (11) and the Department of Employment (19) each took fewer people that year
than the Diplomatic Service, whose intake was 20. This was the
number assigned to the Department of Health and Social

Security, with the Ministry of Defence (40) and the Department of the Environment (55) making much bigger hauls. But
people do not, as a rule, aim for a particular branch of the
Home Civil Service with the same deliberation as they aim for
the Foreign Office: they sometimes list their preferences, but
they apply to join the Home Service in general and, if successful, they are offered jobs as and where the government needs
them in a given year. The needs fluctuate, appreciably in the
case of some Home departments, as much as government
domestic policy does. Foreign Office candidates are much more
concentrated in their ambitions, and there are always a lot of
them. It is estimated that no more than 3 per cent of those
hoping to reach our diplomacy do, in an average year, make
it.

Nobody gets through any of this process without an honours
degree, and anyone heading for diplomacy must also have
shown an aptitude for languages, even though he may not have
studied one since he was at school. The qualifying test is
designed partly to find out how he manages his own language,
partly to find out how his mind works – and how quickly. It all
happens in one and a half exhausting days, with one paper
following another in rapid succession. A passage of 1,500 words
must be reduced to a précis of 350. A solution must be found to
a problem of sociological, political or economic dimensions.
Confronted with a set of statistics, the candidate must write a
report illuminating the significant points. Offered a sentence
with two words very subtly misplaced, he has to reorder them
to make more sense – and repeat the exercise 25 times in 15
minutes flat. On, then, to synonyms (sweater = j——y) with
50 blanks to be filled in 15 minutes. And so on ...

Trial by CSSB is an exhausting business, too, and it lasts
longer. As in the age of the old country house parties at Stoke
D'Abernon, the process stretches across a couple of days, but
now it is conducted in less salubrious surroundings on Northumberland Avenue. The motley battalion of candidates, with
their various ambitions, who turn up on the first day, are
parcelled into groups of five or six, and each group is assigned
for the rest of the time to a panel of three assessors. Some of
these belong to the permanent staff of CSSB; more often
they do not. The panel chairmen are normally senior civil servants, active or recently retired – a former Permanent Secretary

to the Home Office here, an ex-Ambassador in Tokyo there; and any group which includes an aspirant to the FCO usually gets a diplomatic chairman. A so-called observer is generally a working civil servant, in his or her thirties, with a solid career already established and a bright future ahead. The trio is completed by a psychologist, sometimes from the civil service, but more often from industry, a university or a management consultancy. Together and separately, they proceed to take the candidates apart, in the deftest and gentlest and most agreeable manner possible.

The trial starts with a group discussion, for which no marks are awarded, the chief purpose being to take tension out of the candidates while they accustom themselves to a crucial moment in their lives. As they argue whether Britain any longer has any influence in foreign affairs or what price the social contract, the assessors sit watching as the first signs of character are laid on the table: from the boy who tries to dominate the others from the outset, from the lad who says very little but is really rather sharp, from the girl who exudes warmth but not much originality. These characteristics will matter later on when they go into the committee exercise, when each in turn has to chair a meeting of the others and steer them towards a recommendation without bulldozing them to his own private conclusion. The basis of this exercise, and several others that are performed individually, is a complex dossier called The Background Story, which has taken the permanent staff at CSSB several months to prepare and is used for a whole year of competitions. It postulates an imaginary area of Britain positively heaving with problems of local government, legal entanglements and occasional international interests. The candidates are armed with this dossier at the outset and given time to study it before having to start coming up with answers. What it calls for in the first place is fierce concentration and a very clear head to master its intricacies. After that it is all a matter of acumen and straight common sense working against the clock. The candidates have to write a policy appreciation from it and, besides the committee exercise, they must also draft a letter whose object is to resolve a problem in the best way possible. The dossier being deliberately loaded with pitfalls, each exercise demands the balancing of contradictions and the achievement of compromises; which is the art of politics and the craft of civil service.

There are cognitive tests, similar to those already faced in the qualifying exam, which stretch a candidate's capacity to understand words and figures, and measure his intelligence. There are also interviews, each candidate being confronted solo by each assessor in turn. While the psychologist is peering into the inner recesses of character, the observer is concentrating on intellect. Candidate and observer each chooses an arguable proposition and they bat them out together. The chairman, meanwhile, is indulging in the nearest thing that Northumberland Avenue can offer to a fireside chat. He invites the candidate to talk about his reasons for prospecting the civil service, he explores the candidate's interests, and he finds out what the candidate's views of the world are – intensively if he is looking towards diplomacy. It is a completely informal conversation, but an extremely penetrating one, with only a flicker of authority from the distantly paternal figure seated behind the desk. '*Hassan* – that's an odd choice of production for Cambridge, isn't it? Much more pictorial than intellectual?' The questions are hung out innocuously, the answers digested equably.

At the end of each day, when the candidates have trooped limply home, the assessors gather in their threesomes to compare notes. The observer reckons that Candidate A, whom she has interviewed this afternoon, wasn't incisive enough. 'Let's see how he is tomorrow,' says the chairman. 'If we gentle him along maybe he'll relax more.' The chairman is a former Ambassador and he has been confronted this day with a diplomat's son, who wants to follow where father went. 'He's got a fine Diplomatic Service façade,' says the chairman, 'but his drafting exercise lacks judgment. Miss X is much less sophisticated, but her finishing is much better.' Diplomat's son is not, in fact, going to make it; not this year, anyway. Nor is Miss X, who is handicapped by a heavy cold, for which the assessors keep making small allowances (the chairman rather nicely drops a packet of cough lozenges into her lap at the start of Day Two). The boy who tried to corner the group discussion is still competing over-vigorously at the committee stages. 'He should be chastened,' says one assessor. 'Give him The Foreman's Dilemma (a committee topic) in the morning, it's by far the hardest.' The psychologist reports that Candidate B fails to make emotional contact, partly due to losing his father when a child. The chairman, voicing a largely diplomatic thought, wonders whether this might be something he would grow out of. Dodgy, says the psychologist. They discuss performances on the diagrammatic tests, which require the extreme mental agility of youth. 'I could do the first one,' says the chairman, 'but after that the door shuts. It needs a logical, ordered mind, which God knows I haven't got.'

When it is all over, when the assessors have read all the information available to them about each candidate – his headmaster's comments, his university tutor's comments, the background material he has supplied himself, the report of the examiners at the qualifying stage – there is another meeting. They are adjudicating now not only on what they themselves have tested over a couple of days, but on the complete record of every candidate. Their instructions are quite specific on this point:

> CSSB is committed 100 per cent to giving a final mark which is NOT simply the result of the time spent here. If the final mark for practical purposes represents merely, or almost entirely the result of the time spent here we are not playing fair by candidates and we could, I suppose, be almost prosecuted under the Trade Descriptions Act.

So Miss X, whose sinuses have clearly muffled her conversations with the assessors and her committee work, has been allowed something on the strength of her university pastimes, in opera and theatre groups. There is a difference of opinion on where to place the diplomat's son. The chairman has eventually rated him a near-miss, the other two have marked him firmly below the required level. The chairman goes through the young man's papers again, rereads his background material and finally unseals the report on a previous performance at CSSB, action which is permissible only when a candidate's current performance has been assessed. Then he joins his colleagues with a lower marking.

Things are ordered differently, and much more briefly, at the Final Selection Board. No candidate reaches the FSB unless CSSB's conclusion is that he is still in with a chance and, while figures differ somewhat from year to year, the number of borderline cases is suggested by the fact that in 1974 some 58 per cent of Diplomatic Service candidates who got as far as the

FSB were not subsequently offered jobs; 30 per cent of the Home candidates. Yet the Civil Service Commissioners reckon that very rarely do they significantly change the CSSB marking one way or the other after admitting candidates to the final board. In a flight of self-examination the Commissioners decided that in 1971 and 1972 CSSB's standards might have been set a shade too high, particularly in the case of aspirants to the Home Civil Service; and they tried to allow for this in subsequent competitions. But the allowances were made at the level of the FSB, not at CSSB. Guidelines for members of the FSB are illuminating on this point: 'Whenever FSB decides to alter the CSSB mark it must do so on the basis of the evidence as a whole and not on how the candidate has performed at interview: there will, indeed, be occasions when the candidate's performance at interview will be so much worse than his record overall that it will be appropriate for it to be ignored altogether.'

What the FSB is up to almost as much as anything else, is an attempt to demonstrate impartiality, by including even more rank outsiders in the adjudicating processes of the civil service. There are five members of this board, which is generally led by the First Commissioner of the Civil Service, at present Dr Fergus Allen. He is a twinkly Irishman from Dublin, a civil engineer and poet who was Chief Scientific Officer at the Cabinet Office before he took up his present position. Two other people from the civil service sit with him and two more from the world beyond; a captain of industry and a trade union leader are frequent combinations, though one man is almost invariably an academic. Within a month of getting the thumbs up from CSSB, a candidate finds himself joining this squad of judges around a large circular table in the Old Admiralty Building behind Whitehall, with just enough extra space between his chair and those on his flanks to indicate that he is there with a difference. He is there for thirty cordial minutes, which slip away endlessly on a clock behind his head.

All members of the board have a thick file on the candidate; the material CSSB started with, the results of the CSSB tests, and reports written by the psychologist, the observer and the chairman who assessed him. They do not interrogate him. Each man simply asks a few rather casual-sounding questions apparently designed to provoke easy conversation. This is deceptive, for they seem in different ways to be putting their fingers on the singularity of the candidate. One, who fancies himself as a diplomat, has been working in commerce and making far more money at the age of twenty-six than anyone in the FCO below the level of a senior Ambassador. The drift of the questioning is a polite, why on earth ... ? (motivation is in any case scrutinized more closely with would-be diplomats than others). Another candidate arrives at the FSB with a record quite frightening in its brilliance ever since childhood. As he jauntily enters the room, the board is still blinking a bit over the documentation of his remarkable capacities, collectively wondering perhaps whether it is quite up to handling this prodigy. For the next half-hour he treats five men at the top of their various trees to a series of dissertations on anything they care to mention. There is silence as he steps confidently away again. After a moment the chairman clears his throat pointedly. 'Do you realize, gentlemen,' he asks, 'that if we had seen Mr X just five weeks ago, he would have been nineteen years old?' One day he will enter the Diplomatic Service, unless industry or commerce – which he is also canvassing – step in with a more attractive offer. But he is not marked A1, either by CSSB or by the FSB. CSSB has been just a little worried by his manner. Five minutes are now spent worrying whether or not CSSB has worried too much. The board passes him A2, which means that it believes he is likely to reach at least the diplomatic rank of Counsellor; A1 would have rated him a potential Under Secretary.

The young man who follows might have come from another planet. His manner is not in the least practised, he sits down nervously, and while there is nothing of defiance in him, there is something about the way he has not sunk into his chair that suggests he has taken guard before in similar circumstances, ready for someone to bowl the first bouncer. When he opens his mouth, flat midland vowels emerge, marvellously intact after a lot of higher education which has not included the slightest effort to coax them into No Man's Land. This is a geographer from a provincial university, with a fine record; but it does not approach the general brilliance of Mr X. The CSSB chairman (a diplomat, as it happens) has had this to say about him:

F

As the psychologist indicated, Z has had to work hard for everything that he has achieved in life. Because his father was often on night shifts, while his mother also worked a good deal part-time, Z saw little of his parents and had to fend for himself. There was little active encouragement at home for his university studies. What has emerged in Z's case is a most engaging and impressive personality ... He has a strong desire to serve his fellow countrymen in the public service: the Diplomatic Service attracts him because his contacts with foreigners on his enterprising trips abroad have shown him that he can get on well with them, and he is keen to learn their languages well. I have little doubt that he could become a very useful member of the Home Civil Service or the Tax Inspectorate and think his chances of making the fast stream good enough to rate him A3 rather than B. Whatever he does, he will need some training in structuring his thoughts, and he is not instinctively an Organization Person, though he is a very good citizen. He would find much that was wholly unfamiliar in diplomatic life and it would take some time for him to adjust to it. But I believe that if sympathetically handled he would do so; that he would be a most valuable member of any Diplomatic Service community; that he could cope very well in relationships with foreigners, particularly if he were to start his career in underdeveloped countries (he is not yet ready for sophisticated capitals); and that ultimately he might have a great deal to offer on the management side. So with some hesitation, because he needs a good deal of polishing, I join my colleagues in putting forward Z as a possibility rather than as a near-miss for the Diplomatic Service.

Z doesn't get any bouncers from the board. He affects them, as X did, but in a different way, so that there seems to be a fragile nervousness all round the table for the next half-hour. But this, in them, is a thoughtful thing, not a patronizing one. Someone cracked a mild joke when X was in the room, with a wry undertone which X, in spite of his great sharpness, might just not have noticed. Someone else makes a jest in front of Z, but this one is to be enjoyed for its own sake, an invitation to everyone to laugh at it together. The talk hovers vaguely over motivation for a while and then is largely about Z's long vacations in Europe and the friendships he made there. When it ends, there is no question of altering CSSB's verdict. Z may or may not become a diplomat. It will all depend on how many people the FCO needs next year; and how stiff the competition.[1]

No one who has watched the selection machinery working at CSSB and the FSB can fail to be impressed by it. If any part stands out from the rest it is the scrupulous fairness of assessors and board members towards the candidates. The entire operation sometimes seems to be nearly bent over backwards in its desire to take account of whatever is the best that any candidate has to offer. At the same time this is, of course, to a high degree a self-perpetuating system, which the inclusion of outsiders on CSSB and the FSB can only modify. Civil servants are essentially selecting potential civil servants in the image which the selectors have formed of themselves. This is not a unique habit, and they can hardly be expected to detach themselves from it completely. Doctors select other doctors, academics choose other academics. The loudest voices heard in the National Union of Journalists for some time now have argued vehemently that no one but a card-carrying member should be allowed the faintest participation in the editorial construction of a newspaper.

The Diplomatic Service may be more sensitive than any other part of the civil service to criticism of the incestuous element in the selection process. Its highly suspect tradition of recruitment in the past and its occasional exhibitions of defensiveness even now have alone ensured this. A cynic is very likely, as a result, to hail the CSSB chairman's report on Candidate Z ('he is not yet ready for sophisticated capitals ... he needs a good deal of polishing ... ') as clear proof that the Foreign Office has not mended its ways, that it still functions on basic snobbery and class prejudice. Yet this is to confuse utterly a caste mentality and an appreciation of what diplomacy, in fact, involves. It consists in dealing with foreigners, above all other things, and particularly in reaching agreements with them, in not allowing relationships with them to be grinding with friction any more than principle necessitates. It is no more realistic to

---

[1] This candidate was, in fact, successful and joined the Diplomatic Service.

suppose that diplomacy can be conducted at all times by a man speaking his mind bluntly and honestly, than that a court of law sits with every man in the chamber uttering the truth, the whole truth and nothing but the truth, in all its multitudinous shapes and forms. What the morally immaculate may regard as dishonesty is nothing more nor less than the way of the diplomat's world. In some areas more than others, this still demands a degree of 'polish' which those who do not have to endure it in their own lives may reasonably regard as grotesque. It is something to be worn in the interests of an agreeable international relationship; which, provided it has not been based upon some catastrophic fake, like Munich, leaves us all better off. What it does to the diplomat's soul is his own affair. It cannot judiciously be abandoned by any diplomatic apparatus at a greater pace than governments in general throughout the world abandon it. If we do not always get the diplomats idealists would like, diplomacy at least tells us how far the social rearguards have reached.

British diplomacy has been in social transit for some years now, and almost all the old pariahs have been admitted. It has yet to recruit its first Black man, though 1974 saw the arrival of someone who would not have passed muster with the South Africans. Decades have gone by since Jews began to enter the Foreign Office and several years ago one of them was appointed Ambassador-designate, in a splendidly unaware moment, to Saudi Arabia: unfortunately, the *Jewish Chronicle* spent a lot of proud space on his antecedents and, before apoplexy struck Jeddah, the official concerned was discreetly sent to represent Her Majesty's interests in a less sensitive capital. As for rank outsiders of unimpeachably Aryan blood, men with regional accents have been around long enough now to be observed working their way steadily into the higher reaches of the FCO. They are, as yet, no more than a leavening at that altitude but more are surely on the way. There was, in 1975, a head of department in London whose speech bore much more resemblance to Billy Connolly's than to that of the Permanent Under Secretary.

In every sense, the collective voice of the Foreign Office has acquired shades and tones that, not so very long ago, it would scarcely have recognized as proper, let alone diplomatic. The chromatic scale now can be represented by the views of two officials fundamentally separated by almost a generation in age and different traditions of education. A First Secretary in a North American mission, who came out of a grammar school and a redbrick university some ten years ago, was invited to summarize what he saw as the strengths and weaknesses of the Foreign Office today. 'Well,' he said,

> we tend to be an adjustable, flexible lot, fairly quick to pick up new skills, willing to accept responsibility, with an analytical approach to things. The outfit is still small enough for people to know each other and the old-boy network is still very useful. On the other hand, we suffer sometimes from excessive confidence, an excessive assurance that what we do is necessary. There's a bit too much of doing things because that's the tradition – and the bureacratic hierarchy is still pretty structured.

He mentioned that the FCO paid 1,000 dollars a month in rent for his accommodation and he seriously wondered whether the taxpayer got value for that sort of money.

The other man was situated deep inside the diplomacy of the European Community, and nothing in his career had exhilarated him more than the chess games of Brussels, which were not remotely dreamt of when he emerged from his private school and his highly distinguished university college. 'I could be Ambassador to Bongoland,' he declared, 'but it wouldn't be as interesting as this place. Here you can nip foolishness in the bud by a word in the right ear.'

4 Careering Upwards

In the last week of August, a handful of young men and women assemble in the Curtis Green Building on Victoria Embankment. On the desk in front of each is a nameplate, a pad of paper and a copy of *The Complete Plain Words*. The atmosphere of slightly frivolous attention would become a first meeting of university freshmen, but this is the Introduction Course for the annual intake of new Administrative entrants to the Foreign and Commonwealth Office, and it is just about to begin with a breezy welcome from a sort of diplomatic don. Remote personages of very high rank are instantly brought within hailing distance by the careful flippancies of this course chairman. 'The Chief Clerk', he says, 'used to perform certain functions with distinction; functions now performed with even greater distinction by Xerox machines.' And continues in the same manner, which is intended to convey the impression that everyone is going to get along quite famously together. So some of them are. Among these novices is probably the next British Ambassador but ten in Washington, and the PUS who will be trying to steer the nation safely past whatever international rocks may loom ahead in thirty years' time. It sobers a man considerably to contemplate his children's security in such a blend of inexperience and ambition, which seems to place so heavy a responsibility upon the stabilizing influence of Sir Ernest Gowers.

For the next fortnight, this cream of high intelligence will be indoctrinated in the first mysteries of British diplomacy. Heads of department will descend to discourse on the peculiarities of their organizations. Lectures will be delivered on Defence and Foreign Affairs, East–West Relations, Trade Promotion, the Third World and Development Problems and a squadron of other Large Issues. A politician will arrive from across the road to tell what a Foreign Office Minister expects of his professional helpers. Someone from the Cabinet Office will sketch the machinery of central government. The new entrants are towed off to Matthew Parker Street to enjoy a conspiratorial afternoon with Security. They are introduced to the musty splendours of Gilbert Scott's building and offered a sherry before lunch by the Permanent Under Secretary himself.[1] One day they go to be tested in languages just round the corner in Bridge Street. They are given small exercises, in drafting telegrams properly and handling Parliamentary Questions. But most of all, during this fortnight, apart from a swither of activity with national insurance cards, identity documents and other wotnottery, they are given a series of talks by civilized men in a civilized manner on a civilized profession, much lubricated with quotations from Lords Birkenhead, Birkett and Gore-Booth and — most of all — from the ineffable Sir Harold Nicolson. When it is all done they are deposited, one by one, on the doorsteps of the departments to which they have been assigned for the first stretch of their careers. They start work on Monday morning, at 9.30 if possible, and henceforth they are part of Britain's diplomatic response to the rest of the world.

There may not be another country among the developed nations which throws its new entrants into work as decisively as that. The twenty-eight months of training which the French give their men through ENA are not, it is true, specifically designed for diplomacy; but the diplomatic end-products are apt to make British politicians who have seen them in action wish they had all that talent working for them. West Germans join their Foreign Service for a probationary period of between eighteen months and two years, spent alternately in Bonn and at missions abroad, but then they have to face a conclusive examination. A young American starts his diplomatic career with five months of training at the Foreign Service Institute in Washington, which also runs a course for wives of married entrants. It has always been the custom of the British, though, to size a man up, accept him, and teach him the ropes as he goes along. The rawest Third Secretary is quite liable to find that, within the first week of that Monday-morning start, he is drafting a submission which will float upwards through the

[1] Yet another sign of how times have changed — for the busier. When Sir Robert Vansittart was PUS, just before the war, he would invite each new recruit, individually, to lunch.

works and result in £200 worth of footballs being donated by Britain to deserving causes in Uruguay. Before he has even drawn his first pay cheque, he will thus have participated in something with an International Repercussion – even if this is no more than an agreeable cry of 'Bobby Charlton' on the playing fields of Montevideo. From his very first day, when the head of his department kindly takes him out to lunch at the club and talks to him as an elder brother, a pattern is set which will continue for the rest of his career. It is one of being told and shown how to do something and then very swiftly having to do it himself by imitation and for real. Coaches will be awaiting him in the diplomatic nets wherever he goes in his early years, and their philosophy is an extremely simple one. 'It's better', according to a Head of Chancery, 'for one not to ejaculate prematurely if the junior can get on the job himself.' Which is a very Foreign Office way of putting things.

Of formal training there is hardly anything apart from teaching young diplomats to speak foreign languages. A general course is dismissed as something that would stale people who have just completed fifteen unbroken years at school and university. Intensive study of specialized skills is disdained on a variety of grounds: that if a man specializes too early he's handicapped when he reaches the top of his profession, or that the academic mind of the specialist is almost the biggest handicap a diplomat might have, as it would commit him morally too much to what he was doing. Judgment, the new entrants are told in their introduction course, is the single most important qualification in this career. 'At the end of the first year', says a senior, 'our men know a helluva lot about the making of foreign policy, unlike a lot of Continentals.' There are a number of courses which people can take at various stages of their careers, like the drilling in economics which some get at the Civil Service College after their first tour of duty abroad. But generally, such affairs amount to not very much more than the fortnight's civilized discourse which introduced them to their profession at the start. A man who suggested that he should be attached to the Department of Trade for a couple of months, so that experts could tutor him in the intricacies of the General Agreement on Tariffs and Trade, was laughed at as though he were joking; which, being bound for the economic maze of Brussels, he wasn't.

Languages, however, are seriously attended to. British diplomats can speak seventy different tongues between them, and for twenty-six of these there are varying degrees of full-time training. They are the hard languages, a small handful of which will be studied by half an average year's intake of new entrants, though not usually until after twelve months' labour in the FCO, learning a helluva lot about the making of foreign policy. The most celebrated course is the one in Arabic at the FCO's own Middle East Centre for Arab Studies, to which students are dispatched for a sixteen-month stretch, though this isn't the longest by any means. A man specializing in Burmese puts in a full academic year at the School of Oriental and African Studies in London, followed by nine months in Rangoon; a Chinese expert will have done a year at Cambridge University and another in Hong Kong or Peking; someone opting for Japanese also has a couple of years ahead of him, divided between SOAS and Kamakura. Some of the harder languages are taught on much shorter courses: like Swahili, which is handled in three or four months between SOAS and the Church Missionary Society in Nairobi, and Polish, in nine months divided between London and Warsaw, and Amharic, which involves two terms at SOAS and three months in Ethiopia. London, meanwhile, is littered with expatriates from every country in Eastern Europe, who are on the Foreign Office payroll to give private tuition for months on end in all the tongue-twisting syllables known to man between the Urals and the Oder. But so-called easy languages, like French and German, get comparatively short shrift at the Diplomatic Service Language Centre in London, which is organized so that people can put in a laboratory hour on the way to work in the morning or in place of a more natural lunchtime conversation in English.

The FCO puts a great deal of thought and money into the training of its hard linguists: the Service's needs in this direction are at present projected to the end of the century, and some £10,000 is spent on, for example, every student of Chinese. The greatest investment of all, however, is made in the supply of Arabists to British diplomacy, not only in the running of the one specialized language school belonging to the FCO, but in the financial inducements which are offered all diplomats who remain proficient in the language of their (or the Service's) choice: when all the language allowances have been handed out each year the Arabists, quite simply, have more money in their pockets than anybody else. They are, within the Diplomatic Service, easily the biggest of the hard-language sects, which is scarcely surprising when more foreign governments naturally speak Arabic than those speaking any other hard language. In 1975, there were 182 fluent Arabists in the Foreign Office, compared with 159 Russian experts and 35 men who could talk easily in Chinese; figures which suggest that, if anything, it is the number of Foreign Office Russians which is disproportionately high.

TABLE 3 *Hard-language Training*

Language	Usual Training	Examination taken at end of course
Amharic	Nine months: two terms at SOAS in London and three months in Ethiopia.	Intermediate
Arabic	Usually sixteen months at MECAS, Lebanon. The Long Course lasts ten months and leads to the Intermediate exam. This is usually followed by the Advanced Course lasting five months, leading to the Higher exam.	Intermediate (LongCourse) Higher (Advanced Course)
Bulgarian	Six to nine months with a private tutor in London, with additional classes at the School of Slavonic Studies.	Intermediate
Burmese	Nine to twelve months: two terms at SOAS, followed by three to six months with a private tutor in Burma.	Intermediate
Czech	Six to nine months with a private tutor in London.	Intermediate
Chinese (Mandarin)	Two years: forty-week intensive course at University of Cambridge and one year at a language school in Hong Kong.	Advanced
Finnish	Ten months: four months with a private tutor in London and six months with a private tutor at Jyväskylä in Central Finland, living with a family.	Intermediate

Greek	Ten months: five months in London with a private tutor, and five months with a private tutor in Greece, living with a family.	Intermediate
Hebrew	Seven months at the University of Jerusalem supplemented by private tuition.	Intermediate
Hungarian	Nine months: two terms at School of Slavonic Studies, and three months with a private tutor in Budapest.	Intermediate
Hindi	One year: two terms at language schools in Dehra Dun and Mussoorie and periods with a private tutor in Benaras and Delhi. If necessary, tuition may commence at SOAS or with a private tutor in London.	Intermediate
Indonesian	Three months: six weeks with a private tutor in London and six weeks at a residential college in either Bandung or Jogjakarta.	Lower
Japanese	Two years: one academic year at SOAS, and one year at a language school in Kamakura near Tokyo.	Higher
Korean	One year at the Franciscan Myong-Do Institute in Seoul, with possibly a second year leading to the Higher Examination.	Intermediate
Malay	As for Indonesian, but residential training has not yet been arranged.	Lower
Persian	Fifteen months: two terms at SOAS, and nine months with a private tutor in Iran including a period in the provinces (normally Isfahan or Shiraz).	Intermediate
Polish	Six months with a private tutor in London, the last are two months living with a Polish family; and further part-time tuition in Warsaw.	Intermediate
Romanian	Six months with a private tutor in London.	Intermediate
Russian	Ten to twelve months (October–July) at Army School of Education, Beaconsfield, and if practicable	Intermediate

	followed by a short course in Russian conversation at the DSLC and one to two months' residential training in Paris.	
Serbo-Croat	Five months with a private tutor in London, and one month living with a family in Yugoslavia.	Intermediate
Sinhala	Eighteen months: two terms at SOAS and six months in Ceylon.	Intermediate
Swahili	One term at SOAS, followed if practicable by a short course at Church Missionary School in Nairobi.	Lower
Thai	Eighteen months: two terms at SOAS and one year at a language school in Thailand, including a period in the provinces.	Higher
Turkish	Twelve months: two terms at SOAS and six months with a private tutor in Turkey (Bursa or Istanbul).	Intermediate
Urdu	One year: two terms at SOAS or six months with a private tutor in London, and six months in India/Pakistan.	Intermediate

(*Source*: FCO.)

In addition to these courses, the Diplomatic Service Language Centre in London also arranges full-time residential training in some European languages–including French, German, Italian and Spanish–for diplomats whose work will demand a very high degree of fluency. These courses usually last at least one month, and students are sent to live with a family in the country concerned.

The forcing ground for Arabist talent, the Middle East Centre for Arab Studies (MECAS), has been a Foreign Office property since 1947. It is situated in the hills about twenty miles outside Beirut, in the Christian Arab village of Shemlan, which overlooks a Druse community, with the Mediterranean just beyond. After a windy first season in old army huts, the Centre moved into an abandoned village school, and there it has remained ever since.[1] Every October, a small clutch of new entrants

[1] In 1975 it was temporarily moved to Jordan for security, during the civil war in the Lebanon.

arrives here from London to start the Long Course, which runs until the following July, and the best of them continue on the Advanced Course, which keeps them in Shemlan until the January after that. There are shorter courses, as well, for people who wish to brush up their Arabic in mid-career after a posting to a non-Arabic job, or for those whose natural ability in hard languages has been proved elsewhere and who are asked to add Arabic to their existing skills. There are courses, too, for diplomatic wives. And, mixed into any class of British diplomats at MECAS, there is generally a collection of foreign diplomats and businessmen, whose fees help to pay for the FCO's upkeep of the place. Beirut is notoriously one of the world's great espionage centres and the flippant know MECAS as 'The Spy School' — particularly since it was here that George Blake was caught working undercover for the Russians.

The Training Department in London is wont to boast that by the time anyone has passed through the Advanced Course at MECAS, he could grace any chair of Arabic in a British university. The booklet which MECAS itself issues to prospective students more precisely claims that,

> The student who does well on the Advanced Course should be able to read with little help from the dictionary any article from a newspaper and any document which he might be expected to meet in the normal course of work. He should be able to check the accuracy of any translation from his own language into Arabic, though it would still be beyond him to write faultless Arabic. He should be able to understand a speech or talk given by an educated man and should be able to take part in, or to translate, conversations over a wide range of subjects.

He is expected to have added much to the vocabulary of 3,000 words he will have learned on the Long Course.

There is no doubt that MECAS produces some brilliant linguists. One of its most impressive old boys is Sir Donald Maitland,[1] who became Director of the Centre in the 1950s. In this capacity he composed, on the instructions of Sir Anthony Eden, a leaflet which was dropped by aircraft before the Suez

[1] Since October 1975, Britain's Ambassador to the EEC in Brussels.

adventure, informing all readers that Britain had no aggressive intent in the Middle East. It is said that, in creating this piece of propaganda, he made one small error of Arabic punctuation, and was taxed with this by an Arab some years later, when the memories of Suez had died down and friendly relations had been restored. Sir Donald is a very brisk man, and his reply was right in character. 'Glad to see you're on your toes,' he replied. But Maitlands do not come ten a penny, and some outside experts in Arabic and Islamic studies can be very sniffy about the standards of MECAS, and of Foreign Office Arabists as a whole. Even old boys of MECAS will concede that sixteen months there do not equip pupils for instant communication anywhere in the Arab world. Most of the teaching is in Classical Arabic, which is the language of the Koran, not of the streets or even of the editorial page in most Arabic newspapers. What vernacular is taught at Shemlan is the Lebanese of the surrounding district —and that will be as intelligible to the average Iraqi, say, as Lancashire dialect would be to a taxi-driver in the Bronx. MECAS gives its brightest pupils a very good grounding, but they have to put in a great deal of work alone later if their expensive new skill is to be more than marginally useful. The surprising thing to an outsider is how often he is told that such and such an Ambassador (in an Arab post) 'can probably just get by' with his Arabic. In the Cairo embassy they will even tell you that they hardly need to speak it at all, for all the Egyptians they deal with speak excellent English. The second in command there in 1975 was not an Arabist of any description, which was explained as a deliberate step to counterbalance their introspective view of the Middle East. A non-Arabist at another Middle Eastern embassy told me that he had not heard any of his nominally qualified colleagues utter a syllable of the local tongue, excusing themselves on the grounds that this was not the Arabic they had learned at Shemlan. 'There should be one top Arabist in every post,' he argued, 'not half a dozen half-baked Arabic speakers.'

A very special cachet, however, attaches to being an old boy of MECAS. People in Middle Eastern posts who have not passed through Shemlan can be so defensive that, when you casually wonder why they never attended the Centre, they say it was because they had no wish to go there; though later you discover that, for the second year running, they have just failed the most elementary of the FCO's language tests. Successful products of the Centre, who subsequently spend a great deal of their careers in Middle Eastern posts, share many of the subtle caste marks of every private school in the world. They identify each other as 'ABCD men', who rotate round the 'soft' postings of Amman, Beirut, Cairo and Damascus; or as Gulf men, who sweat it out in Kuwait, Bahrein and Abu Dhabi; or as the really hard fellows whose tastes and aptitudes take them along the sandy circuit of Jeddah, Aden and Sana'a. They even have a MECAS old boy's tie, a slim jim of a thing which no other group of hard linguists has attempted to imitate. And when they are not in those faraway and romantic places, or doing time (as they often do) in some embassy where Arabic is of not the slightest use except to chat up a couple of other embassies in town, they are frequently to be observed occupying influential positions in the headquarters of the FCO. At one point in 1975, Arabists were the Private Secretaries, the diplomats closest to, the Foreign Secretary and three of his four subordinate Ministers. Some people outside diplomacy see this Arabist influence as part of a Foreign Office plot to weight policy against Israel; and even inside the Diplomatic Service there is enough of sectarian rivalry to produce the occasional caustic comment about Arabists on other grounds. 'They are apt', said a very senior non-Arabist, 'to talk about Middle Eastern affairs as though it would take too long to explain them properly to a jerk like me.' The Shah of Iran, no less, has been heard in his less neighbourly moments to complain that the British Foreign Office is populated by White Arabs. British Ambassadors in Tel Aviv have been known to explode every six months or so about some of the assumptions Arabists make about the Middle East (Arabists, on the other hand, are likely to say that every British diplomat emerging from Israel has been brainwashed into an excessive appreciation of the kibbutz and Marks & Spencer). There is no doubt at all that no Arabist sees Britain's interests being best served by friendship to Israel *and* hostility to Arab nations. This is not by any means the same thing as an attitude of hostility to Israel, though it can include an exhausted feeling that if only Israel weren't there, the Middle East would be a much simpler place. It would be misguided to see anything very sinister in the proximity of so many Arabists to the Foreign Office politician. They are not always so close to power as they were in 1975. When they are, this probably has far more to do with the preponderance of these specialists at every level of the Service, and the likelihood that a very bright Arabist is going to be adept at any diplomatic job.

There are exceptions to the rule that every new entrant to our diplomacy has a first year in London before being posted overseas or bundled off for hard-language training; there are exceptions to almost every statement that can be made about the British Diplomatic Service. One man found himself *en route* for Japan within a month of joining the FCO, to live with a family in Tokyo for two years before being attached to the embassy there for another three; one result of this instant and protracted absence being that when he finally returned to London he had some difficulty remembering just where along Whitehall the Foreign Office was situated. But, in general, a diplomat's career from the outset looks rather like a football team's fixture list, with a series of home and away appearances, each of which usually lasts for three or four years. An FCO booklet offering guidance on graduate careers in diplomacy cites the example of someone who started in the American Department in London before learning Thai for eighteen months and then spending time in the Bangkok embassy. After that he came back to the Eastern Department in Whitehall, and three years later was sent to Berlin, to work in the British Military Government mission there. This kind of varied movement is commonplace. If it suggests a certain wastage of a linguistic skill laboriously and expensively acquired, it also shows why some diplomats modestly refer to themselves as eternal apprentices.

They are apprenticed at the very beginning to a profession with a strong sense of rank and hierarchy. This is true of the civil service as a whole, of course, which is infatuated with the grading system that automatically settles all salaries and promotions. It is more emphatically true of the Diplomatic Service, which abounds in a far greater variety of labels than does the Home Service. Some of these are ostensibly no more than job descriptions (like Consul), but in reality tell insiders much more than that about the man who wears them. Give a diplomat a man's age, his grading and his title, and he will offer you an outline of the fellow's education, his experience and his prospects that corresponds very closely to the truth.

The grading is basically the reference to what a man earns and where he stands on the ladder of promotion. The title describes the job he's doing and the status that goes with it. Only the first of these coincides with the designations of the Home Service, the equivalent titles running as shown in Table 4.

TABLE 4 *Equivalent Titles in the Administrative and Executive Streams of the Civil Service*

Rating	Diplomatic Service	Home Civil Service
Grade 1	Permanent Under Secretary *or* senior Ambassador/High Commissioner	Permanent Secretary
Grade 2	Deputy Under Secretary *or* Ambassador/High Commissioner	Deputy Secretary
Grade 3	Assistant Under Secretary, Ambassador/High Commissioner, Minister *or* senior Consul-General	Under Secretary
Grade 4	Head of FCO Department, Counsellor, Ambassador/High Commissioner *or* Consul-General	Assistant Secretary
Grade 5	First Secretary *or* Consul	Principal
Grade 6 (Executive stream)	First Secretary *or* Consul	Senior Executive Officer
Grade 7A (Administrative stream)	Second Secretary	(No equivalent)
Grade 7E (Executive stream)	Second Secretary *or* Vice-Consul	Higher Executive Officer
Grade 8 (Administrative stream)	Third Secretary	Administration Trainee
Grade 9 (Executive stream)	Third Secretary, Vice-Consul *or* Attaché	Executive Officer
Grade 10 (Executive stream)	Registry Clerk *or* Attaché	Clerical Officer

(*Source*: FCO.)

G

An immediately striking thing about Table 4 (and also Figure 1, showing the promotion pyramid) is the existence of civil service class (or, as they now prefer it, *stream*) distinctions between the Administrative and Executive officers. They rise upwards in the Diplomatic Service in two distinct channels to start with, the Executive usually beginning at the bottom (Grade 10), the Administrative entrant coming in at Grade 8. If you really want to examine the foundations of the diplomatic structure, of course, you have to go burrowing below both of them. At the very bottom of the pile, upon a subsoil of Whitehall cleaning ladies, come messengers and kindred dogsbodies. Above them, at an approximately equal level, are the security guards, the communications officers and the secretaries. The guards are generally ex-Servicemen from the sergeants' mess, picked for muscle power and solid reliability to protect the diplomats and keep unwanted visitors out of embassies. The secretaries come in with their shorthand (100 w.p.m. minimum) and their typing (50 w.p.m.) and their hopes of being posted to Singapore, Kuala Lumpur or somewhere round the Mediterranean; but not, if they can avoid it, to Tokyo, which is reputed to be big and dirty. The turnover of these girls is high, though it has been known for one to become a vice-consul and quite a lot become diplomatic wives. The communications men are usually old sailors, and we shall hear more of them in Chapter Seven.

The Executive class is a distinct cut above this level, but it is also inferior in many ways to the Administrative class. When a young man joins the Diplomatic Service as an Executive officer, he is usually equipped with nothing more than O- or A-levels, though men with degrees occasionally start as Grade 9 Executives, too; between 1966 and 1970, 50 came with university or polytechnic qualifications, between 1971 and 1975, another 55. Whatever his educational background, the Grade 10 entrant invariably begins work either in the FCO bagroom or else as a registry clerk. The bagroom, as the name suggests, is where the diplomatic bags are filled and emptied between delivery runs made by the Queen's Messengers round the British missions abroad; and a Grade 10 Executive working there is about as usefully employed as a Post Office sorting clerk. The registry is diplomatic jargon for the filing system without which no mission overseas or department in the FCO

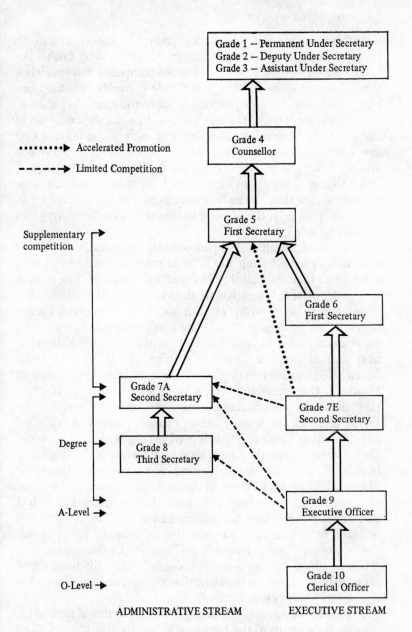

Grade 1 — Permanent Under Secretary
Grade 2 — Deputy Under Secretary
Grade 3 — Assistant Under Secretary

Grade 4
Counsellor

Grade 5
First Secretary

Grade 6
First Secretary

Grade 7A
Second Secretary

Grade 7E
Second Secretary

Grade 8
Third Secretary

Grade 9
Executive Officer

Grade 10
Clerical Officer

•••••••• Accelerated Promotion

------ Limited Competition

Supplementary competition

Degree

A-Level

O-Level

ADMINISTRATIVE STREAM

EXECUTIVE STREAM

FIGURE I   *The Promotion Pyramid*

(*Source*: FCO.)

would be able to function for five minutes. Both jobs can be soul-destroying for anyone with imagination, and both take some getting out of. There is a limited competition by which a Grade 10 man can move up to Grade 9 twelve months after entry, but a very high proportion of competitors fail this on interview after passing the written test. In some departments of the Home Civil Service, men linger in each of the bottom two grades for about five years, but in the Diplomatic Service a Grade 10 man who has not passed the limited competition is liable to stay at Grade 10 for a full decade at least, with another ten years after that before he would expect to rise out of Grade 9. Not surprisingly, the wastage of Grade 10 people in 1975 was over 60 people.

It is almost as difficult to proceed into the middle ranks as it is to hoist yourself from the bottom rung of the ladder. It is possible to take an examination that will allow you to cross a bridge from the Executive to the Administrative class, with consequently better prospects, but the examination is by invitation and not by application. If you don't cross that bridge, then movement upwards on the Executive side is a painfully slow and limited process. There is nothing at all in Diplomatic Service Regulations that prohibits a man who has started at Grade 10 from reaching Grade 1 – at least in theory. In practice, however, no Executive has yet been known to rise higher than Grade 3 and, within memory, only two have become heads of missions. This is a withering outlook, in spite of the fact that, once they have shaken the dust of the registries from their feet, Executive entrants can be found working at almost all the jobs allotted to Administrative men of comparable grades. In a few cases, men who have started as Executives and crossed the bridge to Administration have even been sent to learn hard languages, a springboard from which they are poised to dive into the intensely political work of the chanceries. Their old Executive colleagues are much more likely to spend most of their time in administration proper, or in commercial, immigration and consular work.

A senior Ambassador told me quite forcibly that if he had his way, every entrant to the Diplomatic Service would be obliged to start at Grade 10, irrespective of his qualifications. This would, he declared, ensure that some of the Administrative luminaries who now get a flying start at Grade 8 at least understood some basic skills that they frequently do not seem to appreciate properly. All men would thereafter rise as fast as their abilities justified. There is little doubt that such a system of promotion from scratch would also remove a sense of inferiority and resentment that quite often lurks among Executives beneath all the informal civility and bonhomie of the Diplomatic Service. Too often, they say, you can watch an Administrative man forging ahead at twice your pace when you have been producing similar results from similar work. A Grade 6 First Secretary on the Executive side gets a lower rate of pay than any First Secretary in the Administrative stream, who is automatically rated Grade 5, a distinction that might arguably be defended on the grounds of initial qualifications. But if two such men are serving in the same embassy, the Administrative First Secretary invariably gets larger allowances than his Executive colleague, sometimes superior accommodation as well, which seems to place rather a lot of weight upon conjectural differences between diplomatic sheep and goats.

Not nearly as many obstacles stand on the way to the top for the ambitious entrant to the Administrative class, which numbers 968 men and women at home and abroad, compared with the 2,500 or so in the Executive class. Not only does the Administrative entrant start off a couple of grades higher than most Executives, but he joins the Diplomatic Service in the knowledge that he should at the very least achieve Grade 4 before he retires, while the brightest and the best of the new recruits are marked from the beginning as men who should become Assistant Under Secretaries unless they blot their records catastrophically in between. Thus assured, and fortified as well by his Queen's Commission – a credential given to diplomats alone, which other civil servants do without – he may make his way up the relatively secure but complicated ladder of his profession. It is not by any means a straightforward ascent.

Progress essentially depends on the report everyone gets at the end of each year. This is a searching document which is completed by a man's superior before being deposited with the Personnel Department[1] of the FCO, whose nightmare function

---

[1] There are, in fact, three separate Personnel departments dealing with various aspects of FCO man-management: Operations, Policy and Services.

is to deploy thousands of people in several hundred different places on earth to the best advantage of Her Majesty's Government, and at the same time to take care that as many as possible are tolerably happy in their work. The reports which gradually thicken in a diplomat's file in the Personnel registry leave little to the imagination about him (and about his wife, if any, whose merits and idiosyncrasies are also noted quite carefully) in the course of the next twenty years or more. Chief Clerks confess that, when the time comes to adjudicate upon the candidates for the very highest ranks, they feel a bit shamefaced at how much is known about these claimants. A superior's report on an inferior is required to assess the man's foresight, his powers of analysis, his judgment, his political sense, his ability to think constructively, his organization of his work. Is the fellow easily thrown off balance, unreliable even under normal pressure, or can anything be chucked at him on the assumption that it will be neatly fielded and played safely? Is he liked by his colleagues, by the local British community, by the inhabitants of the country to which he is posted? Does he make life difficult for his own juniors or does he get a particularly good response from staff? These and many other questions have to be answered, quite apart from such objective evidence as will indicate whether or not a man is keeping up to scratch with his Urdu. The pages of a report read like an affidavit of the Inquisition before they are even filled in, though they can rarely be as bleak as they might be. Two poor reports in succession are tantamount to asking Personnel to post a man elsewhere at once, which is very rarely the way of this easygoing and civilized institution. Gone, it is said, are the days when an Ambassador might blacken a man's record because he had affected brown shoes, the hallmark of a cad. They do not yet, however, encourage the genuine iconoclast.

By the time someone has been filed for the first time he will, quite apart from having learnt something of foreign policy-making, have acquired some sense of the strategy needed if he is to fulfil his ambitions. Unless he is ridiculously self-sufficient, he will have taken that first lunchtime hint from the head of his department and joined a club, wherein the topmost Whitehall confidences may be exchanged more naturally than they can be in public places. Just as Treasury officials are apt to gravitate towards the Reform Club, so diplomats have always congregated at the Travellers' more than most other places – and the club itself would find life much harder if it could not rely on a steady income of diplomatic subscriptions. From time to time, Foreign Office notice boards carry reminders from the PUS that aspiring Travellers can readily be put up to the committee by their colleagues. The United Oxford and Cambridge enjoys no such official touting, but is nevertheless a fairly strong runner-up for diplomatic clubability; and very senior, very self-assured diplomats sometimes spend their lunchtimes in less fashionable clubs like the East India, so as to escape from other diplomats for a couple of hours in the day.

The strategy of ambition includes, as much as anything, an appreciation of where to be posted so as to make the most favourable impact on authority. It might be thought that Personnel has its work cut out merely computing with detachment the position of so many diplomatic pieces on its global checkerboard; making sure that when a job in an Arabic-speaking country becomes vacant, there is an Arabist elsewhere of the right grade and due for a move, who may be shifted into the vacancy. The department's life, however, is not nearly as simple as that. It sometimes has to bend to outside pressures, from bodies like the Royal Society, which perpetually whisper in the right ears that a particular project overseas should be more fully supported by diplomatic manpower. It also prides itself on its avuncular interest in every officer's personal fortunes. On New Year's Day each year, diplomats are invited to state where they want to go next, and which places they wish to avoid like the plague. The EEC delegation in Brussels is much fancied nowadays ('good career stuff') though, in general, a large mission – being a heavily populated team operation – is not a posting in which the ambitious expects to shine irresistibly until he has reached the conspicuous level of Counsellor. 'The ideal situation, if you want to collect an AA report rather than a B-plus, is a small post where you're No 2 and where the head of mission is not himself after an AA.' Quite a lot of men are disappointed when their next postings are eventually announced; someone who has pestered for experience in the Third World may find himself spending the next three years in Washington. But by and large, they say, Personnel are really quite accommodating in such matters. A Third Secretary may not cut much ice with the department, but by the time he has

risen to First Secretary, it's surprising how much he can steer
his own career, provided his work is up to the mark. Higher
still, it sometimes looks suspiciously as though parts of the world
are his for the asking. Sir Sam Falle, an Arabist with a long
experience of the Middle East, was in 1974 appointed to his
last post as Ambassador in Stockholm; which was not, perhaps, entirely unconnected with the fact that his wife is
Swedish.

Movement from Third Secretary to First Secretary goes much
more with age than is the case with comparable grades in the
Home Civil Service, where the very bright whizz up much
faster and the rather dull ascend more slowly. After that, promotion becomes intensely competitive, though the ambitious
pushing and shoving generally shows for the first time among
senior Second Secretaries and First Secretaries in their mid-
thirties, who know that so far they are well up with the clock.
You can be eating a midday meal with the Ambassador in his
residence when his Head of Chancery (a First Secretary) bursts
in with a piece of paper which is evidently tormenting him. 'I
go berserk', he splutters, 'when I have to break lunch to receive a
message of this sort.' It happens that the Ambassador's No 2, a
Counsellor, has lately flown to London for conferences, in the
course of which he has voiced some infelicitous assumption
about local politics, which has now produced a puzzled query
from the relevant FCO department on the embassy teleprinter.
His Excellency, who is well aware of undercurrents passing
through his senior staff, smooths the matter away without
pausing much in his digestion, and watches the Head of
Chancery depart, slightly mollified. 'Neurosis!' he shrugs, as
the dining-room door closes.

It's remarkable what some people get up to. Diplomats will
sometimes cultivate back-bench MPs, priming them with the
Parliamentary Question that will give the politician himself a
welcome place in Hansard and, hopefully, attract the Foreign
Secretary's attention to the diplomat's own departmental
subject. Ambitious second-raters have been known to rewrite
in their own style a draft submitted by a brighter junior, em-
bellish it with their own initials without a clue as to its origins,
and send it higher up the command in the hope that it will
dazzle their own superiors. Men who do not need to crib anyone
else's work have been noticed writing to influential persons

(such as the Prime Minister's Private Secretary) on the following lines: 'In the dispatch received from my Ambassador (which
I, in fact, drafted) you'll discover some stuff which you should
find interesting.' It is said that this sort of thing, even though the
recipient recognizes it as a blatant piece of self-promotion,
generally pays off in the long run.

Such ploys occur because what happens to a man in the years
immediately following his promotion to First Secretary is of the
most crucial importance to his future. By the time he has
acquired that title, the Administrative entrant will have been a
diplomat for ten or a dozen years. His abilities will have been
demonstrated at home and abroad and he will know most of
what is to be known about career strategies. It is the next
stretch of his life that will determine whether he is going right
to the top, and how quickly, or whether he is destined to move
up only one more rung in God's good time and cling to it until
retirement comes at the age of sixty. It is at this point that the
Personnel Department puts the most promising men on a formal
list of flyers, whose postings in future will be most carefully
chosen with an eye to formation for much higher things. The
names of these men soon become gossip throughout the chanceries and the departments of the entire institution, and they
are watched enviously by smaller talents who lack most of the
things they've got except the ambition. They become Counsellors at the age of thirty-eight or so, whereas the normally adept
reach Grade 4 some two or three years later; and others, without any future to speak of, do not get there until they are fifty
or more, by which time the rank of Counsellor is little more
than a consolation prize for long service and blameless conduct.
A typical flying case-history sees a man who joined the Foreign
Office in 1949 make Second Secretary in 1953, First Secretary
in 1958, Counsellor in 1965, Minister in 1972 and Deputy
Under Secretary in 1975. You have to be very good and eye-
catching to push along at that rate.

The age of thirty-five or thereabouts becomes something of a
plateau in the diplomatic life. This is the time when men who
know they are good, but are not sure quite *how* good, who are
uncertain about their future in diplomacy and frustrated by
some of its activities, are tempted by outsiders to pull away and
start new careers with attractively higher pay or other vaguely
better prospects. The merchant banks and big commercial

companies come nuzzling round them, hungry for well-connected men of ability, particularly men fluent in foreign languages. Surprisingly few diplomats of this age leave the Administrative stream for such winsome offers; in 1972 only a couple, in 1973 half a dozen, in 1974 just five.[1] Very rarely, perhaps once or twice in a generation, someone will resign on a matter of principle. In 1970, the head of the Arms Control and Disarmament Department asked to be transferred to another post as a personal protest against the British decision not to outlaw CS gas. Two men left the Diplomatic Service altogether over the Suez Canal issue in 1956, one of them being Evan Luard, the subsequently Labour MP (and, since 1976, Minister of State at the Foreign Office).[2] It is even known for men to resign and later rejoin the Diplomatic Service, though no one's record is remotely comparable to that of the astonishing Sir Con O'Neill. Having first entered the Service in 1936 and worked as a Third Secretary in Berlin, he removed himself in objection to Chamberlain's appeasement of Hitler and joined the army. By 1943, however, he was back in the Foreign Office and stayed until 1946, when he departed once more to become a leader writer on *The Times*. That lasted for twelve months, before he returned to the diplomatic fold and applied himself to solid advancement for the next twenty years. By 1968 he had become a Deputy Under Secretary and was due for a final posting before retirement. He badly wanted to finish as British Ambassador in Bonn but the Foreign Secretary, George Brown, wanted him to take charge of the Common Market negotiations. Whereupon Sir Con, over a glass of George Brown's sherry, resigned for the third time and became a banker with Hill, Samuel & Co. Within a year, the Secretary of State him-

---

[1] It is instructive to compare these figures with those of refugees from the Executive stream — between 65 and 111 per annum over the same period — who are not usually bound for plum jobs with merchant banks or anything else.

[2] The figure of two Suez defectors has never been officially admitted. When, on May 22nd, 1957, an MP tried to elicit the information in the Commons, the written answer to his question was characteristically opaque. He was told that in the accounting year 1956–7 (which covered the date of Suez and its aftermath) five members of the Diplomatic Service's Branch 'A' — diplomats from the Administrative grades in today's terminology — had resigned. This was no more than the average annual number for that decade.

self having resigned, O'Neill reappeared as Deputy Under Secretary to do more or less the EEC negotiating job that had been asked of him in the first place. His recreations are shooting and fishing.

Much less independent customers with similarly engaging capacities are very content indeed if an unbroken association with the Foreign Office has landed them in the box seating of Grade 4, with its stimulating little perks. Like First Secretaries below them, they enjoy rather better office furniture than is provided for men of comparable grades in the Home Civil Service. If, as Counsellors, they are also heads of departments at the FCO, they appear in the next edition of *Who's Who*, and thereafter their immortality is assured. When they entertain a small posse of official visitors to lunch, the occasion is noted on the Court Page of *The Times*. If their department supervises the British embassies in a particular segment of Europe, it is not thought amiss of them to make an annual visitation in a leisurely fashion by car, taking the wife along just for the ride. They are, after all, the coming men, with distinctive diplomatic aptitudes, which do not consist so much in intellectual brilliance as in competence and driving power. They are men poised for greatness, of energy, ability and judgment; men who, as Personnel likes to put it, 'can be relied upon not to do anything silly in a crisis'. With a bit of luck, such men will be into Grade 3 by the time they are forty-seven, and ambassadors with Grade 2 embassies of their own in their early fifties.

Yet, if the mid-thirties at Grade 5 can be described as something of a career plateau, the early forties at Grade 4 are generally a watershed. There are, simply, far too many Counsellors sculling around at any one time for all of them to be usefully employed; a medley of everlasting youths with the best still to come, of the diligently middle-aged with a little more progress still to be made, and of the sadly disillusioned whose fondest hopes now lie in the pensionable years ahead. This is one reason why so many are tucked away for a year or so on convenient sabbatical leaves. The Royal College of Defence Studies or the Institute for Strategic Studies are very useful parking places for brilliant men who have to mark time until the right vacancy in the diplomatic scheme of things is open to them. All Souls, Oxford, is generally willing to provide a Fellowship so that someone can spend twelve months distilling his thoughts on Soviet internal politics into a paper that no one outside the upper ranks of the Foreign Office may read for the next thirty years. While all such exercises can be means of keeping first-class minds in trim, of enlarging horizons to the ultimate benefit of British foreign policy, the coldly administrative fact is that they are largely ways of dealing with the diplomatic middle-aged spread. It is estimated that not until 1980 or thereabouts will the Diplomatic Service have naturally lost the excess of manpower which has produced its present obesity and which originates in the cumbersome dismantling of the British Empire. People whose careers began in the India Office, the Colonial Office or the Commonwealth Service could scarcely, according to the protective philosophy of the civil service, be told to go hunting for a new profession when their old one became re-dundant. They had to be found comparable employment inside the related organization. For nearly a quarter of a century after the war, as one departmental merger followed another, large numbers of men were automatically incorporated into what had been, essentially, the *Foreign* Office. Even though the Office assumed greater responsibilities with each merger, these have not always been commensurate with the extra manpower it acquired at the same time.

When a politician declares that something in the air of the FCO seems to turn a lot of brilliant First Secretaries and Counsellors into deadbeats by the time they are in their fifties, he is usually thinking of those who have never made the list of flyers but who have at last got as far as Grade 3, as Ambassadors abroad or Assistant Under Secretaries in Whitehall. They have done pretty well for themselves, but they know that they are not going to reach the two highest grades, with their superior emoluments and prestige. Some, doubtless, begin to take life more easily at this point, devoting rather more of their thoughts and energies to the business of spotting the country cottage in which they will eventually retire, and rather less to the baffling imponderables of foreign affairs. Men in many other walks of life behave in the same way: people do run out of steam in their fifties, to a degree they would have thought inconceivable in their thirties. Diplomats in particular use up a great deal of steam in twenty or thirty years of shuttling round the world, with all the apprentice adjustments involved, not to mention the domestic upheavals. They have spent some time in jobs that do not extend them, which induces a lassitude of its own sometimes hard to shake off when the thoroughly demanding task replaces the unexacting one. It is arguable that our most distinguished diplomats reach the heights of their profession not so much because they have greater abilities and finer judgment than rivals who get left behind, but because they have more energy and large appetites. They are men with a fastidious gusto for life.

These are the ones who are still jostling among themselves in the top three grades. By then, the strategies for success are more refined, the ploys subtler, the outflanking movements more devious and difficult to detect. And by then the most ambitious will have attracted at least the corner of the Foreign Secretary's eye, which is always a help. Although Her Majesty's Secretary of State can make any appointment he wants to make from top to bottom of the Diplomatic Service – he doesn't *have* to bother about seniority, or even whether a man has been a diplomat before – he usually involves himself only in promotions to the top three grades. Two of his subordinate Ministers sit on the Senior Selection Board, together with the Permanent Under Secretary, the Chief Clerk and his Deputy, all the Deputy Under Secretaries, the Foreign Secretary's Principal Private Secretary, and the heads of the subdivided Personnel Departments. This is the appliance which decides who shall represent Britain's interests in the most important capitals of the world, who shall effectively run the diplomatic machine in London, whose careers shall be decorated with the most lustrous public images, and who shall emerge with the most glittering prize of all – that of Permanent Under Secretary in the Foreign and Commonwealth Office and Head of the British Diplomatic Service. And while that ultimate appointment provokes its own peculiar internal excitements – rather like nominating the new Archbishop of Canterbury – the process itself is essentially the same when it's time to decide who shall be our next Ambassador in Washington or Moscow or at the Court of the Common Market in Brussels.

A number of factors are involved in choosing the PUS, aside from the Foreign Secretary's own preferences. The Chief Clerk, as head of administration, is the diplomatic kingmaker here, amassing those embarrassing files on all the likely contenders for a year or more before the old PUS has actually retired. The first thing to settle is the quality of the heir-apparent; his ability, his reputation inside the Service, whether he is good with Ministers – which, to the diplomat, means a mixture of persuasiveness and toughness in standing up to them. But admirable men have been passed over because the job they were doing overseas was thought too vital to be disturbed; bring a man home to become PUS, and a whole chain of ambassadors has to be mended, with some switching of links. Others have lost their chance because they were born in the wrong year, or they have been given it because they were born in the right one; Sir Thomas Brimelow got the job in 1973 for a couple of years because there was no one else as suitable who would not have been there for far longer than is usually thought proper.[1] The technical complexities of the exercise are well illustrated by the experience of Sir Morrice James, who became PUS of the Commonwealth Relations Office in 1968, only to have the job abolished within a fortnight when the CRO was merged with the Foreign Office, which had a perfectly good PUS of its own (Sir Paul Gore-Booth) in the middle of his term. Sir Morrice was thereupon shunted into the first available job at the right grading (High Commissioner in New Delhi) and never did manage to make his way back to Whitehall.

Much more than in the case of the Civil Service Selection Board, this is a self-selecting process: but the casting vote is in the hands of an outsider who can, if he wishes and is strong enough, defy any prearranged plan to give Buggins his turn. There is only one recorded instance of politicians dismissing a PUS after appointment: Sir Robert Vansittart got the push from Neville Chamberlain because he contested the Prime Minister's German policy.[2] But there have been one or two examples of Foreign Secretaries insisting on their own choice, when the senior diplomats had a totally different name in

[1] The average post-war term of Permanent Under Secretaries in the Foreign Office has been fractionally under four years.

[2] Vansittart was kicked upstairs, in effect, on New Year's Day 1938, when he was made Chief Diplomatic Adviser to the Foreign Secretary, Sir Anthony Eden, who resigned his own office within the month. Vansittart's place as PUS was taken by Sir Alexander Cadogan, Eden's by Lord Halifax. Vansittart's new role was purely nominal and two years later he was seconded to the Ministry of Economic Warfare. In 1941 he resigned from the Foreign Office. There has not been a Chief Diplomatic Adviser since.

mind. In 1964, when Sir Harold Caccia was on his last lap as PUS, it had been virtually settled that he would be succeeded the following year by Sir Patrick Dean, an appointment approved by the Foreign Secretary, R. A. Butler. But there was a change of government before Sir Harold's retirement and the incoming Foreign Secretary, Patrick Gordon Walker, decided that Dean was not the right man for the job. After toying with the idea of Sir Con O'Neill (dropped because he was too young) Gordon Walker settled on Sir Paul Gore-Booth, and Sir Patrick Dean was sent as Ambassador to Washington. Another Foreign Secretary with a mind of his own, George Brown, overruled the professionals when it came to picking Gore-Booth's successor. They had confidently awarded the plum job to Sir Denis Wright, then completing his fifth year (a long time as these things go) as British Ambassador in Teheran. George Brown instead gave it to Sir Denis Greenhill, one of the Deputy Under Secretaries, who had never been an Ambassador anywhere. This meant that Sir Denis Wright stayed even longer in Teheran, a post that was upgraded at once as a compensation of sorts, so that at least he shouldn't feel out of pocket. His only tangible loss was the peerage that almost always goes to a PUS when he retires.[1]

One day – maybe – a woman will make it to the top, following where Dame Evelyn Sharp led in the Home Civil Service. It is only just over a generation since they were admitted to diplomacy at all, in the face of all the stereotyped male prejudices. Even today, only 1 British diplomat in 70 is a woman (compared with 1 German in 13, and 1 American in 16), though that may be partly explained by the same inhibitions that produce a comparatively low ratio of men from the grammar schools and provincial universities. Nevertheless, while two former grammar schoolboys (Sir William Strang and Sir Thomas Brimelow) became PUS, no woman has yet reached Grade 1. The late Dame Barbara Salt (The Downs School, Seaford, and Munich University) would have become the first British Ambassador of her sex in 1962, had she not been prevented from taking up her post in Tel Aviv by illness. As it was, the appointment of women at that level had to wait until Miss

[1] Thus, Sir Thomas Brimelow retired as PUS in October 1975, and four months later was introduced to the Upper House of Parliament as Lord Brimelow.

Jean Emery (Western Canada High School, Calgary, and Glasgow University) became High Commissioner to Botswana in 1973; and three years later Miss Anne Warburton (Barnard College, Columbia University and Somerville College, Oxford) became British Ambassador in Copenhagen.

A classic old Foreign Office view of women in diplomacy was offered by an Ambassador just as they were about to be admitted.[1]

> In diplomacy we bow to the inevitable, we accept injustices which revolt us if we allow ourselves to think about them, we are courteous to men who utterly disgust us, we accept compromises despite all logic, we burden our minds against our consciences and we are right to do so. At the same time, if we aspire effectively to serve the State, there must subsist under a heavy armour of cynical pose, a hatred of injustice, a contempt for the despicable, a loathing for bad compromise. I believe this sort of mentality to be utterly alien to the vast majority of women; they are not likely to make good diplomats.

It is doubtful whether anyone today would indulge in such fruity humbug about honour, but there are probably some Ambassadors still who would be inclined to fight some sort of rearguard action if they thought there was any danger of a woman taking her seat on, for example, the Senior Selection Board. Impediments of one kind or another have been removed very grudgingly over the past thirty years. At first, women were admitted for as long as they stayed single. The 1970s had arrived before they were allowed to marry and remain diplomats, and until 1974 they were effectively obliged to choose between husband and career on their first foreign posting after the wedding day. By the middle of 1975 there were still only nineteen married women in the Service—from Grade 10 upwards—but at least one woman from the middle reaches (Grade 6) had gone off to a foreign mission, taking her non-diplomatic husband with her.

As even keenly feminist diplomats will concede, this is one profession where there are genuine difficulties in appointing a

---

[1] Quoted Busk, p. 206.

woman to certain jobs. There is no question of sending them to Arab countries, for example, where governments might refuse to treat with them at all, or would at the very least be unlikely to take them seriously. There are inconveniences in the most emancipated places, and clothing is one of them: while it is easy enough for a man to slide straight out of his office into the evening's round of cocktails, the woman diplomat must somehow make a quick change into party dress in between. The signs of the times, however, are against any discrimination which is not forced upon diplomacy by outside circumstances. Diplomatic Regulations have been discreetly revised to substitute the word 'spouse' for 'wife'; and when heads of department give you a summary of their staff and its organization, this is usually so blissfully sexless that not until you arrive for the departmental meeting do you realize that two of the half-dozen or so 'officers' are, in fact, bonny young things clad in twinsets or slacks. Thus far have we come today. But even in those suspicious years following the first female recruitments, women were treated without discrimination in the area which usually generates the largest sense of grievance among feminists: they were paid the same salary as men of comparable grades.

There is no subject, apart from that of origins and educational background, which turns diplomats so defensive as the amount of money they enjoy one way or another. Their salaries are exactly the same as those of Home civil servants in comparable grades: so are their retirement pensions, to which they do not contribute while they are working, which they are entitled to collect at the age of sixty, and which, since 1971, have been automatically proofed against the effects of inflation. The hot national debate of 1975 on these salaries and pensions began when envious outsiders took note of substantial civil service pay increases in the first few months of that year, which ranged from 26·1 per cent to 42 per cent. The critics, contrasting this liberality with the strict £6 increase applied to the national work force in general, were not attacking diplomats in particular, but the civil service as a whole. The Society of Civil and Public Servants was so stung by the attacks that by 1976 it was taking half-page advertisements in national newspapers under the heading 'The "Whitehall Millionaires"?' and the sub-heading 'Putting it all in Perspective'. In only one respect are diplomats better off than Home civil servants when they are

H

based in London. Their children's education at boarding schools continues to be handsomely subsidized from public funds. At the end of 1975 this subsidy ran to £1,200 a year, tax-free, for each child; and with 1,879 children of 1,003 diplomatic fathers involved, this meant an annual disbursement of £2.2 million. That too had its fierce (sometimes vicious) critics, who paid less attention than they might have done to the fact that the boarding school education is a necessity for most children whose parents are serving abroad, which can scarcely be discontinued when they are subsequently posted to London. 'Nobody', said one man in the Foreign Office, 'owes diplomatic children a public school education; but the country is under obligation to see that they have a decent and uninterrupted one.'

It is when diplomats are abroad that their by no means stingy salaries are supplemented by a complex system of allowances, which produce a standard of living that is more often than not markedly higher than what the diplomats enjoy at home. They are roundly told as soon as they join the service that 'It never was and is not now the intention that you should live abroad on your allowances and save your salary.' Yet it is possible to come across a Grade 9 officer in a small post who admits that he does exactly that, and that his Ambassador probably banks half his salary, too. If Home Civil Servants grumble a lot about diplomatic rewards – and they do, just about as much as outsiders grumble about the civil service as a whole – it is partly because the facts of diplomatic life were long since transmitted round Whitehall from Home officers who briefly hit the same jackpot when serving on attachment to the larger British missions overseas. 'It feels', said a man from the Ministry of Defence somewhere in Europe, 'like perpetual Christmas. You get a message saying don't pay the central heating bill, just fill in this form and the Foreign Office will take care of it. And so on … ' A young Treasury official at another embassy confessed: 'I can't get over a slightly guilty feeling about how much money I have here; it's an absolutely fabulous, rich feeling.' That was twelve months before the allowances at that post were increased by 42 per cent to take care of inflation.

Diplomatic allowances come in various shapes and forms. There is a *Local Allowance* to cover the extra cost of living abroad; an *Indirect Representational Supplement* to take care of servants and other extra household expenses; an *Entertainment Allowance* to provide guests with food and drink; a *Diplomatic Service Allowance* 'to provide a margin to meet items of UK expenditure and commitments, some of which cannot be foreseen'; an *Enhanced Diplomatic Service Allowance* 'paid during service at certain posts when staff are subject to exceptional stresses or harassment or other exceptionally difficult conditions'; an *Outfit Allowance* and a *Climatic Clothing Allowance*; a *Transfer Grant*—which is paid whenever a diplomat changes posts, but has nothing to do with the expenses of shifting his possessions or freighting his car, which are separately subsidized; and a long-winded little thing called an *Accountable Indirect Representational Supplement*, which enables a nanny to be paid for looking after children while diplomatic parents are attending diplomatic parties. All these come on top of the *Boarding School Allowance* and the reimbursement of air fares, so that children may fly out to join their parents for two of the annual school holidays. The diplomat also has his accommodation provided free of charge while he is abroad. When the diplomatic central heating breaks down, the diplomatic kitchen becomes infested with cockroaches, these are fixed free, gratis and for nothing. In addition to these moneys provided by the British government come the other perks of diplomatic life—like the tax-free concessions that are offered diplomats in many parts of the world by local authorities and tradesmen. In Washington, for example, diplomats are provided with cards which exempt them from paying District of Columbia sales tax on anything they buy in the local shops.

Some of the allowances are calculated as a percentage of a man's salary, while others come in fixed sums which are adjusted from time to time to keep pace with inflation and other alien factors. There is variation—sometimes quite sharp—from post to post, as will be seen from Table 6, p. 109, showing a random sample of allowances paid in mid-1974.[1] Heads of mission have their allowances calculated on a slightly different basis from everyone else; in their case all the allowances are lumped together in one sum which is glorified with the title *frais de représentation* and usually looks even more impressive than it sounds. In the early 1970s, the British Ambassador in Paris

[1] This is the date of all the figures in Tables 5 and 6. Galloping inflation, between going to print and publication, would have made nonsense of any more recent figures.

drew a salary of £9,800; his *frais* at that time amounted to £26,755 a year. By the beginning of 1976, when his salary had risen to £18,000, the *frais* had inflated to £50,000. Few other countries take such great care of their diplomats abroad. As a candid official remarked in 1975: 'No American career diplomat could possibly be US Ambassador in London, because he simply doesn't get the money to live as he's expected to live in that post. I, on the other hand, can become British Ambassador in Washington because my government looks after me tolerably well.'[1] A lot of British taxpayers felt, by 1975, that they paid quite stiffly for the privilege of not being represented abroad by the political placemen of this world.

Diplomats emerge so comfortably from the economic hurly-burly partly because the government places a high premium on their integrity; and we may be very thankful that this is so. But they also do well for themselves because they have become very militant trade unionists, with a professional skill in negotiation that might leave the TUC leadership gaping with admiration. There are three main unions involved in the manpower of the Diplomatic Service. Clerical and secretarial staff belong to the Civil and Public Services Association, which represents the bulk of the 500,000 non-industrial civil servants employed by the government throughout Britain. Diplomats in the Executive grades are members of the Society of Civil and Public Servants, which negotiates for men and women in the Home Civil Service as well. Only Administrative people are admitted to the much more influential Diplomatic Service Association, which was founded twenty years ago against some opposition from the hierarchy, but which has proved itself so useful to all senior hands that Sir Thomas Brimelow only relinquished the chairmanship in 1973 so as to avoid any risk of having to ride two horses at once when he became PUS, as his immediate predecessor, Sir Denis Greenhill, had done.

The DSA, like any other trade union, interests itself in the general welfare of its members, and over the years it has become particularly effective in lobbying the government on salaries and allowances. It played its part in general civil service pressures that resulted in those substantial salary increases of January and

---

[1] The American Ambassador in London in 1975 received £20,000 salary and £12,000 in allowances.

April 1975, which effectively dissolved the fleeting illusion of a social contract, and which many people believe were conceded because the government was so worried by increasing evidence of anarchy at home that it wished to secure the confidence of the Civil Service in the event of a national emergency. To see more clearly how the DSA operates, however, it is better to recall a much earlier episode which also, as it happens, illustrates those problems of diplomatic career structure which are still likely to plague the Service into the next decade. This is the sequence of events in 1969 which became part of the FCO's internal mythology, known to diplomats as the affair of 'The Thirty'.

It was a beleaguered time for the diplomats. The Treasury was known to be angling for a 20 per cent cut in the Foreign Office vote and many people felt that Harold Wilson's Labour government, with certain well-bred prejudices of its own, would be very happy to see the Service get it in the neck. As has always been the case since the war, there was a surfeit of manpower in the upper reaches of the profession, with the usual queue of Counsellors awaiting their turn to proceed to the higher grades justified by their abilities. Contrary to some public opinion, diplomats tend to do what they are told by politicians when they are told to do it, and the administration of the Diplomatic Service produced a very simple solution to pacify the Treasury and quench any thirst (real or imagined) among Labour politicians for diplomatic blood. They would sack thirty senior men; though the operation would be called, more delicately, 'premature retirement'. This master-stroke would also, it was thought, solve for the next few years the perennial problem of the bulge. One of the chosen thirty was in Grade 1, a couple were from Grade 2, Grade 3 supplied twenty-three, and the other four came from Grade 4. Their names, of course, were hardly to be made public, or even to be whispered round the corridors of the FCO. The matter was arranged with such confidentiality that when one of the thirty put a speculative notice in *The Times*, hoping that his comrades in adversity might reveal themselves so that they could form a purely private protest group, he received only a couple of religious tracts in reply, his quarry having to a man decided that some clever journalist was merely trying to work up a scoop.

They were never quite such a collection of hard cases as the bald facts imply. Several were within months of retirement anyway, and several more were quite glad to be getting out early with the reasonably generous terms of compensation offered. None who needed a well-paid job outside the Diplomatic Service went looking for one for very long, and three were actually re-employed in lower grades of the FCO. But the howls of protest that went up from the ranks of the DSA when the news of the sackings broke could be heard from one end of Whitehall to the other; and they did find their way into the newspapers, as they were intended to. The burden of complaint was that the compensation was inadequate compared with the golden bowlers handed to retired officers in the Armed Forces, and that the security promised civil servants as a condition of their service was jeopardized for all by one stroke at the thirty. That the second of these was the much greater grievance is suggested by the fact that the loudest noises were made by people who would instantly profit by the removal of the thirty —bright Counsellors and First Secretaries, who imagined a similar fate befalling them a few years later. Nor was authority alone vilified by the protesters. The DSA committee, too, was subjected to their wrath, because it was found that some of its members were part of the administrative unit which had selected the thirty, and had acted as obedient diplomats rather than as solid trade unionists by not letting the membership at large know what was afoot. No one actually called them scabs, but the chairman at one meeting completely lost control of the gathering as many other undiplomatic utterances were hurled deafeningly at the platform.

Eventually a delegation marched in to see the Foreign Secretary himself, Michael Stewart, who said that in a fairly extensive experience of different government departments he had not known anything like it before. As well he might; for there was Sir Denis Greenhill facing him like an angry shop steward, rather than as the Permanent Under Secretary of the FCO. A very senior delegate told the Secretary of State of his concern that reports in the press had given the impression that ill-temper had entered the dispute, which would do the Service's reputation no good. A Deputy Under Secretary, sticking more to the point, observed that when he was fifty-five one of his children would be thirteen and another twelve, which demonstrated the plight diplomats could be in when they had to go begging for better compensation. When they withdrew, the members of the delegation could only say—like many a trade union team before and since—that they had been given a sympathetic hearing by the boss. But the pressure continued less spectacularly and less vociferously behind the scenes. Two years later the terms of compensation for the thirty were quietly increased, leaving every man the better off by several thousand pounds.

The most profitable thing about the affair, however, was the subsequent revelation of very widespread discontents among rising diplomats. The DSA committee, stung by criticisms from the members, set out to canvass people under forty years old for their views of the Service, and some of these were disconcerting. Over half of them had seriously considered resigning within the previous five years and almost as many within the preceding twelve months. Poor promotion prospects were the major grievance, but a lot of people felt that they simply weren't stretched enough on service abroad. The Duncan Committee had lately reported its conclusion that the Diplomatic Service was bound to shrink in proportion with Britain's reduced international role, and the rising diplomats welcomed this; they only wished that Duncan had taken as searching a look at the FCO in London as at the representation overseas. The most curious revelation of all was that large numbers were, in spite of their noisy protests at the sacking of the thirty, quite prepared to accept even more sackings at even lower grades—provided the money was right. What they were chiefly after was greater job satisfaction.

The wounds of the affair are still worn bitterly by senior diplomats today, though most of them came up a notch as a result of it. They speak of the brutality of the operation and hope that nothing like it is ever allowed to happen again. In fact, it has been unobtrusively happening ever since; between 1971 and 1975, another fifty-eight men from Grades 1–4 were 'retired prematurely' with compensation large enough to be accepted without a murmur of protest. Yet, in spite of the 13 per cent reduction of Diplomatic Service manpower that has occurred since 1965, progress towards the top is still a pretty long and slow shuffle for most people. And while this is endemic in any institution as devoted to hierarchy as diplomacy, it also has something to do with the precious security built into the whole of the British Civil Service. The most damaging criticism of the Foreign Office is not some platitude voiced by an outsider, jealous of the clubable rules whereby Buggins gets his well-shod turn at regular intervals. It is something said by a senior insider somewhere in 1975. 'You get into trouble', he remarked, 'if you lose the Queen's secrets or money. But if you commit a diplomatic gaffe, it's unlikely seriously to impair your career.'

TABLE 5   *The Financial Rewards of Diplomacy:*
Salaries

Salaries

Grade 1	£16,350
Grade 2	£11,100
Grade 3	£9,410
Grade 4	£7,110 — £9,260
Grade 5	£4,770 — £6,185
Grade 6	£4,166 — £4,952
Grade 7A	£3,741 — £4,572
Grade 7E	£3,363 — £3,995
Grade 8	£2,229 — £3,192
Grade 9	£1,797 — £3,192
Grade 10	£1,237 — £2,293

Some comparative salaries
Managing directors — £11,043; chief foreign exchange dealers — £7,951; senior Army colonels — £6,946; public company secretaries — £6,596; family doctors — £6,147; senior industrial chemists — £6,300; architects (principal partners) — £5,650; company chief accountants — £5,590; works managers — £5,399; NHS dentists — £5,650; investment analysts — £5,067; junior chartered accountants — £4,000.
Average of all male manual workers — £2,761.

Figures for the Diplomatic Service are as at April 1st, 1974.
The comparative figures are for November 1974. On January 1st, 1975, civil service increases raised the Grade 1 salary to £18,675, the Grade 2 salary to £14,000; those of other grades were raised either in January or April by varying proportions.

(*Source*: FCO.)

TABLE 6   *The Financial Rewards of Diplomacy:*
Some   Overseas   Allowances   (a   random   selection,
Summer 1974)

Grade		£ pa	
		Married	Single
Washington			
4	Local Allowance	2,620	1,229
	Indirect Representational Supplement	1,149	833
	Accountable Entertainment Allowance	2,124	2,124
5	Local Allowance	2,620	1,229
	Indirect Representational Supplement	1,032	973
	Accountable Entertainment Allowance	1,067	1,067
9	Local Allowance	2,127	1,174
10	Local Allowance	1,964	1,155
Kuwait			
4	Local Allowance	2,319	1,041
	Indirect Representational Supplement	1,072	714
	Accountable Entertainment Allowance	1,123	1,123
5	Local Allowance	2,319	1,041
	Indirect Representational Supplement	1,072	714
	Accountable Entertainment Allowance	976	976
9	Local Allowance	2,319	1,041
	Accountable Entertainment Allowance	199	199
10	Local Allowance	2,319	1,041
Havana			
4	Local Allowance	2,808	1,194
	Indirect Representational Supplement	1,556	1,587
	Accountable Entertainment Allowance	1,258	1,258
5	Local Allowance	2,808	1,194
	Indirect Representational Supplement	749	476
	Accountable Entertainment Allowance	934	934
9	Local Allowance	2,457	1,194
	Accountable Entertainment Allowance	287	287
10	Local Allowance	2,344	1,194

		£ pa	
Grade			
Dacca		*Married*	*Single*
4	Local Allowance	1,915	829
	Indirect Representational Supplement	478	Nil
	Accountable Entertainment Allowance	1,170	1,170
5	Local Allowance	1,915	829
	Indirect Representational Supplement	478	Nil
	Accountable Entertainment Allowance	662	662
9	Local Allowance	2,063	977
	Accountable Entertainment Allowance	98	98
10	Local Allowance	2,063	977
Delhi			
(In Compound)			
4	Local Allowance	873	153
	Indirect Representational Supplement	13	85
	Accountable Entertainment Allowance	974	974
5	Local Allowance	873	153
	Indirect Representational Supplement	13	85
	Accountable Entertainment Allowance	378	378
9	Local Allowance	947	227
10	Local Allowance	947	227
Kinshasa			
4	Local Allowance	2,621	1,037
	Indirect Representational Supplement	656	220
	Entertainment Allowance	1,579	1,579
5	Local Allowance	2,621	1,037
	Indirect Representational Supplement	346	Nil
	Accountable Entertainment Allowance	1,252	1,252
9	Local Allowance	2,241	1,037
10	Local Allowance	2,112	1,037

		£ pa	
Grade			
Blantyre		*Married*	*Single*
4	Local Allowance	1,021	454
	Indirect Representational Supplement	47	Nil
	Entertainment Allowance	736	736
5	Local Allowance	1,021	454
	Indirect Representational Supplement	47	Nil
	Accountable Entertainment Allowance	430	430
9	Local Allowance	1,080	513
	Accountable Entertainment Allowance	38	38
10	Local Allowance	1,080	513
Ankara			
4	Local Allowance	760	143
	Indirect Representational Supplement	677	945
	Accountable Entertainment Allowance	1,088	1,088
5	Local Allowance	760	143
	Indirect Representational Supplement	509	381
	Accountable Entertainment Allowance	819	819
9	Local Allowance	819	202
	Accountable Entertainment Allowance	132	132
10	Local Allowance	819	202
Valletta			
4	Local Allowance	834	217
	Indirect Representational Supplement	154	690
	Accountable Entertainment Allowance	819	819
5	Local Allowance	834	217
	Indirect Representational Supplement	266	334
	Accountable Entertainment Allowance	623	623
9	Local Allowance	947	325
	Accountable Entertainment Allowance	55	55
10	Local Allowance	942	320

		£ pa	

Grade		*Married*	*Single*
Budapest			
4		N/A	N/A
5	Local Allowance	864	183
	Indirect Representational Supplement	928	826
	Accountable Entertainment Allowance	1,000	1,000
9	Local Allowance	864	183
	Accountable Entertainment Allowance	123	123
10	Local Allowance	864	183
Tokyo			
4	Local Allowance	2,768	987
	Indirect Representational Supplement	2,013	1,805
	Accountable Entertainment Allowance	1,713	1,713
5	Local Allowance	2,768	987
	Indirect Representational Supplement	1,649	1,547
	Accountable Entertainment Allowance	1,503	1,503
9	Local Allowance	2,492	987
10	Local Allowance	2,398	987
Moscow			
4	Local Allowance	2,388	720
	Indirect Representational Supplement	2,444	464
	Accountable Entertainment Allowance	1,640	1,640
5	Local Allowance	2,388	720
	Indirect Representational Supplement	1,269	464
	Accountable Entertainment Allowance	1,028	1,028
9	Local Allowance	1,747	686
10	Local Allowance	1,530	671

(*Source*: FCO.)

5 The Whitehall Machine

The London end of British diplomacy calls for the instincts of a navigator and the dogged persistence of an explorer in anyone who sets out to investigate it. There is nothing more complex in the whole of Whitehall than the FCO, with its multitude of subdivisions, its intricate lines of communication and its subtle internal rivalries, all of which must somehow be fused in the creation of foreign policy, and the production of 'the Foreign Office view'. Nor is there anywhere else in the machinery of British government so permanently charged with high energy, a curiosity which caught the attention of the Duncan Committee in a report which was otherwise confined to the action of our diplomacy abroad. On glancing at the FCO's metropolitan activities, the Committee was 'struck by the fact that this work, which is primarily political in content, absorbs a surprisingly large workforce'.[1] It found that half the Diplomatic Service's 6,000 people in 1969 were labouring in London and that, if you assessed the Administrative and Executive classes together, 1,000 officers were employed in the capital compared with 1,700 spread around the rest of the world. The emphasis on quality control in Whitehall was even heavier if you noted the figures for Administrative men alone. With 687 of them overseas, there were 376 at home – a domestic muster which made the Treasury (126 Administrative officers) and the then Board of Trade (323) look somewhat anaemic in comparison. What Duncan gently went on to hint, before hurrying away overseas again, was that the FCO in London was just a bit top-heavy in skills.[2]

[1] Duncan, p. 56.
[2] It is in the manpower at headquarters that the most telling differences exist between the strengths of British, French and German diplomacy. There are 3,500 people working for the FCO in London, compared with

The figures are but marginally different today. There were 63 separate departments of the FCO in the middle of 1975. By now there may be 64, or (less probably) 62, for the shape of this conglomeration changes from year to year as a result of pressures inside and outside the institution itself. In 1973, for example, there was a European Integration Department, which supervised all matters relating to the Common Market. By 1974, this had developed into the European Integration Department (Internal) and the European Integration Department (External), with separate staffs and separate departmental heads, the former looking after Britain's affairs in the Common Market, the latter her part in joint Common Market policies towards the rest of the world.

A very broad division of those departments which are not concerned with the administration of the Service itself is that between the geographical and the functional ones. In almost every office of the FCO there is a wall map alongside the ubiquitous dark green tin cupboard of civil service. It is a projection unknown to Mercator or any other cartographer, with a world segmented by heavy black lines which separate one geographical department's sphere of influence from another's. Half a continent is controlled (in a manner of speaking) by the East African Department, which must not miss a British trick anywhere in Kenya, Uganda, Tanzania, Mauritius, Ethiopia, Somalia, Zaire, Rwanda, Burundi, or the French territory of the Afars and Issas, while at the same time keeping a friendly eye on the Organization of African Unity and the East African Community. The great wedge above this area, consisting of Egypt, Libya, Sudan, Algeria, Tunisia, Jordan, Syria, Lebanon and Israel is, meanwhile, the province of the Near East and North African Department. Thus is the globe divided into cohorts of foreigners with whom the British must treat, though certain countries, like Rhodesia and the Irish Republic, have managed to corner separate departments which attend to them alone. All these geographical departments continuously exchange advice and information with their groups

---

2,300 for the Auswärtiges Amt in Bonn and 1,650 for the Quai D'Orsay in Paris. Comparisons between the three diplomatic services overseas are difficult to make fairly, because they are organized in different ways — but in 1976 the total strengths of home-based staffs working at home and abroad were: Britain 6,400; France 4,800; West Germany 4,300.

of British embassies afield, and deal whenever necessary with the foreign embassies in London. They get involved, too, with visitors, both coming and going. The North American Department in particular is for ever receiving tips from British consuls in Boston and points West that mayors, airport managers and other influential people are coming over and should, if we want to get maximum mileage in local trade promotion, be taken care of; which, in the case of the more neurotic civic leaders from the more restless American cities, usually includes the co-operation of the Metropolitan Police. Nothing, however, is allowed to deflect a geographical department from its chief business of briefing its clutch of embassies, taking advice from them, occasionally issuing stern injunctions to them. The department's standing in this relationship has been immortalized by Lord Trevelyan:[1]

> The British ambassador knows that his destiny is in the hands not of ministers nor even of the press but of his department at home, which must be the object of his assiduous attention. He will be well advised always to write to the head of the department on serious matters and to the ministers or more senior officials who proliferate in the corridors of the FO, only on purely trivial questions such as ministerial visits or the more flagrant misdemeanours of his staff.

The geographicals are concentrated on good relations with foreigners. The functional departments exist basically to put Foreign Office policy into the decision-making machinery of Whitehall. They bear titles which at once identify their particular concerns—Defence, Financial Relations (not to be confused with the Finance Department, which worries only about how the FCO spends its own money), Trade Relations and Export, or Marine and Transport. This is the area where the Diplomatic Service's traditional reluctance to recruit specialists puts it at its greatest disadvantage, for the people in the functional departments are perpetually dealing with other civil servants and professionals outside the civil service (like bankers and brigadiers) whose expertise is an accumulation of special-

[1] Trevelyan, p. 100.

ized knowledge. In the Science and Technology Department of the FCO, for example, one desk officer is expected to keep the diplomatic end up in a liaison with the Department of the Environment on a variety of issues splashed across the Atlantic and the North Sea, like oil dumping and the sources of land-based pollution. The same FCO department was concerned in negotiations for the establishment of a radio telescope in Australia, its contribution being the kind of diplomatic skill scientists don't normally possess, which would ensure not so much that the telescope was sited where the scientists thought best, but that the whole enterprise would redound to British credit in Australia.

Neither geographical nor functional departments ever operate in total isolation from each other; their spheres overlap far too much for that, sometimes irritatingly so. During the Cyprus crisis in 1974, the Southern European Department thought little of the extra labour involved in having to inform European Integration (External) of events on and around the island – almost hourly at one point – though they were happy to use the diplomatic leverage supplied in return: the ability to tell Greeks and Turks alike that not only did Her Majesty's Government take a particular view, but that Britain's European partners thought the same way, too. Nor do departments work under comparable pressures, at similar paces. The bright young men of the FCO talk about the 'go-go departments' like Western Organizations and European Integration, to which, although he might be run off his feet for most of an average week, it behoves the ambitious to secure a posting while he is still a First or Second Secretary. No such sapling would relish being transplanted to one of the comparative backwaters; like Guidance and Information, which for unfathomable reasons is liable to find itself briefing the British Embassy in Islamabad with material on fishing disputes in Icelandic waters; or like Cultural Exchange, which is into, among other things, town-twinning.

Nowhere in the FCO is life as leisurely as before the war, however, when diplomats proper did not start work until their underlings had deciphered and registered the overnight swag of telegrams, and 'eleven o'clock diplomacy' was the rule in Whitehall. As the civil service medical authorities have noticed when diplomats are given a searching overhaul on reaching the age of forty, it is those working in London who show stress symptoms, not the ones posted in embassies. Thrice each day do folders full of telegrams land in the departmental in-trays, and they are only part of the grist which is then laboriously ground to refinement in the policy-making mill. The starting place for everything in a department is with the three or four junior desk officers in the so-called Third Room (to distinguish it from the notional First Room of the departmental head, and Second Room inhabited by his chief assistant). Each of these juniors is made responsible for particular areas of the department's work and their basic skill is that of drafting the nursery thoughts on an issue that might result in an international utterance by the Foreign Secretary himself. What the junior needs is clarity as his thoughts are committed to paper in a stylized procession, led by Problem, followed by Background, Argument and Recommendation (an order which George Brown reversed, so that he could quickly see whether he agreed with a decision and, if so, didn't then have to wade through the supporting verbiage). That highly-prized judgment is desirable at the outset, too; the judgment whether to consult another department before passing the submission to the assistant head, or whether to consult someone else in one's own department, or whether confidently to carry on solo and risk making a mistake in the process. Not that chastisement is noticeably severe in the Foreign Office. An incoherent or fallacious submission is at the worst probably going to produce no more than a weary call for elucidation from the departmental head; more usually it is returned with a polite query alongside the senior's initials in the margin.

Paperwork is the backbone of the FCO, although it is customary for most departments to have at least a weekly meeting when everyone sits round a table to discuss what they're all up to, rather in the manner of a newspaper's editorial conference. They give their accounts, very pointedly balancing their evidence for any opinions they offer, with a great deal of 'on-the-one-hand-this-on-the-other-hand-that'. They season these solemnities with the occasional levity: 'I think it's all a publicity stunt by MOD (the Ministry of Defence) — did you read that extraordinary correspondence in *The Times*?' Interventions from the head of department are minimal. 'I don't want Downing Street brought into this yet ... ' is the strongest lead he will probably offer. No one actually asks him what ought to

I

be done about anything; even the junior Third Secretary is likely to observe that he's proposing to take some course of action which is patently mined with potential embarrassment for the nation, and all his chief says is 'If I were you I'd be a bit careful on that ... ' It's all very civilized, though some departmental heads will have none of it on the grounds that it takes up so many man-hours a week which can be more profitably spent at the desk and that, anyway, people can dip into the departmental float of incoming and outgoing telegrams and letters if they really want to keep abreast of all that's happening.

Eventually, something resembling the nursery thoughts of the Third Room lies in the head of department's out-tray, embellished with sets of initials which indicate that it has already risen through three levels of this hierarchical society. It may or may not acquire even more yet. It is reckoned that between 80 and 90 per cent of what starts with the desk officers is translated into action as soon as a head of department has had his say in it. More often than not the action is a telegram or letter to an embassy on the following lines, with each paragraph rigorously numbered:

1. Decision has now been taken to withdraw ...
2. Basis of a formal note to the government of —— is in transit. At the same time as transmitting it, you may wish to consider speaking to Mr —— so as to ensure that there is no misunderstanding of the reason for the decision.
3. In speaking, you should express our great regret at having to take this decision and emphasize ...
4. Please emphasize the concern of our experts ...
5. Please report by telegram when you have arranged an interview. The —— Ambassador will be called in at about the same time. Please also confirm by telegram when the Note has been handed over so that a notice can be prepared for the *London Gazette*.

The signature at the bottom is the Foreign Secretary's. Everything that is officially communicated by the FCO is done in his name, even though he mightn't have the foggiest notion what anyone was talking about, were he to be taxed with half of it.

Whatever is the exact percentage of work that rises above the departments, it immediately enters the hazy world of the Under Secretaries. Nothing, apart from questions of how some decisions are actually arrived at, is more indistinct than the relationship between the Deputy Under Secretaries and the Assistant Under Secretaries; and the two subjects, of course, are very closely linked. You can ask a very senior man in British diplomacy what a DUS does and how this differs from the work of an AUS and he will reply as one whose normal fluency, much above the average, has quite deserted him for the time being. An AUS, says one, manages; the DUS directs. 'The DUS', says another, 'should be trying to see things as a whole; should spend more time than he in fact does, away from his desk, trying to think about things. The AUS is more in the nitty gritty.' An Ambassador with a weakness for all forms of hierarchy puts it this way: 'The head of a department is the parish priest, the AUS is a bishop, the DUS is a cardinal ... '; and then, in afterthought, ' ... the DUS should have one piece of paper on his desk at a time, *thinking* about it'. These stumbling attempts make Assistant Under Secretaries sound like supernumerary heads of department, though each of them oversees anything up to half a dozen. Whether, between them and the Permanent Under Secretary, it is also necessary to have a row of Deputy Under Secretaries maintained for hypothetical cerebration, is something constantly in doubt; not least, in the minds of diplomats themselves. The Duncan Committee said that the number of Under Secretaries was too large and suggested that 'in principle there should not be more than one Under Secretary (whether of grade 2 or grade 3 rank) between the grade 4 Head of Department and the Permanent Under Secretary; and that each Under Secretary should be solely responsible for the supervision of at least two or three departments and preferably more.'[1] As it is, scarcely any Under Secretary is solely in charge of anything. Almost every department has two or even three Under Secretaries supervising it, and every Under Secretary supervises several departments. In theory this sounds like a splendid network of intelligence by which every department is made aware of everything faintly relevant to its work; but it can also mean a confusion of signals, hampering the approach to clear and decisive thought. It is not as though this preponder-

[1] Duncan, p. 57.

ance of topweight has always been thought necessary to our diplomacy. In recent years, there have been as many as nine Deputy Under Secretaries overlooking twenty or more Assistant Under Secretaries; but just after the war, before various amalgamations produced career problems, there were but three men in the Foreign Office with the rank of DUS – one in charge of administration, another taking care of politics, the third supervising economics. 'It is not necessary for a head of department to report to an AUS, then to a DUS, then to the Minister; that's wasteful. He should report to one or the other.' It was a Deputy Under Secretary who said that, a man who knew that he was able enough to survive any surgery that might be performed on the present system.

Here or hereabouts, Foreign Office policy is constructed in committees which are regularly convened, in meetings which are hastily gathered, in quiet chats along Gilbert Scott's corridors, in confidential twosomes sunk deep in the upholstery of the Travellers' Club. Every morning it is assessed in the Permament Under Secretary's meeting at 10.30 sharp. Each month a select band of seniors peer at it long-sightedly in the deliberations of a Steering Committee, after a somewhat larger group of officials have contemplated it in a Planning Committee. There is also a permanent planning staff, which operates from day to day like any other FCO department. Its handmaiden is the Research Department, whose seventy members have usually been recruited by processes different from those applied to other diplomats. They generally have postgraduate degrees, they tend to be historians or specialists in international relations as well as linguists, and they are distinctly academic, reflective men, devoid of customary diplomatic ambitions and definitely not ambassadorial material. From time to time, one of them may be detached to assist some other department under pressure, and there may be as many as a dozen posted to various embassies, to do their digging in the field. But their own department is where they really belong, among their sources of information – FCO archives, press cuttings, academic papers, and what they blankly refer to as 'various kinds of intelligence'. Among a lot of other things, they keep potted biographies of the famous and the obscure throughout the world, filed in volumes devoted to their country of origin. The book on Mauritania is a slim thing of 25 pages; the one for the Soviet Union – the biggest—runs to 500-odd, with two and sometimes three people listed on each page. The details are skeletal, ending with thumb-nail characterizations: ' ... Speaks Spanish and some Arabic. Rather taciturn.' There is also a large room full of card indexes, with what might well be several million entries on individuals who could conceivably be of interest to British diplomacy. A researcher flicks one open at random, to reveal a name and a jumble of references meaningless to an outsider. He studies it for a moment, interested. 'Hmm,' he grunts. 'She must have been useful to someone.'

The Plowden Committee was highly critical of Foreign Office policy planning. 'Some of the most intractable inter-national issues in which we have been involved in the last two decades', the report said, 'could, in our view, have been handled better if their implications had been explored more fully in advance.'[1] So could some other things requiring foresight; it was on Foreign Office advice that the Attlee Government declined to accept the German Volkswagen factory as war reparations, on the grounds that the car's design had no commercial future. Boners of that magnitude were perhaps scarcely surprising in a Foreign Office that didn't even have a planning section until 1957. Even then, it consisted of a solitary First Secretary for the next four years, by which time he was joined by a colleague of the same rank to work within the Western Organizations and Planning Department. A separate planning staff was quickly cobbled together in 1964 when the Foreign Office saw the proofs of the Plowden Report, a month before it was made public, and has remained unchanged ever since. It is still small, but it is relatively high-powered, the Assistant Under Secretary in charge leading three First Secretaries, a man from Research and a supporting secretarial staff. Through this group of men comes the pipeline leading to the FCO from all those outside influences on the making of foreign policy—from university experts in international affairs, from meddlesome bodies like the Royal Society, and from institutes that were created for this very purpose. The Institute for Strategic Studies is one, though it has more obvious and closer links with the Ministry of Defence. The Royal Institute of International Affairs (alias Chatham House, after Lord Chatham's residence in St James's

[1] Plowden, p. 55.

Square) is the other. Founded in 1920 by rich men like Lord Astor, it runs largely on American capital, is firmly fixed upon a mid-Atlantic view of the world, attracts professionals and dilettantes in roughly equal proportions to its lectures, discussion groups, luncheons and sherry parties, gets on with quiet researches of its own, and is directed by one of the Duncan report's authors, the economist and ex-journalist Andrew Shonfield.

The planning staff of the FCO has therefore a very considerable amount of external opinion to draw on, quite apart from the brain-picking it can conduct among the diplomats themselves and the drudgery it can whistle up from the Research Department. Its immediate patron is the Planning Committee, consisting of the PUS, all the Deputy Under Secretaries, the FCO Legal Adviser, the head of the Research Department and the Foreign Secretary's Private Secretary. The head of Planning is always there, too, and individual Assistant Under Secretaries and heads of other departments are summoned when particular topics seem to call for them. This is where the collegiate view of the world is formed before it is tried out on the politicians, and part of the formation consists of the papers sent up by the planning staff. These do not normally attempt to look much further than five years ahead and anything beyond fifteen years falls into what is regarded as the dubious field of futurology. The argument of the planners against very long-range forecasting is that if you take an existing trend and try to extrapolate it to the future, the further ahead you go the more alternatives come up, and in the end you have too many different possible scenarios to consider realistically. Nevertheless, they were in 1974 preparing a paper entitled 'The End of the Rainbow', which set out to consider what effect the final exhaustion of our North Sea oil reserves would have on British foreign policy. But when the Ministry of Defence (a regular customer) asks them what the international situation will be like in 1990, so that it can work out its arms programme in advance, it is likely to get the tart reply that if MOD will forecast the domestic scene in 1990, then the FCO will come up with an international prophecy. Sometimes the planning staff produce their own ideas and beaver away at them for months before allowing anyone else into the secret; and sometimes these are dropped and forgotten because more urgent conjectures are required by orders from above. More often than not, the Planning Committee flicks an idea into their laps at one of its monthly meetings. That was the origin of a paper on Britain's policy towards India between now and the end of the decade, provoked by the first explosion of an Indian nuclear bomb in 1974. The planners proudly estimate that thirty minds were applied to that speculation before it was circulated round the hierarchy and filed for future reference. But their most stimulating moments come 'when we hear a phrase of ours being used by some head of department who at first fought the concept tooth and nail'.

An alarming thing about the forecasters is that they do not really believe in contingency planning, asserting that if a crisis occurs, perhaps 75 per cent of the circumstances are unforeseen. This seems a strange thing to hear in the heart of an organization with listening posts in very nearly every country in the world. But at least, when crises occur, the FCO is fairly well equipped to react to them with an appliance whose operation could not be further removed from the protracted conjectures of the planning staff. During the Middle Eastern Six-Day War in 1967, a number of departments got their lines of communication, their briefings and their information terribly tangled—basically because they were working in their separate offices dotted around the building. It became clear that, if Britain became involved more closely in an international upheaval, the result might be crippling. So the Emergency Unit was devised for future needs, which in practice have arisen almost every year since—at the time of Bangladesh's birth, during the Indo-Pakistan war, when Jordan went through crisis, when Cyprus was in dispute. A suite of spare rooms high in the roof, overlooking St James's Park, was set aside; and that is where all the relevant FCO action took place for a fortnight after that Saturday in 1974, when the Turkish fleet raised steam from Mersin and dropped anchor off the Cyprus beach heads.

The Samson coup on the island had occurred on the previous Monday morning and the political situation deteriorated throughout the week. At Friday morning's daily meeting of the FCO seniors, the PUS, Sir Thomas Brimelow, decided that things looked gloomy enough to justify the unit being manned that night. This meant that the entire staff of the Southern European Department—in whose province, Turkey, Greece and Cyprus lie—left home and established themselves upstairs, among the teleprinters, the pneumatic tubes, the television sets, and the battery of telephones: the red instruments of the government's Federal exchange, and the ones called Pickwick and Belgard, which will transmit the most enormous indiscretions quite safely because their scramblers are changed with tiresome frequency, and they cannot be tapped. People from a number of other departments were drafted in, too, to help take the strain, for once the Emergency Unit starts working it keeps a twenty-four-hour watch until the crisis is over. There are two or three adjacent rooms where people may sleep, and a small kitchen where food may theoretically be prepared, though if you want a cup of coffee out of it you must (this being an accountable civil service) pay the catering lady for it on the spot.

The first night of the Cyprus Emergency therefore got off to a flying start—for everyone, that is, except the Foreign Secretary himself. When it became clear to the diplomats on duty, sometime in the early hours of the Saturday morning, that the Turks were not on this occasion simply going to cruise round the island as they had done before, a lot of senior people asleep round London had to be summoned to work. Unfortunately, the Foreign Secretary's chauffeur could not be found to bring him in from his home in Kennington. So Mr Callaghan, being a resourceful politician, walked into the street, hailed an early-morning delivery van, and had himself conveyed to the Foreign Office by a surprised Portuguese driver, courtesy of Homepride Bread. He did not, naturally, remain with the unit for the rest of the Cyprus crisis; but it was only just up the lift-shaft from his own room and easy to visit when he wanted to watch the state of play. The diplomats there were gathering intelligence on events round the Eastern Mediterranean from every available source; from BBC bulletins, as well as from the high commission in Nicosia and from the embassies in Athens and Ankara. When Ministers—and several had a departmental interest, besides the Foreign Secretary—telephoned for briefing or advice, the diplomats gave them the latest score, presented the apparent options available to the government, and took instructions. Sometimes a First Secretary on the telephone would in this way find himself steering the politicians singlehanded, sometimes he would summon a more experienced hand to the helm. Sometimes a Minister would say, 'What do you think?'; more often, 'Do this or that', having already come to a conclusion in talks with his own colleagues. What everyone was bent upon, in pure national self-interest, was the evacuation of British holidaymakers in a fashion that could not possibly be interpreted by either of the combatants as British military intervention. The Turkish Prime Minister had said that the evacuation plans were reasonable in Ankara's eyes, but in the Emergency Unit there remained niggling worries: would Ankara's views have been transmitted clearly enough to its troops in Cyprus, would every military commander accept Ankara's views when he heard them ... and so on. International crises largely boil down to clear communication in the emergency units of this world: stylized communication between diplomats and their political masters, straightforward communication between headquartered diplomats and their embassies, roundabout communication between contestants routed through third parties, garbled communication with combatants in the field, and intriguing communication with people who don't seem to have much to do with the business at all. Some 20,000 telegrams flowed in and out of the British diplomatic machinery during that Cyprus crisis. And when it was all over there was to be seen, among the post-critical detritus of Rooms 117–220, the telltale marks of other communications as well. On a noticeboard, above the silent teleprinters, the empty television screens and the abandoned plastic coffee beakers, were the memoranda of important telephone numbers that might have to be dialled in a hurry. The one that told where Sir John Killick (a Deputy Under Secretary) would be dining at seven o'clock one evening. The one that would get the Hotel Beau Rivage, Geneva, in quick time. And the one that would instantly connect you to the President of the United States, in San Clemente, California.

The Head of the Diplomatic Service, the Permanent Under Secretary, can sometimes be curiously detached when his men are grappling with international crises. Sir Paul Gore-Booth was in Italy when Russian tanks reached Prague in August 1968, and he did not allow the agonies of the Czechs to interrupt his holiday there. It is perfectly arguable, of course, that a PUS who is confident of his machine's smooth efficiency does not need to be at his desk, even when catastrophe threatens; though a more plausible explanation of Gore-Booth's absence in 1968 is that British diplomats and politicians alike had already made up their collective minds that what happened in Czechoslovakia was not, for the second time in thirty years, of the slightest concern to Britain or her interests. The PUS is, as an outsider has remarked, 'the supreme pourer of oil upon troubled waters in a profession devoted to doing just that';[1] and most of the lubrication is conducted where no one but the closest insiders will ever notice it happening. He is also, as Sir Frederick Hoyer Millar once explained, the man who sees to it that the Foreign Office speaks with one voice to the politicians. 'In a properly managed Department (of State), as we understand it, if there is any sort of dispute between departments or Under Secretaries or Deputy Under Secretaries, I have to settle it first. We try to avoid ever going to the Minister and saying that half the Foreign Office thinks this and the other half thinks that; will he decide it?'[2] This, too, is a discreet role. Permanent Under Secretaries, unlike Ambassadors, are rarely in the public eye except for occasional extra-curricular activities as curious as the Gore-Booth Presidency of the Sherlock Holmes Society, which once involved him in a costumed re-enactment of the struggle with Professor Moriarty at the Reichenbach Falls.

Only in modern times has the PUS been very much more than an Office manager. Lord Salisbury never consulted his PUS, Sir Philip Currie, about anything of importance and often kept secret from the Foreign Office his dealings with other governments; while Currie's successor, Sir Thomas Sanderson, thought it improper to offer advice on policy to his Minister. Since the creation of the FCO in 1968, its PUS has been supreme commander of the Diplomatic Service; but immediately after the Plowden reforms (i.e. the creation of the Diplomatic Service), that distinction rotated between the PUS of the FO and the CRO in turn. Until 1956 the PUS wasn't thoroughly in control of anything at all if the Head of the Civil Service – who might be a very insular man with his origins in the Inland Revenue – decided to exercise his full authority, which extended to the diplomats. But in that year, when Sir Norman Brook succeeded Sir Edward Bridges at the Treasury, he was gazetted as Head of the *Home* Civil Service, leaving diplomats to drift away on their own devices.

[1] Boardman and Groom, p. 58.
[2] *Sixth Report from the Select Committee on Estimates, Session 1957–8*, Question 1507.

Even today, diplomats manage to convey the quite erroneous impression that the PUS has very little to do with creating policy. To some extent this probably results from a tribal loyalty to the office, for although they can be quite savagely critical of Ambassadors, one never hears rude noises about any PUS — with the solitary exception of Sir Ivone Kirkpatrick, who was deeply implicated (painfully for the Foreign Office) in the Suez adventure of Anthony Eden and Selwyn Lloyd. Yet it is, all the same, remarkable how a PUS is mentioned only for his general presence, or for the adjustments he may have made to the diplomatic machinery. Sir Frederick Hoyer Millar is thus remembered for an air of comfortable common sense which helped to transform a panic into a mild irritation; Sir Denis Greenhill for enormous confidence in dealing with his politicians and for being, so the story goes, the only PUS who didn't make the Queen feel she was being lectured. Sir Paul Gore-Booth is recalled for introducing the idea of a PUS's morning meeting, whereas his predecessor, Sir Harold Caccia, had simply asked individuals to drop in when he thought there was something worth talking about. Sir Thomas Brimelow was known as an austere and ungregarious man with a disconcertingly retentive memory for the most obscure and distant details, which he would recite with the steadiness of a metronome, his eyes fixed on the wall opposite, his fingertips just touching at nose level in an emphasis of precision. It was characteristic that, just before retiring in 1975, he started to learn Classical Greek, purely for amusement in the years ahead.

Brimelow was, in fact, one of the FCO's great experts on Communist affairs, having been a Minister in Moscow and Ambassador in Warsaw on his way to the top job. He had also been a member of the Secret Intelligence Service, whose men are seeded in unmentionable numbers among the more innocent components of the Diplomatic List. As PUS he was a great delegater of authority, who encouraged people just below him to accept more responsibility than most Permanent Under Secretaries have cared to, partly because, as a relatively short-term caretaker, he wished the politicians to have a full sight of potential successors. There was never really much doubt that Sir Michael Palliser would step into his shoes, however, once the referendum on the Common Market had sealed our membership earlier in 1975. He was one of two Ambassadors whose names, together with those of two Deputy Under Secretaries, were most frequently canvassed as successors to Brimelow for months before the decision was actually taken – and Palliser from the beginning was clearly the popular choice within the Office itself. In many ways he is a complete contrast to his predecessor, an urbane ex-Guards officer, an admiral's son, replacing a withdrawn polymath. His career rose along one of the most dazzling routes possible – private secretary to Sir Ivone Kirkpatrick when he was PUS, first head of the Planning Staff, private secretary to Harold Wilson at No 10 for three years and, penultimately, Ambassador and Permanent Representative to the EEC in Brussels. Brimelow started as a Vice-Consul in Danzig just before the war, grafted away at unfashionable jobs like that of Commercial Counsellor in Ankara, and was rarely where he would obviously attract attention – apart from three stints in Moscow – until his later years; perfect spy cover, in fact. Palliser's credentials are basically those of the brilliant Whitehall operator and the totally committed European; he even married, impeccably, the daughter of Paul-Henri Spaak. His Catholicism is maybe an oblique sign of the times, too (though it allows the irreverent thought that the theology of the PUS is rotated like a crop, Sir Paul Gore-Booth having been a Christian Scientist and Sir Denis Greenhill having come from Congregationalism). Whatever direction British diplomacy takes with Palliser as its chief professional, it cannot avoid being deeply marked by his influence. Having become PUS at the age of fifty-three, he is, unless he retires early, going to be in office far longer than anyone before him since the war.

But no PUS can ever feel he has the entire diplomatic operation in his grasp; it sprawls too much in too many different directions for that. He can lie abed of nights with awful forebodings of what would happen if NATO collapsed, or if someone in the Middle East became impossibly aggressive; or he can coolly decide to live easily with problems that can't be solved by the British, including the one in the Middle East; that Armageddon in any case certainly won't come from that direction ('because politicians do not lead their people to certain destruction') and that the pressures imposed on the Western world by the oil producers in 1974 could not possibly be as effective an economic and political weapon if applied a second time ('What you basically bank on is the willingness of parties to moderate their demands'). Recent Permanent Under Secretaries have thought variously on such lines. The very most any PUS can hope to do is to make sure that his machine is highly polished for any work required of it; to press the Foreign Office view upon the politicians in the most effective way possible; and to see that the diplomats have their oar into anything remotely relevant to them that flows up and down Whitehall. It is with this last end in view that a PUS spends a considerable amount of his time in the company of other civil service chiefs, quite as much as to enjoy any collective sensation of rarefied power. Twice a year, all these men congregate for a special meeting at the Civil Service College in Sunningdale. Much more frequently, half a dozen at a time may drop in for morning coffee at one another's suite of offices. The business of shared government is not confined to the Cabinet.

It is not a perpetually friendly affair between the civil servants, any more than it is between politicians of the same party; though, even when the widest differences appear among the former, backed by the deepest feelings, they are probably cloaked in greater civility than similar arguments among Ministers. Their disagreements certainly do not get anything like the same airing in public. But one does not need to dabble in the sub-political process of government for long to discover all manner of rivalries and suspicions between the different departments of state. Home Office people have a powerful contempt for the Ministry of Defence, for example, and diplomats reckon – not too lightly – that they'd sometimes rather deal with foreigners than with some of the other ministries in London. 'Moscow is as nothing compared with them in some cases,' said a former Ambassador there. 'There are far longer and sharper knives in Whitehall than ever you find here,' echoed a colleague in Brussels. The fact that the Diplomatic Service's work is so different from that of other ministries makes it an obvious potential adversary for the rest, surpassed only by the Treasury, whose calculating eyes all other civil servants feel boring into the back of their necks. Treasury influence is not confined to apportioning available funds among the other ministries; it extends, whenever possible, to the insertion of various levers in the works. One of these was the Organization and Method approach to life, which was thrust on the FCO in the mid-1960s and resulted in working instructions – hitherto codified in the Foreign Office Order Book, a communications manual and Foreign Service Regulations – being increased from those three volumes to the present forty-seven volumes of *Diplomatic Service Procedures,* an unwieldy epic of advice which the Diplomatic Service inspectors have ever since been trying to reduce to more manageable and more digestible proportions.

It is not only the substance of diplomacy which sets the FCO apart from other ministries. There is, beyond this, a studied singularity about the diplomats. Alone, they are self-administering instead of being organized by the Civil Service Department. They become and remain diplomats for the whole of their careers; unlike Home civil servants, who may start their working lives in the Department of the Environment and finish it in Energy or the Ministry of Defence. The diplomats insist on those slightly higher performances in the Administrative entrance exams at CSSB. They have their own honours system, the Order of St Michael and St George. They even enjoy better health than Home civil servants; more liver complaints, it is true, but half as many of the troubles that show up on electrocardiographs, and an expectation of life that is greater by four good years. Such unassailably distinguishing marks are heavily greased by the application of myths. New young diplomats are very pointedly told that no one knocks on anyone else's door in the FCO, and experienced diplomats will say that in the Home Service, not only do the closest colleagues knock before entering, but that almost everyone is hailed as 'Mr ——' as well. A Home civil servant will flatly contradict what these observations imply. Diplomats, he will say, are *much* more deferential to their superiors than we are; they are not nearly so ready to ask themselves or authority 'Does this make sense?' Beneath all the professional amiability of Whitehall, there are strong feelings of distinction, and opportunities are not often lost to point them out to the discredit of others. A Commercial Counsellor abroad told me that 'a fairly *relaxed* man from the Department of Trade could do this job as well as I can'; and 'relaxed' was quite clearly crucial in his eyes. Lord Trevelyan told a story in one of his books, with a great deal of relish, about a group of officials from the Inland Revenue inquiring on the streets of Bonn the way to the British *legation.*

Barricade noises will be heard now and then in every department of government. Novice diplomats hear them for the first time on their indoctrination course, when a lecturer points out that a high priority of the FCO is not only to co-ordinate all other ministries in their dealings with foreigners, but to influence their relevant policies: 'We must be there from the start, helping to shape those policies.' Another speaker is even more emphatic. 'It's the interface with Whitehall', he declares, 'that's really crucially important to the future of this Office.' There is a deep Foreign Office belief that Home civil servants as a whole are apt to think that all policy is evolved by them, leaving the diplomats to explain it to the foreigners. The diplomats are the last people to resist the notion that at every turn they must stand between the Home men and all aliens, and they cite examples of the damage that can be done when they do not occupy this frontier position. There was an occasion, several years ago, when another ministry produced a faultless analysis of one African national economy, but it was expressed in terms which offended the Africans considerably. Diplomatic anxiety to avoid offending foreigners is professionally paramount, and accounts for the FCO's considerable displeasure when the Home Office introduced immigration laws that had Australians and Canadians, much more than Indians and Pakistanis, complaining bitterly that they had been cheated of a birthright. But diplomatic concern to be involved in all policy-making, and not merely in its interpretation abroad, seems to spring as much as anything from a deeply insecure feeling that otherwise they will, as a group, be pushed more and more towards the periphery of all events. They worry a lot about the traditional inadequacy of their specialized knowledge, which prevents them from challenging the specialist departments of state as effectively as they might. They fret over the weakness of their organization, which scarcely leaves any man in London long enough at a stretch to achieve a totally commanding position on any brief which may be shared with another ministry. They wriggle uneasily at the thought that, in the many interdepartmental committees of Whitehall, the only subject on which the FCO leads — by producing the basic information, the inspiration and the clout from which other ministries take their clue — is the Law of the Sea. This is an important lead to have; but it is not enough to ensure diplomatic survival, should another James Burke come to transform the whole appliance of government.

The closest other departments to the FCO are Defence and Trade, which are also largely outward-looking. But overlapping interests, and some duplicated efforts, occur almost all along the line in Whitehall: and that is to disregard for the moment the special case of relations with the rest of the European Community, in which virtually every ministry is highly involved. When the Channel Tunnel still looked like a going concern, both the FCO and the Department of the Environment had teams of men working on it. Concorde spawned working relationships between the FCO, Industry, Environment and the Department of Education and Science. The Law of the Sea Conference, which has for almost twenty years perambulated under United Nations patronage from one inconclusive venue to another, has thrown up a British alliance consisting of the FCO, the Ministry of Defence, the Ministry of Agriculture, Fisheries and Food, the Department of Energy and the Department of Trade. Even something as remote as East African Railways can have a proportion of Whitehall making tracks together with the diplomats: the Railways, a joint possession of Kenya, Tanzania and Uganda, have been greatly in debt to the World Bank for years, but the British government happens to be a guarantor, which brings Trade and Overseas Aid into the Whitehall equation alongside the FCO. Pressures from the world outside, such as these, have thrown the civil servants of Whitehall together into joint negotiating teams much more than ever before in British history. This is an aspect of what the Duncan Committee called the New Diplomacy. Yet it may be a fairly recent sense of national crisis, a subconscious laager mentality, which has gradually developed since and as a result of the loss of Empire, which had, quite apart from New Diplomatic requirements, resulted in a certain amount of cross-fertilization in Whitehall. A number of diplomats in the past two or three years have been posted on attachment to other government departments. The highest-ranking woman at the London end of the Diplomatic Service, Gillian Brown, has been working since 1974 as an Under Secretary in the Department of Energy, which has one other fairly senior diplomat on its books. There is a Grade 4 diplomat in the Ministry of Agriculture, a First Secretary attached to the Treasury, and several FCO people working among the Tradesmen. At the FCO itself, there is a non-diplomatic Chief Economic Adviser, and Home civil servants have for donkey's years been scattered as Attachés in various British missions abroad.

On the face of it, the insecure barricade cries of the diplomats are hardly to be taken seriously. Not only do they have closer links with all other departments of state than any ministry but the Treasury, but they are also firmly placed at the controlling points of decisions. The Chief Executive of the Overseas Trade Board, a very weighty collection of people from inside and outside the civil service, including Lord Briginshaw and the Duke of Kent, is a diplomat. Someone from the FCO is always one of the four Private Secretaries to the Prime Minister at No 10. A diplomat is on the Central Policy Review Staff, the 'think tank'. Another dozen or so are situated elsewhere inside the Cabinet Office, which is quite the most important place to have them outside the FCO. Started by Lloyd George in 1916 as nothing more than a secretariat for Cabinet meetings, this organism grew over the years into something much more potent, and almost as large as some of the smaller ministries: there are close on 700 people under orders from its HQ in William Kent's Old Treasury Building, on the Whitehall corner of Downing Street, which separates it from the FCO. Its declared task is to serve the Cabinet collectively with information and advice from the full range of Whitehall departments, and in this process the Cabinet Office runs to no fewer than (at the last count) 118 official committees. But it has great independent power, and a rare public exhibition of this came with the long wrangling, in and out of the Law Courts, over the publication of R. H. S. Crossman's diaries. One could never be sure whether Sir John Hunt, as Secretary of the Cabinet, was merely the frontman for politicians who wished to be saved from an old colleague's indiscretions, or whether he was acting as a spokesman for all civil service chiefs who preferred that the vitals of government should stay secret to them and their political masters. It was perfectly clear that, had the Law Lords not disagreed with Sir John, the Cabinet Office—not the government per se—would have blocked the full publication.

The diplomats appointed to this intriguing appliance are never of lower rank than up and coming First Secretaries, who will be restored to the FCO and the embassies as Counsellors. Mixed up with comparable officials from other state departments, they spend their time in one or other of the Cabinet

K

Office's subdivisions, like the European Unit, which co-ordin-
ates the complex British operation at the EEC in Brussels, or the
Assessment Staff, whose job is to feed Cabinet Ministers with
advice on almost everything else under the sun. For the time of
their service in William Kent's building, they are expected to
rid themselves of instinctive genuflections they might normally
make in the direction of their superiors in Gilbert Scott's palazzo.
People who have found themselves in this interesting position
for three or four years say that the habit comes quite easily and
soon, and indeed that you get quite a kick out of thumbing
your nose obstreperously at the old Office. Contact between
these diplomatic outriders and the FCO does not, of course,
break down; but it is for the time being certainly transformed.
For any appraisal of foreign policy made by the diplomats
working in the Cabinet Office overrides any appraisal of the
same situation that might emerge from the Foreign Office. An
example of this occurred when the Americans were preparing
to withdraw from Vietnam. A Cabinet Office assessment was
made of the implications of US withdrawal for British foreign
policy. The FCO made its own assessment, based on the latest
briefings it had obtained from the British Embassy in Washington. The Cabinet Office paper, besides being placed before
government Ministers, was passed on to the FCO, where the
official receiving it agreed that it was probably sounder than
the FCO's own product; and it continued on its way to Sir
Peter Ramsbotham, the British Ambassador in Washington. A
little later, however, a Deputy Under Secretary in the FCO
advised Washington to take no notice of the Cabinet Office
assessment, and to act on the FCO's line of thought (which, in
effect, meant that the Ambassador was to follow his own instincts). Somehow, word of this subversion got back to the
Cabinet Office. As a result, the PUS got a rocket from just up
the street, and the Deputy Under Secretary was diplomatically
trodden on.

If this suggests a permanent state of tension between Cabinet
Office and FCO, then it is misleading. But it is an indication of
where—when all the smooth relationships of Whitehall have
served their purpose, when all the informal contacts have produced mutual aid in interdepartmental problems, when all the
civil service chiefs have supped morning coffee together and
agreed upon a common posture to set against or alongside the

political stance of the moment—just where, when all this is done, the whip hand really lies. There can be no doubt that the genuine teamwork of Whitehall has reached a greater pitch in the last few years than any civil servant could have imagined a quarter of a century ago. The trend is increasingly towards joint effort and away from an insistence on independent departmental existence which produced, among other things, such daft anomalies as a Commonwealth Relations Office which until the day it expired, was technically part of the Home Civil Service because of an administrative decision taken in 1782.

The teamwork, however, will have to be refined a great deal before the lines of communication along Whitehall are completely insulated against the possibility of those explosive short circuits that happen from time to time between the closest of departments. One involving the FCO and the Ministry of Defence burst into the public prints in October 1974, over the perennially sensitive issue of the Simonstown Defence agreement. According to newspaper reports, the Ministry of Defence was 'steaming with indignation' at the Foreign Office's accusation that 'the Navy had overdone its part in the latest round of sea-borne exercises with the South African forces'.[1] Mr Callaghan was said to have apologized to Mr Mason, the Defence Minister, across the Cabinet table for this diplomatic incivility; and the nation mostly licked its chops at the spectacle of confusion in high places, while the back-benchers of the Labour party prepared to make the most of a God-sent opportunity to revive debate on Britain's relationship with South Africa. Anyone not totally concentrated upon the morality of apartheid, however, was much more stricken with curiosity at how such an internal muddle among the British could possibly happen.

The manoeuvre of ten ships belonging to the Royal Navy in South African waters was inevitably well scrutinized long beforehand by the Cabinet. On Ministerial instructions, indeed, two vessels which the sailors had planned to include in the exercise (one of them the royal yacht *Britannia*) were forbidden to participate, and never got anywhere near Table Bay. The Cabinet's guidelines on what was to be a limited weapons exercise, topped up with a courtesy call at Simonstown, were

[1] *Guardian*, October 25th, 1974.

issued both to the Ministry of Defence and to the FCO well in advance of events; long enough for them to be passed by the FCO to all British missions in Africa. The word eventually came back from the missions to the FCO that local African opinion was not unduly perturbed at the prospect of the exercise (though British press reports subsequently said that Black Africa was deeply offended by happenings at the Cape). On this basis, the exercise went ahead as planned.

It is possible that nothing more would have been heard of it had *The Times* correspondent in South Africa not done what any journalist in his right mind would have done in the same position, which was to report the fraternization of British sailors with South African girls in the byways of Cape Town – something that hadn't been seen in a long while – and to add that the South African press, for good political reasons of its own, was making the most of this amity. He also mentioned that the British ships had loosed off twenty-one-gun salutes to the South Africans as they steamed into harbour. It was this incident, entirely in accordance with Queen's Regulations and Admiralty Instructions, that produced the upheaval in London. It had the Foreign Secretary demanding an explanation from the Ministry of Defence, word of this leaking in time for the second edition off Fleet Street, and a great deal of sharp telephoning in the next few days between the Ministry and the FCO. Basically, the public was treated to combat in Whitehall because Whitehall's internal communications system had not worked as well as usual. A shortage of general knowledge among the diplomats had left them ignorant of standard naval practice in foreign waters, which was odd in a profession which devotes much of its life to such niceties of protocol, odder still when it happened at that moment to be led by a politician who was himself once a naval stoker. At the same time, the Ministry of Defence had made the large assumption that *everybody* knew about the firing of twenty-one-gun salutes. That small but reverberant detail had never been mentioned by anyone in all the painstaking plans that had been laid long before the fleet sailed for Simonstown.

It is possible that the FCO is less wholehearted about combined operations with other departments of state than the majority of British civil servants – though this is something that Sir Michael Palliser may well seek to correct after his experiences in Europe. The FCO has for a long time accepted the infiltration of Home men in its missions abroad, and at the EEC delegation in Brussels it has taken part in the clearest possible demonstration that a jumble of men from several ministries can work effectively together. It has always been accepted that a diplomat who, for reasons of health or domestic difficulty, cannot face any more postings abroad, shall be detached permanently to work out the rest of his career in some part of the Home Civil Service. But the senior administrators of the FCO tend to recoil nervously if they are asked why there cannot be a much greater transfusion of Home blood into the Diplomatic Service at home and abroad. They say, for a start, that Home civil servants are reluctant to be posted abroad.[1] They argue that the language qualification is vital to everyone working in the diplomatic machine, which it clearly should be overseas but hardly so, one might have thought, in Whitehall. They talk about different casts of mind required in the two branches of government service, the Home men developing administrative skills, the diplomats having always to be questioning assumptions – a *non sequitur* which an outsider has some difficulty in following. But, when pushed to it, they invariably fall back to an argument about different career structures, about different speeds in promotion: 'It's fast early on in the Home Civil Service, it's fast later on in the Diplomatic Service. Amalgamation would mean that someone got the best or the worst of both worlds, and that would be disastrous for general morale.' The thought that one day the office of Permanent Under Secretary at the FCO should be interchangeable with, say, the Permanent Secretary in the Ministry of Agriculture, as that post can be now with the Permanent Secretary at the Department of Health and Social Security is, quite simply, unspeakable anathema to the diplomats.

Whether or not it is because the Home civil servants feel that the diplomats are much readier to spread themselves abroad in Whitehall than to allow Home men more participation in foreign affairs, the truth is that, underneath the increased teamwork, the jealousies persist. The Department of Trade suspects the diplomats of wanting to run the export programme and is not gratified when a new Whitehall committee, to thrash out

[1] The number of unsuccessful Diplomatic Service aspirants who accept alternative appointments in other government departments after passing muster with CSSB, however, would seem to suggest otherwise.

external economic policy, is launched from inside the FCO. A memorandum is put up by a bright man in the FCO suggesting that this international information service should supply an adviser to the chief officials of every other government department; it never even leaves the FCO because it is assumed that no other department will look at it. When a lustrous job in such combined operations as we have goes to a man in one department, it must quickly be balanced by some *quid pro quo* elsewhere. This was the case in 1975, when Sir Michael Palliser was nominated as the new PUS at the Foreign Office. In Brussels his No 2 was a Deputy Secretary from the Home Civil Service and for months before Palliser was recalled to London the Department of Trade had pushed heavily for one of its men to become the new leader of the delegation to the EEC. Interested parties in other places were also stirred by opportunity and called for a political appointment next time, like the placing of Sir Christopher Soames in the Paris Embassy in 1968. The Foreign Office, naturally enough, did not propose to yield this ground easily if it was going to be a matter of push and shove (it had to think in terms of career rewards for its own men, quite apart from anything else) and in the end it won the subterranean tussle for preferment. Palliser was succeeded by Sir Donald Maitland, one of the Foreign Office's great all-rounders, an Arabist who had been Britain's Permanent Representative at the United Nations and then the Deputy Under Secretary in charge of FCO economic policy, the man responsible for the diplomatic contribution to the Whitehall External Economic Policy Committee. Had the national referendum on the Common Market gone the other way, a different talent would have been needed to conduct the dismantling operation in Brussels, and, instead, Maitland would very probably have found himself the new British Ambassador in Cairo when the job changed hands that year. But we stayed put in Europe, he went to lead the EEC delegation, and it is extremely doubtful whether a candidate as suitable could have been put up from any other quarter. Within a few weeks, at least one of the contesting parties was placated by an appointment in London. During Palliser's time in Brussels, the European Unit in the Cabinet Office was headed by Patrick Nairne, who had been drafted in from the Ministry of Defence as Sir John Hunt's second in command. Nairne now left for an independent empire of his own, as Permanent Secretary at the Department of Health and Social Security. His place as London's chief supervisor of British activities in Brussels, was taken by Roy Denman, a Deputy Secretary in the Department of Trade.

'There's a general feeling round Whitehall, which still persists,' said one diplomat of the norm in departmental attitudes, 'that if we tell them that, they'll use it against us.' For all the increasing co-operation of the past generation, for all the superb teamwork that has been developed in response to the Common Market, the business of government is still heavily influenced by pecking orders and defensiveness, which show up in public when draconian Budgets are in the offing and departments begin to make plaintive or aggressive noises in anticipation of cuts in their own programmes. The noises, of course, are not usually made by civil servants, but by politicians. The alliance between these two species of authority is what matters most to us all.

6 The Politicians

It was a Permanent Under Secretary in the 1940s, Sir Alexander Cadogan, who expressed the most pungent view ever recorded by a diplomat about politicians. 'Silly bladders, self-advertising, irresponsible nincompoops! How I *hate* Members of Parliament. They embody everything my training has taught me to eschew — ambition, prejudice, dishonesty, self-seeking light-hearted irresponsibility, black-hearted mendacity.'[1] An extreme response, of course, to what had clearly been a long and trying association, possibly to both sides. At this distance its chief interest is its demonstration of the feelings that can accumulate when civil servants, like royalty, are obliged to keep their mouths publicly shut about what matters most to them when it is happening. But, even allowing for its excess, it suggests the high degree of tension that is built into the relationship between the nation's elected governors and their professional advisers. Between them they shape our destiny, yet they alone know exactly what each has contributed to its final form. Each group knows the other's strengths and weaknesses, brilliance and worthiness, vanities and stupidities, far better than the most diligently inquisitive journalist and it is to their mutual advantage — and sometimes, no doubt, in the national interest — that a

---

[1] Cadogan, *Diaries*, March 1st, 1945 (though the quotation is given in full only in the editor's introduction, p. 18). The PUS could be just as intemperate about journalists. On December 8th, 1944, he wrote:

While waiting for dinner, I read ... article in the *New Statesman* — a thing I haven't done for two years or more. How anyone can write such distorted, biased and dishonest muck passes my comprehension. The *NS* is addressed, I suppose, to more or less educated people. Are their readers really taken in by such dishonest and libellous trash? I suppose so, if the *Times* readers can swallow the swill dished up to them ... Barrington Ward is not capable of running a mussel stall.

great deal of this shall not be publicly revealed until the ener-vating passage of thirty years or so. The politicians, being (like writers) exhibitionists by definition, do have a certain licence to speak impromptu, which the civil servants lack; but they must use it, according to the unwritten rules, with extreme caution. George Brown's criticisms of the Foreign Office a few years ago were innocuous compared with Sir Alexander Cadogan's strictures; they were precisely aimed at specific points in language as civil as, though less stilted than, that of an official report. But within twenty-four hours of their being made public, the former Foreign Secretary had a load of lately retired diplomats down on him in print like a ton of bricks.

The relationship between diplomats and Foreign Office politicians is even more inbred than the one between Home civil servants and their Ministers. The Home civil servant cannot draft a paragraph in any submission without being well aware that there will be innumerable public checks on his work by many MPs and lobby groups – not to mention, as often as not, by campaigning local if not national newspapers. The Second Secretary in the FCO rarely works under such inhibitions. If it is true, as some politicians assert, that diplomats can be shockingly ignorant of life in Bethnal Green and West Brom-wich, it is equally true that the East End of London and the south side of Birmingham are largely oblivious of what SALT amounts to, and mightn't think about it very deeply if they were informed in some detail. There are not many votes to be obtained by questioning the Foreign Secretary sharply in the House of Commons; and it is perhaps small wonder that, when diplomats complain that politicians are obsessed with the sover-eignty of Parliament, they sometimes add that Parliament is not competent to make judgments on foreign affairs when it spends so little time considering them. Successive British governments must take the blame for that, for conducting their foreign affairs in a way that obscures them from the nation almost as much as if they were run by the most suppressive totalitarian regime. We have nothing comparable to the United States Senate Committee for Foreign Relations, which regularly examines what American diplomacy is up to. The House of Commons Expenditure Committee (more precisely, that committee's Defence and External Affairs Sub-Committee) has a very res-tricted role in comparison with practice across the Atlantic. It meets infrequently and, empowered only to scrutinize financial matters, it can inform itself only about the condition of the diplomatic machine: it cannot review the direction in which it is travelling, except by limited inference. Apart from senior politicians in the Cabinet, therefore, British MPs are just about as restricted in what they may learn of Britain's diplomacy as any intelligent reader of the newspapers. Even in the inner sanctum of government, a great deal of information is confined to the small number of Cabinet Ministers who sit on its Defence and Overseas Policy Committee, a half-dozen or so in a Cabinet of twenty or more.

On the third Wednesday in every month, however, it is the Foreign Office's turn to face a full hour of Question Time in the House. It was an ancient tradition that this bout should be held on a Monday, until Sir Alec Douglas-Home once missed it, being otherwise engaged at the monthly meeting of the Nine in Brussels. The first supplementary question in the House that day was 'Where do the Foreign Secretary's loyalties lie?'; and the reply was to the effect that, as junior member of the Common Market, Britain could scarcely ask her colleagues to shift their well-established date for her convenience; so a disgruntled Mother of Parliaments was forced to yield instead. Ever since, the third Wednesday has occasioned the most frantic activity the FCO generally experiences between one month and the next. There may be anything up to ten days' notice of written questions and there can never be less than thirty-six hours in which to prepare answers to them: it is the speculative orals and the artful supplementaries that have the Office ajiggle with nervous anticipation on the Wednesday morning. Young diplomats tune in to the early-morning radio bulletins and to the fruitful 'Today' programme before leaving for work, knowing that back-benchers will be searching the same sources for a topic which can be tossed at the government later in the day. Guessing what may be asked, before the prepared oral questions come over from the House in mid-morning, is among the arts of briefing the Minister adequately, so that when he enters the Chamber just before 2.30 his large transparent folder is not merely thick with answers, but has handy little comments scribbled in various margins as well. 'It's So-and-So's hobby horse', to guide him through an imminent gust of back-bench flatulence; and 'On no account should you make a commitment on this because we are still bargaining with Ruritania', to steer him past a more serious hazard. Classified information must be carefully excluded, and newcomers to this business are given one other tip about supplying answers to Ministers; 'Don't try to make funnies; they like to make their own.' A handful of acolytes is always in the House, lest the Minister should get into desperate trouble with his papers, and this was always a test for the diplomats backing Ernest Bevin, who sometimes forgot to take his brief into the Chamber with him. 'But even if he were still holding it when he rose to speak,' wrote one of them later,[1]

> he would end by putting it down and forgetting about it, while if, exceptionally, he followed it approximately as he spoke, its text emerged from his lips so gravely transformed that it was all but unrecognisable to its several authors, nervously huddled in the Box in the north-west corner of the Chamber reserved for Government advisers, and vainly straining their ears for the reassuring sound of their meticulously chosen generalisations, equivocations and evasions.

All civil servants understand their duty to lie in the promotion and support of government policy, by giving their Minister the best information they can lay their hands on. They are advised on recruitment to rid their minds of any notion that they can serve the national interest better by doing anything beyond this. Yet, while there can be no question of the real integrity of that advice, there is a sense in which Question Time and the monthly preparation for it is merely one example of a game which is played continuously throughout the length and breadth of Whitehall and Westminster, between various teams and on adjacent or overlapping pitches, whose object is to achieve the most resounding credit for the participants. In this sense, so far as the Foreign Office is concerned, foreign affairs are simply the ball used in a number of matches. There is the one played between the Office and Parliament, when the diplomats are captained by the Foreign Secretary, and the one between the Office and a Combined side from the rest of the civil service,

[1] Valentine Lawford, 'Three Ministers', *Cornhill Magazine*, No 1010, (1956–7), p. 93.

when the PUS leads his men on to the field. The most import-
tant match of all to the spectators on the touchlines is that between the Office and the government, in which the Foreign
Secretary's role can be curiously equivocal. For, although he is
apparently with the politicians, he sometimes puts through his
own goal in a surprisingly determined fashion; and once in a
while he is barged off the ball from behind by the equally surprising tactics of his Prime Minister, or flattened in a headlong
rush of Cabinet colleagues. Stripped of the metaphors, with
very serious intent replacing the gamesmanship, that is the
reality of government.

It was not R. H. S. Crossman, but a Labour politician of an
earlier generation, Arthur Henderson,[1] who after experience at
the Foreign Office said that 'The first 48 hours decide whether
a new Minister is going to run his office or whether his office is
going to run him'. There have been many politicians in the
second category, and they are remembered with little enthusiasm by the civil servants. Ernest Bevin was distinctly a commander of his men when necessary, and he didn't take long to
demonstrate it. It is said that on his first Friday night as Foreign
Secretary, his Principal Private Secretary left a pile of red boxes
on his desk with a note on top which read, 'The Secretary of
State may care to peruse these documents over the weekend'.
The boxes were still there when the diplomat returned to work
on Monday morning, and so was the note, with Bevin's post-
script at the bottom – 'A kindly thought, but erroneous'. As
Lord Chalfont (himself a Foreign Office Minister in the 1960s)
has remarked, this symbolized a decisive moment in the life of
any politician:[2]

> his first encounter with that silky, steely and beautifully
> articulate machine, the Diplomatic Service. The first trial
> of strength, which is sometimes no more dramatic than the
> handshake of two boxers, often decides whether the poli-
> tician is eventually able to control the machine and use it
> effectively, or whether he falls into the works and comes
> out the other end bearing a remarkable resemblance to
> a rubber stamp.

[1] Foreign Secretary 1929–31. Quoted in Clark, p. 8.
[2] McDermott, p. 9.

The gearbox of the works, which the politician must manipulate deftly if he is to drive the machine, is his private office.
Each Minister of State has a posse of attendant officials, with
whom he sorts out the subjects allotted to him by the Foreign
Secretary, who pass his instructions down to the relevant departments and who convey departmental and other diplomatic
advice back to him.[1] These anterooms of power are miniatures
modelled on *the* private office, which is arranged about the person of the Foreign Secretary himself. Apart from its secretarial
staff – the eight women who, besides typing and taking shorthand notes, are most highly valued for an ability to find the
right document in five minutes flat – the Foreign Secretary's
private office reflects the schizophrenic nature of any government Minister's life. It includes three people who have entered
the Foreign Office with him, a reminder that he is, above all,
a politician. One is the lady who takes care of affairs in his constituency. Another is his Parliamentary Private Secretary, an
MP who, although based in the Commons, is brought into
some of the Foreign Office meetings. The third is his Political
Adviser, who sits, all the time, very close to his boss. A lot of
the Adviser's efforts go into writing the first drafts of the Foreign
Secretary's speeches, but that is the least important of his roles.
He is the man from the party, attached to the diplomatic
machine to make sure that the party line is never forgotten.
Sir Alec Douglas-Home's Political Adviser was Miles Hudson,
from the Research Department of the Conservative Central
Office; James Callaghan's was Tom McNally, who was International Secretary at Transport House. The Adviser will call
himself, diffidently, an extra pair of hands and eyes for his
superior. His access to the purely diplomatic deliberations is
considerable, though the most sensitive papers are carefully
routed past him and he is not allowed to take part in staff
discussions. But he occasionally attends meetings of the Planning
Committee, and, besides putting up papers of his own to the
Foreign Secretary, he is licensed to scribble comments at the

[1] These vary in number from one government to another. There were
three Ministers of State at the Foreign Office when Sir Alec Douglas-Home
was Foreign Secretary under Edward Heath, but there were only two under
James Callaghan in Harold Wilson's Government. In addition, there are
the so-called 'junior Ministers' – Parliamentary Under Secretaries of State.
Callaghan had two.

bottom of other people's submissions. He is there, above all, to make sure that the Foreign Office takes account of all the options acceptable to the party in government and to head off the diplomats from those which will be utterly unacceptable, a waste of the Foreign Secretary's precious time. An emphatic and uniquely public demonstration of the Adviser's essential role occurred in February 1976 when, after the civil war in newly-independent Angola was over, the British government made its first contact for a long time with the Smith regime in Rhodesia. After preliminary soundings had been made in Africa by one of the Deputy Under Secretaries from London, Sir Antony Duff, the Foreign Secretary sent a three-man team to meet Ian Smith in Salisbury, to find out what his position was after the latest turn of events on the continent. Since Smith illegally declared independence in 1965 and diplomatic relations between London and Salisbury were broken, no topic has been more likely to rouse passions within the Labour party than Rhodesia, and Callaghan picked his envoys very carefully. He brought Lord Greenhill (the former Permanent Under Secretary) out of retirement to lead the team. The head of the FCO's Rhodesia Department went with him. So, too, did Tom McNally.

There are generally four diplomats in the Foreign Secretary's private office. The dogsbody among them is invariably a promising Executive officer with the temperament of a saint, which he sorely needs in supervising the Foreign Secretary's engagements and enduring trial by telephone from start to finish of every day. Much of the more rarefied work is done by the two Assistant Private Secretaries, who are handpicked First Secretaries with rising careers ahead of them. Yet no one in the entire Diplomatic Service is chosen more thoughtfully than the Principal Private Secretary, a Counsellor whose distinguished future is thereby well assured. James Callaghan's first PPS left, after he had served his time in the private office, to become Ambassador in Luxembourg at the age of forty-five, while his successor, forty-two on appointment, came in from Brussels, where he had been Sir Michael Palliser's Head of Chancery at the EEC – a small and tight relationship of people and places which indicates, among other things, the intense commitment of British diplomacy to Europe.

The PPS represents the continuity of government, to offset

the interruptions of democracy which occur when one political party takes charge from another. He is not transferred to another part of diplomacy when an old Foreign Secretary moves out and a new one moves in; he stays put, until he has completed the normal term of his own posting, and it would be a very foolish politician who wanted things otherwise, for in his early days with the Foreign Office he has much to learn from this official above all others. The PPS, for his part, makes his own discoveries about the nature of British democracy when a new chieftain arrives. To one PPS[1]

> it came as a shock to find that such a very large proportion of the letters of condolence written to Lord Halifax when he was transferred from the Foreign Office to Washington in 1940, and of congratulation to Eden on his being appointed in Halifax's place, no less than the letters of commiseration to Eden when he in turn left the Foreign Office in 1945 and the letters of congratulation to Bevin on succeeding him, were from the self-same members of the public. It was a lesson in versatility that I might scarcely have been privileged to learn, had it occurred to the writers that in each case their letters would actually be opened, and the replies thereto drafted, by one and the same man.

It is only a small exaggeration to picture the PPS as the most influential diplomat in the entire machine. He alone is perpetually in the company of his political boss. He is the man in the room next door when the Foreign Secretary is in the FCO, the man who goes with him on all his foreign travels, the man we see in the quick television snapshots of the Foreign Secretary on the move, already standing by the open door of the car as the politician gets out, walking just a few paces clear of him as the cameras swivel towards the aircraft steps, bending near his shoulder at the treaty-making publicity. The Permanent Under Secretary is merely a nodding acquaintance by comparison, for, although he can gain access virtually at will, he probably doesn't see the Foreign Secretary in practice much more than twice a day and sometimes not for two or three weeks at a time. The PPS, moreover, has a seat in every consultation that counts

[1] Lawford, op. cit.

in the building, whether or not the Foreign Secretary is present. He is at the 10.30 meeting chaired by the PUS each morning, at the coven of planners once a month or more, and at all the other confabulations that go to the making of policy. When he sits alone with other diplomats he is the interpreter of his master's mind, and when he returns to his master he is the vehicle of the Foreign Office view. Where he himself stands is of some importance to the balance of power between the politician and the diplomats. 'It is more important to get in well with him', according to a former Foreign Secretary, 'rather than the PUS in some ways, certainly if you're thinking of making an impact on the Office.'

The PPS has another intermediary role, even more delicate at times, which is to act as a linkman with No 10 Downing Street. The relationship between a Prime Minister and his Foreign Secretary is always a potentially strained one, for there is no grander part for a politician to play than that of the man who (singlehanded, etc. ...) brings home the bacon from overseas. Stanley Baldwin is probably the only occupant of Downing Street who has been utterly indifferent to foreign affairs, and the past half-century alone has been littered with examples of Prime Ministers who peered just a bit too intently over the shoulder for the Foreign Secretary's comfort. Chamberlain dominated Eden and Halifax, Churchill stole Eden's thunder, Eden got his own back on Selwyn Lloyd, while Harold Wilson's supervision finally caused George Brown to throw in his hand altogether. Brown resented the Prime Minister's interference in the Vietnam problem, with the dispatch of an obscure backbencher on a farcical mission to Hanoi.[1] Nor did he think much of the joint tour he made of Common Market capitals with his leader in 1967 ('it would have been logical for such a tour to be made by the Foreign Secretary alone ... '[2]). He criticized No 10's attempts to maintain 'a private Foreign Office', as a result of which the official Foreign Office 'could quite easily find that the seconded FO official was simultaneously advising

---

[1] Harold Wilson's memoirs of the 1964–70 Labour Government provided an interesting sidelight on the Prime Minister's own wish to be recognized as an international figure. The book contained nineteen pictures of him posing with foreign or Commonwealth statesmen. Only seven photographs showed him in a purely British context.

[2] Brown, p. 205.

the Prime Minister on the same subject and on a quite different network'.[1] It is an important function of the Foreign Secretary's PPS, and of the diplomatic Private Secretary at No 10 (who, in the Wilson–Brown days, was the up and coming Michael Palliser), to prevent their masters from reaching cross-purposes even though, as a last resort, the man at No 10 is empowered to tell the Foreign Office where it gets off – just as the diplomats in the Cabinet Office are. 'But if it becomes too tense,' according to a man who has done time in both these places, 'then it's the fault of the private offices. A private secretary is not just there to shuffle papers – you're there to advise your Minister; that's your job.'

Everything is done to stop friction with and between politicians. Private Secretaries are the collision mats of the civil service as a whole, and among diplomats generally there is a deeply professional instinct to avoid all things that go bump in the night; or day. Apart from anything else, a healthy sense of self-preservation causes the professionals to dodge the head-on clash, for the politician does have the power to hire and fire in the restricted terms of civil service; a Foreign Secretary can transfer anyone below the PUS on his own authority without consulting the Prime Minister. George Brown used to tease those who argued most fiercely with him that he'd have them posted to South Yemen if they didn't shut up; and diplomats before now have ended up in Ouagadougou after getting badly on the wrong side of their superiors. But the craft of diplomacy in the most literal sense is required when dealing with the politicians. What matters most of all, say the diplomats, is the *presentation* of policy, the *style* in which you present your case; and that differs from man to man, and from government to government. 'A Foreign Secretary may not need nudging, but arguing into a position,' says an old grand master in the game. 'But if a Minister is more difficult or ignorant, then you have to push him. You certainly try to prevent the Foreign Secretary from getting it wrong.'

It is said by some diplomats that nine times out of ten the politicians act upon the advice the professionals have given them, and many a First Secretary is sustained in the drudgery of an average week's paperwork by noting that Her Majesty's

[1] Brown, p. 134.

L

Principal Secretary of State for Foreign Affairs has just made a
series of observations at an international conference which
originated on his own desk. The highly critical Mr Crossman
himself once said, of government in general, that Ministers
made only about 10 per cent of all policy decisions, these covering the topics that a man was particularly interested in; the
rest, implicitly, being made by the civil servants and given little
more than a nod by the politicians. In foreign affairs especially,
perhaps, it is virtually impossible for even the four or five
politicians involved to absorb all the information available,
enough to contest with complete confidence any proposition
put to them by their advisers. Of policy-making in general,
Sir David Kelly wrote:[1]

> I have many times seen purely personal likes or dislikes,
> personal health, vanity, prejudice, *or just lack of time for
> proper consideration* decide important issues. The men who
> take the decisions usually rationalise them later, and I
> cannot doubt that casual and accidental factors of this
> kind have played a far greater part in history than appears
> from the textbooks.

The sheer exhaustion that builds up in a politician's life
alone weighs heavily against his determination to handle everything decisively. An average day for a Minister of State at the
Foreign Office starts at 9 a.m. and the morning is wholly spent
in half-hour meetings with resident officials or visiting Ambassadors, but on three days a week he has to set a couple of hours
aside for his constituency affairs. On four days in the week he
has to attend official luncheons. Between 3 p.m. and 5 p.m.
each day he has more official meetings at the FCO. Then he
struggles over to the Commons for an hour or so. If he gets
home and finishes his supper by 9 p.m. he is doing quite well;
but then he has to face anything up to three hours of reading
through his red boxes full of official papers. That is a day on the
soft side of his work, and it is likely to be softer at all times than
a Foreign Secretary's day. Foreign Office politicians are expected to go abroad now more than ever before in British
history. In 1974, Minister of State Roy Hattersley made over

[1] Kelly, p. 1.

twenty visits to Brussels alone; in 1975, James Callaghan was abroad for ninety-five days. It is not surprising that there are a number of issues which any politician does not wish, in the sense implied by Crossman, to be bothered with. 'If I were a politician,' said a diplomat, 'I'd *want* the Foreign Office to solve whatever problem is still inherent in the Berlin Wall without asking me what I think about it.'

The Crossman diaries have left a strong impression that, in his experience, civil servants spent a certain amount of effort not merely in exerting every pressure they could on him to produce a particular decision, but in trying to alter his decisions once they had been made. He cited the example of a man who drafted a speech which would have had Crossman saying exactly the opposite of what he had indicated in the notes he had given the official before the draft was written. It is impossible to find a politician associated with foreign affairs who reports the same experience. Foreign Office Ministers past and present are liable to say that in the FCO, more than elsewhere in Whitehall, the machine will operate quite easily without your presence. But they also say that the diplomats will pursue you hotly if they think you haven't noticed something: 'It's assumed', according to one, 'that I haven't read something if I haven't put my name on it – things aren't just shifted from an in-tray to an out-tray.' They say that there is far less shifty work behind the politician's back in the FCO than in other departments of state. But it does happen. 'The trouble starts', in one politician's experience, 'when you don't argue your case; when you simply say to them "Do this".'

Diplomacy's way of getting round the politicians is much subtler than the practice of R. H. S. Crossman's civil servant, mentioned above. Lord Chalfont has described one of the processes, involving the straightforward submission of advice that has been concocted out of the amalgamated brainpower of Third, Second and First Secretaries, departmental heads, Assistant and Deputy Under Secretaries, with a seasoning of ambassadorial influence as well. The submission is[1]

always lucidly presented, persuasively argued, and formidably monolithic. Dissent and reservation is carefully ironed

[1] Quoted in Clark, p. 50.

out at the official level; what is presented to the Minister is the considered, agreed, Foreign Office view. If he is disobliging enough to reject it, the process has to begin again; and in case Ministers should disrupt the machine by trying to initiate policies themselves, they are kept busy with an endless stream of telegrams, despatches, Cabinet papers, Parliamentary questions and miscellaneous correspondence.

It is the easiest thing in the world, in a ministry notoriously addicted to much more paperwork than any other, to bury the politician beneath a largely irrelevant pile of it, so that he is eventually too bleary with scrutiny to think straight about the document that really matters to his own precious concepts. It was to reduce the risk of this hazard that George Brown used to have people in his room to thrash problems out before the arguments were committed to paper, a tactic that met with only limited success:[1]

> It didn't reduce the written work all that much, but it did mean that when the files came to me ... I had enough knowledge from our discussions to be able to assess the personal opinions offered. It also meant that I developed a scheme of management in which people were always having to come up, always having to defend, and decisions could be given – and were.

An earlier Foreign Secretary, Patrick Gordon Walker, had devised a similar method of trying to penetrate the anaesthetic verbiage of diplomacy, sometimes calling in young men well below the heads of department, and letting it be known that he wanted a note if anyone of reasonable position had seen his view overruled by someone higher up the ladder in the course of a file rising towards the Foreign Secretary. In ploughing through his boxes at night, Gordon Walker would also sometimes scribble at the foot of a telegram 'Why was I shown this?' – which worried the diplomats far more than the more urgent comment 'Why *wasn't* I shown this?' But neither politician made any lasting impact upon the FCO's way of handling its

[1] Brown, p. 162.

Ministers. It still takes willpower, when the diplomats present you with their written advice and its supporting evidence on all the colossal complexities of Mutual Balanced Force Reductions, to tell them to hold on a bit, while you spend the weekend picking a few independent brains in order to get your bearings.

There are even more devious ways of forcing the Office view into practice. When a politician has managed to keep his head above the tidal waves of paper, and when he has resisted all diplomatic invocations of the traditional approach to the problem (backed by argument which, when pressed, they will occasionally admit in private to be specious) he can still be foiled by other manipulations. It is possible for diplomats negotiating overseas to keep things out of Ministerial vision almost long enough for him to be presented with a *fait accompli*; long enough, at any rate, for him to reverse a process already started and involving other nations only at the expense of some international disturbance. If a politician is not directing an operation in person then the theory of government is that his officials are supposed to be getting on with it; having kept him less than completely informed, they can always plead, if it comes to a show-down, that he ought to have taken a greater interest on the evidence available to him. A device used by Ambassadors from time to time, when immersed in a subject they have reason to suspect will produce political hostility to the Foreign Office view, is to mark their relevant telegrams and dispatches 'For the PUS only'. This can be no more than a holding operation, for sooner or later the Foreign Secretary will have to be let in on the secret; but it can be a very useful one, giving the diplomats in London the maximum time in which to marshal the finest possible argument that can be placed on the ignorant politician's desk.

The Whitehall network can also be recruited profitably, particularly nowadays, when there is more interdepartmental collusion in foreign affairs than ever before. If, for example, a Foreign Secretary were obdurately resisting a Foreign Office attitude which the diplomats knew was viewed sympathetically by another member of the Cabinet, the tactic would be to provide the private office of the sympathetic Minister with the best possible briefing, which would then be used in Cabinet to attack the position of the comparatively ill-briefed Foreign Secretary. This ploy was used successfully in reverse on a number of occasions in the months before the referendum on the Common Market, when the Foreign Office and all the other departments of state represented at the EEC headquarters in Brussels, together made sure that James Callaghan, like every other Minister in favour of Britain's stay in the Community, was significantly better equipped for debate than Mr Peter Shore and Mr Anthony Wedgwood Benn. Diplomats who have been involved in such tactics say that you have to be very careful not to overload your case, for that can quickly be detected. No group of men and women, however, has ever been more adept in concealing a deep and abrasive purpose beneath an appearance of benign compromise. They bank very largely on the inability of politicians to consider many horizons beyond that of the next Parliamentary session, and on their unwillingness to contemplate hypothetical questions in general. The more ingenuous among them allow that no Minister can ever know what diplomats in negotiating positions have really been up to, unless the diplomats themselves wish to inform him. Plenty say that a basic civil service weakness, not confined to diplomacy, consists in being too good at explaining why X, Y or Z can't be done, leaving the politicians little room for manoeuvre. The ones who would die rather than concede that manipulation and subterfuge can sometimes be applied by the Foreign Office in its dealings with the Foreign Secretary and his Ministers say, 'If a man knows what he wants to do, he can usually get the apparatus to do it. Our difficulties arise when he doesn't quite know what he wants to do.' This rings with a great deal of truth. But political control depends on a powerful amount of attention, energy and willpower vested in one man.

The mythically 'anti-Labour Foreign Office' is, of course, a simplistic caricature. There is no doubt that, when socialism first became a ruling option in Great Britain, the diplomats were as dismayed as anyone in the land. 'My God,' said Curzon, when Ramsay MacDonald was about to form his 1924 Administration, 'fancy a Labour Minister in the Foreign Office!' Even today, it is possible for a diplomat, in an unguarded moment, to be heard referring to 'a more natural relationship' between the Foreign Office and a Tory government; and when Harold Wilson returned to power in 1974, one Ambassador thought it necessary to parade his entire staff and remind them that they were servants of the British *Government*. They were told that if anyone was heard making critical comments about the change of governing party to outsiders, he would be in deep trouble with His Excellency the moment news of it reached the British embassy. British communities overseas are more often than not hostile to Labour governments, for complex reasons of their own, and see in the embassy or high commission a band of likely allies with whom they can share the derision and contempt they feel for what they still sometimes call (revealing amnesia as well as fear) the *new* masters. When George Brown was in office, it sometimes happened that an embassy reception would be held so that these people could meet the Foreign Secretary on his travels, as one of their inalienably British rights. At these functions, it was known for adolescents to come swaggering up to him at the buffet and inquire with truculent familiarity how he was doing. At a luncheon in Copenhagen once, some fairly steady adult sniping at Brown continued until the courageous wife of an embassy Counsellor informed the marksmen that her father had, in fact, been a founder-member of the Labour party, but had always prized good manners even above his politics.

A tradition of breeding and education, held in common until quite recently, may continue to lubricate most relationships between diplomats and Tories. There is manifestly still a deep suspicion of diplomats held by the Labour party at large, which is aired crudely every time a general policy document is composed. Labour politicians arrive in office with a very wary look in their eyes. It was quite typical that, when James Callaghan first stepped inside the FCO, he should announce (breezily, but quite serious underneath) that he supposed the Foreign Office to be pro-Arab, pro-Catholic and pro-Europe almost to a man. He was stiffly told that the Office deeply resented the rumour that it fostered an Arabist Mafia – and got on quite well with his closest advisers ever after. This itself can produce difficulties. Every Labour Foreign Secretary finds that, if he strikes a good relationship with the diplomats and is prepared to back them on any issue against the consensus of Labour opinion, he is at once accused by his political colleagues of ratting on his basic philosophy, of being seduced by the blandishments of a traditional foe.

Senior diplomats have been known to regard Labour Ministers as much ruder men than Conservatives; by which, being them-

selves fellows who sometimes mistake glib speech for a caste mark
of civilized behaviour, they probably mean blunter. They will
sometimes admit that they find Tories more to their taste
because the Tories tend to fuss less over the details of policy-
making, which allows the diplomats to get on with things themselves, unimpeded by what they regard as over-direction from
above. Yet it is very curious that in the majority of post-war
memoirs written by retired diplomats, whatever warmth is
shown towards politicians, as distinct from approval of their
policies, is almost always offered Labour and not Conservative
Ministers. When I drew the attention of a senior man to this
phenomenon he was mildly surprised and, raising his eyebrows
dramatically, said 'Well, there's more joy, I suppose, in heaven
over the sheep that was lost ... ' The generic difference between
Foreign Secretaries has been most neatly observed by Lord
Trevelyan, who had experience of several politicians in high
places. Writing about the Minister's personal relations with the
office, he remarked:[1]

> If he is a large landed proprietor, they will come easy to
> him. He will treat the PUS like his factor, the Assistant
> Under Secretaries like his farmers on a day with the hounds,
> and the heads of department like his gamekeeper. The
> Private Secretary will rank high, like his trainer, the
> Assistant Private Secretaries like his jockeys. It will all be
> very natural. If he has not been born with a Georgian
> silver spoon in his mouth, he may be suspicious that they
> are all reactionary members of the Establishment, bent on
> obstructing his progressive policies.

Though either party, on taking over government from the
other, may come to office with a distinctively different approach to foreign affairs, the international facts of life tend to
reduce these differences drastically in practice. Unlike his colleagues on the Home Front, the Foreign Secretary controls
nothing but an appliance which is itself nowadays little more
than a reactor, rather than an instigator. It is within the very
narrowest margins that initiatives can be taken which have any
hope of an effect on the world outside and which are instituted

---

[1] Trevelyan, p. 147.

for some more substantial purpose than that of purely domestic approval. According to Sir Cecil Parrott, a former Ambassador to Czechoslovakia:[1]

> Whatever politicians may say when they're in Opposition, they soon find out when they get into office and read the confidential papers that they can't possibly do what they said they would do and must instead follow the line of their predecessors in office, because there's just no other line any Government can follow.

'What's more,' says the collegiate voice of British diplomacy, 'we, the officials, tend to move towards the position held by the politicians and they tend to move towards our position: the facts of whatever is the situation abroad are a great leveller.' This is not to say that such compromising movements are achieved without a fairly constant tension between the two sides, particularly when Labour is the governing party.

Most people Left of centre who have had dealings with the Foreign Office claim that the diplomats take a very restricted view of what is British self-interest, usually adding that it generally seems to be limited to immediate economic returns. 'The FCO', said one, 'has the narrowest and most foolish view of national self-interest – selling arms to white South Africa without considering the odium for a long time afterwards from Black Africa.' The diplomats, for their part, become very impatient with an emphasis on morality purveyed by Labour politicians, and what they regard as naive notions about the brotherhood of man. They do not forget that it was the innocent socialism of Sir Stafford Cripps that presented the Soviet Union with a couple of Rolls-Royce Nene aero-engines at the end of the war, a gift that, with the passage of many fraught years, seemed to them increasingly eccentric. They have, however, from time to time, redressed such tendencies since. During the first Wilson Government in the 1960s, the Labour party urged that Britain should join the countries of the Third World in demanding that the Americans disengage themselves from Vietnam, but the diplomats argued successfully that we could not afford to offend our principal ally. There was a great deal

[1] *Sunday Times*, April 14th, 1968.

of emotional support for Biafra in 1969, which the Foreign Office managed to drain out of the government on the grounds that Nigeria was one of the most important countries in Africa, an oil producer on whom we needed to rely, and that – in the words of a man who helped to formulate the policy – 'it was going to win anyway'. Occasionally, the diplomats have been less successful than they might have wished. They reckon that, given their own way, they would have brought Britain closer than she is to Czechoslovakia today because the Labour party in general still takes a dusty view of the men who supplanted Dubček. The Foreign Office was utterly hostile to Labour's decision to hold a national referendum on the Common Market. It is constantly braced for the next disputation, the struggle for supremacy between the engagingly optimistic philosophies of socialist masters and what it sees as its own humane realism. It sighs inwardly with vexed anticipation as it contemplates the Iberian peninsula at the end of 1975, knowing exactly what arguments it will muster – and why it will be necessary to muster them with a Labour government in office – if the Portuguese pull out of NATO and a transatlantic voice suggests that Spain should come on as substitute.

It is bad enough serving a government saddled with a universal conscience. There are times when diplomats also feel they could do without the public opinion by which politicians occasionally justify themselves. At such moments, the British imply that theirs is a unique handicap from which their French counterparts on the Quai D'Orsay are happily free. This may not be so. Indeed, an informed outsider has noted that in 1973 'A French academic patiently explained to a conference in London ... that the British must understand that, although their own Government exercised effective freedom in conducting its foreign policy, the French Government had to pay more attention to public opinion.'[1] Foreign Office men, however, will readily cite examples of what they mean when they refer to an absence of domestic inhibitions on the Quai. Paris, they say, does not subscribe to the Nuclear Proliferation Treaty because it does not feel enough moral obligation to sign it ... When nine countries recall their Ambassadors from Franco's Madrid to mark their disapproval of the execution of Basque

[1] Wallace, p. 271.

nationalists, the French merely arrange for their man to slip home 'on leave' so that, while Paris shall not appear to condone, it can nevertheless plead, should it be convenient to do so, that it did not join the condemning throng. Other diplomats besides the British see French foreign policy as an utterly selfish thing, festooned with amicable gestures only in matters inessential to France. None, however, see this more intently than the men in the Foreign Office, who will say that 'We, on the other hand, have a vague feeling – to an extent we can't afford – for global problems; we aren't prepared to *wreck* on the whole for the sake of British interests; to some extent we're always fighting the French with one hand tied behind our backs.' Yet, in spite of such reservations, the diplomatic instinct to reduce friction is always paramount. First Secretaries in the FCO may fashionably speak of Concorde as the politicians' sex symbol; but from the outset, the Foreign Office backed the project as enthusiastically as Mr Wedgwood Benn, so anxious was it to promote some kind of co-operation between Paris and London, that would counteract and outlast the dogged anglophobia of General de Gaulle.

Britain may realistically have done no more in recent years than cheer Dr Kissinger from the sidelines of the Middle East problem, yet no area of foreign affairs illustrates the divergent philosophies, the implicit challenges, the careful sparring and the eventual compromises that exist when the diplomats find themselves serving a Labour government. George Brown broke the pattern of this sequence in relation to the Middle East. He transferred an Ambassador from Tel Aviv because he decided the man was becoming too much of an apologist for his host country – a diplomatic weakness which can and does occur anywhere in the world. Brown took the view that, belonging as he did to a party with strong traditional sympathies for Zionism, being also married as he was to a Jew, he could very well do without the Israeli argument being rammed down his throat in every dispatch coming from his man on the spot.

There was to be nothing like that from James Callaghan, after he reached the Foreign Office, voicing his reflex suspicion of the FCO Arabists. Arriving not long after the October War had established Israeli forces on the banks of Suez, and after the consequent oil embargo by the Arab producers, he none the less reacted in the classic Labour party manner. The diplomats were at once given to understand that a high priority of the new government would be an effort to recover the middle ground between Israel and the Arabs; they most certainly were not to expect any repetition of Sir Alec Douglas-Home's Harrogate speech during the preceding Conservative administration, which had inclined Britain heavily towards the Arabs. For the first three months of the new Labour government the struggle on this issue rolled back and forth around the Foreign Secretary's office at the FCO. Callaghan and the other politicians were quite adamant that the Labour party had historic links with Israel which could not and would not be washed away; they were quite unwilling to make those gestures which – sometimes much more than substance – come as manna to the Arab soul. The diplomats were equally insistent that the overwhelming priority was to avoid another oil embargo, and that this meant a very clear pro-Arab policy. The Arabists generally argue that they take their line on the Middle East from very hard-headed considerations such as these. They scoff at suggestions that they are a bunch of romantics, pointing out that the most senior of them have usually at least once in their careers had to evacuate their embassies in Arab capitals with a demonstrating mob in the front garden – 'which soon drums the romance of the area out of you'.

Gestures of a kind were eventually agreed upon in the struggle between the Foreign Secretary and his advisers. The TUC would be encouraged to have greater contact with Arab countries, and this indeed has happened to a limited extent in Egypt. At the same time, the Foreign Secretary thought it would be a good idea if diplomats who had served in Tel Aviv were later posted to Arab capitals. This is a small policy decision which, as Lord Chalfont might say, seems to have fallen into the works. Beyond that, it was tacitly agreed that the diplomats should get on with securing Britain's economic interests in the Middle East as best they could without affronting Israel more than necessary; she, in fact, was to be mollified somewhat in the spring of 1975 by an economic agreement with the EEC, to which Britain was a party.

Unfortunately for the blood pressure of the Arabists, the former Prime Minister, after a few months in office, made a gesture of his own, when he embraced Mrs Golda Meir publicly in a kiss of friendship from one Labour party to another. The

Foreign Office was furious at the tactlessness of this, for it was precisely the sort of thing they thought they had persuaded the Foreign Secretary to avoid. The gloom of the British Embassy in Cairo was fairly typical of the general diplomatic feeling. The morning after Harold kissed Golda, their picture appeared in *Al Ahram*, though Cairo generally treated it as a bit of a joke. But then the extremely hostile reactions of other Arab countries began to drift into the Egyptian government. Next day, *Al Ahram* published a leading article vilifying the kiss as scandalous. On Day Three, the Egyptian National Assembly passed a resolution condemning the incident, after a question asking what measures could be taken to dissuade Great Britain from such a close relationship with Israel. One measure taken instantly involved a number of commercial contracts between Britain and Egypt, which were on the point of being signed, but were not signed. 'That kiss', said a despondent fellow in the middle of it all, 'undid about nine months of work in this embassy.' In saying this, he was doubtless indulging in a touch of diplomatic hyperbole: this is frequently used, with the very finest calculation of effect, to colour the passions of the moment. British salesmen in various commodities were that very week bustling fruitfully round the Middle East. In June 1975, some of them secured a contract worth £1 million from Saudi Arabia, in exchange for an education programme, with the possibility of much more to come later. In November 1975 President Sadat came to London where, although the Prime Minister did not kiss him, the two men appeared to get on pleasantly and afterwards agreed that Britain should supply arms to Egypt worth considerably more than £400 million. This still left a Foreign Secretary uneasy at his policy; but, unable to think of a viable alternative, he was obliged, like other members of the Labour Cabinet, to thank God for a windfall when the nation most stood in need of one.

Diplomats do not, on the whole, resent what they may regard as wrongheadedness in politicians. They will resist it with every means at their disposal and they may even sneer at it sometimes privately in the Travellers' Club. But perverseness is a fact of their life from time to time in the relationship with their own government, just as it is an even more consistent factor in their dealings with foreigners. It is their profession to handle it and the things they esteem in politicians do not include complaisance. Their ideal Foreign Secretary is a decisive man with a mind who will, if he thinks it necessary, argue the diplomats away from their own positions; a man who will back them to the hilt once a decision has been reached and agreed between them; a man who has sufficient power inside Cabinet to ensure that these agreed policies are carried out. They acknowledge that the politician expects them to be aware of the political realities he faces as a member of the government and his party, and as a representative of 'the people'. They expect him to accept the limitations they face overseas, to understand the significance and importance of what appear to be the most trivial ploys of diplomacy. Sir Alec Douglas-Home fell somewhere short of the diplomatic ideal because, like Edward Heath, he would bestir himself to Heathrow Airport to meet or wave away only the most impressive visitors when, as everyone in the FCO knows, President Podgorny, no less, is prepared to lumber out to the icy tarmac of Sheremetyevo merely to flatter the Grand Duke of Luxembourg. No politician has been a greater source of exasperation to the Foreign Office than Mr Peter Shore, who did everything he could to prevent Britain staying in the Common Market. He was among the British politicians, led by the Prime Minister, who went to Moscow for the Anglo-Soviet negotiations in February 1975, when the debate on the Common Market referendum was raging most hotly in Britain. Just before one of the sessions in the Kremlin began, Mr Kosygin addressed himself to Shore on the follies of the Common Market which would, he declared (knowing full well where Shore stood in the debate) do Britain's real interests no good at all. 'But of course,' he added, with a po-face and an artful shrug, 'that's an internal matter for you to decide and I mustn't interfere ... ' At which Shore, sitting across the table, looked Kosygin straight between the eyes and replied: 'You're quite right, Mr Prime Minister. It is an internal matter, and we shall settle it democratically.' The watching British diplomats gave him very full marks for that.

There is a lustre attached to the position of Foreign Secretary that is unequalled elsewhere in British political life below the level of Premier. It is derived from a past when the country carried great weight in the world, from periods when, paradoxically, it was the Prime Minister and not the Foreign Secretary who dominated foreign affairs (whoever now recalls that the 15th Earl of Derby was Disraeli's Foreign Secretary during most of the imperial 1870s?). It is the association of ideas that gives the office an extra spit and polish that other Cabinet positions seem to lack. Technically, the Home Secretary has always been second in command to the Prime Minister. But even in these diminished times it is a toss-up whether the ambitious politician who may yet hope for a Higher Thing would most prefer, for the moment, to occupy No 11 Downing Street as Chancellor of the Exchequer or to leisure himself whenever possible out at Dorneywood. This is the 1920 Tudor manor house in Buckinghamshire which was bestowed upon the nation by Lord Courtauld-Thomson for the convenience of its Foreign Secretaries, just as Lord Lee of Fareham had left the genuine Tudor of Chequers for the benefit of Prime Ministers. (The Foreign Secretary also has an official residence at No 1 Carlton Gardens but, in practice over the years, it has been little used except for luncheon parties and other official entertainments.) When it comes to image, however, there is no choice to make between state finance and diplomacy. The Foreign Office represents glamour, exotic horizons, and just the faintest echo of a bar or two from 'Rule, Britannia ... ' carried on the dying winds of change; whereas the Treasury has never really amounted to anything more than boring sums, blasted bills and an intermittent hole in the trouser pocket.

George Brown has said that, more than any of the other Ministries he worked in, the Foreign Office brought home to him the exciting and frightening responsibility of political power. This had something to do with the fact that the Foreign Secretary *is* privy to more state secrets than anyone else but the Prime Minister. He is required to swear an oath about secrets not only before starting work, but another one on leaving office. Politicians don't, in fact, much enjoy this sort of thing; some of the secrets can be too hair-raising for that. Brown has also pictured the FCO as a place where the officials, more than in other parts of Whitehall, are apt to coax the politicians through arcane rituals that cover the most mundane events. On Brown's first day at the Office, he entered the building through a small doorway near the Park which is reserved for the use of Ministers and very senior diplomats. Unknown to him, a great deal of Foreign Office topweight, together with the press, had assembled

by the main entrance in Gilbert Scott's quadrangle to welcome
him officially – a performance that neither the Ministry of
Works nor the Department of Economic Affairs had bothered
to mount for Brown's previous excursions into government. The
new Foreign Secretary had scarcely sat down in his room upstairs before 'a very impressive but worried PPS' came after
him. 'He suggested, in the way which the FO has, that it would
be rather "nice" if I went out again and came in through the
proper door.'[1]

All part of the Service, whose attention to detail can sometimes irritate the politicians with its fussiness, but sometimes
impress them as do few other things in the business of government. There is nothing to equal the briefing a Minister gets
about the foreigners he is to meet on a tour overseas: those
ubiquitous card indices and national potted biographies down
in the Research Department are ransacked so that the Minister
may be informed, before each encounter, where the man went
to school, what kind of scholar he was, what he has done since,
what his weaknesses are ... Thus armed, the politician sets off,
with his subsistence allowance to take care of tips and flowers
for hostesses and all the other expensive incidentals of good
foreign relations. And never a moment thereafter, unless he
demands it, are his officials more than an arm's length away
from him, steering him this way and that, prompting him at
every pause, ready and more than willing to pick up the pieces
discreetly should he drop something with a crash.[2] He certainly
doesn't have to think for himself unless he particularly wants to,
for the right phrases and the proper concepts will be supplied
like everything else, *sotto voce* and *prestissimo*, at the faintest hint
of a glazed look in the eyes. All is attended to without a trace
of vulgarity, even when the pressure is extreme, when the
matter is of the utmost urgency. As one much-travelled
politician recalls, ' "*No doubt the Minister will wish to say this*"
means you'd bloody well better.' Sometimes the helmsmanship
of the officials is absolutely vital to success, and sometimes it

[1] Brown, p. 127.

[2] The custom is not confined to British diplomacy. When Adlai Stevenson
was the American Representative at the United Nations, he complained to
J. K. Galbraith that the State Department 'advises him more or less at
what hour to see Gromyko, when to interrupt to go to the men's room, and
how long to stay there'.

can result in the most devastatingly awkward consequences. Too often the diplomats assume that the politician will study his papers thoroughly while flying to an international conference, only to find that the chap prefers to chat with cronies in mid-air and merely scans the relevant documents in the car from the airport. Harold Macmillan was once supplied with a brief which included a summary of things he should on no account mention to the Italian politicians he was about to face, but which he unerringly declaimed, with many majestic references to his papers, the moment he rose to his feet in the conference hall.

The impact these men have had on the Foreign Office follows no party pattern; and diplomatic applause or coolness depends as much on a Foreign Secretary's character as on his politics and the extent to which he controlled or was controlled by the machine. Herbert Morrison is spoken of by those who remember him as a man without the slightest instinct for foreign affairs, and they have nothing more to say. Only R. A. Butler is served shorter than that, for he is the one post-war Foreign Secretary whose name is never mentioned in the Office of the 1970s. They talk of Michael Stewart as a man of deep convictions, unspectacular but strong enough to withstand great political pressure during the Nigerian civil war: which is a rather more generous tribute than you hear from some of his old political colleagues, who reckon he so scrupulously read everything put before him that he was too exhausted to make decisions. Selwyn Lloyd is seen by some as a tetchy individual with chips on his shoulder that possibly issued from his Prime Minister, Eden; by others as a funny, cryptic fellow—'everyone liked him but you never felt you had got to know him'. He is credited with the vision to have created a post at DUS level in 1956, to concentrate exclusively on economic problems; but, on the whole, it is thought that he probably found his true métier later as Speaker of the House of Commons.

No Foreign Secretary has divided diplomatic opinion nearly as much as George Brown. Even his strongest critics at the FCO warm to the memory of what they call a brilliant opening speech he made to the assembled seniors on his first day at the Office, when he said that they were together going to run Britain's foreign affairs from that building. Nothing that happened in the rumbustious and sometimes tortured relationships of the

M

next nineteen months ever caused them to doubt his determination to create policy by intense teamwork. When it was all over, and a lot of people had fallen back exhausted by the experience, there were some who felt they had just seen a very nearly great Foreign Secretary. These men today say that George Brown had a remarkable sense of the way things were going, or were likely to go in international affairs. They admired, particularly, his assessment of the Common Market and his judgment of the Middle East, the steps he took in the United Nations to do what Britain could do about the Arab–Israeli conflict. They will even tell you that he was one of the very best things that ever happened to the Foreign Office itself, because he swept away (for the time he was there) a lot of its hierarchical structure. He would go over senior heads to get information from knowing juniors. He left a more flexible operation which others subsequently allowed to ossify again; and, worse, which reverted to a habit of reacting to outside events, rather than of seeing objectives clearly ahead and making for them as decisively as the nation's health would allow.

Others contest all these views strongly. They deny that Brown's judgment was all that good, when he wanted the East Germans inside the EEC and seemed to think that the Bonn government would be willing to act as a gangway. They are still horrified by some of his unorthodoxies. He was in Moscow in 1966, at a time when diplomatic relations between Britain and Egypt had been broken off. Discovering that President Nasser's right-hand man, Hakim Amer, was also in town, Brown simply picked up the telephone and spoke to Amer at his hotel, an action which curdled the blood of the British officials when they heard of it. So anxious was Brown to patch up the quarrel with Egypt that he employed Sir Humphrey Trevelyan (as he then was),[1] who had retired after many distinguished years as an Ambassador in the Middle East, to go to Cairo as an emissary to Nasser because 'I thought that the more the FO was kept out of things officially at that stage, the better. If things went wrong, it would be preferable to be able to disown my efforts as a private episode.'[2] A fine and original thought, but it was unlikely to endear a Foreign Secretary to his chief official advisers,

---

[1] Since 1968, Lord Trevelyan.
[2] Brown, p. 238.

who prefer to know exactly what is going on. As for his meddling with the structure of the FCO, well, say Brown's critics, 'He didn't destroy the Office, but he didn't use it properly'.

His biggest fault, though – and his supporters see it as the thing that stood between him and greatness – was his temperament. He was too emotional by half, with a very low flashpoint; an incredibly nervy man who, even after years of political life, would be physically sick just before making a speech. Some say that he had a mean streak, too, that could wound people intensely. Yet even those who disliked George Brown most (and he is the kind of man who produces strong reactions in others) do not fail to comment on some characteristic that struck them as out of the ordinary: 'He was one of only two post-war Foreign Secretaries (the other was Bevin) who showed any interest in financial problems ... For the first two or three hours of every day he was so mentally agile you had to run to keep up with him ... He hated pseudo humility and had no time at all for yes-men ... He could be bloody-minded and many other unwelcome things, but he appreciated you if you stood up to him with your opinion.'

He was not in the same class as Sir Alec. Everyone at the Foreign Office calls the *ci-devant* 14th Earl of Home 'Sir Alec', even though, after being recycled for a second time, he has been known as Lord Home of The Hirsel since 1974. When Harold Macmillan made him Foreign Secretary in 1960, the *Daily Mirror* said it was 'the most reckless political appointment since the Emperor Caligula made his favourite horse a Consul'. This was harsh on a man who had just put in five years as Britain's Commonwealth Secretary, and whose contact with government went back to before the war, when he had been Chamberlain's Parliamentary Private Secretary.[1] Yet Lord Home had, oddly, always been something of a background figure. As Foreign Secretary, however, he rapidly emerged as a strong-minded man with a profoundly landed antipathy to Communism, a rather well-bred version of John Foster Dulles. The hostility was still unflinchingly there four administrations later, by which time Sir Alec had led his own government and then served as Foreign Secretary again, in which capacity he ordered a massive

[1] In those days Sir Alec was Lord Dunglass, heir to the 13th Earl of Home.

clear-out of the Soviet Embassy staff in London, in 1971, on security grounds. His professional obituary appeared in March 1974 in that peculiarly glossy publication *The Diplomatist*, which does for the diplomatic corps in London what *The Tatler* does for the rest of society. 'Let us face it,' wrote the editor (whose unnerving task is to avoid giving offence to Israelis and Arabs, Russians and Chinese, British and French in approximately equal measure in every edition that goes to press),

> Sir Alec Douglas-Home was respected in almost all CD quarters, liked in most but found difficult to deal with in quite a few ... Sir Alec's almost innate distrust of the aims and methods of communism was a main stumbling block in these diplomats' efforts to strengthen and improve relations with the UK.

A neater epitaph would be Sir Alec's own comment on the Duncan Committee's recommendation that the British passport should have limp covers, like most others, so that it could be processed automatically. 'Over my dead body,' said the former 14th Earl.[1]

The outstanding mark he left on the Foreign Office was that of a thoroughly nice man. He was exactly the same genuine soul with everyone he met, whether it was King Hussein or the lady who cleaned the office (his successor, James Callaghan, was said to be rather nicer to the cleaning ladies). Sir Alec would shake everybody's hand in every group of officials accompanying him anywhere, including that of the policeman sent along to take care of him. He would have his PPS, complete with wife and children, up to stay at The Hirsel, the ancestral headquarters of the Homes on the Scottish Borders. He had a reputation for hard work, sometimes arriving at 5 o'clock in the morning to start dealing with papers at his desk. He could be even slower to make up his mind than James Callaghan, whose canny instinct was always to take away a problem for reflection and maybe outside discussion, rather than tackle it cold in private with his officials. But Sir Alec was very shrewd about people, difficult to fool. He would not have dreamed of inter-

[1] In 1975, however, Mr Callaghan's Foreign Office announced that the passport change would soon be made.

fering with the FCO's established batting order, like George Brown. He took his advice, more often than not, simply by bringing in a Deputy Under Secretary to discuss something alone with himself and his PPS.

In the end, he had been around too long for his own, or foreign policy's good; he got away with a lot of things the diplomats would have reacted strongly against in others, because he was Sir Alec and much liked. More and more frequently, in his latter days in Whitehall, the diplomats would have to hasten round to foreign embassies the morning after an utterance by Douglas-Home, to assure Ambassadors that the Foreign Secretary hadn't *quite* meant what he had seemed to imply the night before. He did not take the same trouble as he once had with his speeches. And he was only once really tough with his own people, when at a Conservative conference he had to convert the party faithful to the diplomatic view of Rhodesia; or rather exhort them to accept it. Someone who worked near him for several years said: 'He wasn't great at anything, but he had a fine mixture of integrity, commonsense and decency. His big weakness was that he was a little slow.'

The once darling boy of the Foreign Service, of the whole nation, has become with the passing of the years the most painful figure of all in the diplomatic pantheon. By the end of the last war, Sir Anthony Eden's image was probably more enviable than that of anyone in British public life excepting Winston Churchill, in spite of the fact that the electoral vote went astonishingly against the pair of them in 1945. He was the man of principle, as well as of judgment, who had resigned office rather than compromise with evil. Even he did not realize until years later the extent of Chamberlain's readiness to settle with Hitler and Mussolini while Eden was still Foreign Secretary, but it had involved negotiations through the Italian embassy in London without the knowledge of the Foreign Office. There was another side to Eden, though, besides that of principle, and British diplomats who served him during his three periods at the Office (1935–8, 1940–5 and 1951–5) were very well aware of it. The man was a *prima donna*, temperamental and rather difficult to work for. His officials never knew, when they came to work each day, whether they were going to be charmed out of their pants or abused for inefficiency. He would explode with fury when the slightest thing went amiss – a car breaking down, a scrambler on the telephone ceasing to work properly – or even when arrangements weren't quite to his taste, as when a bevy of photographers appeared unexpectedly in his path. Such things 'sometimes threatened to assume the proportions of a hideous departmental *faux pas* or a major diplomatic reverse'.[1] He had the strongest objections to being left unattended for ten minutes by his PPS. He was also exceedingly vain. Although he hardly ever wore a hat during the war, he kept his famous black Homburg – for ever associated in the public mind with his gallantry before Munich – on a sidetable in his room at the Office, where the charladies dusted it reverently each day.

There have, however, been other difficult Foreign Secretaries, and diplomats usually take them in their stride and sigh with relief when it's all over. It is what the man of principle did when he became Prime Minister himself that turns them very cool indeed on the subject of Anthony Eden. Lord Gore-Booth, who was a Deputy Under Secretary in the Office during the Suez catastrophe in October 1956, has written of it thus:[2]

> Just as Mr Chamberlain did not choose to have full advice from the FO in 1938, so did Sir Anthony Eden tragically avoid it in 1956. In general, Conservatives tend to be less touchy about advice than their opponents, and it is sadly ironical that on the occasion of our two foreign policy disasters in my time, it was the Conservatives who did not so much reject advice as decline to hear it.

That is only part of what rankles with diplomats today. Among the more senior of them there is a nostalgic grief attached to Suez; for this was the watershed in Britain's foreign policy, the irredeemable proof to the world that she was no longer a great power who could have her way by resorting to arms if need be. They were, moreover, deeply insulted by politicians who preferred to conduct foreign affairs behind their backs, particularly in an episode that would have produced a massive weight of dissuasion from the professionals had they been consulted beforehand. But, worse than this, they felt they had been betrayed by the Head of the Diplomatic Service himself, Sir Ivone Kirkpatrick, who was PUS at the time.

[1] Lawford, op. cit.
[2] Gore-Booth, p. 231.

Two diplomats, in fact, besides Kirkpatrick, knew of the impending invasion of Suez while it was still at an early planning stage. The moment Nasser nationalized the Canal at the end of July 1956, 'Eden and Selwyn Lloyd gave three of us at the FO, of whom I was one, top secret instructions to prepare with the Chiefs of Staff a plan to remove Nasser by force.' That is Mr Geoffrey McDermott—who was the head of the PUS's Department of the Foreign Office at the time—writing nearly twenty years after the event.[1] The top secrecy held to a quite remarkable degree, considering that a number of civil servants in the Ministry of Defence must have been aware of the planning, too, not to mention a handful of politicians besides the Prime Minister and his Foreign Secretary, and many military officers. But Sir Humphrey Trevelyan, the British Ambassador in Cairo, was not informed and subsequently, after thinking of handing in his resignation, was very glad that he had known nothing of what was afoot until the air-raid sirens sounded outside his residence one night. Uneasy rumours, however, that something inexplicably important was in the air, began to move about Whitehall, and drift even farther afield. The Regional Information Officer in the Middle East was so worried by them that he asked the Foreign Office if he might fly home from Beirut for discussions.[2] On reaching headquarters he found that none of his diplomatic colleagues seemed to be any wiser than he was, so he went in search of some politicians, but they were peculiarly elusive. Eventually, he managed to obtain half an hour with Mr Dodds-Parker, the Joint Parliamentary Under Secretary, who assured him to forget about the rumours, in which there was no truth at all. A few days before the Israeli invasion of the Sinai Peninsula on October 29th, which preceded the first Anglo-French bombing of Egyptian airfields by forty-eight hours, the British Ambassador in Tel Aviv, Sir John Nicholls, sent a telegram to London recording a conversation he had just held with Mr Ben-Gurion. Something the Israeli Prime Minister said implied that he had spoken to British politicians of things that neither Sir John nor his regional department at home knew about. When the telegram reached London, that section of the message was removed before the

[1] McDermott, p. 120.
[2] Seventeen years later, as Sir Philip Adams, the officer was to become British Ambassador in Cairo.

document was put into its normal classified and limited circulation round the Office: and, to this day, no one knows who made
the excision. On October 30th, at the very moment Sir Anthony
Eden was telling the House of Commons that Britain had issued
an ultimatum to Egypt, a spokesman in the Foreign Office was
innocently telling journalists that Britain's policy was to invoke
the Tripartite Agreement opposing the use of force.

There was outrage when the news broke, even more intense
in the Foreign Office than in the country outside. For the
diplomats now knew, as nobody else did, that for months the
Prime Minister and the Foreign Secretary, in collusion with
their own Permanent Under Secretary, had been working in
secret alliance with Israel and France while at the same time
quite deliberately directing every other diplomat involved in
Middle Eastern affairs towards a policy of curbing Israeli aggression. Sir Paul Gore-Booth 'wrote, after several attempts, a confidential note to the PUS ... I thought it important for those in
authority to realise that the overwhelming majority of people
in the Office felt that our action had been a big mistake.'[1] It is
Gore-Booth's recollection today that Kirkpatrick never con-
fided his thoughts about Suez in anyone after the event. Four
months later, the PUS retired and, later still, wrote poignantly
that 'To leave a Service in which one has spent one's life is
rather like dying'.[2] In his memoirs, Kirkpatrick refused to discuss Suez; except to make it clear that he thought the events
leading up to it had been inspired by the Russians and that
Egypt under Nasser had become part of a Communist plot
against the West. By the time Kirkpatrick had gone, the worst
sense of outrage in the Foreign Office had died down. In those
first few days after the invasion it had been so great that a
number of people had spoken of leaving British diplomacy in
disgust; so many, in fact, that although only two men actually
left, the administrative chiefs sent round a circular reminding
everyone of the terms of service, and pointing out that resignations en masse would not alter what had been done, anyway.
Senior men felt so strongly that they had been compromised in
the eyes of the world that they drew up an official account of
the diplomacy and management of the Suez operation, as soon

[1] Gore-Booth, p. 229.
[2] Kirkpatrick, p. 269.

as they were able to work it out for themselves. This document was so sensitive to the feelings of the governing Conservative party that Harold Macmillan, who succeeded Eden as Prime Minister, took the extraordinary step of ordering that it should be locked in secrecy not for the normal thirty years, but for a full century. Everything about Suez left a streak of bitterness that still marks the FCO today, matched only by the lingering resentment of the way 'The Thirty' were sacked thirteen years later.

The other outstanding folk memory is that of Ernest Bevin, which persists in spite of the fact that no more than a handful of people in the Diplomatic Service today were around during his five and a half post-war years as Foreign Secretary. When he first reached the Office, many diplomats viewed his appointment with much the same disquiet as Curzon had voiced in 1924: a trade union organizer who had belligerently led dockers on strike was an unwholesome prospect to men who had been prepared almost from birth for a cultivated existence in the chanceries of the world, even if he had served Churchill as Minister of Labour in the war Cabinet. But, as Gore-Booth has recorded, 'We were in for a highly favourable surprise ... in my diplomatic lifetime, no Foreign Secretary engaged the loyalty and affection of the whole Diplomatic Service as Ernest Bevin did.'[1] In the words of another contemporary, Lord Trevelyan, 'He was a man loved by all who worked for him, genuine, honest and full of courage.'[2] Patronizing Sir Alexander Cadogan, PUS when Bevin took over from Eden, was actually impressed before the new man had even started work, for he had seen him in action under Churchill. 'I think we may do better with Bevin than with any other of the Labourites,' he wrote in his diary.[3]

> I think he's broadminded and sensible, honest and courageous. But whether he's an inspired Foreign Minister or not, I don't know. He's the heavyweight of the Cabinet and will get his own way with them, so if he can be put on the right lines, that may be all right.

[1] Gore-Booth, p. 149.
[2] Trevelyan, p. 146.
[3] Cadogan, July 28th, 1945.

The American Secretary of State, James Byrnes, met Bevin at the Potsdam conference. At first he found him 'so aggressive that both the President and I wondered how we would get along with the new Foreign Secretary', but soon came 'to respect highly his fine mind, his forthrightness, his candour and his scrupulous regard for a promise'.[1]

So notorious did the unlikely alliance between Bevin and his diplomats become, that it fuelled already deep suspicions of the man held by many people in the Labour party. He had never had much time for Left-wing intellectuals like Hugh Dalton (who was considered as Foreign Secretary before Clement Attlee finally decided on Bevin) and the feeling was mutual. When he was locked in ideological Cold War battles with Vyshinsky and Molotov, the hatred of the *Tribune* group of Labour politicians made Bevin the most heavily abused man in the country. He was, to them, a traitor to the working class of his origins and to the party which had given him power. Even today, extreme Left-wingers in the Labour party find it very difficult to accept the legend of Bevin at the Foreign Office as anything other than clear proof that he had been seduced by smooth diplomacy.

They forget that, long before he got anywhere near White-hall, he had shown high diplomatic talent among his own people. He spent ten painstaking years trying to persuade four-teen separate trade unions to amalgamate before he succeeded, with the creation of the Transport and General Workers Union in 1922. He knew as well as any Ambassador what difficult negotiations involved. His Left-wing critics conveniently over-looked the fact that, while he blocked what he saw as Soviet imperialism, he was not at the same time some folksy lap-dog of the Americans. He might advocate a merger of the British and American zones in Germany in 1947, in order to promote German regeneration and reduce receptiveness to Communist ideas. But in the new NATO Council in 1949 he argued strongly against the Americans that it was useless to try to buttress the regime of Chiang Kai-shek in Formosa. He saw the American eagle on one side, the Russian bear on the other, and (as he inimitably put it once), he believed it part of his duty to try to stop these two gorillas from tearing each other and the rest of the world to pieces. He had, as *The Economist* wrote at his death

[1] Quoted in Bevin, *DNB.*

in 1951, 'learned to combine a sense of the possible with a regard for the visionary objective'. And he had done so before he came to the Foreign Office.

He was not completely open-minded, though when Robert Birley left a government job to become Headmaster of Eton, he told him to keep sending Etonian recruits, because diplomacy couldn't do without them. Bevin didn't take kindly to criticism from anyone, and he was a terrible man for holding on to a grudge. He put diplomats in their place when he felt like it, and if they didn't keep their minutes to one side of one sheet of paper, they were usually told off to go and try again; or ignored. It is probable that he had his own suspicions about them before his arrival, the corollary to theirs about him. It is likely that he was flattered by their appreciation as soon as it showed, which in itself would have warmed up the atmosphere. But the appreciation on both sides was based on something much sounder. He found that in the Foreign Office, whatever Labour party myths might have held to be true, people worked as hard as anyone in the trade union movement, even though some men in Bevin's own union would not have regarded diplomacy as work. The diplomats found that, besides the considerable political strengths of Bevin, there was a rare humanity in the man. His abysmal handwriting (which resembled Amharic script), his capacity to depart from their carefully-prepared briefs, his power to force their policies through Cabinet —none of these things mattered so much as the born and bred character of the man. He used to dictate speech notes to a young woman, which rambled semi-coherently so much that he would eventually catch her look of bewilderment and concern. 'Never mind, Missy,' he would say on these occasions, 'just get it down like I say and Lawford here [his PPS] will try and put it into English for you.'[1] He was quite capable, at a state banquet whose tedium had run far too long, of humming softly to himself; and, when a disapproving silence spread over his immediate neighbourhood, of asking blithely, 'Why don't we all have a bit of community singing?' These were the reasons why the British Diplomatic Service used to call him Uncle Ernie —behind his back.

One of his memorials at the Foreign Office is to be found just

[1] Lawford, op. cit.

inside the exclusive little doorway near St James's Park. A lift there conveys Foreign Secretaries up to their room and, in Bevin's time, it had to be slowed down because he had a bad heart. For some reason, the engineers were never able to restore its former pace, so that it still lumbers and rattles frustratingly up to the floor where he commanded. The other memorial is the bust by E. Whitney-Smith on a lower corridor, commissioned with subscriptions from the Diplomatic Service when he died. Only Lord Hammond, who was PUS from 1854 to 1873, was ever commemorated by contemporaries like that.

But the finest tribute of all paid by diplomacy to Ernest Bevin, and the one that touches most carefully the unique thing that was in the Foreign Office while he was there, happened on his seventieth birthday, just a month before he died, which was also the day Herbert Morrison took over as Foreign Secretary. The Office gave him a party on the proceeds of a collection made from top to bottom of the Service. Writing a quarter of a century later, Sir Roderick Barclay (who by 1951 had taken over from Valentine Lawford as the Foreign Secretary's PPS) thought, none too certainly, that everyone subscribed two shillings for this event. Bevin's biographer, Francis Williams (who was much closer to the old man and, in a sense, to those last days) records it differently. According to him everyone contributed sixpence, no more and no less – the old docker's tanner of Ernie's trade union days – from the Permanent Under Secretary downwards. Ambassadors tipped up their coins from all over the world, like everyone else in the embassies. So did the whole hierarchical society in London. So did the telephonists, the secretaries, the messengers and the cleaners. They had dancing, with that great dying bulk of a man beaming at them all from his chair. They had a bit of community singing. They had a cake with candles on top. And when it was all over, Bevin said it had been a marvellous time.

7 Matters of Communication

As any politician of wide government experience will tell you, there is much more to read in the Foreign Office than in any other department of state. When he says that, he is talking about those sheaves of paper that cross his desk each day, constituting various stages in the professional advice, which always has been a wordy business. Other Ministers of the Crown are subjected to approximately the same trial by persuasion, of course, but none of them belongs to an organization with something approaching 350 outposts of one sort or another spread around the globe. Communication lies at the philosophical heart of diplomacy, and communication in a material form comes to the FCO every day from the British missions overseas in an endless flow of cables, letters, dispatches, phone calls and items transmitted by teleprinter and telex: and is returned, in due course, whence it came. Well might Home civil servants say of diplomats, as they sometimes do, with no unkind intent, that few of them make decisions but all all of them pass messages. There is nothing very much more impressive than the way the diplomats put the word about.

It used to be quite a leisurely affair. Just before the war, urgent messages were sent from Whitehall to India by air, and not so urgent messages by sea. The telegraph was resorted to only in moments of dire imperial crisis. That wondrous device had been employed since the middle of the nineteenth century for the emergency situation and every British embassy suitably equipped, as well as the Foreign Office in London, was identified in the telegraphic address books of the world as PRO-DROME, which is Classical Greek for 'forerunner'. One hundred years later, telegrams to the Foreign Office from abroad are still addressed thus but, such is the welter of transmitting and receiving stations throughout the world, so great the potential confusion inherent in a vast cascade of signals to and from all points of the compass, that some British missions have had to settle for titles less corporate. The embassy in Teheran is merely PROD. The high commission in Kingston, Jamaica, answers to a gnomish UKREPKIN. Our men in Athens are known as LION DR. The British Consul in Palermo is resoundingly BRITAIN.

A few charming relics of the old days remain in the farthest-flung outposts, which still have to make do with nothing more sophisticated than a morse set. But much higher forms of technology are employed elsewhere. Half the embassies enjoy wireless, while several major missions such as Washington, Brussels, Paris and Bonn are linked directly to the FCO with private telegraphic circuits. Two-thirds of all traffic travels in code, a high proportion of it by an electronic device called Piccolo, which emits euphonious melodies at its destination that mean something fairly stern to His Excellency once they have been rendered into words again. Apart from anything else, the advent of Piccolo has helped to brighten many a diplomatic Christmas overseas. For, just as it has long been the seasonal habit of teleprinter operators everywhere to transmit a load of gobbledegook which emerges from receiving machines in the pictorial shape of Santa Claus, so the instrumentalists in the FCO have caught the knack of playing carols on Piccolo to cheer their comrades in Moscow and other listening posts. More practically, the machine has speeded up one side of diplomacy remarkably. At the end of the war, a telegram of 1,000 words would have taken ten hours to encipher by book code, five hours to transmit by morse, and another ten hours to decipher at its destination. Piccolo can do the lot in forty-five minutes; and the record transmission of a telegram, from the moment it was signed by a departmental head in London to when it was opened and read abroad, is said to be eight minutes. Where they have not Piccolo, however, they still have to plod through the code books. In the tiniest missions this task is sometimes entrusted to the Ambassador's secretary, a lady whose quietly maturing years have so far probably been confined to shorthand and typing, but who has been trained in codework before being posted from London. It sounds an intriguing procedure for, as one of them describes it, when a Top Secret message comes for

His Excellency, 'I have to decipher while he conceals the result from my gaze'.

The techniques of communication, however, are basically in the hands of specialist operators whom the Foreign Office largely recruits – simply because they are the most available – from men who have served as telecommunications ratings in the Royal Navy. They run the wireless relay station at Hanslope in Buckinghamshire. Another body of technicians mans that temporary-looking hut which has now been lodged in the FCO's Durbar Court for a quarter of a century, and the establishment at Crowborough, in Sussex, from which half the BBC's External Radio Services are broadcast– the half that is transmitted to the Middle East and Communist countries. Other specialists are placed in the high-security Government Communications HQ at Cheltenham which, it is said, is mostly populated by 'boffins, mathematicians and first-class chess players'.[1] They serve in all but the smallest posts overseas. And wherever they are, their constant anxiety is lest the line should break down, lest communication should be interrupted, leaving the Ambassador and his men in some troubled place with a queer and demoralizing sense of being alone in the world. The biggest threat of all comes from industrial disputes, which foreigners endure just like the British, from the possibility that strikers in Ruritania will pull out all the plugs in the local power station. This is a surprisingly rare occurrence. Even during the coup which overthrew President Allende in Chile, the British Embassy in Santiago was only blacked out for an hour or so.

The traffic has become colossal as the techniques have been improved. In an average year now, something like 600,000 telegrams are transmitted between London and the diplomatic missions abroad. This flow, naturally, is heaviest where most of the diplomatic action is thought to be. In 1974, the British Delegation to the EEC was dispatching between 20 and 30 telegrams a day to the FCO while, just down the road at the British Embassy in Brussels, the average was little more than 1. In the first nine months of that year, the embassy in Washington handled 3,000 telegrams, the embassy in Paris 1,000. But even in a remote place like Mogadishu, five months in 1975 saw 20 telegrams coming in from London and 70-odd going out. It is

[1] McDermott, p. 142.

an enormously expensive business of perpetually escalating costs, and the most extortionate bills can result from isolated occasions that superficially seem to be but an oblique exercise in diplomacy. When Concorde flew round the Middle East in 1974 on a test run lasting a fortnight, the Foreign Office spent £8,000 on telegrams. The pilot would be delayed in leaving point A for point B because of some technical trouble, and foreign dignitaries awaiting the plane at point B would have to be advised to go home and come back later. At every trifling turn of the flight, telegrams took off from the FCO in a number of directions, while others sped home from the embassies abroad, all in the interests of good relations. But the really crippling sums are spent consistently in traffic which is much more humdrum and, sometimes, less necessary. A fairly small embassy like the one in Kuwait can find, when it has done its accounts, that one-third of the incoming groupage from London in a year consists of a summary of the British newspapers dispatched by the Central Office of Information each day, in spite of the fact that the papers themselves arrive by air twenty-four hours after publication. It has been estimated that, of the telegrams which come into each FCO department every day, averaging between 60 and 90, the vast majority simply amount to useful information about the world in general; 20 of them will convey tidings of no great urgency about that part of the world which particularly concerns the department and only 5 will necessitate action on their contents. In 1973, Sir Alec Douglas-Home demanded what successive politicians and Permanent Under Secretaries had been urging for years: that somehow the flow of telegrams must be reduced, not only on the grounds of cost, but because the system was being clogged by inessential traffic which delayed the movement of vital messages. In the next twelve months, the flow subsided by 10 per cent. But it is still colossal and expensive.

It is in its control of the communications network between Britain and all British officials overseas that the Foreign Office can exercise, if it wishes, a powerful hold over the whole apparatus of government. All written messages from abroad, whether destined for the FCO or some other department of state, are in its hands until the moment they arrive on the recipient's desk; and vice versa. It is a major operation merely to arrange the circulation of telegrams once they have been received in the

Office. There are almost fifty different distribution lists for telegrams, though they break down into three broad types of distribution, quite separate from security classifications. One is the very limited, marked 'For X only', which may result in only a handful of copies being made for the files apart from the original going to an individual. Another is confined to general FCO distribution, plus one or two outsiders, which can mean 150 copies being made. The third is for general circulation round Whitehall, in which case about 400 versions have to be run off and distributed. It is a cumbersome cottage industry to provide this service, which would have been automated in the mid-1970s if the national economy had not collapsed. But in effect it means that the FCO sees everything, and can therefore intervene in everything, that passes between any branch of government and its officers overseas. The Home civil servants in Brussels, where they outnumber the diplomats these days, complain that far too often instructions coming from their departments further up Whitehall are delayed because they have to be routed through the FCO.

One reason why so many telegrams are committed to the network is that they are much easier to compose than letters. Telegraphese is discouraged for clarity's sake, but in the name of economy these messages are sent 'as from a miser to a fool', according to someone much practised in the art. For some curious purpose that no one in diplomacy seems able to explain, the transmitted telegram finishes its journey printed in a typeface devoid of lower case lettering, so that it could quite easily be read in half-light by a myopic rhinoceros. Another reason for this enormous traffic may have something to do with the diplomat's notorious devotion to writing things down. Whitehall as a whole reckons that if a man from, say, the Treasury wishes to communicate with a fellow in the Ministry of Defence, his reflex is to pick up the telephone; or even, if it is likely to be a long-winded conversation, to step up the street for a *tête-à-tête*. Not so your average diplomat, they say; his immediate instinct is to draft a minute. It is true that some diplomats get an extra-curricular kick out of creating the artful telegram, which occasionally causes them to indulge in a boyish spoof. A highly respected head of chancery, when serving in the mission to the United Nations some years ago, concocted a convincing document on the future of Guinea-Bissau, before that region had yet

N

been independently dubbed as such. The telegram went into general circulation from New York and the Dutch, joining in the fun, added seventy-three amendments of their own and sent the document even more impressively into orbit. The Danes, having playfully transmitted it to their own foreign ministry in Europe, called the joke off when they received serious instructions from Copenhagen in return.

The man utterly addicted to composition, however, has much more scope for his talents in a letter travelling the good old-fashioned and highly romantic way. In spite of the unimaginable number of telegrams that must circulate the globe nowadays from every foreign ministry to its representatives abroad, the diplomatic bag or pouch, in the custody of the diplomatic courier, still provides the backbone of every communications system. In its time, the diplomatic bag has also provided many a fiction writer with a serviceable sub-plot, worked out against a pulsating beat of pistons and a trailing plume of steam aboard the Orient or Stamboul Express. Not all these period pieces have been far-fetched, for bags have been known to convey items generally excluded from the protective clauses of the Vienna Convention. During the 1930s, foreign diplomats of ardent disposition would smuggle the latest Paris fashions into Moscow for the benefit of ballerinas. Bits and pieces of archaeology have found their way out of South America in the same manner. Some years ago, the proverbial international gang bribed a courier from the Italian embassy in Paris to cart 2,000 Swiss watches into London, where he was caught because an astute and feeling Customs officer decided that no Ambassador on earth would allow one of his men to rupture himself under such a weight of correspondence. There has been at least one attempt to smuggle a living body in a diplomatic bag, from the Egyptian embassy in Rome to Cairo. Small arms and ammunition have been concealed within the canvas covers of diplomatic privilege. This is why Special Branch officers at Heathrow now run portable X-ray equipment alongside diplomatic baggage flying in and out of London.

The British reputation is comparatively law-abiding. The rules explicitly ordain that, to justify the normal immunity from interference by third parties, nothing but correspondence and confidential matter like code books shall be included in any nation's diplomatic bags. But it has always been tacitly understood that if the ambassadorial spectacles or the head of chancery's watch should be broken in some outlandish place lacking a reliable optician or jeweller, no one is going to raise any objection to replacements travelling in the bag; not even the Customs man who drops in on the FCO bagroom once a week to check that contraband is not slipping into and out of the country the easy way. Just occasionally the rules are bent fractionally further, here and there, on what might be called compassionate grounds. A naval attaché some years ago, thinking little of Moscow's laundering facilities, used to ship his dress shirts home in the bag so that the collars could be pressed into conformity with Queen's Regulations. Great is the joy in many a zealously Islamic land when bag day is due, for the embassy knows that, along with the official instructions and the tittle-tattle from home, the dear old courier will be bringing in the bacon. People posted to adjacent countries which tend to be short on high living frequently come to a mutually agreeable arrangement, which takes advantage of the courier's flight from one to the other in the course of his long perambulation from London. The administrative officer of a coastal embassy will slip a pair of fresh lobsters into the courier's bag for the benefit of his opposite number 500 miles away in the fruitful hinterland, who settles the account when the courier retraces his steps, with half a dozen juicy pineapples.

We have had official couriers since 1485, but the Queen's Messengers of today generally see themselves as descendants in a line given particular blessing by Charles II. During his exile in the Netherlands, the King made much use of messengers to maintain contact with his supporters in England. To each of them he gave a small silver greyhound, broken from a dish which (as every courtier at home knew) had belonged to his father. This became the token by which each messenger was at once identified as a trustworthy loyalist, and it is the symbol of their successors now. It is woven into an exclusive tie. It hangs as a small medallion from a coloured ribbon, which is worn on ceremonial occasions. On the Grand Staircase at the Foreign Office, below the Goetze frescoes, there is a glass caseful of these objects, all of them collectors' pieces. They are minted afresh with every reign, which gives them a distinctive value, for scarcely any two greyhounds cast over the past four centuries have ever been quite alike. Much more important in a practical way to any modern Queen's Messenger, however, is his special passport. Diplomats proper have passports indistinguishable from those the rest of us use. But the courier's document comes in maroon covers instead of blue, with *Queen's Messenger* at the top and *Courrier diplomatique* at the bottom: and on the inside cover, as well as the usual florid injunction from Her Britannic Majesty's Principal Secretary of State for Foreign Affairs, an extra solemnity informs all readers that the bearer has been *charged with dispatches*. One might think that if such a testimonial will not carry a Queen's Messenger unhindered across all frontiers, then his legs cannot. But it is simply not enough in the suspicious world of the twentieth century. Visas have to be obtained, too, as by ordinary mortals. This is why every QM owns five passports; so that, while he is using one, the other four can be doing the rounds of foreign embassies in London, collecting their stamp marks for subsequent journeys.

There are about fifty of these men, and they have a lot of battle honours between them. The majority are old soldiers who were bowler-hatted with a colonelcy. There is always a smattering from the RAF and two or three ex-policemen or former District Officers; but rarely are there more than a couple of old sailors. Picked in the first place because they are reliable and pretty durable, with a habit of command that still comes in handy on occasion, they tend in the course of their new profession to acquire the knowing look, the wry twinkle and the blasé manner that is commonly found among the overseasoned travellers of this world. At 230,000 miles a year, which is what every Queen's Messenger logs on average, these caste marks develop quite quickly. They belong to men who will not be pushed around too easily by officials who do sometimes try to push them around, as though diplomatic immunity had never been conceived. There has not yet, within living memory, been an occasion when the bags have been seized in even the most unpleasant places, but there have been times when the QM has had to stand his ground against some stroppy fellow, much girt about with leather and metal, who wanted the bags to be opened up. But, as one of them says, the rule is that 'if it's a question of being opened or beating a retreat, you beat a retreat'. Aside from professional pride, no messenger would dare lose control of a bag, for if he did he would automatically lose his job as well, with no right of appeal. Only once has this happened in recent years. A QM reached Tokyo after a long and exhausting flight, and only when he arrived at the embassy did he find that he was a bag short. At that moment the airport rang to say that it had been found untouched under the unfortunate man's seat, where he had forgotten it in his weary disembarkation. No harm was done, except to his second career; though a kindly Office helped him to a third by providing the references that long service and impeccable conduct had deserved.

There was a rather rough passage during a muscular moment of the Chinese Cultural Revolution. Colonel Constantine was bringing the bags home from Peking and found, when he descended from the train at the border crossing into Hong Kong, that a jeering mob of young lusties was offering a Red gauntlet which he would have to run for a hundred yards or so between the station platform and the frontier gates. The bags were piled on to a trolley whose wheels gave way under the weight, and the Colonel had to hand-haul his cargo while he was jostled and tripped and given several sly kicks on the shin, though no one so much as laid a finger on the diplomatic bags themselves. Unpleasant, but not nearly as exciting as the episode involving Commander Woodhouse, who attracted trouble more often than most of his colleagues. He was once ordered off a train in Eastern Europe by a drunken Russian colonel waving a pistol. Later, in 1951, he was aboard the SS *Hupeh*, sailing from Hong Kong to Tientsin, when it was attacked in the Formosa Strait by pirates in a motorized junk. The Commander was about to heave the bags overboard when the *Hupeh* came about, presenting him with the inconvenient prospect of the pirate's deck instead of the sea. So he went down to his cabin and stowed the bags behind some garments in a cupboard. By the time the boarding party reached him he had invitingly strewn his money and private valuables on top of his bunk; and, after relieving him of these things, the marauders went on their way rejoicing, allowing the diplomatic bags to proceed safely. Bags almost always do. The only ones that have come to grief have taken their custodians with them. In 1947, Colonel Simpson was killed when the aircraft in which he was flying to Santiago crashed in the Andes. In 1949, Colonel Fane died in an air disaster at Dallas. In 1963, Colonel Drake went down in another crash in the Cameroons.

The journeys the couriers make today have obviously lost

much of the tingling spirit they once had, because we no longer inhabit the world of Phileas Fogg. In those days, the Queen's Messenger travelling from the Foreign Office to the British Ambassador in St Petersburg would take a train to Berlin, where he would hire a carriage and horses. These he would load on to another train, which conveyed him as far as Warsaw. Then he would take to the road, and ride pell-mell for nine days until he reached his destination. There are just one or two bag runs in the 1970s which recapture the flavour of that age. Thrice weekly a courier leaves London (Victoria) for Paris (Nord) on the night sleeper, and the railways are also used to reach Brussels, Luxembourg, Strasbourg and The Hague. Even on the longest of his flights across the world, the courier is liable to come to earth for a while to cover one stretch by train. There is a run from London to Kabul and back, by way of Turkey, Iran, Lebanon and Jordan, which involves an overnight ride out of Istanbul on the Ankara Express. And there is PUB 26, quite the most glamorous schedule of all and easily the most extended, so that the messenger completing it has ten days of leave when he returns home. He flies out of London for Damascus at the start, then to Doha, Colombo and Singapore, delivering his bags wherever his plane lands. On the seventh day he takes a train from Hong Kong to Canton, and then flies up to Peking. There he boards the International Train, which carries him through the Chinese Customs post at Erlian and the neighbouring frontier station of Dzamyn Ude. For the next thirty-six hours he rattles romantically across the steppes of Mongolia, bringing the considered instructions of the Foreign Secretary (and perhaps a few kippers wrapped in tinfoil and plastic) to Our Man in Ulan Bator. Eleven days out of London he has been, when finally he steps into the residence at 30 Peace Street. And they do say that, as often as not, on those last few miles across the plains of Central Asia, the Queen's Messenger, on looking out of his railway carriage window, may observe wild horsemen riding companionably alongside the train, upon shaggy little beasts whose breeding goes straight back to the days of Genghis Khan.

Most of the time, however, the couriers shuttle around the world in the most tedious fashion ever contrived by man. The job would be quite insupportable if it were not for the fact that almost all the long journeys are broken with rest nights at intermediate embassies. But the messenger does not always take his bags into town when his plane lands at a passing capital. The very first run any QM makes when he starts the job is to Cologne, where men from the Bonn embassy await him at the aircraft door and relieve him of his burdens on the spot, after exchanging documents which, by a prearranged code, assure each side that the other is what he seems to be, and not some spymaster's lackey. A sense of security is the reason, more pressing than patriotism, why the Queen's Messengers travel by British aircraft whenever possible. The incontinent courier feels just a bit happier, as he makes his way aft, if he can leave his bags for a moment or two under the eyes of a nicely trained girl from Surbiton, rather than any more tantalizing variety of stewardess. On foreign airlines, as the watchful traveller may note, those chaps with a heap of baggage in the next seat rarely indulge in liquid refreshment. On flights to Communist countries, in fact, the messenger is always accompanied by an escort, just to be on the safe side. But the general view of these things is that the traditional immunity of couriers is such a deeply embedded principle with all nations, that the risk of a bag being tampered with in transit is almost nil; and that, if it were, reprisals could always be taken. All the same, the British feel that the Americans are just a bit too easy-going in these matters today. At one time their messengers used to have the bags tethered to their bodies, something the British have never done. The practice was discontinued after a ghastly accident, when a plane made a crash landing in which all the passengers, including the courier, managed to escape through doors and windows: only he, poor fellow, couldn't get his bags through the opening after him, and was burned to death in the fire that followed. Since then, men from the State Department have ridden in aircraft like every other passenger, and their diplomatic bags have been stowed in the belly of the plane, with all the other luggage.

The deadliest run of all is reputed to be the one round the West African missions, because so many deliveries and pick-ups are packed into such a short time. After flying out of Heathrow on a Tuesday morning, the courier has called at Rome and Accra by nightfall. Wednesday sees him moving on to Lagos and Kinshasa, and Thursday back to Lagos again. But then, from 11 a.m. on Friday, he flies without a break, except for airport meetings, to Accra, Abidjan, Monrovia, Freetown, Banjul and Dakar, where he arrives at teatime; and, six hours later, staggers on to a plane which reaches Gatwick just before breakfast on Saturday. He gets five days rest after that lot, and sorely needs them. Even the greater leg-room of the first-class compartments, where the couriers sit on journeys outside Europe, are of little relief in a sequence like that. After a day or two of intensive air travel, the chances are that a man is becoming too strained with fatigue to concentrate on one of his mid-air pastimes – which tend, among the Queen's Messengers, to follow the direction taken by many other long voyagers: needlework and cartooning and studying languages. Yet concentrate he must, on staying awake, without benefit of conversation. Plenty of fellow passengers are willing to strike up an acquaintance with a man who sits, surrounded by huge parcels, like Father Christmas in mufti. Americans are particularly prone to come roaming down the aisle, amiably wondering what it all amounts to – especially that cute little bag (for they come in eight different sizes, all by courtesy of HM Prisons) perched right there on top of the pile. The most experienced QMs cover the heap at their elbow with a blanket. When the next blue-rinsed matron pauses inquisitively by their side, they assume their most mournful countenance and mumble something rebarbative like ' ... Wife passed away ... few days ago ... taking body Home as she would have wished ... ' And this invariably guarantees them solitude for the rest of the flight.

The ideal journey takes three days, between Tuesday and Thursday, which means that the relevant desk officers at the FCO, and their opposite numbers abroad, can clear their joint material within the same week. But the frequency of bag day in British missions varies considerably. At the EEC delegation in Brussels it comes round five times a week, at Washington four, at Paris and Bonn three. The embassies dotted round South America are visited every two weeks, and the PUB crawl to Peking and Ulan Bator is fortnightly, too. The most infrequent run of all is, oddly enough, to Iceland, which sees the Queen's Messenger only once a month. The most welcome one has become the weekly trip to Moscow, not only because it is an easy run for the courier, who has a day of leisure between his two journeys, but because it now represents a lucky break for embassy staff as well. Moscow may be a fascinating professional experience for any diplomat, but it is regarded as a trying post otherwise, with far fewer fun and games to be enjoyed than in most places, and a tendency towards a laager atmosphere in the foreign community. When Sir Terence Garvey was Ambassador there, he decided that every one of the hundred people in his command would feel the benefit of a long weekend in London, to punctuate the posting, by flying as the Queen's Messenger's escort. The FCO huffed and puffed a bit at the idea, pointing out the hypothetical impropriety of a bowler-hatted colonel and a young girl secretary sharing a suggestive night in the open (and be damned to the diplomatic bags) should their plane make a forced landing somewhere in Schleswig-Holstein. But imaginative Ambassadors usually get their way in the end and, one after the other, from top to bottom of their ranks, the Moscow staff now take it in turns to fly home in time for supper on Wednesday, coming back to work near the Kremlin the following Monday.

Every embassy, in truth, owes a lot of its better morale to the couriers. For, quite apart from delivering his official swag of letters and instructions for the Ambassador and his men, the Queen's Messenger is also the postman for every family in the mission. Bag day means hectic activity in the chancery, as the diplomats rush around, trying to get their last thoughtful words and their most recently considered opinions sewn up in time to catch the London-bound flight. But in every diplomatic household that night, it usually means a nostalgic half-hour reading Auntie Maud's spastic handwriting, or catching up with what the son and heir has been doing at that faraway boarding school of his. It is possibly because diplomatic families turn in on themselves on bag days that the courier, their harbinger of news, is usually left out of things a bit. He may have some bachelor buddy in this or that mission, with whom he has a night on the town during the stopover, in which case the friend will almost certainly be an Executive who administers, or one of the security guards, who is an old soldier himself and understands. Any outsider in a British embassy on bag day has little difficulty in spotting the Queen's Messenger. He is that rather crumpled-looking figure who appears to be in familiar surroundings, but who clearly does not belong. He gets friendly nods and greetings as he wanders down corridors and pops his head round doorways, whiling away the time until he must be off again. But the affability of the diplomats comes from a distance. He's a damned good chap, and where would they be without him. Quite as indispensable as Piccolo has now become. But he's not really one of them.

It's a lonely life.

PART TWO

8 Far-flung Outposts

High above the Golden Horn, which was once the crossroads of the known world, is the British Consulate-General in Istanbul. On the roof it is possible to stand enraptured by one of the most intoxicating scenes ever created by man. For on the Horn's opposite bank the late afternoon sunlight streams down past a thicket of domes and minarets and towers, belonging to the biggest mosques and the Topkapi Palace. In straight dusty shafts it slants into the waterway, where time seems to have lost its way not later than the turn of the century. Ferry boats swash back and forth, belching out smoke as they did when Florence Nightingale was labouring at Scutari, on the far side of the Bosphorus. Old men trot across the Galata Bridge, bent double under loads that look as if they might cripple a donkey. The waterside heaves with people hosing down fresh fish in boxes, humping sacks of coal, selling bootlaces and lottery tickets, whipping up nags to gallop along with rattletrap carts, making a din with hammers and chisels against sheets of rusty metal. The nose, down there, twitches in a perpetual breeze of spices, roasting food, carbon, steam, fish scales, axle grease and ozone.

The consulate-general is not quite of a piece with all this, though the streets beyond the great iron gates have a ragamuffin charm of their own. Directly opposite is the Çiçek Pasaji, the Passage of Flowers, where the discriminating diplomat may sit almost alfresco beneath a curved glass roof, while he munches shrimps cooked in ten different ways, sips raqi, lends ear to the gossip among the marble-topped beer barrels, and watches the vagabondage of the town pass him by in a knockabout and Byzantine version of the Burlington Arcade. Lunch over, he can be back at his desk in half a tick in what (but only if he is a tiresomely staid fellow) he may refer to as his office. For Her Majesty's consulate-general is otherwise known as the Pera Palace, and looks every inch the part, as it was meant to do by Charles Barry, who designed it in a splendidly Florentine mood, before practising his Gothic on the Palace of Westminster and something less easily describable on Halifax Town Hall. Moreover, for a century or so, when this was a proper embassy, its inhabitants lived up to its grandeur of pedimented windows, private chapels, ballroom and formal English garden sweeping downhill towards the Golden Horn. It was from his study in the Pera Palace that Stratford Canning fenced with the Czar Nicholas over the disputed Holy Places of Jerusalem, and arranged for Layard's priceless discoveries at Nineveh to be shipped home to the British Museum. And for decades after Canning had thankfully retired to Frant, to contemplate Virgil and Alfred the Great in old age, his successors in the embassy here manipulated the fag-end of the Ottoman Empire with rather more dexterity than the long line of Sultans they entertained to supper.

They lived like grandees themselves. As well as the establishment at Pera, there was an alternative embassy at Therapia, on a point overlooking the Bosphorus, where wave-sloshed villas sadly decay at the water's edge, just before it opens out into the Black Sea. The British would betake themselves there when summer fell upon the land, just as their distant colleagues in India migrated from the steamy heat of Calcutta to the refreshing hills of Simla. Down at the Horn their private steam yacht was anchored, ready to convey them between their two homes, or to entertain gracious boating parties in trips along the coast. Such things changed only a little when the Ambassadors were first obliged to strike camp in Istanbul and move off behind Atatürk to the lunar bleakness of Ankara. The British assigned Consuls-General in their place, to keep the home fires burning in Pera. And this they still do, though it is many years now since the *Makook*, the last of the yachts, quietly foundered with senility; and the 1960s probably saw the last British Consul-General who would ceremonially board one of Her Majesty's warships (showing the flag in Istanbul), dashingly costumed in his full dress uniform of frock coat, cocked hat and sword.

To be precise, they keep half the home fires burning at Pera, for the palace is now divided between the diplomats and the British Council. The men from the FCO still have a weight of responsibility to discharge, for Istanbul is still some kind of crossroads. Something like 20,000 visitors call at Pera Palace in an average year; 500 of them sit down to meals, and another 2,000 are summoned to cocktails. That's what comes of trade promotion, of soothing distraught Britons on cruise liners, of sorting out idiot adolescents who have ignored the rule that you must not carry pot through Turkey, of keeping a weather eye lifted for the next Soviet cruiser nosing down the Bosphorus, to sail brazenly in the wake of the United States Sixth Fleet. The grandeur of the Pera Palace is not much different nowadays from the grandeur of the FCO itself. It's a bit more faded and considerably dustier, that's all. Nothing but bygone potted palms grace the great Palm Court today. Earnest young Turks study *In Britain Now* and *The Lancet* beneath the immense chandeliers of what was once Stratford Canning's ballroom, but which has been turned into the British Council's library. Someone has kept the garden in good order, though. And at the entrance to the drive, where policemen occupy a sentry box, the letters 'VR' are still entwined defiantly upon the gates.

There are many times, in plenty of places around the world, when a British diplomat needs to have his feet placed firmly upon the ground if he is not to succumb to a *folie de grandeur* induced by his immediate surroundings. The Pera Palace is not by any means the only sumptuous building retained by the Foreign Office abroad, and most of them are kept in a more glittering state of decoration and repair, which is not shared with the British Council or anyone else. They are the shop fronts of a nation of shopkeepers, and they set a great deal of store by the cultivated distinction of their window dressing. Occasionally, a British Ambassador still has the run of two establishments in the same capital city, as in the old days at Istanbul. For most of the year, the British Embassy in Teheran is located in what can only be described as an encampment, which is fenced off from the most appalling traffic in creation charging along one of the city's main roads. The chancery and other working offices are here, the Ambassador's residence is a few hundred yards away across a lawn, and dotted among trees are the homes of other diplomats as well. But, come summer, the Ambassador moves up the hill to Gulhek, half an hour's drive away, where he and twenty-two others can coolly situate themselves in the middle of forty acres, just as if air-conditioning had never been introduced along the Avenue Ferdowsi. At Addis Ababa there is an even greater need to spread the embassy around – over seventy-one acres there – for the British government's estate includes a small village which was built to accommodate all the servants.

The most sumptuous embassy of all is generally acknowledged to be the one in Paris, which is said to be a far more lavish establishment than No 10 Downing Street. There is manifestly nothing stingy about a residence which runs to twenty-three bedrooms, ten bathrooms, a three-roomed flat for a private secretary and nine rooms for servants. But it is the style as much as the scale of Britain's representation in Paris that puts it at the top of the lists. The mansion inhabited by the Ambassador was the town house of Napoleon's sister, Pauline Borghese, until the British bought it in 1814, after the Duke of Wellington had first looked it over and decided it would do. It has a courtyard in the rue du Faubourg St Honoré, a long garden running to the Champs-Élysées and rooms which, Anthony Sampson has remarked, 'it is not easy to find anyone big enough and confident enough to fill'.[1] The embassy's offices are just down the street, adjacent to the Élysée Palace. Before the war, business was conducted entirely from a chancery located in the gatehouse of the residence; but now this has become merely the Head of Chancery's home. Stylishness of that sort is to be found much lower down the diplomatic pecking order. Like a lot of European posts, from which an influential tide has receded in the direction of the EEC, the Brussels Embassy is a rather sad place these days, its self-confidence especially undermined by the knowledge that, in its case, most of the action is going on just up the road, where an entirely different squad of British diplomats is doing its best for the nation. The embassy offices are as undistinguished as a post-war insurance building, but the Ambassador's residence is another thing altogether. You walk straight into the eighteenth century there, with Savonnerie carpets on the floor, Louis XV chandeliers up above, Beauvais tapestries round the dining-room walls, and white and gilt panelling by the Frères Rousseau in the drawing room. At mealtimes, a flunkey circulates the table with what looks like Aladdin's lamp, an antique silver touchpaper with which he lights the cigarettes. There can be but a handful of English

---

[1] *The New Anatomy of Britain* (Hodder & Stoughton, 1971), p. 293.

dukes who live in a household such as this, and those that do probably have funfairs and chimpanzees in the grounds to help pay for it all. But in the rue Ducale everything is utterly refined and all is conducted in perfect taste, from the moment the hapless visitor, having almost gone full-length across the raised doorstep, warmly thanks a morning-suited gentleman for his kind invitation, only to discover that the gentleman in question, puzzled by this effusion, is merely come to take the visitor's coat, and that His Excellency is somewhere within, toying conversationally with a cut-glass bumper of sherry.

There are embassies which are not only grand, but superbly sited into the bargain. At Cairo, the offices look like some awful misjudgment by the old Ministry of Works, which indeed they were, having been built just before the Suez affair on a rambling scale which has failed to correspond with Britain's local influence ever since. But the residence near by is impressively classical, still charged with the history that was schemed by some of its occupants. Cromer ruled Egypt from its library. Allenby and Kitchener were here as well. In their days, the lawn ran straight down to the water's edge of the River Nile, but was halved as a reparation for Suez, to allow the passage of a main road. All the same, it is still big enough to accommodate an open-air swimming pool and garden parties of 1,200 and more. In 1974 it saw jollifications with a ducal touch, too, when the Ambassador threw a charity fête, with coconut shies and roundabouts and tours of the residence conducted by the Head of Chancery, the first time the hoi polloi of Egypt had ever been allowed inside the place. For it was built for powerful men who prized seclusion and ran things the way they wished. Though the pale green stucco frontage of the residence is a little dwarfed today by the bulk of the new Shepheard's Hotel on one side, and of the Nile Hotel on the other, there is no diminishing the outlook His Excellency enjoys from his own suite of rooms. The embassy is set upon an island midstream of the Nile, which is very wide at this reach, so that the buildings on the far bank are distant and intriguing, and there is a long and sweeping view both up and down the river, of lapping waters, drooping palm trees, and feluccas gliding by with the wind leaning firmly into their lateens.

Moscow is just as captivating. This may be the most gorgeously odd embassy of all, the product of a nineteenth-century

o

Russian sugar magnate's haphazard tastes. One British Ambassador there, Sir David Kelly, described the interior as 'a mixture of Gothic cathedral and a Munich beerhouse', though the visitor is more immediately struck by the Scottish Baronial of the entrance hall, with a massively oaken staircase leading up to the Ambassador's home on the first floor. This is a rare arrangement, for in most British missions the residence is carefully detached from the working offices, sometimes being located on the other side of town. Until the First World War, indeed, it was thought improper for any Ambassador to enter the chancery building without an invitation, which was not often extended by a junior staff more than content that His Excellency should not emerge from his lair as a caparisoned mouthpiece until they had finished their diplomatic spadework on *bouts de papier* and *notes verbales*. The conjunction of residence and chancery in Moscow, however, gives the place a homely air, in spite of the Soviet camera lurking behind a ventilator on an adjacent roof, which tempts any healthy man marching up the front steps to turn round and offer it a V-sign. The domestic and the professional life is so contiguous that the ambassadorial dog is also a household pet for the embassy guards, posted by their closed-circuit television set in the lobby. This modish security is but one of the adjustments that have been made since the sugar magnate built his folly. The ballroom upstairs, which is something of a cross between Versailles and a Spanish Cartuja, now flickers decadently from time to time with the latest example of Western cinema, which would otherwise not be seen nearer than Helsinki. The library below, which closely resembles the mustier corners of the Bodleian, is the daily workshop of a Third Secretary from Research, scrutinizing *Izvestia* and *Pravda* for the faintest hint of internal Soviet changes that might eventually cause the world outside to wobble in response. Even in the front bedrooms, where visiting Prime Ministers and Foreign Secretaries are lodged in old-fashioned splendour, there are timely warnings that 'Speech on this telephone is NOT SECRET'. Yet the most captivating thing about the Moscow Embassy has scarcely been touched by all the upheavals that have otherwise shaken every building in the city to its foundations in the past three-quarters of a century. Directly opposite, 500 yards or so across the river, is the Kremlin, still wildly romantic with its palace and cathedrals poised above the long crenellated walls. Gold glows from the onion domes, as it did when the embassy was built. But now, thanks to Comrade Lenin, Her Majesty's Ambassador and his guests, should they wake up in the middle of the night, may not only enjoy the entire and superb spectacle by floodlight, but the transcending touch of stars picked out in red neon on the pinnacles as well.

Not every embassy is pickled in its glorious past, like Cairo and the Pera Palace. There are some whose greatest local fame has nothing at all to do with the British; like Jakarta, whose residence is where the Japanese surrendered in 1945 to the infant Indonesian Republic. There are others, sometimes very grand, which have no history of any description worked into their fabric. An expensive new building went up in Rio de Janeiro in 1950 (it was later described in the House of Commons as 'a magnificent monument to Ernest Bevin') and everyone had just nicely settled in when the natives disobligingly shifted their capital to Brasilia, which meant that the Ministry of Works had to start all over again. Dilapidations of one kind or another are for ever occurring in some part of the globe. There has been an embassy overlooking the moat of the Imperial Palace in Tokyo for a century, a site uncommonly prone to earth tremors and very damaging to ordinary bricks and mortar, which has caused the most recent building to be laced throughout with steel rods in a style known as 'shock-proof Queen Anne'. In the days of the Baghdad Pact, the British Ambassador to Iraq had his base by the Tigris burned down by a revolutionary mob, its eventual replacement being much more modest than the original – and fireproof.

But any embassy which has been a going concern for a generation or more has an accumulated history of its own, which has nothing to do with its diplomatic relations. In Belgrade there is a stone by the garden wall, with the inscription 'In memory of Rufus. A golden labrador, born Sedgwick 1926, died Belgrade April 1934', which means that Sir Neville Henderson was also here, sometime before his unfortunate posting to Berlin. Not far away, by the Vice-Consul's window, is a magnolia tree under which, it is said, a fairly new Third Secretary asked a young woman to marry him some thirty years before they set up house in the residence together as Sir Dugald and Lady Stewart. Nor is it forgotten that, in the bustle to make the place fit for the Queen's state visit to Yugoslavia in 1972, the entire embassy had to be evacuated one lunchtime because the lorry delivering oil for the central heating pumped petrol into the system by mistake. In such moments – mournful, intimate and serio-comic by turn – the internal lore of the Diplomatic Service is born, to be nurtured fondly later on over many a loquacious gin and tonic in the Travellers' Club in London. Other legends can be seen more slowly in the making. It is not so long since the Cairo embassy contained a First Secretary destined for memorial gossip from the moment he arrived on post. He was the somewhat diffident holder of the MBE (military division), which he acquired on National Service as commander of the first tank to roll ashore at Port Said in 1956. Unlike his colleagues, he profoundly disliked city life, preferring to live in a mouldering house by the Pyramids, where he could ride horses or camels every morning before breakfast, and sleep on all but the coldest nights of the year at the bottom of his garden, in a tent which bore a strong resemblance to Sir Richard Burton's mausoleum in Mortlake Cemetery.

In some places a mission's links with its past are maintained through innumerable and complete staff changes, in the person of a local and long-living legend. Such is the case in Kuwait. The embassy there is set on a headland, where its veranda will catch the slightest whiffle of breeze that may come off the Persian Gulf. In a corner of the Ambassador's office, a model of Concorde is perched upon an old and brassbound Arab chest; and this juxtaposition wryly mocks the topsy-turvy world the Ambassador and his men find themselves in here, since oil turned Kuwait into an extravagantly opulent place which makes any British town look like a grubby museum piece. Very little of tumbledown and mud-walled Kuwait remains, though just along the seafront, across the road from the dhow harbour, stands a slightly ramshackle dwelling, which represents the most poignant British traditions in the region. It was the last home of Lt-Colonel Harold Dickson who, in the early 1930s, when Britain mastered the Gulf, was the Political Agent here, a post he sandwiched between a period as Guardian to the Maharaj Kumar of Bikaner and his final profession as chief local representative of the Kuwait Oil Company. It is still the home of his widow, Violet Dickson, MBE, who lives in it by grace and favour of the Ruler, is supplied with a free car and petrol by the oil people, and is otherwise provided for by her

pension from the Foreign Office. She has stayed because anywhere else would be an alien land to her, and because she is so
gratifyingly a figure in the landscape here. The Ambassador
includes her in cocktail parties on his veranda from time to
time. First Secretaries invite her to their supper tables, to remin-
isce about the past. She remembers when she and her husband
used to entertain Royal Navy officers, whose ships had dropped
anchor offshore to give the washing a better chance to dry than
in the sopping atmosphere of Bahrein. In those days Kuwait
was but a strategic interest to Britain, ignored by almost everyone else, but now, she says, 'they have Ambassadors here from
every Tom, Dick and Harry of a country – terrible!' Now they
also have wealth undreamt of in the 1930s, a transformation
which Violet Dickson patronizes as a sort of *ex officio* First Lady.
Shortly after President Sadat had travelled into town from the
airport on an official visit in 1975, she found herself, quite by
chance, bowling down the same road in her chauffeured
Mercedes. The soldiers who had been lining the presidential
route were still there, loafing in small groups before the order
to dismiss. She waved at them as she went by; and they, not
quite snapping to attention, gave her salutes in return, part
reflex, part friendly, but totally in recognition.

Less dazzling transformations than that in Kuwait have
occurred throughout the world in the decades since the Second
World War, which is one reason why the number of British
missions abroad is so rarely constant from one year to another.
The first thing any territory does when it declares its independence is to establish diplomatic relations in its own right. In the
case of even a small new state like Oman, this has meant that,
since 1970, more than thirty other countries have had to respond
by starting fresh missions of their own in the capital at Muscat.
The British were among them, as they have been elsewhere.
Yet, while some British Ambassadors have been appointed to
set up shop for the first time in some city which has only just
become intoxicated by freedom, others have found themselves
rolling down the shutters for the last time in response to other
influences. Occasionally the closures have resulted from relations breaking down between the two countries. In 1965 we
parted company with Mauritania and Mali and, though the
quarrels were repaired three years later, the British embassies
never returned to either Nouakchott or Bamako, diplomacy

having since 1968 been conducted on a basis of flying visits by the British Ambassador and his staff in Dakar. But a lot of British posts have been abandoned because we have had to take a fresh look at the world and decide just where we could afford to spread our diplomatic representation in our newly-straitened circumstances. Thus, while there was a great vogue for creating new posts in the 1960s, in response to other people's independence, there has been a tendency since then to close missions down because of our own poverty and lack of power. Between the Duncan Committee reporting in 1969 and the beginning of 1975, the Foreign Office closed more than twenty-five of its posts abroad. In 1975 the Foreign Office decided to close four of its embassies abroad for economic reasons.

It is in the smaller and younger capitals of the world that British missions may be found whose buildings are neither sumptuous nor reeking with any kind of history worth speaking of. The embassy offices in Mogadishu, for example, fulfil anyone's boyish expectations of a distant outpost of the Crown. The outside walls are whitewashed to throw back the drilling sunlight of Somalia, and they are decorated with travel posters and other British propaganda, the only thing that distinguishes the building from its neighbours along the street. Out of office hours, large wooden doors are laboriously opened by the native gateman, in response to the right combination of toots on a car horn. A Land-Rover is parked in whatever corner of the courtyard offers shade. A wooden staircase climbs, in the open air, to a doorway on the first floor. Gunga Din should have been here. The arrangements inside are modest by anybody's standards, with plaster coming adrift from some of the rooms. Without the air-conditioning and the fans, diplomacy in this corner of the globe would be an unenviable business. In places such as this, in fact, postings are generally shorter than is the rule in general: a couple of years on duty with a home leave in the middle, instead of the three to four years normal in more comfortable and less remote spots. They are run on the sort of shoestring that is even more commonplace in French diplomacy except in old French colonial territories. Their Ambassadors are more workaday souls than they will become when they have acquired the airs and graces of experience on subsequent promotion to more senior posts. When Britain opened its new embassy to Mongolia in the early 1960s, the Ambassador came to his command with no great flourish or fanfare, but rather hot and sticky after the long train journey from Peking, which he made alone except for a Reuters correspondent, and a suitcase crammed with £500 worth of currency in order to establish British solvency from the outset of his mission.

The British embassy in Mogadishu is a five-man affair, and almost our smallest representation abroad – though Hanoi is a two-man post, and Lomé was a three-man effort until the embassy there closed in 1975. But when the Foreign Office speaks of five-man or two-man posts, it is speaking of personnel whose home is in the United Kingdom, and disregarding the number of people locally engaged to back them up by typing letters, driving cars, running errands, cooking meals, waiting on table and doing all manner of less impressive jobs; a figure which can be disproportionately high in the smaller embassies and which is substantial everywhere. In Mogadishu, the diplomatic quintet is supported by eighteen Somalis engaged on the spot. This means, in effect, that such an embassy spends 60 per cent of its energies in self-administration. One of the diplomats can pass most of the morning trying to arrange for local workmen to mend the broken air-conditioner belonging to one of the other two diplomats, sighing in the aggravated knowledge that, just across town, the pampered Americans are comfortably above such frustrations, because their embassy runs to its own motor mechanic and air-conditioning engineer. It is not always clear to the outsider to what end the diplomats in such comparatively tiny posts are applying the rest of their energies, the 40 per cent that goes on pure diplomacy. In Mogadishu the answer seems to consist largely in lending a hand with a modest EEC aid programme and in observing the local influence of the Russians at one of their most secure footholds in Africa. Although trade between Great Britain and the Somali Democratic Republic is virtually non-existent, our mission there must bring great joy to at least the British bunting industry. For, in spite of the fact that the Union Jack is dutifully hauled up and down the embassy flagstaff at sunrise and sunset (unlike the practice of other nations, who tend to keep their standards flying at all times) both it and the little emblem fluttering on the bonnet of the ambassadorial car have to be replaced eight times a year, so corrosive are the salty winds blowing inshore from the Indian Ocean.

It is all so different in the biggest embassy of all, which attracts more public attention in Great Britain than almost all the others put together. The headquarters of British diplomacy in America, the command post for some twenty separate missions spread throughout the United States, has been situated at the top of Massachusetts Avenue in Washington DC since 1926, when a substantial acreage was purchased by the British government for a cool ten bucks. On this site Sir Edwin Lutyens created a neo-Georgian residence (complete with Lutyens lions, who growl at passers-by from the Ambassador's gates) that is first cousin to many an expensive dwelling along Millionaires' Row at Kenwood in London. At a respectful distance uphill there arose a great conglomeration of offices less impressively designed, not unlike a custom-built comprehensive school, which now culminates in a large glassy rotunda, where wholesale cocktail parties and other enormous jamborees can be housed. There is nothing along the length of Massachusetts Avenue to compete with the scale of the British Embassy, though the avenue itself contains very few buildings that are not diplomatic in purpose. The British are out on their own, however, enfolded in parkland on every side, with a statue on the pavement outside the residence which only emphasizes their aloofness: Sir Winston Churchill as ever was, brandishing two digits at all-comers from lower down the hill, a gesture which, together with those Lutyens lions, must be rather off-putting to well-disposed strangers unfamiliar with the ambiguous ways of the British. Their nearest neighbours are the Brazilians, a quarter of a mile downhill, who inhabit a marvellously modern box constructed of little but smoked glass, through which Latin American diplomacy may be dimly observed functioning inside. After the Brazilians comes a regular cascade of embassies on both sides of the avenue, the least of which is pretty grand. Even the Indonesians operate from what appears to be a seventeenth-century French *hôtel de ville*.

The only thing a man can say with complete confidence about the size of the Washington embassy is that it is the biggest we have or that Washington knows. For the size and the expense of running the place are probably the touchiest subjects in British diplomacy and figures are very jealously guarded, those available being arranged in such a complicated fashion that no one but a graduate in applied mathematics could be expected to appreciate just what they represent. The United

States State Department's Diplomatic List for the city in May 1975 put the British representation at 77 (compared with 53 Frenchmen and 60 West Germans) but that nowhere nearly logs the true working population. The top three floors of the offices house a British Defence Staff which is practically un- accounted for in the Diplomatic List – and that doesn't include the two or three score men of the British Naval Staff who are attached to the United States Naval Headquarters across the city at Arlington. Substantial numbers of civil servants are similarly unremarked, on the payroll of the Foreign Office and just about every other ministry in Whitehall. There are many underlings of the locally engaged staff as well. The evasiveness of the Foreign Office when asked for such information was well illustrated when officials were interrogated by the Parliament- ary Expenditure Committee in March 1975:[1]

Question: Would you please say what reduction has been made in the number of Service Attachés since 1969 ... What is the current strength of the BDS Washington?

Answer: There is close interdepartmental consultation on Service Attachés but accounting responsibility for all these questions rests with the Ministry of Defence.

The total population at the embassy must run into hundreds, and it feels like a minor version of the FCO in Whitehall. People are so numerous that a fair proportion know each other only by sight, and they are so sealed into their specialized com- partments that they can be quite remarkably ignorant of what some of their colleagues are up to. In all but the smallest em- bassies there is a regular coming and going of diplomats and other home-based personnel, as some of them end their period overseas and their replacements arrive on post. In Washington the annual movement in each direction is about fifty people, which is something like the total strength of a fair-sized British mission anywhere else in the world. Manpower here is so lavish, its consumption of everything so considerable, that outside contractors supply things in great bulk for its use alone. Even packets of sugar for the tea breaks are specially labelled 'British Embassy, Washington DC'.

[1] *Eighth report from the Expenditure Committee; Session 1974–5,* p. 125.

What it all costs seems to be anybody's guess as well. When a journalist in mid-1974 suggested that more than £6 million a year was spent on running the Washington embassy, with another £1·4 million provided for the Defence staff, he was challenged very vaguely about the accuracy of his figures. Twelve months later a Labour MP took it into his head to report the Foreign Office to the British Ombudsman for profligate spending on Massachusetts Avenue, and mentioned £2·7 million. The nearest thing to an official leak on the subject came some years before either of these quotations when Mr Anthony Barber, as Chancellor of the Exchequer, in grappling with a supplementary question in the House of Commons, seemed to be saying that the Washington embassy cost the British taxpayer only a shade less than the emoluments of Her Majesty the Queen. This is conceivable, given the extent and nature of the government's holding in the American capital. Quite apart from the running costs of the work there, together with the salaries and allowances involved, we spend a small fortune each year on accommodation and property.

When the majority of British diplomats go home each day, they are bound for Georgetown, or somewhat farther afield in salubrious parts of Maryland and Virginia. Now, Georgetown is one of the most civilized urban areas on earth. Its highly cultivated clapboard charms run to classical porticoes and coach lamps on the doorposts, to orange trees grown out of tubs and a mural by Chagall on somebody's garden wall, to a cryptic neighbourhood of 'N' and 'O' and 'P' Streets, to a great deal of wealth and breeding, with an Italian delly and a Chinese laundry just round the corner. It is All American Old Colonial, but if you mixed the polished manner of South Kensington with the side-streets of Hampstead you might come up with approximately the right image. Property here comes at pretty prices, and nowhere in Washington fit for the diplomatic community is anything on the cheap, or depreciating in value. The British government owns no more than twenty homes, which have cost anything up to $125,000 apiece. The rest of the accommodation required to house its considerable task force is rented, and in 1974 the going rate was anything between $220 a month for a one-bedroom apartment considered suitable for a Secretary's secretary, and $750 a month for a four-bedroom house judged adequate for a Counsellor. Other overheads add to the collective cost of living by the Potomac. In 1973 a start was made on a renovation of the Ambassador's residence which was so thorough that two successive incumbents and their families were lodged for a total of twelve months, while the work went on, in the Sheraton Park Hotel, whose charges are not meagre either. Everything about the operation in Washington is inflated. James Callaghan was putting it politely when, on his first visit to the embassy, he breathlessly described it as a Rolls-Royce of a place. Others, inside diplomacy as well as out, can be much ruder than that. But somehow it continues to roll along in style, purring imperviously at all its critics, though the loudest noise most of them hear is the deficit ticking of the clock.

The pattern of these British investments generally throughout the world is haphazard in the extreme. We have acquired our embassies and other missions, the land on which they were built and the appurtenances of their trade, by a combination of power, bounty and straightforward commerce. We came by some of them because they were simply given to us in the first place. Tunis was gifted by the Bey there in 1850, and Addis Ababa by the Emperor Menelik in 1904. We have others on lease, like the residence at The Hague, which really belongs to the Roman Catholic Church but has housed British Ambassadors since 1861. Athens was bought from the widow of Premier Venizelos when she was stuck for ready cash in 1936. Kuala Lumpur is a reach-me-down from the glorious past. It was built by Frank Swettenham when he was Resident-General of the old Straits Settlements, and secured for the Crown by perpetual lease; which at one time its creator seemed likely to enjoy himself, for he went East the year Stanley met Livingstone and yet managed to survive the Second World War. New buildings raised in the less glorious and more recent past in various places may lack history but at least have given the heirs of Barry and Lutyens a chance to show that Britons still have some sort of flair. Basil Spence has left his mark on the chancery in Rome, and Lionel Brett his on the residence in Lagos. Other post-war structures are merely serviceable, like the brick edifice created in Warsaw by the Polish State Building Organization out of the Ministry of Works. Regarded as real estate, however, the sum of British missions abroad would probably set our balance of payments straight if they were to be put on the market, though some are considered much better investments than others. Bangkok stands somewhere near the top of this list. When we were given the land by the King of Thailand in Queen Victoria's day, it was in the middle of empty paddy fields. Now it is bang in the centre of a costly city.

The Treasury, of course, would take a great deal of pleasure, not all of it disinterested, if some of these Foreign Office properties were disposed of. It keeps a very sharp eye on the capital expenditure of the diplomats when a new mission is opened, sometimes putting its foot down quite heavily, from its position in a joint committee, on their own proposals for how they intend to live. It was responsible for painfully reduced standards when a home for the first High Commissioner in Swaziland was built at Mbabane in 1968, though the place still cost £50,000 when all the argument was over. It has been doing what it can for several years now to get the Foreign Office to sell its present residence in Copenhagen and move to less expensive premises. The Ambassador there inhabits what was once a prosperous merchant's house when it was built in the eighteenth century, which we bought at the turn of the twentieth. It is in the middle of the Danish capital and far grander than any British Ambassador's responsibilities today. The Foreign Office resistance to selling (because, as one diplomat put it, 'the money would only go to the Treasury and not into the FCO vote') has so far been successful because, as much as anything, both the British and Danish royal families have let it be known that the idea does not much appeal to them. Almost anything can still be done if royals are involved. The High Commissioner's residence in Singapore suddenly acquired an extra drawing-room in 1972, because the Queen was about to drop anchor there for a couple of days.

The Department of the Environment also has a finger in the diplomatic pie overseas, for one of its responsibilities is the Property Services Agency, which attends to the construction and maintenance work required by all government departments; as the Ministry of Works was until it was transmuted. The agency's engineers have been extremely busy men this past year or two, supervising all the safe areas that have laboriously been built into almost all missions since diplomacy became a prime target of the urban guerrillas and other international bully boys. So hard-pressed were they for time at one embassy that they flew out again before anyone realized that, should the Ambassador and his staff have to work from the self-sealing wing of their building for any length of time, this might be uncomfortable, as the gents from London had quite forgotten to incorporate a lavatory there. Besides its construction work, the agency looks after all the paraphernalia needed to furnish the embassies and diplomatic dwellings abroad. It has a depot in Savile Row where it stores all the pictures that will hang on office and drawing-room walls from Finland to the Falkland Islands: the prints, such as may be bought at Boots, that will do for the secretary girl's flat, the lithographs that will attract casual attention at a Counsellor's cocktail party, the period portraits of old imperial masters that were brought home from some residence when diplomatic relations were severed and never found their way back again. Genuine new masters are not neglected and John Piper is particularly favoured for display to the foreigners, his gently decaying churchyards hanging in the British Information Services office in New York, and a tapestry decorating the embassy in Helsinki. The Property Services Agency mounts its own exhibitions from time to time, so that diplomatic wives may inspect the latest line in curtains they will have to live with on their next postings, the tables they will dine off and the armchairs they will sit on, as designed for the conforming middle classes by G-Plan and Schreiber. Standard issue is standard issue and follows the flag wherever it may fly, even though there are places, like Peru, where the local carpenters can turn out chairs and tables that are just as good and much cheaper than anything consigned (strikes permitting) from the docks at Tilbury. The agency is said to be very sympathetic in dispatching garden furniture on request, and various other implements that can help transform a compound in New Delhi into a corner that is for ever Haywards Heath. It sometimes takes a little time, that's all, and much sweat by the Queen's Messengers; the lawnmower file for Belgrade can become quite ridiculously thick. Distinguishing marks altogether are very few and far between one outpost and the next, if you discount the buildings themselves and the localities in which they are set. In the offices they scarcely exist at all, apart from tiny details which have not always been issued by the agency. At the EEC delegation in Brussels they use ashtrays that look as if they have been commissioned from a sculptor;

the embassy in Teheran appears to have been given a handout by Messrs Rothman.

Although it resists as best it can pressures from the Treasury and other quarters to keep within tighter cost-of-living limits, the Foreign Office conducts its own scrutiny of expenditure in the missions. The Ambassador, in the first place, is responsible for how much money is being spent at his post, and heavy are the sighs arising from many a residence breakfast table when the day comes round for His Excellency to tackle the monthly accounts yet again. More effectively, the FCO has a group of inspectors based in London, who descend on missions in small teams once every three or four years. A weakness of this system is that these officials, being diplomats, are assigned to the job in rotation, just like any other posting, which means that they do not have the chance to visit the same mission twice. But their examinations are extremely thorough, even if they could gain something from continuity. A small embassy can occupy a team for ten full days, while Washington's inspection goes on for a couple of months or so. Every aspect of a mission's life and work is scrutinized and subsequently reviewed in the report bound for Whitehall. 'Totally air-conditioned' – runs a typical commentary on a Far Eastern embassy – 'the Main Block has chilly offices where the staff cannot in any way control the ambient temperatures, open windows, hear the tropical birds sing or listen to the rain fall. All that can be heard is the dull uninterrupted factory-like hiss of the air-conditioned system.' Nor are individual performances overlooked: 'We recommend that Miss X, the present LEIII Commercial Department Receptionist, who tends to be harassed and is occasionally sharp, act in future as a backstop in the Reception Area.'

The head of the mission gets a copy of the report, so that he may contest it with London if he has a mind to, and operate its recommendations if not. Three months later, in any event, a check is made to see if these have been carried out. Always, some of the recommendations are financial. The first thing the inspectors do after they have introduced themselves to the Ambassador and his henchmen, and after they have settled into their hotel (where they stay so that they shall be beyond hypothetical corruption by old friends) is to start questioning everyone on the post about money. For it is on the inspectorate's judgments that the diplomatic allowances overseas are based.

To this end, they are not above sending their own travelling secretaries round the local market place to price the goods, so that they shall not have to rely wholly on information supplied by diplomats and their wives who are feeling sorry for themselves at the time. The inspectors have been known to reduce the allowances here and there. But they are never sent out from London with a brief to cut down on things; only to estimate maximum efficiency. 'Live peaceably with all men,' said one fellow who did the job for a while, 'that's my motto.' This may have been good news from St Paul, but it may occasionally have helped an inspection to get some of its sums badly wrong. It is not so long ago that a First Secretary in Athens, on reaching the end of his term there and discovering that £300 of his allowances were still unspent, blew the lot in one evening on a party which shocked even his Greek guests with its lavishness.

Diplomats complain about the surveillance of their affairs by the Treasury, and they are not wildly enthusiastic about Environment's minor role in deciding where and what they shall build overseas, either. Three years before the Property Services Agency was established, the Duncan Committee had recommended that an Overseas Diplomatic Estate Board should be set up to own property abroad and manage it on commercial lines. It would have been accountable to Parliament like a nationalized industry, and the diplomats would have been its tenants. The idea foundered largely because the Foreign Office opposed it on the astonishing grounds of its public accountability, though Article 42 of the Vienna Convention was also invoked as a tripwire over which, it was argued, the Board would be bound to go sprawling in the matter of diplomatic immunity. Duncan's reasons for proposing such a board was, as much as anything, to propel the diplomats with greater urgency than they had so far shown towards Lord Plowden's earlier recommendation that Britain should take steps to own at least two-thirds of all the staff accommodation abroad, instead of perpetually draining the foreign currency reserves of huge sums in the payment of rents to local landlords. The Property Services Agency, an anaemic substitute for the stillborn Overseas Diplomatic Estate Board, has been unable to exert such pressure. By the start of 1975, we still owned no more than a quarter of overseas diplomatic accommodation, in spite of the fact that by then we were almost half-way through a building and buying programme for diplomatic property which by 1981 – even if prices were to be frozen at 1974 values – will have cost the nation £67 million in ten years.

For all their irritation at meddlesome outsiders, however, and in spite of the thoroughness built into their own system of inspection, diplomats do not on the whole give the impression that budgeting and economy are matters which figure highly in their priorities. Someone inside the Foreign Office told me that 'Diplomats are very bad handlers of money'. This was certainly no imputation of dishonesty and not even, I think, of wilful neglect. It was much more to do with the distinction that exists between the essentially literate and the essentially numerate mind. But it was also a reflection on a way of life in which people are obliged to worry about their personal spending much less than most others. MPs sitting on the Expenditure Committee are almost always left gaping by some new revelation of this blind spot when they have questioned diplomats about their work and their resources. In 1971 it was the discovery that the FCO did not employ a single chartered accountant. 'We are fairly small spenders of money,' an official told the MPs, ' ... it is in a sense purely a housekeeping accounting operation.'[1] When he said that, the FCO was directly responsible for spending £78 million in the year.

That Parliamentary committee spent some time investigating the baffling affair of the Villa Wolkonsky. This is the residence inhabited by the British Ambassador in Rome, a building described by one MP as 'a fascinating place', which it is, quite apart from its architectural merits: the Claudian Aqueduct wanders through its extensive gardens, and during the war it was the local headquarters of the Gestapo. At one time the chancery of the British Embassy was contained in buildings alongside the residence, but was later shifted to a site some distance across the city at Porta Pia where, since 1971, it has been housed in the structure designed by Basil Spence at a cost of £850,000. The committee was particularly interested in our diplomatic presence in Rome because Her Majesty's Government is the owner of much unused land in the city, and at the same time pays heavily in rents each year for the accommodation of its staff. The Villa Wolkonsky stands in the middle of eleven acres.

[1] *Fifth Report from the Expenditure Committee*; *Session 1971–2*, p. 32.

At Porta Pia, apart from the Spence chancery, there are some two acres of empty ground. In 1971, meanwhile, British diplomats and their families were housed in about fifty premises dotted round Rome, which were costing £107,000 a year to rent and maintain.

To the MPs, intent on economy, some fairly obvious rationalizations seemed possible. The Villa Wolkonsky site could be sold and a new residence built on land adjacent to the chancery at Porta Pia. Or both sites could be retained, with the spare ground at each put up for sale or lease. Alternatively, one parcel of unused ground could be sold to outsiders, the other employed by the British for the development of their own staff accommodation, which would mean a greater saving in rent money in the long run. The diplomats saw various impediments to each of these courses. Allowing outsiders to build close to either residence or chancery might, it was suggested, produce security problems. The Roman authorities might very well refuse planning permission, particularly on the antique site of the Villa Wolkonsky. Outsiders, in any case, might not be in the market for any offerings the British cared to make. The notion of His Excellency having to live in a new house at Porta Pia was scorned on the grounds that he would be brought unnaturally close to the neighbourhood washing, hanging out to dry on the balconies of adjacent flats. Yet all talk of such impediments was pure speculation. For a quarter of a century the British had possessed this substantial acreage of unused land in Rome, and in that time not one inquiry had been made of the Roman authorities about possible planning permission, not one decision had been taken by the British about use of the land in future, not even a feasibility study had been made by the Foreign Office itself. The MPs conducted part of their investigations in Rome and at one stage in the proceedings this exchange took place between the chairman, Colonel Sir Harwood Harrison, and the Ambassador, Sir Patrick Hancock:[1]

Chairman: The other alternative, if one is being quite commercial about this, is to sell that land. Have you any idea what the selling price of that land would be?
Ambassador: Do you mean this bit of land here?

---

[1] *Fifth Report from the Expenditure Committee; Session 1971–2,* p. 57.

P

Chairman: Yes.

Ambassador: No, I have no idea.

Chairman: The Foreign Office have never asked you to get it valued?

Ambassador: No.

Chairman: Is anything happening about possibly converting the old chancery at the residence into flats or making some other use of any of these buildings?

Ambassador: Nothing is happening at the moment.

Another MP said, when the committee was interrogating other diplomats in Whitehall, 'If this were a commercial property, the shareholders would be clamouring for the heads of the officials in charge.' Three years later, a feasibility study had been made, and inquiries had produced a mixed response from the Roman authorities. In the light of which the Foreign Office confessed that it was 'faced with a serious dilemma in deciding our best course of action for the future'.[1]

By then, inquisitive Parliamentarians had turned up the even more remarkable case of the Villa Said. This was a new residence for the British Ambassador to the Organization for Economic Co-operation and Development in Paris, situated in the Avenue Foch, not far from the Arc de Triomphe. The British delegation to the OECD in the French capital is a small one, but important enough to be led by a Grade 3 diplomat, who for several years lived in an apartment on the Avenue Victor Hugo, in the same part of the city. Fairly soon after taking up his post in 1971, however, a new Ambassador, Mr Francis Gallagher, complained that the level of noise surrounding his residence had become impossible to live with; moreover, tenancy agreements in the building had altered, and what had been dwellings near the ambassadorial apartment were gradually changing hands and becoming offices. The FCO agreed with him that another residence must be found as soon as possible. The newly constituted Property Services Agency set to work, and by March 1973 had found the Villa Said. The Ambassador by this time was describing his plight in the Avenue Victor Hugo as 'desperately urgent'[2] and the PSA responded by getting a local archi-

[1] *Eighth Report from the Expenditure Committee; Session 1974–5*, p. 10.
[2] Ibid., p. 45.

tect, a Frenchman who had done much work for the British government in Paris over the previous twenty years, to make a survey. On the basis of his report, the Villa Said was bought three months later for £235,480 and the Foreign Office prepared to turn in its tenancy in the Avenue Victor Hugo, which had been costing £4,500 a year in rent.

It was seen at the outset that, on top of the purchase price, some £72,000 would have to be spent on the villa, to convert it to ambassadorial requirements. The actual bill, however, eventually came to £146,000 and a number of things were responsible for the difference, quite apart from economic inflation. Not only had the French architect seriously underestimated the general dilapidation of the property, which necessitated unexpected repairs to stonework, plasterwork, roofing and floors, but he had also misplaced a decimal point in calculating Value Added Tax, working it out at 1·76 per cent instead of 17·6 per cent, an error that no one in the Property Services Agency or the British delegation in Paris spotted, and which cost the British taxpayer some £9,000 more than anticipated. The same officials overlooked the architect's failure to provide for cooking equipment and light fittings. The original estimate was knocked even further sideways because the Ambassador came up with his own ideas for changes between March 1973, shortly before the purchasing contract for the villa was signed, and the following November, five months after signature. Improvements were made to a servant's flat; a second servery and a food lift were introduced; decorations were gingered up to 'the necessary representational quality' even after decorations had already been settled; a completely new heating system was installed to serve the main residence of five bedrooms, three bathrooms, three reception rooms and a study, as well as the staff accommodation. All that amounted to another £20,000, which might have been more had the Ambassador's wishes been fully satisfied. He asked for, but was not allowed by some brave soul somewhere along the line, a marble floor for the gallery, tiling on the terrace at the front of the second floor, and extra obscured glazing in the annexe—all of it after the contract had been signed, when he had already been told, before signature, that he could not have yet another bathroom on the second floor. In this whole extraordinary business, maybe the most remarkable thing is that no suggestion was made in any quarter that

British heads should roll for incompetence, or for spending the taxpayer's money with the prodigality of a drunken sailor. As for the French connection, far from the architect's services being instantly terminated, his future was evidently still in the balance some eighteen months later. 'You are not going to employ him again?' asked an MP in March 1975. 'There is', said a man from the Agency, 'a large question mark over him at the moment.'[1] The committee's final, maybe dumbfounded comment on the affair was 'We hope this case is exceptional'.

Almost certainly it is exceptional, though the same report detailed two other property deals, in Johannesburg and Geneva, which bore similar marks of poorly co-ordinated activity by the officials concerned. As in the cases of Rome and Paris, these seem to have been abetted by an attitude of mind that would have been more proper in the heyday of British rule overseas. The attitude is still strong enough in some areas of British diplomacy to provoke MPs in 1975 to the warning that 'Considerations of prestige alone should not be decisive, and in our present economic situation the United Kingdom should not seek as a matter of course to compete on equal terms with the wealthiest nations.'[2] In that year it was exceptional to find a diplomat who did not applaud the prospect of Britain's representation abroad contracting to a more realistic size, and being dimmed to a more sober display. People in London would indicate on the staff list of almost any embassy they knew personally, just which jobs could be shorn without a significant loss of efficiency. People overseas would sigh heavily as they recounted the more ostentatious forms of representation diplomacy still thrust upon them. Everyone was of the opinion that British high commissions in the old imperial lands were overstaffed and sometimes far too grand for their own good. Yet the outsider was left with a feeling that this highly responsible chorus was sometimes paying no more than lip service to what it did not genuinely believe; or that perhaps it believed genuinely enough until it observed a conflict with self-interest, at which point it was left stammering with indecision. Ever since the Plowden Report of 1964, there has been regular talk of reducing Britain's diplomatic manifestations abroad in keeping with the nation's

[1] Ibid., p. 59.
[2] Ibid., p. xv.

real position in the world. Reductions have indeed taken place, but they appear to have happened rather more in the diplomats' own good time than might have been expected in the circumstances. In 1969, the Duncan Committee proposed that, with very few exceptions, British missions outside the Area of Concentration should be manned by no more than three officers whose homes were in the United Kingdom. By the beginning of 1975, when there were 120 full British embassies and high commissions spread around the globe, as well as 200-odd other posts of varying size, no more than a dozen embassies had been reduced to the three-man target set by Duncan.

9 Colonies Surrounded by Natives

There is a way of life attached to a diplomatic mission unlike any other devised by man. It has something in common with the life of the journalist abroad in that it is very difficult for anyone to say with certainty which parts of it are work and which are play, for there are times in the occupations of both diplomat and foreign correspondent when the two are inextricably mixed. Severe and highly professional strains are built into it, disguised by activities which others regard as clear evidence of the grossest self-indulgence. But, unlike journalism, diplomacy is formal and hierarchical in the extreme. Every member of a mission knows his place in an order of precedence and is acutely aware of just when and where and how he must defer (sometimes quite humbly) to another human being, and whom he may look straight in the eye at all times, as though distinctions of rank had never been thought of. There is a degree of responsibility carried by every diplomat which is also exceptional, and the higher up the order of precedence a man stands, the greater this burden tends to be. A Third Secretary might just get away with an offhand or careless remark at a cocktail party that, coming from an Ambassador, could involve his government in the most severe embarrassment. Foreigners, as all mankind knows, are a peculiar lot. Living in the middle of them for years on end turns diplomats into a fairly rum collection, too. Not wishing to offend their hosts, which is part of their profession, they frequently become apologists for them, to the irritation of their compatriots at home. At the same time they are apt, like many expatriates, to exaggerate their own national idiosyncrasies in front of the foreigners; and while this is partly because they wish to satisfy an expectation they assume the foreigners have, it is also to reassure themselves about their own true identity. They are not, by and large, simple folk. If they have not been born with a calculating streak, they rapidly acquire it in their way of life. If they have a patron god he should be Janus, who looked both ways at once and supervised the doorways of the world.

A mission is a colony surrounded by natives, some of whom it employs, while the rest are usually kept at bay as much as possible, except for those of the influential caste with whom it is necessary to treat for survival and for reasons which justify the diplomatic existence. As such, a diplomatic mission must at all times be careful of its collective conduct, and injunctions by authority about behaviour in front of the natives are rather remarkable, given that they are addressed to very sophisticated adults and not to unpractised children. One of the formative documents in the career of anyone belonging to the British Foreign Office is the *Handbook on Diplomatic Life Abroad*. It was first composed many years ago by Sir Marcus Cheke, sometime Minister to the Vatican, who offered the inspiring advice that funerals presented admirable opportunities for making contact with influential foreigners. This observation commended itself little to Ernest Bevin after some Westminster hearty inquired whether he had been to any good burials lately. Cheke's tone of voice fell into disrepute some time back and the handbook has gone through two less ponderous editions by different authors since his day. It mostly concerns itself with the excruciating niceties of diplomatic etiquette that will operate almost solely within the profession. But it also spends time considering mundane topics like grumbling about the locals, non-involvement in local politics, and avoidance of those sharp customers who run black markets in duty-free beverages; as well as the bracing British virtues of Loyalty and Team Spirit.

There are places where a British mission feels not only surrounded, but as remote and isolated as any garrison in the early outposts of the Victorian Empire; like Mogadishu, where apples in 1975 cost 75 pence apiece and fresh food generally is hard to come by unless it has been caught in the sea, slaughtered by a butcher or laid by a hen. There are posts as hazardous as the most frightful places in Ulster, like Beirut during its civil war of 1975–6, and like Aden a few years earlier, when the insurance companies charged twice their normal diplomatic premiums. There are places where gunfire is never heard but where life in the mission is beleaguered to an extent that leaves its mark on people for a long time after. This is still the case in Moscow, even in the comparative warmth of détente. There are some peculiarities of the Soviet system that are just a damned nuisance to foreigners, like the absence of telephone directories, which are classified documents. But there are other things which produce perpetual strain in any outsider living there for any length of time. It is some years now since a robustly heterosexual member of the British embassy woke up after a party to find himself lying naked on a bed several miles away, alongside another naked man, both their bodies blotchy with love bites: but in the first six months of 1975, a dozen attempts at sexual blackmail were made on foreign diplomats in the city. When the embassy typists go off to Leningrad or Kiev for a weekend, they travel like old-fashioned nuns, in pairs, chaperoning each other for a security which has nothing to do with the possibility of rape or other violence. When someone parks his car he does so most carefully, for the policeman with a parking ticket may be the thin end of an official wedge bent on prising information from the diplomat. When a First Secretary invites an academic home to supper, to talk about a possible lecture and study tour of Britain, the invitation is invariably refused. 'What do you want me to do, Mr X,' asks the Russian, 'visit Britain officially or see you in your home?' When any object has broken down, it is never allowed back into the embassy again; there is no question of having it repaired locally, just in case the KGB has invented a bugging device which defies normal methods of detection. The first thing the visitor there spots, after he has been amiably saluted into the forecourt by the militiaman on the gate, is the *Gibraltar and Fulham Diocesan Gazette for the Continental Churchman*, stacked on a table just inside the door. The second thing is the closed-circuit television monitor where the security guards sit, an oblique reminder that almost all walls in the building have ears, as in all the flats and houses where the diplomats live. It doesn't help to know that Soviet diplomats in London are in much the same crazy state. When people have served in Moscow, they find that for quite a while afterwards they are still filtering everything they want to say before opening their mouths, to a degree they do not experience in any other post. People who have served in both places say that Belgrade under Tito's form of Communism is a holiday camp by comparison.

It is the laager mentality, inevitable to some degree in every diplomatic mission abroad, that produces a variety of recreations which are distinctly meant to exclude the foreigners. In Moscow they play a winter game of their own invention called broomsky, with a bouncy ball and sawn-off hockey sticks, six-a-side upon the frozen embassy tennis courts; and in summer they generally manage a cricket fixture with the British Embassy in Helsinki. All but the tiniest missions have their own social clubs, where the lower orders of British diplomacy – the Executive classes, the security guards, the communications men and the secretaries – do their own thing, uninhibited by the sometimes stifling habit of the chanceries. In Belgrade, the Embassy Club holds dances every quarter, runs a darts league (with two tickets to London as first prize) and, in its bar, serves bread and cheese with the local beer and the imported Whitbread; and the diplomatic plebs muster a football team, which the Head of Chancery occasionally cheers on like a housemaster from the touchlines. The lingering caste system of the profession is underlined in Washington, where the social club's members caustically style themselves The Diplonots. It is extended to even lower orders of society elsewhere. Down in the Persian Gulf, the visitor from home may enjoy a splendid whiff of nostalgia from the productions of the Kuwait Players, where the amateur dramatics of the British and Americans fluctuate between *Julius Caesar* and *Arsenic and Old Lace*, in which the British Ambassador's wife may appear as leading lady. The Embassy's Amenities Club, however, is the regular playground of the other ranks, as in Belgrade, and it has its own astringent sense of who's who. The staff of the British Council in Kuwait are very welcome to use it, provided they are thoroughly British; the council's own underlings there, who tend to originate in Pakistan, Iraq or Palestine, have been excluded by the vote of people ranked at Grades 9 and 10 in the British Diplomatic Service.

There is a strangeness in all foreign places, quite separate from anything decreed by local politics, with which the diplomats must live and to which they must accommodate themselves in some way. There is a formality in Russians which doubtless springs from Soviet organization and which may mean that when an appointment has been arranged, the diplomat finds his opposite number awaiting him by the street door of the state office concerned. But there are also habits essentially Russian rather than Soviet, like the custom of eating a buffet supper at 5 o'clock immediately after leaving work. South Americans, on the other hand, show little appetite for any solid food in the evening until midnight is near. If you throw a party, the Finns will probably show up five minutes before opening time, while the Swedes will walk up and down outside, glancing at their watches every ten seconds until the appointed hour precisely, when they will make a general rush for the door. Africans may turn up an hour and a half late, or not come at all. The British peculiarity is to circulate the port with cigars round the men after dinner, the women obediently taking themselves out of earshot, as in homely days gone by. Arabs like to drink for a couple of hours, Koranic injunctions notwithstanding, then eat a large supper and go straight off to bed.

Alimentary considerations have to be borne in mind constantly in a profession which spends so much of its time eating and drinking on a bountiful official scale. But there are subtler customs that must be well understood by the residential outsiders in the interests of agreeable international relations. A thumping extrovert, however winning, will probably do more harm than good in Arab society, which does not take kindly to the backslapping approach. Endless patience is the cardinal rule here, for all conversations are pursued to exhaustion and business must not be mentioned until the introductory circumlocutions and the coffee served with them are finished. It is somewhat the same in Thailand, where you never ask anyone a point-blank question, but engage him in a long talk, in the course of which all will, with luck, be revealed. Many a stripling diplomat from the West has come to grief during his first weeks in Bangkok, because he ignorantly patted a child on the head, or sat cross-legged with one foot pointing at the person with whom he was conversing; both of which are awful solecisms in the local culture. The trouble is, say the diplomats, that before you go out to foreign parts for the first time, no one at headquarters ever briefs you about the nuances of correct behaviour among the ordinary people you may meet, although much wordage is lavished upon the most trivial details of etiquette in the diplomatic community. A fairly senior man who has come to Kuwait after experience in Nairobi can find himself baffled by all the sidelong glances he seems to attract until, after a few days, his Ambassador takes him aside and points out that the bare legs and shorts which were thought rather becoming in East Africa really won't do on the Persian Gulf. Even an Ambassador can come unstuck if he isn't careful and ready to take advice on the spot, particularly when something so complex and so alien to British nature as the Japanese concept of courtesy is concerned. Several years ago a British airliner crashed into Mount Fujiyama and the mayor of a village at the foot of the mountain performed prodigies in organizing a rescue operation which, in the end, meant bringing down a lot of bodies. The British Ambassador in Tokyo, Sir Francis Rundall, who had not long been at the post, decided that when the mess had been cleared up he ought to visit the village and thank the mayor for all his efforts. Ah, no, said his Head of Chancery, who had been in Japan for some years. The visit would be a capital idea, but it should be made to *apologize* to the mayor for all the trouble he had been caused. So His Excellency went with three aides, all toffed up in their diplomatic braid aboard the ambassadorial Rolls, to present to the mayor a great scroll of parchment with a very civil expression of regret from Her Majesty's Government, in Japanese script. This went down so well that there was nation-wide coverage in the newspapers to the effect that the British were surprisingly sensitive people after all. That is, alas, not always the case. There are embassies where the British diplomats have little to do with the populace except in a master-servant, a shopkeeper-customer relationship, and where they hold themselves aloof even from those they employ in the mission; or condescend to them, which can be even worse. A young man, a local graduate, who had been in such a position for years, in spite of which an enthusiasm for Britain remained unspoilt, confessed something about his employers that would have been less surprising in an imperial age. 'They treat us lightly,' he said. At that mission a senior man reckoned there wasn't any need to speak the local language 'unless you want to find out what the taxi driver thinks', which he appeared to regard as unimportant.

The home comforts enjoyed by the diplomats once their work is done mitigate many of the nuisances and the jarring peculiarities of existence abroad. There are missions where the economic gap between the general run of local society and the diplomatic community is so wide that even junior diplomats are living in much the same style as the upper middle classes of London a century ago. The British tend to complain that their accommodation and other domestic endowments compare unfavourably with those provided for their American counterparts, but they are all probably living in more comfort than they do when based in Whitehall, much better provided for than people of comparable social and professional levels who never leave the United Kingdom. They may be heard from time to time complaining, or at least hinting, what a frightful bore it is, having to cope with the servant problem; implying that a remaining attraction of dear old England is that there such problems now virtually no longer exist. It is surprising how infrequently, when they speak of the diplomatic life abroad, they mention what might have been thought an outstanding attraction of the job: the opportunity to visit places most people dream of seeing but never reach, to wallow in a different culture. Some diplomats approach strange places with enormous zest even after decades in their profession; but far more seem to have their minds on other things after a single foreign posting. This apparently tepid response to what should be thrilling may sometimes be due to the hazy boundaries in diplomacy between what is work and what is sheer fun and games. An experienced man in the Brussels embassy told me that for relaxation he liked to get out of the city at weekends and go boar-hunting: only later in the conversation, and as an unconnected remark about his work, did he mention that he had spent a lot of time in the previous few months out at the battlefield of Waterloo, officially concerned with the establishment of a Wellington museum there. Not that every mission offers opportunities for the official tourist. In the smallest posts, which are often situated in the least congenial places, the chief relaxation is likely to be steady drinking, to compensate for the comparative isolation and lack of other interests. This pushes up the already high incidence of liver complaints among diplomats as a whole. Measurements recently have shown that, at the level of Counsellor and above, 25 per cent of the people in the Diplomatic Service drink enough to damage their livers, whereas Home civil servants in the same grades produce a figure of only 15·5 per cent.

Everywhere produces a certain strain deriving from alienation and other factors, which is reflected in the number of diplomatic marriages that come to grief—about half as many again as in the Home Civil Service. The strain seems to fall heaviest on the wives of diplomats, judging by the numbers who are shipped home on the verge of nervous breakdowns. It is scarcely surprising that when a man is interviewed by the Personnel Department in London before he goes on his first foreign posting after marriage, his wife is invited along, too. As in the case of the parson and the general medical practitioner, diplomatic couplings involve the woman in the man's work much more than in other walks of life. She is required to be a hostess in what are, to greater or lesser degree, official entertainments mounted on behalf of the government or the Crown; and the higher up the diplomatic scale the household goes, the nearer a full-time occupation that can be. She is also part of an official presence in a foreign land, a representative of her own nation who is publicly displayed as such from time to time. The FCO thus has a distinct and understandable interest in the sort of person she is. 'It would hardly do', as a man from Personnel put it, 'to send some lady with her husband out to an Arab post, if she's likely to swoon at the prospect of kissing an Emir's hand.' A great number of wives resent this scrutiny, as they resent the fact that their characteristics and capacities are noted each year on the personal report filed on their husbands. Their bitterness is perhaps more a reflection on several years of diplomatic drudgery and its many other domestic inconveniences: a failure to recall that at the start, when they were told what marriage to a diplomat involved, the handicaps seemed slight compared with the attractions of a life promising much more prestige, romance and excitement than wedlock shared with a solicitor or a diligent chap from the Ministry of Agriculture, Food and Fisheries, who might take them no farther than Fleetwood, or introduce them to anything more stimulating than the eradication of swine fever in Sussex. Not all diplomatic wives, of course, are British by birth. A high proportion—a third is the usual estimate—were foreigners when they first met their husbands.

There was a time when wives were expected to do nothing but act as hostesses and, dressed crisply for the occasion (complete with hat and gloves), decorate various public functions with their husbands. They were probably bullied much more by the Ambassador's wife than ever their husbands were by His

Excellency, dragooned—without option—into the mulling of strawberries for the Queen's Birthday Party, and into whatever causes Her Ladyship believed best suited to her own public image. Not obliged, or even expected, to perform domestic chores, they filled in the hours between breakfast, the set luncheon and the cocktail party with coffee mornings, sewing bees and afternoon teas. Such times have not completely departed, but they have changed enough for many wives to take jobs when posted abroad, so long as they have secured the head of mission's approval first. Sometimes this is no more than secretarial work within the mission itself or over at the British Council, if that body happens to have an office in the city. But a lot of younger wives are professionally qualified as their predecessors rarely were, and they are sometimes able to pursue their professions in foreign parts. This is not always a straightforward business, for diplomatic immunity from various civil laws, the extent of which differs from place to place, frequently doesn't cover such a situation. The British Home Office is almost exceptional in allowing the wives of foreign diplomats posted to London to take up any work they are able to obtain. The American State Department takes a much more hard-nosed view of things. A work permit is a work permit is a work permit in Washington, and an extremely difficult thing to acquire, whatever your un-American activity may be.

There are other strains for any diplomatic wife, and they are purely domestic. However agreeable the material comforts of your home, the fact is that you are obliged to uproot yourself at regular intervals and start putting the thing together again, from scratch, every time you go abroad. Curious local circumstances occasionally mean that diplomatic families hop from one home to another in the course of the same posting—as many as five times in one recorded instance. The norm of one dwelling per posting makes life difficult enough. The equipment provided by the government is all splendid (Property Services Agency mattresses are said to be particularly comfortable) but families are encouraged to bring as many of their own possessions, including small items of furniture, as their travelling allowances permit, in order to make the house or apartment recognizably theirs and not just another showpiece of British interior decoration. Possessions get smashed or even pilfered in transit, not to mention the damage that guests and servants can cause *in situ.* Some diplomats estimate that three foreign postings are approximately as harmful as one fire in this respect. The odd thing is that (as any female diplomatic officer will tell you), far from being careful in their own use of government property, diplomats generally leave a terrible mess behind them when they return to England, on the blithe assumption that some-body else will clean the place up before their successors move in. Outside the residence itself, somebody frequently doesn't.

The biggest strain of all falls on the wives who are mothers as well. It is bad enough when they are lucky enough to have their children with them, when they have to transfer their energies (in spite of the nanny) from the disorders of the nursery to the rituals of diplomatic representation within the same day. But that relationship too often ends soon after the child passes the infant stage; almost always by the time it is ready for secondary education. There are very few places in the world where a diplomatic child can be educated to standards regarded as minimally acceptable in the United Kingdom. More often than not, they are found only where American representation – diplomatic, commercial or military – is heavy, for such Ameri-can colonies often create their own schools and the British are usually welcome to share them. The British community itself is now large enough in Brussels to run a school system of its own there, which it does with grants from industry but none from the government. Elsewhere education is difficult, and the essen-tial problem would not be much relieved if it were less so; continuity is impossible when parental life is lived in three-yearly postings. This is why some 1,800 children of diplomats are lodged in the boarding schools of Great Britain, seeing their parents, whether they are at home or abroad, only during the school holidays. And while some of the parents are doubtless happy to be rid of their offspring for the same obscure reasons that have always provided the so-called public school system of the British with pupils, there will be just as many for whom the division of the family in this way is quite the most awful thing about diplomacy. It marks the children, too. As the Welfare people in the FCO are well aware, there is a disconcerting rate of anguished behaviour by the adolescent sons and daughters of diplomats, up to and including attempted suicide.

So great is the sense of collective and special identity among these diplomatic women that they are very well organized into a Diplomatic Service Wives Association, whose function is thought important enough for the FCO to provide it with office accommodation in Whitehall. It exists to help morale, to sort out personal problems, to exert pressure on the Office, to offer wives a platform on which they may speak their minds (up to a point) in a way generally impossible for women coated with the suffocating inhibitions of their husbands' trade. This last function is discharged once a quarter in a *Newsletter*, among articles about the care of diplomatic pets, travelogues from far-away places, recipes for whisky mincemeat and other titbits, and descriptions of the London wives' outing to Dorneywood and Eton. The preoccupations of the wives are clearly stated in one issue after another. 'I must soon face up to the problem,' writes someone from Colombo, 'of where to send a 12-year-old for a 10-day half-term in the autumn. I think I am going to throw it back at the school first, and ask if they can't run a camp for those whose parents are overseas.' Another wife ends her piece, 'A final warning: rest assured that with the greatest care and the best will in the world, you may still choose the wrong school, and even if you haven't, your child may turn round one day and say you have. Parents, alas, rarely win!' There is a potted report of a talk to the wives by the Chief Inspector of the FCO, referring to what 'although described as secondary in the Inspectorate's formal terms of reference, is probably of prime interest to us all: the calculation of the overseas allowances'. There is guidance on what to do if the British police stop your car and invite you to take the breathalyser test. Under the heading 'The Need For United Feminine Influence', which is a quotation from *The Times*, there is a short account of a confer-ence organized by the British Federation of University Women, which conveys the impression that there may be a flicker of women's lib illuminating the diplomatic hearths of the British. The advertisements carried by the *Newsletter* are another pointer to priorities, for they offer services which bring regular and handsome rewards in a fruitful marketplace. 'Schooling Problems?' asks the Gabbitas-Thring Educational Trust inside the front cover; echoed by 'Domestic Staff Problems?' from Nash Personnel Services on the back. In between come the likes of Country Cousins and Emergency Mothers, Wild Acres Quarantine Kennels, half a dozen packers, removers and insurers, Louis Silverblatt's Furs of Fine Quality, John Lewington's Properties of Quality in West Cornwall, the Aquila Press and its Engraved and Die-Stamped Stationery, the Design Centre and its offer of 10 per cent discounts to all members of the Diplomatic Service Association who purchase gifts in its Souvenir Shop.

In no area do the wives fulfil their unsalaried obligations to diplomacy more than in the sphere of diplomatic entertainment. Nor is there any part of the diplomat's professional duties which provokes as much scorn in outsiders, who can only imagine what a tippling and a gorging goes on in the name of détente, negotiation and showing the flag; and believe it all to be highly wasteful anyway. Diplomats are rarely as candid as the former Permanent Under Secretary who remarked that[1]

> The stay-at-home British taxpayer is apt to think with envy
> —and even with indignation, since he pays for it—of the
> British diplomatic representative's life as one of perpetual
> carousing at groaning boards. And he is not so very wide
> of the mark so far as representational duties are concerned.

Like everything else about diplomacy, things vary from post to post, between one country and another. In Belgrade, the Ambassador, the Counsellor who is his No 2, the Head of Chancery and the Defence Attaché will each probably spend three or four nights of the week at either dinner or cocktail parties given by Yugoslavs or by other embassies in the city. About once a month they and their wives will be hosts at separate dinner parties of their own, they will throw one large cocktail party apiece and they will each organize maybe four smaller convivial gatherings. At a minor post like Mogadishu, the combined attendance of the three British diplomats will probably not average more than a couple of official entertainments a week of any description. Sometimes such events sweep up a wide range of contacts whose brains may be picked for different pieces of information, or whose senses may be gratified to the diplomat's subsequent advantage; but few places afford such generous opportunities as Washington, which abounds in Congressmen, journalists, academics and other useful quarry

[1] Strang, p. 120.

Q

who are ready and willing to gossip about this and that at the drop of a copperplated invitation card. At some places, however, the partygoing occurs almost wholly within the diplomatic circle. The same faces with similar drinks trickling aboard, the same small talk and the same practised laughter, decorate a circuit of tables which before long become tediously familiar to those bidden to sit there. The same voices are directed at the same ears as servants circulate the cocktails and the dainties, and the same people wish they could take the weight off their poor feet as the duty-free tobacco smoke stains the same living rooms or drifts across the same patios for the umpteenth time that year. The parties are mixed where communication is open and where the diplomatic appetite is to learn as well as to digest. Diplomatic incest flourishes where the lines are bad or where the will is weak. It is generally much easier to share secondhand news with another diplomat than to root it out for yourself by soliciting the acquaintance of someone well outside the diplomatic circuit, whose government may not take too kindly to the idea anyway. 'Did you notice', says the Briton casually to the German at his elbow, 'the line-up of bigshots when Aeroflot flew in yesterday? Must have been expecting someone important.' 'Well, whoever he was,' says the man from Bonn, his eyes dawdling carefully round the room, 'he didn't show up.' By such transactions, do a great number of diplomatic entertainment allowances justify themselves.

It was Lord Palmerston who declared that dining is the soul of diplomacy, and it was Mr Muggeridge who observed that diplomats, like cows, eat standing up. Both quips are perfectly valid, the second never more so than when diplomats ruminate through each other's national days. There was a time when the number of sovereign states on earth was infinitely smaller than it is now, and decent intervals stood between each of these occasions and its nearest neighbour, thus allowing the diplomatic corps in any capital city to ponder the impending event's significance properly, and the intestines a small convalescence after the previous bombardment of food and drink. But now there is scarcely a day in the year when some nation is not celebrating its independence, its revolution, its reunification or some other auspicious moment in its history. The diplomatic community in London spreads itself around no fewer than 411 such annual events, and on some days a fellow laden with particularly heavy representational duties can find himself gliding in and out of three or four different parties in the course of a few hours. By and by, the less resilient begin to wonder why on earth this profession of theirs requires so much internecine gluttony and inebriation, particularly as the national day is primarily celebrated at any embassy so that its own people—inside and outside diplomacy—may gather and enjoy their native peculiarities in a strange land. The answer the British and some other Europeans give themselves is that they would joyfully abandon this non-stop circus if only diplomats from countries less absorbed in the world's work would allow them to; some of whom, they imply, would have very little to occupy themselves with if it were not for the perpetual diplomatic fling. Then these Europeans sigh, and prepare to face the next bout of gormandizing, knowing that it will inform them of nothing more certainly than the law of diminishing returns.

For the British, the Queen's Birthday Party on June 11th is the appointed feast. On that day, lawns throughout the world are (weather permitting) aswirl with expatriates and diplomatic representatives as Her Britannic Majesty's Ambassadors mount the best imitation they can manage of a Buckingham Palace garden party. Unlike the Queen at home, however, they would be a bit startled if everyone they invited actually turned up; a mission which has laboriously dispatched 4,000 gilt-edged cards weeks in advance does not bank on having to cater for more than 1,500 on the day. There are purely local hazards built into the Queen's Birthday Party, quite apart from the catastrophe that could befall any of them should the victuals run out through an excess of patriotism by the local British community. After much experience as an Ambassador, Sir Douglas Busk warned that 'so long as these parties continue, the hosts will be wise to remove all portable objects of value from any room to which guests may gain access and lock the doors of the rest. It is unwise to put too much faith in honesty, even at the most distinguished capitals and in the most affluent society.'[1] High Commissioners in Nairobi some years ago decided that, although it would be splendid to engage the local Police Band to entertain the guests to slices of *The King and I* and *No, No Nanette*, as well as the British and Kenyan national anthems, it was more

[1] Busk, p. 32.

prudent to book the somewhat less accomplished Prison Band instead, as President Kenyatta was always liable to pre-empt the constabulary musicians at the last moment, thus reducing the harmony of the British celebration at a beat. Now and then, a Queen's Birthday Party is enlivened by some diversion unwittingly provided by a guest. In Moscow, the buffet was once garnished with a hundredweight of fresh strawberries, specially flown in from London for the occasion and appetizingly displayed in several bowls among other food by the time the guests arrived. One of these was the Ambassador of some impoverished land in the Third World, who proceeded to help himself to fruit from each bowl until he had a large plate piled high with them. He then moved on to a dish which apparently contained clotted cream, and ladled an unhealthy amount of that on top of the strawberries: only it was not cream, but a cheese sauce; and the British diplomats, who had blankly observed His Excellency's greed, gladly watched the wretched man's attempts to maintain chitchat in the next quarter of an hour, while masticating the prodigiously awful mess on his plate.[1]

In large posts, there are enough servants attached to the combined British diplomatic households to lackey on this occasion. In smaller places, the wives are mustered, together with the semi-detached ladies of the local British community, to handle the preparations. Even in a purely consular mission like Mombasa, where 600 invitations to celebrate the Queen's birthday will bring maybe 400 people into the consul's waterfront garden, this involves much hard labour. Some poor woman from the Ladies' Committee, having volunteered to stuff 300 eggs beforehand, discovers that in practice this amounts to 600 stuffings – and swears afterwards that loyal obedience will not carry her thus far again. The same insurgent feelings, dutifully muffled, are common among many diplomatic wives who, in their various ranks and stations, are more responsible than any of their husbands for managing the whole intimidating range of entertainment, from the jolly dignity of the Queen's Birthday Party down to the quiet and unofficial supper when

[1] In 1976, the Foreign Office instructed heads of mission abroad to give a lunchtime *vin d'honneur* for no more than 200 people. It was expected that, in most cases, this would cut the costs by half. It would probably mean that members of the local British communities would no longer be invited to the official festivity.

a visiting British writer blows in. Making sure that the food and drink come up to scratch is quite the least taxing part of it. Seeing to it that the flowers are blooming on the bureau top, that the cutlery, the crockery and the glasses are immaculate, and that the domestic staff have arranged the furniture just so, is no great penance either. It is in handling the guests properly that the severest test comes.

Many a diplomatic wife, on her first posting abroad, needs all the guidance the Foreign Office can give her (and it is generous) on how not to upset her guests unwittingly, or even to induce an indulgent smile at the Britannic image's expense. She arrives on station with her mind ajuggle with all the correct forms of address she must remember to use. Does she gaily inform her French neighbour that she and her spouse will be dining with the de Chateaubriands next week, or would that be as revealingly crass as to hint that the of Harrows were droppin' by that evening? Yet even that problem will not nag her to the end of her husband's career so much as the everlasting and perpetually treacherous permutations of *placement*. Just as lawyers mouth Latin to obscure some of their purposes from the rest of us, so diplomats relish an abnormal amount of French, as if to remind everyone that their profession has a plane and a dashing style all its own. Of these smatterings, *placement* has been quite the most durable through recent years which have seen off many others. It means precedence at table, and any diplomat whose wife cannot get that right whenever they entertain may as well seek other employment without delay. It has been known for someone to turn over his plate at a dinner party and refuse every course at the meal, because he has felt that the seating arrangements insulted either himself or his country. In such society, it is mighty important to know precisely who is who, and to be sure that he is put exactly in his place, either above or below the salt.

The fundamental rule is that the right-hand side of the host and hostess is a more honoured place than the left, the most highly esteemed female guest sitting on the host's right and the most important male on the hostess's. After that, instruction in precedence is apt to sound like a review of some primitive tribal gathering patronized by missionaries. Number Three Lady is next to Number One Gentleman (on the hostess's right), while Number Four Lady is alongside Number Two Gentleman (on

Herself's left); and so on. The difficulty comes in deciding who shall occupy these positions. For the diplomatic meal does not always consist entirely of figures with unmistakable positions in a hierarchy. It is bad enough having to work out whether a Second Secretary from the Ruritanian embassy outranks his opposite number from the Hydropotamian Ministry of External Affairs. It is much worse when you must make up your mind whether to avoid offending Lord Pompous Ass (a visiting magnate with much pull in Downing Street) at the risk of upsetting Senator Hirem N. Firem Jr (who carries overweight on the Senate Foreign Relations Committee in Washington). Collect three or four problems of that magnitude under the same roof and you are in the predicament of the Ambassador's wife who consulted her husband's protocol expert about her proposed arrangement for the next dinner at the residence. 'Madam,' he said, 'I can only advise you not to give that particular dinner party.'

Nor is the problem of *placement* confined to hypersensitivity about rank. It embraces all the considerations that arise at any intelligently arranged dinner table – the separation of husbands and wives, of gasbags and introverts, of people who patently would find nothing in common if they were to sit together at a Last Supper. The well-drilled diplomatic hostess sorts these things out with a sweetened charm that very often exceeds anything her husband can turn on in his chancery or at the negotiating table. Many an unsuspecting guest has been deftly downgraded over the *caneton* and the *soufflé* because the lady of the house, seizing his arm at the dining-room entrance with a pressure suggesting that there just might be some undiplomatic pact between them, has told him she badly needs his Urdu strategically placed at the bottom end of her table. New diplomatic wives have to acquire such ploys by practice. They come out from London, wondering which of the Nine Table Arrangements, regularized by tradition, they will have to manage first. Will it be that relatively easy Table A, laid for a round dozen, at which women will sit only in their own right, and not as wives? Or will it be tricky Table D, or equally awkward Table E, for eight guests, a number that is to be steered clear of whenever possible? Ten is a figure to watch, too, for that is the maximum number that one servant can cope with if he is to keep the meal running like clockwork; a process that is frequently aided by the concealment of an electric button under the carpet within footsie range of the hostess, by means of which the man's synchronized interventions have done the British diplomatic reputation a power of good in more than one impressionable quarter of the globe. The diplomatic wife soon discovers that such conundrums as these are not often to be solved by a crafty resort to several small tables, so that a party of twenty-four may be deployed at six different points of the room. Connoisseurs of *placement* will take note of which table is on whose right or left; though it is conceded in some diplomatic quarters that sticklers can occasionally be foxed by jumbling people so haphazardly that the querulous can for weeks afterwards still be trying to work out the principle adopted. Only innocents wonder why this should not be the starting point in diplomatic dining, instead of a reluctant rearguard action. And only Foreign Office wives can properly appreciate the thought that, instead of grappling with the permutations of *placement*, they might conceivably have done better to seek their fortunes on the football pools.

Placement, however, is merely the crumbs under the table of protocol, which is to diplomacy what grammar is to language and what theology is to religion: the framework within which the whole operation is conducted. It was all very well for uncomplicated Harry Truman to say that protocol and striped pants gave him a pain in the neck (many an Ambassador has said the same thing, under his breath), but these were the very things insulating him from foreigners whose equally simple ground rules of natural behaviour were sometimes vastly different from his own. Strictly speaking, protocol is concerned with documents, but by extension it has come to mean all forms of understanding between governments about how their representatives conduct business, behave formally and generally avoid accidental frictions and collisions. It is the imperatives of protocol that enable an embassy staff to be evacuated without harm after two nations have started fighting each other, even if that takes several months to accomplish, as it did when the British left Tokyo in 1941 after declaring war on the Japanese. It was the farcical end of the philosophy that once had the protocol committee of the diplomatic corps in Phnom Penh meeting on eight separate occasions to decide how properly to address the new American Ambassador there, who caused the problem by

waywardly being a woman. It is an occasional matter of protocol for the British that, should the head of your mission be so
good as to offer you a lift in his car, you take care not to
sit on his right (*placement* again); though how on earth you
manage, should His Excellency be at the wheel of a two-seater
with left-hand drive, is something that neither Sir Marcus
Cheke's *Handbook* nor Sir Ernest Satow's biblical *Guide to Diplomatic Practice* ever got round to considering.

Those legendary diplomatic calls wheel around the hubcap of
protocol. Like many other things embalmed in the mythology
of this profession, the business of calling and circulating visiting
cards is no longer quite what it used to be. There are plenty of
British posts where, below the head of mission, no one bothers
with it at all except among the embassies representing the other
nations of the EEC; and, of course, with the appropriate
officials in the local foreign ministry. This is a distinct decline
from the not so distant past. Writing in 1949, Cheke was quite
adamant that any new arrival at a post 'must send one of his own
cards to each member of the staffs of all the diplomatic Missions
in the capital according to the Diplomatic List which is printed
and circulated by the Ministry of Foreign Affairs.' His wife,
moreover, was expected to do likewise. Even more recently, it
was commonplace for everyone at the level of First Secretary
and above to bowl round in person to say 'how do you do' to all
his opposite numbers in town; and, in due course, to receive
each opposite number at the British embassy when the call was
returned. He went through the same process again when he, or
anyone else, was leaving the city, which meant that in a large
capital, he could be as perpetually engaged in this task as any
painter of the old Forth Bridge. Diplomats who snort with disdain at straightforward inquiries about the extent of calling today, as though these came from some callow soul who still
believed in Santa Claus, have overlooked the fact that as lately
as 1965 the *Diplomatic Service List* (the annual handbook to who's
where in British diplomacy) spent half a page on the niceties of
protocol which had been unchanged since they were laid down
by the Congress of Vienna in 1815.

The burden of calling and card-dropping now falls on the
head of mission and his wife, and even at that level has been
drastically reduced in many posts, by general agreement of all
the senior diplomats there, who have found the habit a time-

consuming bore. The normally tepid feeling about it was expressed by a Counsellor, No 2 at his embassy, who remarked: 'I don't perhaps call on other people as much as I might. One fellow called on me the other day, mind you; but he seemed to have nothing to say, and didn't want to know anything.' Nevertheless, the mystique is still powerful enough for every British diplomatic couple to be advised in meticulous detail just how to handle their calls and play their cards, should they be luckless enough to find themselves in a capital where these things still matter a lot.

The formal call on another diplomat or another diplomat's wife is a relatively straightforward business; around 11 o'clock in the morning or 4 o'clock in the afternoon for preference, and lasting not a minute longer than half an hour. The card game is another matter, a highly complex one, with almost as many rules to it as bridge. A card may be sent after lunch or a dinner party, but not usually after a tea or cocktail party, instead of sending a thank-you letter. It may be sent as a sort of range-finder to someone with whom it is hoped to make contact, but only after an introduction has been made first. It may be sent on a special occasion to convey a stylized message in the most cryptic form possible, which gives it away for the impersonal thing that the whole business of cardmanship really is. For reasons which may once have had much to do with easy communication, but which time has turned whimsical, these messages are formulated in French, and then encoded even further into a sort of diplomatic tick-tack by abbreviation. The most common of them are as follows, and some pedants reckon that all are improperly transmitted if they have not been written in pencil:

p.p. (*pour présenter*) to introduce someone to someone else
p.r. (*pour remercier*) to thank
p.f. (*pour féliciter*) to congratulate
p.f.f.n. (*pour féliciter fête nationale*) to congratulate on the national day
p.f.n.a. (*pour féliciter nouvel an*) to congratulate on the New Year
p.c. (*pour condoléances*) to condole
p.p.c. (*pour prendre congé*) to bid farewell on leaving post

Cards may be sent by post or messenger, or even delivered by the sender himself, in which case they should be 'cornered', with the top left-hand corner turned down. But there is one way no card may ever be sent, and that is by a woman to a man: and when a bachelor calls upon a solitary wife for some impenetrably diplomatic reason, he will do well to leave a couple of his visiting cards behind – one for her and another for her absent husband. Pasteboard, indeed, is showered like confetti on some occasions. If a diplomatic wife visits another diplomatic wife she must leave one of her own cards and two of her husband's – one destined for the hostess, the other for the missing host. The same cards are left when a married couple call on a married woman alone in the house, while a wife calling on a widow gets by with one of her own and one of her man's.

People at the FCO are more likely than not to declare that they haven't clapped eyes on a visiting card in London for years. The impression they thus convey may well be an accurate one; but it would be misguided to infer from it that protocol in general – in London or anywhere else – is a vanishing trade. A department of the Foreign Office is totally dedicated to its tortuous ways, with a staff of fifty-five working under the Vice-Marshal of the Diplomatic Corps – and that does not include the panel of 'greeters', distinguished military men who are enlisted and posted off to Heathrow Airport in order to provide the correct tone and colour for the diplomatic welcome of arriving VIPs. The Vice-Marshal, who is usually an Assistant Under Secretary at the FCO and not destined to rise any higher, stands in this cosmopolitan arena in much the same position occupied traditionally by Dukes of Norfolk (the Earls Marshal of England) when a Coronation is afoot. He does, himself, have many dealings with the Palace at regular intervals during the year, for part of his duties runs to organizing state visits to London by monarchs and presidents from abroad. These invariably originate in Foreign Office advice to the sovereign about what would be rather splendidly judicious and timely in the national interest as a whole. He is, besides, for ever in and out of the Queen's anterooms as shepherd in charge of the newest flock of foreign Ambassadors presenting their credentials to the Crown, and those tendering letters of recall before moving on elsewhere. He may well be the only British diplomat now who regularly lives up to the popular caricature of bowler hat, grey tie and pin-striped suit, his customary rig of the day when in contact with the royals.

The association with the Palace, however, is but the gaudiest side of the Protocol and Conference Department's business. It is up to its neck in perpetual relationships with all the foreign embassies on such workaday topics as diplomatic immunity from parking regulations outside Harrods, and the organization of duty-free privileges. When a foreign Ambassador is summoned to the Foreign Office to receive a Protest from our government to his, someone from Protocol is nervously in the background, hoping that no one on our side of the unfortunate affair has made any slip that might disturb the dogmatic ghosts who were at the Congress of Vienna 160 years ago. Well aware that their diplomatic speciality is regarded by the world outside as ridiculously old-fashioned and stuffy, the people in Protocol hasten to assure the inquisitive that, far from this being so, the niceties of protocol are most heavily applied and the curiosities of etiquette are most carefully preserved not among old imperial nations like ourselves, but in the Kremlin and among the most self-consciously independent states of Africa. Like all arguments advanced by diplomats about their profession, some that may be heard in this quarter ring with complete truth, while others bear the cracked note of self-justifying humbug. It is doubtless the case that it would be very stupid, and in some instances downright dangerous, if immunity were to be removed from the scores of foreign diplomats who quite knowingly leave their cars parked on double yellow lines in London for purely domestic convenience or merely to exercise their self-importance. A tougher attitude by the British might pacify the Automobile Association and quell annual cries of outrage from jealous local motorists whenever the relevant figures are published, but it would certainly invite reprisals against British diplomats abroad, not always in the matter of car-parking. 'It's one thing to be in London without diplomatic immunity; it's quite another thing to be without it in some capitals one could name.' But then the protocol experts rather spoil this candid effect by remarking in the next breath that 'Diplomats don't get duty-free booze because they are a privileged class, but because one sovereign by international comity doesn't tax another sovereign.'

It is not a vice peculiar to the British Diplomatic Service to indulge in such artful dodging, and every Foreign Ministry on earth has a squad of men engaged full-time in dealing with the codified rules and unwritten proprieties of protocol, though few of them can be as generously staffed as the department in London. In the life of every British mission abroad, protocol of one kind or another shapes each day, from beginning to end. A diplomat and his wife can no more escape this than a monk can separate himself from what is ordained by the Rule of his order and perpetuated in the customary of his religious house. It is protocol, as much as many other considerations, that will cause a Counsellor to confess that 'It's not a particularly demanding office week here, but sometimes the social side is hideous'. With more than 100 embassies in the capital where he is serving, he will not be exaggerating. One man in his mission may well be finding the social side even more trying. For nobody is as completely packaged in protocol and all its works as the Ambassador.

10 Their Excellencies

'No moment in a diplomatic lifetime', wrote Lord Gore-Booth, after retiring from the topmost job in his profession, 'is quite so exciting as taking up one's first post as head of a diplomatic mission.'[1] It is comparable to the sensations of a sailor, who may yet end up as First Sea Lord, when he walks over the brow to commission his own coastal minesweeper; or of a parson, with disturbing thoughts of Lambeth Palace, when he is introduced to the lesser pomps of a suffragan bishopric in a provincial wasteland. It is a sensation that the game, assiduously played for a couple of decades already in the diplomat's case, has only now properly begun. Provided he is on the right side of fifty and isn't about to take command of the outpost in Lesser Bongoland (in which case he really can't hope for much more than subsequent elevation to Upper Claustrophobia) he can anticipate the possibility that the fullest rewards of diplomacy, both active and geriatric, will now be his. He has crossed the gulf that lies between every head of mission and his staff. This is much wider, say some who have made the crossing, than you ever expect beforehand. You find yourself slipping into a slightly different tone of voice, more confident with authority. If you wish to thump the table, no one around you now will tell you not to be a bloody fool, and only a comparative handful of men in London will instruct you to come off it. You are 'sir' at last to most of those you meet, and almost the only people in sight who can safely get away with omitting this deference are foreigners in positions like your own. When a British Ambassador refers to 'my colleagues', he is not talking about those who are closest to him in his own embassy. He means all the other Ambassadors representing their countries' interests in that capital, occupying

[1] Gore-Booth, p. 201.

the same self-conscious perch as himself. They are captains of the
diplomatic corps together; and there never was a more elite
body of men in the world. As a word suggesting rare distinction,
there is nothing to compete with 'Ambassador', judging by the
frequency with which it is attached to first-class hotels, night-
clubs, expensive drinks, cigarettes and other luxuries throughout the world.

A head of mission in a Commonwealth country is a High
Commissioner and as such almost always (according to the fine
distinctions of protocol) represents the British government
rather than the Crown. There is something slightly less formidable about the image of the High Commissioner, than that of
the Ambassador. It doubtless has something to do with a suggestion of bare knees, camp fires and the sturdy innocence of the
Boy Scout, rather than gold braid, ostrich feathers and a polish
that will dazzle any assembly. But there are other details which
add to this effect. There is nothing to choose in comfort between
the residences of Ambassadors and High Commissioners, but no
British Ambassador ever inhabited a building with such a cosily
suburban address as those of the British High Commissioners
in Ottawa ('Earnscliffe'), Colombo ('Westminster House') or
Bridgetown ('Ben Mar'). The Ambassador is a man whom
protocol has placed abroad as the personal envoy of his monarch, even if in practice he spends most of his time trying to
make life easier for her leading politicians. He is the Queen's
Man, as no one else is, and some Ambassadors never let anyone
forget it. He is entitled to a nineteen-gun salute on ceremonial
occasions, which is only two blank cartridges fewer than his
sovereign gets from the Royal Horse Artillery in Hyde Park,
but nineteen more than the Prime Minister gets anywhere. Her
Britannic Majesty's Ambassador outranks every Cabinet Minister once London has been left behind, though no diplomat, well
aware of which side his bread is really buttered on, would dream
of sitting by the Premier's right elbow at a foreign negotiating
table.

The connection with the Palace is established when the
newly-appointed Ambassador goes there to kiss hands before
departing overseas. It is directly maintained at regular intervals
for the rest of the man's diplomatic career, and for some time
afterwards if he does well for himself. He is formally received
by the Queen again when he comes home at the end of his

diplomacy. The Diplomatic Service is allotted 100 places at the three Palace garden parties each year, and people who have reached Grades 1 and 2 are automatically invited (together with wives and elder daughters) for three years after they have retired. Men who are doing a shift in London as Under Secretaries, in between their ambassadorial stints abroad, may find themselves sharing the Royal Box at Wimbledon with the occupants for whom it was designed, for a couple of tickets are sent round to the FCO each day for the duration of the tennis championships. But, gratifying as these occasions must be, none can possibly match that first moment when a new Ambassador is ushered into the Throne Room to receive his sovereign's blessing and exchange some words with her about the appointment. The Queen herself appears to be in no doubt at all about the significance of the encounter. A man who was recently there sensed that the interview was drawing to its close before he had quite got everything he wanted to say off his chest. 'May I just add something else, Ma'am?' he inquired. 'Of course, Mr ——', the Queen replied. 'Now you're one of my Ambassadors you may say anything you like to me.'

One of the things he bears abroad with him is his credential as a royal liegeman, which he will have to present to the head of the state to which he is accredited. It is a florid document which has essentially been unchanged since the time when King James I's old envoy, Sir Henry Wotton, produced the classic pun, much misinterpreted, defining an Ambassador as 'an honest man who is sent to lie abroad for the good of his country'. The phrases in a Letter of Credence vary slightly, depending on the status of the head of state receiving it, but the version addressed to another monarch goes thus:

Sir My Brother

Being desirous to maintain without interruption the relations of friendship and understanding which happily exist between the two Crowns, I have selected My Trusty and Well-beloved —— to proceed to the Court of Your Majesty in the character of My Ambassador Extraordinary and Plenipotentiary.

Having already had ample experience of ——'s talents and zeal for My service, I doubt not that he will fulfil the important duties of his Mission in such a manner as to

merit Your approbation and esteem, and to prove himself
worthy of this mark of My confidence. I request that You
will give entire credence to all that —— shall have occasion
to communicate to You in My name, more especially when
he shall express to Your Majesty My cordial wishes for
Your Happiness, and shall assure You of the invariable
attachment and highest esteem with which I am,

Sir My Brother
Your Majesty's
Good Sister

Manu regia   ELIZABETH R

The assurance that his talents and zeal have been marked in
that particular quarter will have done much to solace many a
lofty fellow who, on arriving at his new post, has discovered
that the reception of credentials is conducted more briskly and
with less sense of circumstance than he might have expected.
When the Honourable Sir Peter Ramsbotham reached Washington at the start of 1974, President Nixon gave him no more
than a regulation three minutes in a procession of new Ambassadors, sandwiched between His Excellency from Haiti and the
gentleman who was going to represent Rwanda's interests to the
White House. There was no gold braid or cocked hats on that
particular parade, and the amount of wear and tear these
things get anywhere in the world nowadays is not at all what it
once was. But it is still extensive enough for full-dress uniform
to be an essential part of an Ambassador's wardrobe if he is to
look a proper Queen's Man in such capitals as Paris, The
Hague, Madrid, Vienna, Tokyo, Kathmandu and a couple of
dozen more cities where a diplomat is likely to be regularly
judged by the cut of his cloth. Only an admiral dressed overall
can possibly match a British Ambassador clad in the height of
his professional fashion, with gold oak leaves at his throat and
cuffs, nine gilt buttons down the front of his coatee, thick gold
stripes down the seams of his pants, and a splendid sash in
crimson and blue (if he has collected the appropriate decoration) to help keep his sword from dangling on the floor.
Certain reductions have been made to this traditional attire
over the years. Some £200 was lopped off the tailor's bill when
a gold scarab at the back of the coatee was replaced by common
gilt buttons. But when an attempt was made after the war to

remove ostrich feathers from the beavercocked hat, so great was the outcry among Ambassadors, confirmed and expectant, that the plumage was promptly restored; but made of nylon instead of bird.

Decorations are not tossed around as liberally as they were when you could count our Ambassadors on your fingers; in 1920 there were only eight, but now there are nearly a hundred. For some years after the war, even, virtually every British Ambassador could be sure of collecting his knighthood either on appointment or very shortly afterwards. This habit impressed all foreigners enormously and there are some radical souls in the Foreign Office who would vigorously sweep away what they regard as many remaining cobwebs, who take the view that it might have been retained with profit. Countries feel slighted, they say, if the Queen's envoy turns out to be almost plain Mr Smith, when they know that the rival state down the continent has been endowed with Sir Someone Orother, and that in each capital the Belgians have placed a Baron and the Swedes a Count. By the mid-1970s more nations suffered this indignity than did not. With patience and application, however, few things in this life are more certain than that an Ambassador will end up with his knighthood as he rises into the senior grades of the Diplomatic Service. From his first appointment as head of a mission, he is making a parallel ascent up the Most Distinguished Order of St Michael and St George (motto: Token of a Better Age). As a Grade 4 novice he will certainly become a Companion in due course, which means that although he remains 'Mr', he at least tacks CMG after his name (pointedly known in the trade as Call Me God). Presently, at a more senior post, he will be elevated to a commanding knighthood with a KCMG (Kindly Call Me God) and, if he has been a very good Ambassador indeed, he will ultimately be rewarded with the Knight Grand Cross of the order (God Calls Me God). It is not possible for ordinary flesh and blood to rise much higher than that. But if a man happens to be running the right embassy at the right time, he will also acquire the KCVO, or some other token of the Victorian Order, which the Queen always leaves as a parting gift to her Ambassadors abroad when she has made a state visit to their territory. Such baubles matter much more to some men than to others. A fully-laden fellow who retired in 1974 complained in his final dispatch to London that the Service

R

now collected only about half its former quota of knighthoods which, he had the nerve to suggest, were a traditional form of compensation for poor pay and impoverished retirement among other things. By some mental process which may have been unique, he concluded that the halving of diplomatic knighthoods was in some way a breach of promise to unacknowledged individuals, who had entered a service which gave a clear expectation of earthly rewards.

A head of mission's life is not always the one of unalloyed grandeur that his royal connection and the dispensation of titles might imply. It can sometimes be very nearly normal. In La Paz, His Excellency has to sleep with an oxygen cylinder by his bed, like every other weakling foreigner in town, in case the local altitude should wake him gasping in the night. There are cracks in the residence wall at Kampala and there was rising damp in Quito. Even in a very senior post, an Ambassador today may feel a bit sorry for himself when he recalls how things once were for men in his position. In Cairo, thirty years ago, when the Ambassador did all his work in the residence and scarcely went near the chancery building, his needs were met by an English staff of eleven, including four aides-de-camp, two diplomats, a confidential typist, an accountant, his wife's secretary, a housekeeper and a butler; now the staff in the residence is entirely Egyptian and His Excellency has to make shift with a single girl secretary during his working hours in the chancery. Ambassadors are prone to such nostalgic comparisons, encouraged by the row of photographs outside their offices, to remind them of whose shoes they are wearing. They are not always kind to these predecessors of theirs, quite liable to pause beside the portrait of one stern-faced fellow (only three years retired) and say 'Yes, well he should have stuck to farming'.

But, whatever his situation, every head of mission is fortified by the knowledge that his immediate world revolves indisputably around him. Things happen to make him comfortable without his having lifted a finger to bring them on. A hi-fi set with all the most advanced twiddly bits arrives from London, like pennies from heaven, and he wonders who had that splendid idea. Servants are at his beck and call and in some places (like Washington, where there are sixteen, and Buenos Aires, where there are eleven) they are so numerous that he doesn't even have to exert himself that much. Even in a small post he can be sure that dear old Hanif will have his polished shoes awaiting him outside the bedroom door before breakfast, his suit pressed ready for the courtesy call up the road in mid-morning, and that his faithful retainer will still be going strong at dinner, which he serves with the BEM proudly on the chest of his white jacket, a small mark of something which an earlier Ambassador thoughtfully extracted from the Birthday Honours after Hanif's twenty-fifth year of sub-diplomatic endeavour. If His Excellency merely wishes to move 500 yards from his doorstep, his car will be ready and waiting at the porch, the chauffeur standing in some attitude of respect alongside. In senior posts the vehicle will most certainly be a Rolls-Royce and in Washington it could even be two, for there the Minister is allocated one as well. In Kuwait the car is a Jaguar, while Our Man in Mogadishu has to endure a somewhat weary Ford Executive, whose playful motion results from the driver's insistence on changing down at least two gears too late. It does, however, have the ambassadorial flag fluttering from the bonnet, as bravely as aboard any Rolls, with the royal coat of arms in the middle of the Union Jack. Like a man riding a camel, several feet above the pedestrians, a man conveyed by a Rolls with its flag up would have something missing if he didn't experience at least a twinge of superiority. It is a feeling that, if anything, can only have been increased in those places where policemen swing in carloads right behind the back bumper of ambassadorial vehicles the moment they have emerged from embassy gates, to discourage hoodlums from trying to kidnap the highly negotiable passenger ahead.

All these forms of solicitude may be taken for granted the moment a man first becomes an Excellency. There are many others. There is a special section of the FCO dedicated to the needs of Ambassadors and High Commissioners alone. It organizes their busy timetables when their appointments are announced, seeing to it that they get round the banks, the important commercial companies, the British Council and the other Whitehall departments – all the London bodies that might have an interest in their destinations abroad and want words with the new man so that he shall not overlook their special concerns when he takes over from someone he will probably pass en route, in mid-Atlantic or high above some Mediterranean coastline. The Heads of Mission Section will continue to pander to his needs when he is safely installed, sending a body down Regent Street to purchase a piece of glass or silver so that he can present someone with a suitable wedding gift Out There. Elsewhere in the FCO, they snap to it when HE's telegram arrives complaining that his distant living room is draughty, or that he really could do with an extra door inserting in the fourth bedroom. Many Ambassadors complain about such things as they become more confident of their powers, and the ones who endlessly demand attention are usually the ones who get it first. In the mission itself, it is the administrative officer (from the Executive class) who bears the brunt of the Ambassador's structural requirements, which are sometimes so insistent that this official will confide that 'everything here takes second place to servicing the boss's house'. It takes a man of great character not to become peevish if something goes amiss when he has ceased to be an Ambassador, so carefully does the system lackey to his every want when he is one. The ease with which he can get anything at all done for himself will be extended to almost anyone he nominates. If his son decides to come out to him overland from Oxford in the long vacation, His Excellency has only to drop a line to all the British embassies along the way, and the youth and his travelling companions will be gently taken care of in a manner befitting the father's position.

This is so exalted by the time a diplomat has reached a senior rank that anyone who retires at Grade 1 or 2 really doesn't have to worry whether his considerable pension rights have been inflation-proofed or not, or whether he and his wife have managed to bank quite a lot of their money on the last posting, to provide for the ambassadorial equivalent of a rainy day. For all manner of entrepreneurs lurk in the City of London, anxious to haul such a man on to the board, where his proven talents and zeal will serve the shareholders as well as they once served the sovereign. Not everyone finds this to his taste. Some Ambassadors are so utterly soaked in the ideals of public service that they offer themselves freely or for a pittance to bodies like the Civil Service Selection Board or the Wates Foundation, and are otherwise content to watch cricket and make their gardens grow in Hampshire or Dorset. Some have so fallen for a country they worked in that they go back there for good: like Sir Ashley Clarke, who used to lecture the Italians on Delius to his own piano accompaniment when he was Ambassador in Rome, and eventually made his home in Venice. Some have moved straight out of diplomacy into the academic world, and of these there are those who returned to their old schools and universities in a commanding role, like Sir William Hayter, who became Warden of New College, Oxford, and Sir Patrick Dean, who became a Governor of Rugby School; and those who exchanged the ambassadorial desk for the professorial chair, like Sir William Barker, who left Prague for Liverpool, Sir Cecil Parrott, who went from Prague to Lancaster, and Sir John Richmond, who switched from Khartoum to a lectureship at Durham. *The Directory of Directors* discloses where all the rest find their feet, though few have done so as successfully as Lord Caccia. After being an Ambassador *and* Permanent Under Secretary, he still had enough appetite left to become Provost of Eton and, simultaneously, Chairman of Standard Telephones and a Director of the National Westminster Bank, the Westminster Foreign Bank, the Orion Bank, Prudential Assurance, and the Foreign & Colonial Investment Trust. He would presumably have found some richly diplomatic retort for the senior Ambassador, a man of quite exceptionally balanced gifts, who on contemplating his own retirement in 1975, told me 'I've no intention of going on anybody's board. You're only wanted as an impressive name on the letterhead, to be dangled like a marionette; and I've never seen myself as that.'

Ambassadors, in fact, as that suggests, are a very mixed bunch; more mixed than most envious outsiders might like to believe. Every one of them, say cynical juniors, likes to give the impression that he's a new broom who will sweep up some things left lying around by his predecessor, though as often as not nothing very much does change. Some Ambassadors will actually say, blissfully forgetful of the taunt attached to their KCMGs, 'One creates the thing in one's own image'. These are the ones who like to see as many names and statuses as possible representing their embassy on the Diplomatic List, the more impressive-sounding the better, with the registry clerk styled as Archivist and the British Council representative drummed up as Cultural Attaché; for a long and weighty roll-call does something for the Ambassador's self-confidence when he has to hobnob with his colleagues of the local diplomatic corps. There are others who much prefer to run a tight little operation, with as little fat on it as possible, and are much more interested in the intellectual challenge of the post than any representational trappings of the

Queen's Man. Some Ambassadors exude effortless superiority so overpoweringly that one wonders how they ever manage to check the habit for a moment or two when they are in the presence of the Queen. But there has been at least one Ambassador, Sir Colin Crowe, who was so nervous even after years of public speaking, that he had to post his wife in every audience to give him the confidence to bring it off. There are Ambassadors who at last command the mission they have served in once or twice before, where they first made a mark as juniors at the start of their careers. Edward Youde became Ambassador in Peking in 1974, a quarter of a century after he was a Third Secretary in the embassy there and walked along the Yangtze for four days to help HMS *Amethyst*, which was stranded on a sandbank as a result of Chinese gunfire. There are Ambassadors who come to their command with no previous experience of the country, though very rarely can they be as completely uninitiated as one man the FCO sent out to represent the Crown in Ulan Bator. Not only was he ignorant of Mongolian when he arrived, but he didn't speak Russian either, and every Queen's Messenger on that outlandish run for the next twelve months was fairly staggering under the load of specialized books plundered on behalf of His Excellency from the shelves of the London Library.

'The days of the Barney's Tobacco kind of man', said someone, 'are definitely over.' Individualists still abound, however, and there are even slightly strange Ambassadors, like the man who used to proselytize for Moral Rearmament wherever he went, as vigorously as if it were part of Her Majesty's Government's policy. No figure in British diplomacy for a long time has been as eccentric as Sir Hugh Boustead. He was never, in fact, an Ambassador: he was one of that almost vanished sub-species who used to administer desert areas of the Middle East when Britain had a controlling interest in the sheikhs, and who headed British missions there with titles like Political Agent, or Resident Adviser. When Boustead was the bossman at Abu Dhabi in the 1960s, he would summon junior diplomats with a code of blasts on a policeman's whistle. And when he finally retired some years ago, laden with exotic honours like Vladimir with Crossed Swords and St George's Medal with one Palm (Ethiopia), so unable was he to detach himself from a world that was partly of his own making, that he accepted employment from a ruler down the Persian Gulf as supervisor of the princely stables; and there, as far as anyone knows, at the age of eighty-odd, he still is. Being an Ambassador encourages any taste a man may have for eccentricity, for there is no one near by who dare mock him for it. These things clearly have limits, though. When Keith Hamylton Jones was Consul-General in Lubumbashi, his entry in the 1970 edition of *Who's Who* ended '*recreations;* reading, writing, walking, tennis, sex (all in decent privacy).' By the 1974 edition, when Hamylton Jones was about to become Ambassador to Costa Rica, someone had obliged him to cut out the sex. Sometimes, a man's foibles can be turned to diplomatic advantage. Sir Andrew Gilchrist once put his bagpipes to splendid use by marching with them before an angry mob outside his embassy in Reykjavik, thus pacifying them on the spot. He subsequently repeated this performance in similar circumstances in Jakarta, before retiring with his music to even more appreciative audiences as Chairman of the Highlands and Islands Development Board.

There will be no profession richer than diplomacy in good stories about senior people, for diplomats are inordinate gossips, particularly about themselves, and senior diplomats provide as much fertile ground as any other form of aristocracy. It is said that when Sir Donald Maitland was Britain's Permanent Representative at the United Nations during the second Icelandic cod war, he received instructions from London to make urgent representations to his opposite number in the dispute. Sir Donald happens to be a very short man, and the Ambassador from Reykjavik at the time was a giant of well over six feet. Maitland bustled into his office in New York, fluttering the telegram from London. 'I have been told', he informed the Icelander, 'to make representations at the very highest level.' And, with a leap, he landed on the startled man's desk top. This did something to take the chill out of the atmosphere. Ambassadors are not always as impish as that, but they can sometimes leave a warm memory behind without having quite intended to. When Sir Oliver Franks arrived in Washington at the height of the Cold War, he was rather taken aback by a telephone conversation he had with the local radio station before he had properly settled into his desk, a few days before Christmas. The man in the studio was welcoming him to the American capital, wishing him well during his time there, and seemed very anxious to know what Sir Oliver wanted for Christmas. Franks, not a man for small talk, spluttered a little as he groped for a seemly idea, and finally came up with something he thought might do. On Christmas morning the broadcasters came on the air, burbling goodwill across the District of Columbia. 'On this hallowed day,' crooned the announcer, 'we have a number of distinguished foreign residents in the capital city of the United States, and we thought it would be appropriate to ask some of them what *they* would like most of all for Christmas 1948. First of all, we asked His Excellency the French Ambassador what his choice would be ... ' The broadcast cut into a tape recording of a Parisian voice, pregnant with sincerity: 'Pour Noël, I want peace throughout all thee world.' 'Then we asked the Ambassador of the Soviets, what he would like most of all today ... ' A dogmatic voice on the tape this time: 'For Chreesmas I want freedom for all the peoples enslaved by imperialism, wherever they may be.' ' ... Finally, folks, we asked Her Majesty the Queen's Ambassador from London, Sir Oliver Franks, what he would prefer this day ... ' The diffident tones of Bristol Grammar School and Oxford came on the air: ' ... Well, as a matter of fact, it's very kind of you, I think I'd quite like a small box of candied fruit.'

Lord Franks (as he has been since 1962) went to Washington at the age of forty-three, an academic who had made his name in wartime administration. He moved into diplomacy for just four years and then came out of it again to enlarge his reputation as a don and a government committee man *in excelsis*. He is still the outstanding example of the non-professional Ambassador who is appointed from time to time to some important post over the heads of careerists from the Diplomatic Service. This has never been more than an occasional practice with the British, in marked contrast to the American habit of regularly awarding some 30 per cent of their plum diplomatic jobs to outsiders; notoriously often because they have backed the Presidential party with a lot of hard cash and loyalty, which was how Walter Annenberg became United States Ambassador in London between 1969 and 1974, and how Mrs Anne Armstrong, wife of a Texas rancher, came to Grosvenor Square in 1976. The majority of the British non-professionals have gone in the opposite direction across the Atlantic. Besides Oliver Franks, Washington in the last thirty years has seen David Ormsby-Gore (a cultivated landowner with private American connections, who later became a television tycoon), John Freeman (once a Labour Minister, and another television chief today), and the Earl of Cromer (a banker); while in 1974 the barrister Ivor Richard, QC (another Labour politician), took over from Sir Donald Maitland at the United Nations in New York, after he had lost his Parliamentary seat in an election. Freeman went to Washington and Sir Christopher Soames (a Conservative politician) became British Ambassador in Paris when Harold Wilson seemed set on emulating President Kennedy's eclectic style of government, Freeman having already fulfilled a similar function in the Premier's first burst of enthusiasm, as High Commissioner in New Delhi.

The professionals have never grumbled too much about these appointments on principle because there has never been the remotest chance that they would be the start of patronage on an American scale. But they do concede that when they hear of an outsider's appointment to their mission, they are on tenterhooks until they have actually met the chap and found out whether he will be an agreeable commander of their team. Usually the thing has worked. Few British missions will have produced happier teamwork than the one at the UN in New York under Ivor Richard, and even though John Freeman scarcely ever entertained other British diplomats in Massachusetts Avenue, he was well respected there as a man with a mind who knew what he was doing. When Lord Cromer left in 1974, however, morale at the embassy was on the low side and it was thought that although he might have done fine work for Britain as far as the International Monetary Fund was concerned, he never really grasped some essentials of an Ambassador's job; one of which is to appear regularly at the meetings of senior staff to discuss policy, which Cromer often passed up. The embassy never quite got over Lady Cromer's early brush with American journalism, either. Asked for her views about Vietnam, she said, 'It's a long and terrible war, but saving face means so much more to Asians than life. Life means nothing, but nothing, to them.'

One difficulty facing every outsider, quite apart from questions of personality, is that, according to one of them, 'You spend a lot of time at the beginning learning the ground rules of diplomacy; learning, for example, how vital it is to settle the exact nuance of the word "deplore" – which is used by the professional diplomat with far more calculation than the rest of us are accustomed to.' An advantage the outsider has over the professional is that, being a political appointment, he probably knows the mind of his political masters rather better than the diplomats and can, in doubt, pick up the telephone and speak to the Foreign Secretary or even the Prime Minister and sort something out man to man with them, instead of having all his communications channelled through senior officials at the FCO in London. He will scarcely ever do this in practice; but it would be quite unthinkable for an Ambassador who has spent decades learning all the proprieties of the Foreign Office. John Freeman sometimes backed his own deep knowledge of Labour government philosophy and threw away instructions he had just received through the North American desk at home; and diplomats who were in Washington at the time say that almost always his judgment of the situation, when he did this, was better than Whitehall's. Ivor Richard's headlined attack on Daniel Moynihan in 1975 was to some extent a product of the outsider's independence from a lifelong allegiance to protocol. Moynihan, as American Ambassador to the United Nations (and another non-professional), had denounced a resolution drafted by Third World and Communist countries, which described Zionism as 'a form of racism'. He called the resolution 'obscene', and went on to picture President Amin of Uganda as 'a racist murderer'. No professional diplomat from the West would ever use such language, however much he might sympathize with the sentiments, because he would regard it as totally inexpedient. Ivor Richard, who knew very well that in diplomacy you do not often say directly what you think, and appreciated all sorts of difficulties that could befall Western nations in the Middle East if a Western representative spoke like that, then attacked Moynihan in a public speech outside the United Nations. He likened the American to a bitter King Lear, and declared that the United Nations was 'not the OK Corral'. He was saying no more than what every man in his mission thought, a view shared nervously by the top brass in the Foreign Office at home and the government above them; and a view that had almost certainly been passed by the censorship of Dr Kissinger, whose appreciation of diplomacy's tortuous ways is as fine as any professional's. But a regular British Ambassador would not have spoken so bluntly. Richard was less inhibited because he was the outsider.

There is a school of thought which quite strongly believes what the Canadian Prime Minister, Pierre Trudeau, once said: 'I think the whole concept of diplomacy today is a little out-moded. I believe much of it goes back to the early days of the telegraph, when you needed a dispatch to know what was happening in a country, whereas now you can read it in a good newspaper.'[1] It argues further that the Ambassador especially has lost his point since highly developed airlines have allowed a country's political leaders to fly within hours to speak to their opposite numbers in person. One thing is sure. The world will never again see the likes of Benjamin Franklin who, from his clandestine embassy at Passy, brought France singlehanded to the aid of the American colonies in their struggles against the British. Nor will there be another Stratford Canning, who per-sonally guaranteed that Britain would fight Russia and Austria if the two attacked Turkey, without dallying for the two months it would have taken to obtain confirmation of this from London. Some very senior men in British diplomacy today can take a considerable amount of personal responsibility for what they say and do abroad. The High Commissioner in Nairobi is author-ized to allot up to £400,000 worth of government aid to any project he thinks fit in Kenya (from an annual aid budget there of between £12 million and £14 million) straight off his own bat. A Grade 1 Ambassador will sometimes take a particular line without instructions from the Foreign Office, that an Ambassador in a Grade 3 or Grade 4 post — with enough career ahead of him to worry about — would not dream of doing unless he had consulted London beforehand down to the last full stop. But, by and large, the power, and the status that goes with it, of every Ambassador from countries with the longest diplomatic traditions, is infinitely smaller than it was even fifty years ago. And the old glitter of the residence is no longer magnetic after twenty-five years of social revolution. The oldest hands say that, although even now the British Ambassador in Paris must bring some weight of social privilege or intellect to his mission if he is to have any chance of penetrating the tightly caste-ridden layers of influential French society, the last time every Frenchman who was 'in' (they are talking of people up to Cocteau's calibre) could certainly be attracted to the rue du Faubourg St Honoré,

[1] Quoted in Clark, p. 1.

was when the Duff Coopers kept its ballroom regularly aswirl with talent for three years just after the war. So what is the general usefulness of the Ambassador today?

'An ambassador', writes Lord Trevelyan,[1]

> need no longer be the first cousin of a great family or figure in the Almanach de Gotha, nor even have been to a good school if he is English, though a readiness to point the right kind of gun at the right kind of bird is still useful, if only for the presidential shoots at Rambouillet or as a convenient alibi when he wishes to see something of a country in revolution without arousing the suspicion that he is surreptitiously carrying silver bars to distribute to agents of the opposition.

That refers to one side of the ambassadorial function, which has been unchanged by time. Among several other things, His Excellency is expected to stick as close as politics and dignity will permit to whoever are the Top People in the country to which he is accredited, and there are still some Ambassadors around who see their role as consisting in little else, though both politics and dignity might decree otherwise. They are, however, a dwindling breed. Only a fool could fail to see the importance of a British Ambassador keeping well in touch with the local rulers, a posture which does not necessarily include ingratiation, or his peculiar characteristic as the Queen's Man. It enables him the better to discharge his sometimes uncomfortable duty as weathercock, visible at all times, even on the cloudiest days, from the Foreign Office. If he is recalled to London by his own government, or asked to pack his bags by his hosts, that is the clearest evidence of a storm brewing. But there are many less public ways of using an Ambassador to show a government in which direction and how strongly the wind is blowing. When Lord Caccia was Sir Harold and Our Man in Washington, it was three full months after the Suez catastrophe before John Foster Dulles would condescend to see him; which told Whitehall a great deal more about American disapproval of the invasion than any number of papers exchanged by the two governments could have done.

[1] Trevelyan, p. 23.

The kind of base an Ambassador establishes is vital to the success of his mission in such company. From it he goes forth to represent his government. In it he is on Her Majesty's sovereign territory and can parley with his hosts as he thinks fit and wise. Here or hereabouts is to be found some justification for the *frais*, the accumulated allowances paid to Ambassadors, which is colossal in the case of the senior men and scarcely cheese-paring for the juniors, abused by some and spent as it was meant to be up to the last devalued penny by others: and some Ambassadors have been known to come home from their last posting in the red, so assiduous have they been in the matter of entertainment. There are even more forms of this for heads of mission than for the other diplomats. Quite apart from dinner parties and cocktail parties, there are grand banquets to be attended and occasionally to be given. At a mere dinner party an Ambassador can be as bored as Sir Bernard Burroughs once was in Ankara, when a lady at his side started talking nervously into his silence about a book she had been reading, which she proceeded to describe chapter by chapter before reviewing at length her conclusions; which caused the Ambassador to look up from his plate at last and say, 'Do you know, I think you've totally misunderstood that book.' But the boredom of the most awful dinner party is as nothing to the crushing ennui that always descends at some stage in the average state banquet, where the speeches are usually distinguished more by polemic than by wit. It was in Moscow, during a particularly long exhortation, that Sir Humphrey Trevelyan fell to dreaming about a speech he might make one day, ten hours long, about the liberation of England from the Danes.

Even banquets are not as taxing as the hospitality expected of the Ambassador who heads a large mission in an important capital. A man in that position finds that his residence is not so much his home as a luxurious hotel with a constant procession of guests. It is slightly beside the point to argue that the Ambassador and his wife enjoy the luxury, too, and don't have to worry overmuch about where the money is coming from to maintain them in it. The point is that they are not often alone in it together, that they cannot enjoy a normal married life there. It is very difficult to have a blazing domestic row when your Foreign Secretary, or even a bigshot from British business, is going to share a nightcap and then the breakfast table with

you. In one recent year in Paris, the Ambassador supplied
visitors with beds on 250 nights, gave meals to 2,000 people and
drinks or cups of tea to another 1,800; and 2,800 assembled in
the residence for the Queen's Birthday Party. In five months of
1975, the guest bedrooms in Cairo were vacant on only two
nights. Not all of these visitors provide congenial company. The
satisfaction of accommodating government Ministers soon wears
off, Parliamentary delegations can be much more demanding
than American tourists, and captains of industry can be remarkably limited in their conversation. Some people can be flattered
by an invitation to stay with the Excellencies; others might be
surprised how frequently Excellencies resent an assumption
that they are basically in the bed and breakfast business. As
always, of course, a great deal of the success or failure at this
end of diplomacy depends on the diplomatic wife.

An Ambassador's wife is as crucial to a mission's success, in
many ways, as her husband is himself. She, too, has her representational role, which is the side of diplomacy most difficult to
assess. Who knows what benefit Great Britain got because Lady
Tomkins, rather than Lord Sieff, opened the new Marks &
Spencer department store in Paris? But generally her influence
is much less direct than the man's, a great deal of it exerted in
the relationship she has with other wives in the mission, with
a consequent effect on everyone's morale. There are some exalted ladies who seem to be doing nothing very much more than
getting their own back for indignities they suffered when they
were junior wives. At one European post the Ambassador's wife
let her inferiors know quite sharply that they had better not
take second helpings at her table, as she was on a diet and had
no intention of watching others stuff themselves. Other women
in her position are quite clearly bent on putting a stop to a lot
of the patronizing nonsense they had to endure years ago; they
make sure that when a new couple arrive on post their home
is spotlessly ready for them, the heating is on, and the re-
frigerator is stocked with food. Ambassador's wives are as
varied as Ambassadors, but they usually give themselves away
more clearly. At one embassy a woman who had at least learned
the obliqueness of her husband's profession, if not its finer points,
said shrilly, 'How very brave of you to be writing a book about
the Diplomatic Service without ever having been a diplomat',
which in her tone of voice meant 'What a bloody cheek!' At

another, the Ambassador's wife took a piece of local handicraft from their mantelpiece as I was leaving, and pressed it upon me as a keepsake.

It is very easy for a wife at this, as at any other, level of diplomacy to become no more than an appendage to her husband. But this, more than anything, depends on her own character. Sir Terence Garvey was an outstandingly fine British Ambassador in Moscow, and Lady Garvey was a winner in her own right, who persuaded the Russians to let her give part-time classes in the city, and encouraged other qualified embassy wives to do the same. But there were other elements in their combined success, and a clue to some of them was what happened when an English girl was about to marry a boy from Georgia. For some reason, the arrangement for the girl's parents to fly from England for the wedding had broken down, and she was at a pretty low ebb when there was a knock on the door of her apartment. A woman she didn't know was standing there. It was the wife of Her Majesty's Ambassador, who said that she'd heard about the problem and that, if the bride didn't mind, she would very much like to stand in for the parents, reception and all. The Ambassador himself could take no part because of diplomatic protocol between two nations with a very delicately balanced relationship. But Lady Garvey made up for a great deal by claiming her own independence from protocol.

The Garveys are not the only couple who have elevated the profession of diplomacy to the level of its highest aspirations. Sir Antony and Lady Duff in Nairobi, Sir Dugald and Lady Stewart in Belgrade, are among others who have been very hard acts to follow. And wherever such reputations occur, they are based on a similar combination of personal standards. While feeling that it's quite nice to be entitled, such people are not much interested in rank, except in so far as it affects their salaries. They are absorbed instead by people and they are curious about places. They have enormous appetites to understand their surroundings and they like to build bridges wherever they go. They are very likely to reduce the domestic staff when they reach a new residence, partly because they don't believe the taxpayer's money should be spent on more than necessities, partly because they don't really feel comfortable with lackeys anyway. What's more, they communicate these standards to everyone in the mission with them. And the outsider walks in to a general atmosphere which includes an air of efficiency markedly different from that in some places he has been.

The real achievements, or lack of them, are very hard to detect until thirty years afterwards, and even what may be read in the Public Record Office does not tell the whole story of an Ambassador's mission. It is very easy, therefore, to dismiss him as a figurehead when all that is known of him is what appears in public; the endless official occasions and the engaging items of newspaper gossip that tell how His Excellency in Warsaw invited the pop group Marmalade home to steak and chips after their one-night stand in the Polish capital, or how the British Ambassador at The Hague ceremonially drew the first pint at the imported Rose and Crown. A man's less obvious workload depends mostly on his own inclination to work, but there are some capital cities where he would find it very difficult to take it easy and allow his juniors to get on with almost everything except the ambassadorial representation. Of nowhere is this truer than at the Washington embassy. This is the outline of Sir Peter Ramsbotham's major engagements between September and December 1974, as they were fixed by mid-August:

September

7–8	Attend ESU Ball (America Cup Races) Newport, Rhode Island
9	Dinner meeting, International Management and Development Inst.
10	Address Brookings Institution lunch
12	Private plane to Illinois. Night Castalia Farms with Attorney-General and Senator Robert Taft
13	p.m. Return Washington by private plane
16–18	Visit of delegation of European Parliament
17	ETD Dulles for Los Angeles (5 p.m.)
17–20	Official visit to Los Angeles
21–2	En route to San Francisco
22–4	Official visit to San Francisco
25	Return Washington – ETA 4.50 p.m.
28	Chancellor of Exchequer and IMF party arrive
29	Reception and buffet lunch by Continental Illinois National Bank & Trust Co for World Bank and IMF
30	IMF/World Bank annual meeting

October

1	Chancellor of Exchequer ETD
4	IMF party leaves?
9	8.30 a.m. Breakfast at residence for members of House Foreign Affairs Sub-Committee on Europe. Dinner for Meridian House Ball
12	12.30 p.m. ETA Duke of Gloucester
13	Duke of Gloucester to Jamestown, but HE need not accompany
14	Duke of Gloucester returns to Washington. Dinner party
15	Duke of Gloucester's lunch with Washington chapter of American Institute of Architects. 6 p.m. Duke's lecture at Smithsonian, followed by cocktails and dinner
16	Duke of Gloucester leaves for Philadelphia
16–18	Duke of Edinburgh in New York privately
17	Mr David Wills, night at residence
19	United Nations concert, dinner and dancing; heads of mission. Dr and Mrs Henry Kissinger, host and hostess
21	Attend Laurence Whistler's lecture
27–31	Official visit to St Louis, Fulton, Kansas City, Omaha (Offutt Air Base)

November

11	HE to Valley Forge to attend British Officers Club of Philadelphia dinner
13	Address British-American Chamber of Commerce, New York
14	Address Council on Foreign Relations seminar on Middle East, New York
16–17	Lord and Lady Chalfont stay residence
18–19	Address National Foreign Trade Convention in New York
20–7	Official visit to Houston and Dallas
27	Joint Churchill Dinner, residence

December

2	Dinner meeting, International Management and Development Institute

s

10   Lunch and talk to insurance world, New York.
        Dinner with Council
14–15   Visit Hoover Farm at Akron. Attend and speak
        at Akron University graduation ceremony

And this is the diary of the Ambassador's engagements for one
day in June that year, as it had been more fully drawn up a few
days beforehand:

9 a.m. Chancellor of Exchequer's party – briefing in residence study
11 a.m. Miss Goodison and Mr Glover (HE signs affidavit)
11.30 a.m. Mr Palombo from Senator Bentsen's office calls
(office)
1 p.m. HE attends Mr Krag's lunch for the Nine
3.30 p.m. Swedish Ambassador pays courtesy call (office)
4.30 p.m. HE calls on Congressman Wilbur Mills (Capitol)
8 p.m. Dinner with Mr and Mrs Marquis Childs (informal)

All this conveys well enough the Ambassador's energy in
travelling around the United States as a British salesman, the
number of speeches he makes to various influential bodies, the
back-up he provides for certain selected Britons, the entrée he
enjoys to high American quarters, and the number of calories
he has to accommodate in the course of his various duties. It
can give no idea at all of how the Ambassador rates as a leader
of his mission, or of his perception and integrity as the chief
linkman between two nations. And on those two things are
Ambassadors chiefly judged by other diplomats.

Occasionally an Ambassador can still pull off a remarkably
difficult enterprise abroad by some personal skill or other. Sir
Denis Wright was widely credited with persuading the Shah
of Iran to renounce his claim to Bahrein in the 1960s, when
pressing them might have left the Middle East in a bigger mess
than it was already. The problem of Asian British passport-
holders in Kenya, which at one time could have produced
bloodshed in Africa or vicious xenophobia in Britain, or both,
was largely reduced to insignificance by the careful diplomacy
of Sir Antony Duff and his consul. Sir Humphrey Trevelyan,
on several missions to the Middle East, seemed to be a one-man
first-aid kit in one disaster area after another. But coups of this

nature are comparatively few and far between. After doing time as American Ambassador in India, the academic J. K. Galbraith said that an Ambassador's job was essentially like an airline pilot's: hours of boredom and moments of panic. Catchy, and sometimes true, no doubt, for a man of a particular temperament. But between the boredom and the panic should come the carefully concentrated times when the Ambassador is really justifying his existence.

He is paid to make decisions, and the decisions that are liable to occur almost every day of the week are what and how to communicate to two different governments at once; his own and the one just up the road. This may not tax him overmuch when relations between the two countries are amicable, but it becomes progressively more demanding (and, for the men of appetite, absorbing) as the international relationship swings towards strain. 'In filthy weather,' according to a highly-skilled practitioner, 'the best the Ambassador can do is to act as honest interlocutor and be known as a man who reports straight. He can also demonstrate that Britons do not necessarily or even ever conform to the local stereotyped image.' If an Ambassador doesn't get his political judgments right he is, of course, disqualified as a useful informant of his own government. His usefulness also depends on the other government's conviction that he is truly representing his own people's position; which is not the same thing as stating it crudely. The greatest sin of an Ambassador is to report what he thinks a government wishes to hear, though such men have existed in British diplomacy and Sir Neville Henderson was one of them at the pre-war embassy in Berlin. The Ambassador who fears to stick his neck out in making a risky judgment and conveying an unpalatable decision to his superiors at home is not worth his salary, let alone his frais.

Most of his decisions and judgments go by telegram to Whitehall, but a proportion of his opinions are saved for his dispatches, which travel in the confidential bag. Estimates vary as to how many of these documents are in fact the handiwork of the Ambassador rather than that of someone below him. The most valuable dispatch is the product of the man with a mind like a jackdaw, who picks the brains of everyone in his mission for every gobbet of relevant information and every possible viewpoint, adds all this to his own knowledge and perception, and then composes a considered judgment on the whole. But some dispatches are notoriously the Head of Chancery's work, which the man at the top has merely redrafted from inertia, boredom or a supervening interest in less cerebral matters. Such efforts, however, are never to be found among the dispatches sent by the men of high ambition with the loftiest peaks in sight, who are not above slipping a memorandum to the right person which suggests that Her Majesty might be particularly interested in the Ambassador's latest account of relations with Her Brother of Ruritania. One other man would never dream of passing off the Head of Chancery's work as his own. This is the Ambassador with a literary flair, who takes great pride in edifying and amusing all stations at home and abroad, to whom it would be pain and grief to see so much as a semi-colon deployed by hands other than his own.

In general, an Ambassador is expected to send a dispatch conveying his first impressions of his new milieu six weeks or so after he has reached his post. After that he composes very much as the spirit moves him, but probably not less frequently than three or four times a year. It is also a tradition that he bids farewell to his surroundings with a final flourish of carefully numbered paragraphs, which are supposed to summarize the state of play for the benefit of his successor and the archives, but which frequently extend to highly personal views on diplomacy in general, particularly if the Ambassador is writing a Valedictory dispatch at the end of his career. He may even, on such an occasion, firmly put the Foreign Secretary in his place with such resonant sentiments as 'Your man, Sir, must appear to have your ear, if he is to speak with the full authority of your voice'; or dismiss any upstart talk of Diplomatic and Home Civil Service equivalence as 'an illogical piece of bureaucracy. We have little in common. Ours, as its name used to imply, is a "foreign" service with quite a different job, different needs and hence different rewards.' That particular view may be held now by no more than a small minority of British Ambassadors; so, too, may the attitude of one senior man, who described the Mosaic tones of many a Valedictory as 'an excrescence'.

Some Ambassadors find it desperately hard to mind the Foreign Office plea for brevity when putting things down on paper. Ernest Bevin once told some diplomats, 'I sympathize with you; you have to encipher your Ambassador's telegrams. But I have to read them.' Many dispatches, extremely informative and useful in themselves, have lost half their value because they have been far too long for very busy men in London to wade through with the concentrated attention they required. The dispatch, more than any other form of communication, can become prolix when a man who fancies his own style has his eye on the FCO Print. This is the service by which the most important, or merely the most memorable, dispatches achieve circulation throughout the Diplomatic Service, so that the whole organization can keep itself informed of what is happening to it all over the world. Plenty of diplomatic cupboards have prime examples of the funny dispatch from the other side of the globe pasted inside their doors for light relief from the solemn drudgery of the moment. Some of these essays are very witty indeed, with a gift of mockery (occasionally extended to their authors) that will not have been surpassed in the heyday of the Cambridge Footlights. 'I called on the French chargé d'affaires, a weary but intelligent professional who, if he had been English, would undoubtedly have been a Wykehamist': that expresses the flavour common to many. There was a classic composed by an Ambassador who had just presented his credentials on a day when the local version of the monsoon broke. As he had been forced to stand in full dress uniform under the downpour for some time before his reception, this ceremony was eventually conducted in a miasma of rising steam and, on retiring from The Presence, the Ambassador was somewhat mollified by the damp patch he had left on his host's gorgeously upholstered sofa. Another celebrated dispatch was entitled 'The ——— Ambassador's Suitcase', and described a wholly mystifying series of events during an official outing of the local diplomatic corps. In many examples of the form, like that one, the dispatch can be seen as a panacea for various ambassadorial ills, wherein the author can say what he really feels about the blasted foreigners without giving them offence.

No author of dispatches in recent years has been as renowned as Sir John Russell, who retired in 1974 after being British Ambassador to Ethiopia, Brazil and Spain. His writings were notable for a superb control of language and a journalist's eye for detail, talents he had demonstrated some time before he went to Addis Ababa. It is said that when he was head of the

British Information Services in New York and Harold Macmillan was Foreign Secretary, one of his compositions found its way on to the Secretary of State's desk; and Macmillan, reading it perhaps with his publisher's rather than his politician's sense, passed it into his out-tray with the scribbled question 'Who is Russell? What is he?' A generation hence, some other publisher could do much worse than to put Russell's Dispatches between hardbacks for, had he not sought a diplomatic career, he might have performed with great distinction as a feature writer on a first-class newspaper. Nothing more readable has ever emerged from the Foreign Office than Sir John Russell on Carnival in Rio, Sir John Russell on the day Lord and Lady Chalfont attended the inauguration of President Costa e Silva, or Sir John Russell on the diplomatic jamboree which culminated in a mishap to one of his ambassadorial colleagues:

> this splendidly bemedalled figure, in a beautiful white uniform and scarlet sash, pardonably tired and perhaps a little unobservant, mistook the ornamental water in front of the Palace for the gleaming wet pavement and stepped right into it, disappearing with dignity up to his Golden Fleece. This restored the evening for me.

A Valedictory dispatch, written just before inflation got under way, calculated that a British Ambassador's time cost the taxpayer something like £300 an hour. If it is true that sometimes the money might have been much better spent elsewhere, it is equally true that other Ambassadors have come very cheap at that price. A few generalizations can be made about these men, but they become very dubious once they are attempted outside the area of status, role and way of life. It is a very daring outsider who attempts an unqualified conclusion about the effectiveness of Ambassadors, or their value, or even the way they go about their job. There is much variety in all these things. There are Ambassadors who complain that they are stifled by the weight of instructions from London, and there are others who lament an apparent indifference to what they think they are supposed to be up to. There are Ambassadors who would still subscribe to every word Sir David Kelly wrote in 1952:[1]

[1] Kelly, p. 118.

The most pathetic fallacy of all is the notion that an Ambassador should cruise around trying to get contacts with the 'man in the street' for the latter, alas, has no more direct personal say in a modern democracy than he had under the Habsburgs or Hohenzollerns; neither has the ordinary professional man.

But there are others who would swiftly point out that the quotation deliberately obscures one prime purpose of every mission, which is to tell London which way a country is heading as well as where it is, and that several British diplomatic failures may be blamed on such obscurantism and the towering elitism that spawned it. 'More ambassadors', said one of them, 'have failed through lack of character than lack of brains, have suffered from the delusion of being a nob when living it up abroad, from lack of intellectual curiosity and, above all, lack of rapport with people.' Someone who may yet reach the heights of his profession said, 'An ambassador's presence pervades the whole mission, particularly if he's a deadbeat – as some are.' The balance between the deadbeats and the rest has always been crucial in British diplomacy. There are still some who are as closed and self-satisfied as any caricature ever drew them. But the best of the Ambassadors, and their wives, have qualities that are rarely equalled in any profession, exceeded in none. The nation, and sometimes civilization beyond it, owes them rather more than it might think possible.

11 Letting the Other Side Have Your Own Way

It says much about diplomacy that so many people have offered such different definitions of it. None of these disagrees with the rest, but they contain enough variety between them to suggest what a sprawling craft diplomacy is compared with most others. Medicine is to do with healing the sick, and there is not much more to be said about it. Diplomacy is far harder to summarize, however, for its very nature is tempered with discretion, loaded with artifice, and always qualified by the extenuating circumstance. The Greek root of the word means 'a doubling', and some people claim to have found dictionaries which, by stealthy degrees, bring the curious down to descriptions of 'uncandid' and 'deceitful'; though it has to be said that in the land of the Foreign Office the OED scrupulously refrains from scoring such easy points. Sir Edward Grey used to say that the aim of diplomacy was to enlarge the area of confidence between nations, and half a century after him Lord Strang described his trade as the art of negotiation and persuasion. Balzac said it was 'a science which permits its practitioners to say nothing and shelter behind mysterious nods of the head'. Some anonymous wit said it was the art of letting the other side have your own way. A German Chancellor before the First World War, Prince von Bülow, settled for 'a first-class stall seat in the theatre of life'. No Englishman has handed down tablets more confidently on these matters – or been quoted more dutifully by successors ever since – than Sir Harold Nicolson, who served in the embassies at Madrid, Istanbul, Teheran and Berlin before turning in his immunity for greater exposure in journalism and politics. How he regarded diplomacy is best conveyed by what he saw as the great diplomatic attributes. He told the first group of Foreign Office recruits after the war that reliability was the most important thing in a diplomat – or, rather, as he always insisted, diploma*tist* – this being a compound of truthfulness, precision, loyalty, modesty and a sense of proportion. Elsewhere Nicolson declared that the ideal Ambassador should be a good linguist, hospitable, a man of taste, patient, imperturbable and tolerant of the ignorance and foolishness in his own government. The Great Mandarin might have found tasteless a quotation which came out of the FCO long after his own days there, to illustrate the most common of all the diplomatic skills. 'I sometimes like to feel', said one British diplomat of the 1970s, 'that if I had to tell a friend he had BO, I could do it in a way that would leave him feeling touched and grateful.'[1]

Diplomacy can be seen as a contraceptive, whose function is not so much to seek solutions as to avoid the worst happening. Diplomats certainly see themselves, in nautical terms, as fenders hanging down the sides of the ship of state, to prevent the paintwork being scratched and hull dented in the event of another vessel barging into it; and, they say, the less room for manoeuvre there may be in the seaway, the more need there is for fenders. For those who argue that improved communications, which enable politicians to meet any time they choose, mean that the diplomat is redundantly fading into a decorative social grin, they have a ready answer. It is that direct dealings between political leaders are dangerous because of their finality. The professional intermediary whose case has been pushed dangerously far can retreat in the next round of talks, without his government losing such public face as when a Foreign Secretary insists on taking a strong line that eventually fails in full view of an international television audience; which happened in 1975, when James Callaghan was to be seen clambering down on the issue of British independence from the EEC at an energy conference in Paris. Lord Trevelyan was not referring to that particular hazard when he claimed that sending special envoys was a bad American habit, but it was a view that covered somewhat the same ground.

It is instructive to note that Sir Harold Nicolson's catalogue of diplomatic attributes did not include the virtue of curiosity; and none of the most frequently repeated definitions of diplomacy appears to take account of it, either. Nor is the word mentioned when recruits to British diplomacy are advised about the

---

[1] Clark, p. 16.

talents they will need most in their new profession, though they are emphatically told to develop their judgment. Yet every official document which reviews the purpose of the British diplomatic machine, considers its reporting job a high priority. 'Her Majesty's Government ... ' said the Plowden Committee, ' ... must be quickly and comprehensively informed about political and economic developments overseas which are of significance to us.'[1] It is not only cynical journalists who believe that, far too often, much greater weight is given in practice to 'significance' than to 'comprehensively' and that judgment of the balance to be held between the two is usually decided by the amount of curiosity the diplomat has about the world he lives in. When the Diplomatic Service Association canvassed members under forty about their profession in 1970, 73 per cent said that the guidance they received on the content and quantity of their reporting was inadequate. A highly experienced Head of Chancery told me that he was appalled by the unevenness of Foreign Office performance in this field. Another man in the middle ranks said that 'journalists can usually tell you at least as much as you can tell them, and frequently far more'. Foreign correspondents who make their number with British embassies at the start of an assignment, to obtain their bearings, are frequently invited to return before going home to tell the diplomats what they've managed to find out on their own account. Many of them conclude by then that this is almost the only source of information the diplomats ever tap outside their own profession and what they regard as 'influential' society; and that sometimes they aren't even very thorough in picking the brains of local journalism.

An Ambassador who snorts derisively at the very idea that he should personally leg it round the country, canvassing the hoi-polloi for information, is begging the question preposterously. The best British Ambassadors, in fact, do exactly that; but they do not need to, with a number of junior men in their missions who might perform the task adequately. *Diplomatic Procedures*, whose numerous volumes regulate the work of the missions abroad, lays down what it calls a 'schedule of external initiative calls'; but that only tells the diplomat how often each week he should be out and about, not which way he should be going.

[1] Plowden, p. 7.

The first thing Sir Peter Ramsbotham told his assembled staff when he took station in Washington, was that they should get out of the American capital as often as possible; but such advice has not always been given in Washington or any other city. Rarer still is an Ambassador's insistence on his men's immersion in their surroundings to the degree laid down by Sir Dugald Stewart in Belgrade. Junior diplomats joining that mission are packed off to live with a Yugoslav family for their first few weeks, partly to improve whatever fluency they have achieved after nine months with a private language tutor in London, but also to get the feel and some understanding of the country from the workaday natives: and, whenever there is an official reception in the embassy, it is an ambassadorial rule that all speeches shall be made in Serbo-Croat, with translations following in English if necessary for the benefit of visitors who don't know the language – up to and including British Cabinet Ministers. As a result of such direction, Britain's standing in Yugoslavia is probably higher in many ways, in spite of political differences, than that of any other country; and no reporting to the Foreign Office from any mission will be more comprehensively well informed of what is significantly happening, or what's likely to happen there.

There was a time when British diplomacy was enriched with specialists who went under the title of Oriental Secretary, though in some places they were known as the Ambassador's dragoman. As the words imply, these were originally situated in Eastern outposts and one of the most famous of them was Lawrence of Arabia's old patron, Sir Ronald Storrs, before he became a Governor and a knight. Their tastes and their gifts were so firmly attached to a particular part of the world that they would remain at the same mission for decades, while less committed men came and went at much shorter intervals. So completely did they belong to their surroundings after a while, so assiduously did they cultivate the acquaintance of everyone who crossed their path, in the market place as well as in the palace, that they became priceless sources of local knowledge to every head of their mission. They were aware of undercurrents sometimes long before a local ruler suspected that he might be swept aside by them. Men with the same accumulated expertise as the dragoman's were to be found eventually in many Western missions: there was Don Bernardo Malley in Madrid, Lance

Pope in Berlin, Michael Winch in Warsaw, Guy Hannaford in
Rome and Charles Mendl in Paris, as well as Walter Smart in
Cairo and Sajjadi in Teheran. The species is not quite extinct
even today. The British Ambassador in Kuwait numbers among
his locally engaged staff a Palestinian who has been on the embassy's pay-roll for the past fifteen years as an invaluable ear to
the ground. He reads the local newspapers every morning and
translates documents for the Consul. But he also attends meetings of the National Assembly, to catch the unedited mood of
local politicians, and drifts through Kuwait's supermarketed
advancement on the soukh. By and large, though, the age of the
dedicated specialists has gone for ever, much lamented by the
old hands. The title of Oriental Secretary was still used in the
embassy at Kabul in the late 1950s; but by then it was worn
only by a young sprig on his first foreign posting, newly acquain-
ted with Farsi, and destined to make his next stop along the
diplomatic line at a more elevated station in Vienna.

It is some indication of priorities today that a great deal of the
information once supplied by the greatest local expert attached
to a British mission is now left to the attention of the most junior
and least experienced diplomat on the staff. It is the Third
Secretary on his baptismal tour abroad, who is generally told
off to scrutinize the local newspapers for anything he thinks may
be of interest at 'morning prayers', the conference to decide
what the day's drift of the mission is likely to be. This is not to
say that the more senior men do not read anything but the air-
mail edition of *The Times*. It is, however, not regarded as their
job to sift the local press thoroughly. Where there is no Labour
Attaché with special skills formed in the Department of
Employment (someone only the larger missions run to), it is the
Third Secretary who is expected to make contact with the local
trade union movement, if it exists, or whatever spokesmen the
local work force have if it does not. It is the Third Secretary who
is instructed to include the police on his beat if, indeed, it is
thought worthwhile to have any dealings with them at all.
Third Secretaries are generally told to keep an eye on student
affairs, which is perhaps the only province in which their experience will provide sounder judgment of what to look for and
how to seek it than ought otherwise to come from superiors
whose college days are much more distant. But in some places,
even the frequently explosive (and therefore influential) world

of the student is left to take pot luck so far as the diplomats are concerned.

There are missions of which everything in the paragraph above will be a travesty; but there are probably far more of which it is a fair summary. The cast of mind it imputes to heads of mission, on whom such matters mostly depend, is frequently to be seen limiting the scope of a mission's collective inquiries in other ways. In spite of Sir Peter Ramsbotham's admirable in-junction to his men to tour the American outback for a rounded view of the United States, local trade union leaders (a very influential group of men in the States) have not been conspicu-ous guests at the residence dinner table, though politicians, businessmen, academics and even journalists have been wel-comed in abundance. Yet, as every diplomat well knows, the most effective way of securing high-grade information, as wel-as of forming useful alliances, is to introduce a potential inform-ant and ally to the flattering attentions of His Excellency's household. Another curious omission in Washington seems to spring from some collective philosophy in the Foreign Office, and stands in direct contrast to American practice in Grosvenor Square. At the United States embassy in London, one officer is detailed to each of the three main political parties, on which he is expected to concentrate the whole of his attention. In Wash-ington, one British Counsellor is posted to keep a general eye on Capitol Hill, but there is no intensive effort to get inside the minds of Republicans or Democrats, by virtually living with them, day in and day out. When MPs asked senior Foreign Office officials in 1975 whether perhaps this was a good Ameri-can habit that might profitably be imitated by the British, they were told 'Our instinct is against it'; but not why.[1]

The value of information picked up inside the diplomatic circle should not be underestimated. But a weakness of some British Ambassadors has been to turn their backs on all non-diplomatic sources of information, occasionally with results that would have been richly comic had they involved only private matters. Some time before the Fifth Republic was proclaimed in France, George Brown – an Opposition front-bencher in 1958 – spent an evening in Paris with an old crony from the Reuters news agency there. The correspondent told him that, from what

[1] *Eighth Report from the Expenditure Committee; Session 1974–5,* p. 79.

he could make out and had heard on his own intricate grape-
vine, it looked as though General de Gaulle was about to rise
as a French phoenix from the ash heap of Algeria. Brown
hastened to the British Embassy next day and told the Ambassador, Sir Gladwyn Jebb, what he had heard. 'Nonsense,' said
Jebb, 'the General is gaga; he commonly refers to himself in the
third person'; and indicated that he intended to convey this
opinion to London by telegram. Ten days later de Gaulle
announced that he was forming a new government of national
safety. There have, of course, been times when diplomats have
warned politicians of impending upheavals, to which the politicians have not seemed to pay the slightest attention. Men with
specialist knowledge of Pakistan spoke to Whitehall of a possible
conflict with India over the East Bengal question some three
years before the eruption of Bangladesh, and two successive
British governments ignored them. But at least politicians can
answer that they are not running a highly organized information
bureau, which has sometimes proved depressingly unreliable.
No one in the Foreign Office predicted the Hungarian uprising
in 1956 when word of its imminence (which could have been
picked up by a mission finely tuned to student chatter) would
conceivably have deflected Sir Anthony Eden from the counter-
attraction he produced a week later at Suez. The overthrow of
Prince Sihanouk in Cambodia a dozen years later was a source
of astonishment in Whitehall, where it was believed that he was
one of the more secure men in South-East Asia. When the Shah
of Iran abolished all political parties in March 1975, the first
the British Embassy in Teheran knew about it was when the
next day's newspapers were opened. Nor is the unevenness of
Foreign Office reporting confined to transmissions from the outposts to London. An Ambassador in the Middle East was startled
one morning in 1975 when, on tuning in to the BBC's External
Service, he was informed that the EEC had just reached a substantial trade agreement with Israel. It was the first he had heard
of it, and he was completely unprepared for the vigorous complaints he would receive from local politicians later in the day.
Yet anyone on three or four different Foreign Office desks
should have been wide awake to the embarrassment the news
would cause every British mission in an Arab country, where
distant early-warning signals are particularly important.
    It is not quite fair to compare the reporting performances of

the diplomats with those of journalists, because the former are always inhibited by one powerful factor which can be completely ignored by the newspaper correspondent. They are expected to maintain at least a working relationship between two governments, and this does not always allow diplomats to behave as they would in a free and civilized society. On many occasions they have little alternative but to cut themselves off from people whose attitudes they might usefully have assessed to the benefit of British government policy. At other times, the diplomatic laager mentality has separated them needlessly from the populace. In one instance, self-imposed isolationism ended catastrophically for the diplomats themselves. In the summer of 1958, one of the Military Attachés at the embassy in Baghdad got wind of an army plot led by Abdul Karim Qasim to overthrow the pro-British Hashemite monarchy and its government in Iraq. Instructions were at once issued that no one in the embassy was to have anything to do with the Qasim faction; which on July 14th, slaughtered the royal family and Prime Minister Nuri es Said – and then marched on the British Embassy, which was burned and looted, one of its staff being killed in the process by a stray bullet.

One has to turn yet again to the eloquence of Trevelyan for the best summary of established Foreign Office dogma on this area of international relationships:[1]

> The sensible British practice is to establish diplomatic relations with any government which has control of a country and looks like keeping it, whether we like it or not ... The Americans, less sensibly, are apt to introduce moral criteria and to refuse to regard a government as worthy of their recognition if they dislike it and hope it will go away ... The American doctrine has been a bad example ... a number of countries in the Middle East and Africa now break off relations because they belong to a group which wants to show disapproval of another country's policy on a particular question ...

As a basic proposition that seems incontestably sane, even though it leaves unanswered the question (unfortunately moral,

[1] Trevelyan, p. 17.

but none the less proper) of the extent to which diplomatic complaisance and even diplomatic toadying shall be admitted into diplomatic relations with a government whose policies are regarded as reprehensible. Some embassies under certain Ambassadors have been undignified by an obsequious approach to their hosts which has been replaced, under the leadership of a new head of the mission, by a more level correctness. If you put morality to even the coolest of Ambassadors, in a land where dissidence smoulders underground as hotly as the sun shines above, he will invariably give you the same retort. It is that he has no business to be getting on terms with the dissidents, however much he may or may not sympathize with their cause, in anticipation of a successful coup. Coups do not always succeed, and to be even distantly implicated in one that backfired would be a disastrous diplomatic gaffe by the representative of a country which can no longer advocate by gunboat. And yet diplomats do temper their responses with considerations of morality, though it is sometimes difficult to determine how much these are controlled by thoughts of national expediency. I asked a man in Belgrade what he would do if, in the absence of the Ambassador or anyone else senior to him, he suddenly heard of a plot to assassinate President Tito which he had reason to think credible. He replied, without a moment's hesitation, 'I'd get on the phone to the foreign ministry straight away, and I'd inform London—in that order.' Other diplomats in other countries whose leaders could come to grief one day said more or less the same thing, though never as emphatically as that. It is possible that in only one capital city of the world, diplomats just might allow human nature to take its course.

Outside examiners have pointed out how finely the diplomatic virtues are separated from the diplomatic vices:[1]

Each of the 'desirable' qualities has its undesirable, but closely related counterpart, for which it may sometimes be mistaken or into which it may sometimes develop. Quickness of intelligence lives close to the substitution of instinct for thought, oral articulateness to glib verbosity, self-confidence to arrogance, equanimity to complacency.

[1] Boardman and Groom, p. 87.

The demarcation between the two is at no point harder to define than in the matter of truth and evasion. Lord Strang has conceded that 'A certain capacity for deception *is* needed in a diplomatist ... ', but then rather blurred the issue by implying that it was needed only as 'in the domain of ordinary good manners'.[1] New entrants to the Foreign Office in 1974 were very firmly told by a senior official 'In this racket one does not and one should not lie', just after another speaker had informed them that 'White lies are part of normal social interchange', adding that it was *sometimes* better to say nothing than to say something that was misleading. In diplomacy, strict honesty and total candour are quite obviously out of the question in some circumstances; more often than not, maybe. But there are techniques of evasion accepted by all diplomats as coming from their universal codebook which the wise ones (in this context, those with the finest appreciation of how self-interest is ultimately served best) will abandon only with reluctance for something more immediately expedient. Political leaders can be as deft as any Ambassador here, and none was better at it than President Nasser. When, in 1956, Sir Humphrey Trevelyan put it to him that he was responsible for subversion in Aden, Nasser replied that he had no agents there, which Trevelyan took to mean that the Egyptian was operating through local dissidents. When the Ambassador complained about hostile propaganda transmitted by Cairo Radio, the President said that he did not control the programmes. Between those two men, this was as good as saying that he had merely instructed the radio director to attack the British government. 'These devices', wrote the Ambassador later, 'did not destroy the possibility of a serious negotiation, because he knew that we would not believe him but would recognise that he could not admit the charge.'[2]

Sometimes, however, such techniques can become positively Byzantine in their intricacy, as many European diplomats reckoned twenty years ago after dealings with the American Secretary of State. 'Mr Dulles, a man of the highest Christian principles,' says Trevelyan,[3]

[1] Strang, p. 170.
[2] Trevelyan, p. 57.
[3] Trevelyan, p. 56.

T

conducted the foreign relations of the United States in a way that led others to look for the fine print on the back of the contract, as many American diplomats acknowledge. In 1954, before the Geneva conference, he tried to make out that Mr Eden was committed to his proposals on South-east Asian defence, knowing that this was not true. In 1956, he told the Egyptians privately that they should look out for the French, who were trying to settle the Algerian war in Cairo. At the same time he was ostensibly backing the proposal to form a Suez Canal Users' Association, with the intention of making it impossible for the British and French to use force, and ensuring that the association would be wholly ineffective.

This was going far beyond a commonplace American evasion, no more than a politeness between gentlemen who understand each other, when its representatives wish to reject something in the least troublesome way possible: they simply say that 'Congress won't wear it', even when they have not the slightest intention of letting the proposal get within a mile of the Hill.

The British like to think that they are not naturally as tricky as some others they could name, though so steeped are they in the oblique ways of their craft that they disguise the vanity of the assumption by saying modestly that when they try a trick or two they are not very good at it; which may well be true, without necessarily supporting the assumption. However strongly they adhere to a philosophy of straight dealing within the rules, the fact is that in their profession, ambiguity is often regarded as a necessity, and tact is frequently carried to the length of guile. Torn between Machiavelli and Sir Ernest Gowers, the diplomats have produced a language of their own, in which nothing need be quite what it is said to be in the clearest possible fashion. This is something other than the muffled incoherence sometimes found in other quarters of the civil service and in local government officers, whose sentences may read as though they had been dictated by a man with his head swathed in seven thicknesses of blanket. Diplomatic language is a highly conscious act and a very artful form of communication. It is carefully balanced with any number of possibilities and it is meticulously structured with loopholes. It can be weightless with uncertainty, but it is never less than well considered. If an Ambassador refers to an agricultural implement, it is because he will not call a spade a spade for fear that it may be mistaken for a bloody shovel. There are parts of the world where it is commonplace to insinuate some form of bribe into commercial contracts arranged between governments and business corporations, and the scandals of 1976 trailing out of the American Lockheed company and the British Petroleum and Shell organizations, gave us some idea of its scale. Some of the industrialized nations now have small official agencies specifically charged with catering for corruption. The British have so far kept clear of this muckiest side of international commerce, maybe out of poverty rather than righteousness. This is not to say that an influential visitor to London will ever fail to obtain the right address in Mayfair or St John's Wood if he solicits the nearest First Secretary in Whitehall. But when an embassy finds that someone proposes to work a backhander into his transaction with the government, it declines to accommodate him as inscrutably as possible. In such cases the jargon maintains that 'The tender has been misunderstood ... '. After a professional lifetime in the deep end of such language and the philosophy it represents, diplomats can sometimes find themselves a little wistful, as though a misspent youth had unexpectedly extended to the threshold of old age. A very sensitive man, asked whether he had any regrets about his way to the top said: 'Just one; being all things to all men.'

It is when all the blandest felicities of diplomatic language have failed that the sterner stuff of diplomatic relations begins. The worst thing a country can do to another, short of declaring war, is to end official contact by recalling its own Ambassador and closing its own embassy, simultaneously telling its opposite number to shove off home. Things have to become bitterly difficult before this step is taken by countries operating on traditional lines; although, as Lord Trevelyan observed, the essential diplomatic violence of this act has been somewhat vitiated in recent years by its use as a form of muscle-flexing in diplomatically youthful capitals. Even before diplomatic relations are broken off, leaving the problem of how to reconnect two countries in better times, a variety of ploys is available to either one wishing to show its displeasure or sense of grievance to the other. The heaviest pressure the British could exert at this stage of affairs would be to instruct Her Majesty's Ambassador to talk directly to the leader of the other government, over the head of the Foreign Minister, while at the same time summoning the other country's Ambassador to the FCO to hear what the Foreign Secretary had to say to him. When an Ambassador meets a head of state or a Foreign Minister, with his government's Note of protest, things are getting relatively serious, even though they are still not beyond recall. The system has any number of devices built into it to regulate the force of such diplomatic impact. A small one governs the exchange of memoranda. If the Ambassador presents the Foreign Minister with an unsigned paper headed '*Pour mémoire*', it is an informal note of what he has to say, and may only be used by the Foreign Minister in making his own record of the encounter; but if the paper is headed '*Aide-mémoire*' then its contents are instantly transformed into an official document, which may be quoted later in official correspondence.

Diplomatic protests, in fact, are generally nothing more than gestures, and no one is more astonished than the immediate participants if they are swiftly followed by the sound of gunfire. They are, moreover, not even always gestures of anger. They are sometimes no more than a way of suggesting injured innocence to an international audience. Occasionally, they can be as tiresome a ritual as that of the footballer who regularly takes a tumble in the hope that some undeserved benefit will be awarded by the referee. Almost always they alarm the rest of us much more than they do the diplomats themselves. When Iceland broke off diplomatic relations in February 1976, during the third cod war, this meant that the British Ambassador alone was declared *persona non grata* that only His Excellency was required to flee Reykjavik. Although he had to close the shop behind him, his entire staff simply moved down the road to the obliging French embassy, where they carried on their daily work of attending to British interests on the island. Nothing can illustrate better than that episode the most remarkable effect modern communication has had on diplomacy. For in the weeks before relations were broken off, British television crews were aboard Icelandic gunboats and inside Icelandic supermarkets, presenting the Icelandic case to the British people. More significantly, the Icelandic Ambassador in London was appearing on our television screens, doggedly advocating his country's cause, in defiance (and with BBC collusion) of all diplomatic protocol.

Long before the diplomats think of waving their protest Notes, however, they are in dialogue with each other on behalf of their governments. Their bread and butter business is the meeting, both formal and informal, the set negotiation, and the walk through the park, carefully dropping hints to each other like a flutter of autumn leaves. 'This', said the Duncan Committee, 'is the basic and indispensable diplomatic function.'[1] Like all ringing phrases, that one sounds as if someone — after a great deal of time and effort spent on less important things — has at last and triumphantly found the simple heart of the matter. This is misleading. The dialogue between governments may be basic diplomacy, but simple it never was.

It matters very much, for a start, who is dealing with whom. Just as there are universal techniques of evasion which may be applied with reasonable confidence in any diplomatic company, so there are special techniques which have to be learned in order to get on with selected foreigners. National temperaments, as even the rest of us notice, are not at all the same wherever you go. Arabs set a great deal of store by the gesture someone makes, often responding to it much more than to the substance of what they offer or withdraw. Nothing could be more alien to the ways of the French, whose gestures are meant to clothe or camouflage a substance which is very carefully weighed. If our men at NATO headquarters in Belgium want a co-ordinated Italian view of the alliance they have to track it down to Rome, because the Italian diplomats in Brussels keep their military men at arm's length; whereas the Germans, like the British, quite often sit on each other's laps. The Greeks will share secrets like a village gossip, but almost all of them can be obtained from respectable newspapers elsewhere. The Americans, on the other hand, are much more tight-lipped than laymen suppose but at least, when they decide to utter, what emerges is usually arresting. As they move from one country to another in the course of a career, the diplomats must sometimes feel as though they are picking their way through minefields of idiosyncrasy which may blow up in their faces if they take one indelicate step. They must remember, at every African post, never to say or do anything that could possibly be interpreted as patronizing one of the locals. As a man in Nairobi put it, 'Aggressively English houses aren't the best places for an

[1] Duncan, p. 18.

African politician to unburden himself in.' In some places, the diplomats even have to worry lest offence shall be given by some Englishman at home in a matter that cannot concern a democratic government. When some unknowing fellow added a camel to his troop of donkeys on Scarborough pleasure beach, and named the beast Mohammed, Ambassadors in some Islamic lands braced themselves to go through motions of grovelling apology. When a judge in the Netherlands was lenient in his treatment of some Iranian students who had rebelliously raided their own embassy at The Hague, the Dutch in Teheran were in the doghouse for months afterwards.

Dealing with the Russians is a performance with rules of its own, different from but not necessarily more complex than those applied elsewhere, except that they are liable to change more starkly from time to time, according to the political weather prevailing at the moment. And that is something over which Soviet diplomats have almost no control, unlike their opposite numbers in the West. The Ambassador, as a species, does not rank very high in the Soviet order of things. It is said that only Mr Dobrynin in Washington is in a position to conduct major diplomacy for his country, by making some decisions off his own bat and by advising his government what to do. His colleagues in other posts do not generally open their mouths at all without first consulting 'the leadership' at home. And 'the leadership', even on its own doorstep, is not often accessible to foreign diplomats. All this means that a British Ambassador in Moscow and his staff are largely straws in a highly variable wind, and there is nothing they can do about it except to seize limited opportunities. When Sir John Killick went to Moscow in 1971 the climate was very bad, Sir Alec Douglas-Home having just bundled 105 Soviet diplomats out of London. The Ambassador was never really much more than a postman between two correspondents who didn't have much to say to each other. By the time Sir Terence Garvey left Moscow some four years later, spring had returned and summer was conceivable, and some marvellous things had been wrought by the standards of the Killick years. A new Anglo-Soviet agreement had been signed, characters from 'the leadership' had occasionally ventured inside the embassy, and Sir Terence and Mr Kuznetsov (a member of the Politbureau) were in a position to say some pretty raw things to each other behind closed doors, like human beings, without any displacement of what the Russians called 'a qualitative shift' in the overall relationship between the two countries. But Sir John might have fared just as well, and Sir Terence as ill, had their postings been reversed. By 1975 it was possible for the British diplomats to make direct contact with a number of elements in the Soviet machine, like the Ministry of Agriculture, the Ministry of Defence, the Central Committee of the Party and the Supreme Soviet itself, which had been quite closed to them in the chilly times of 1971 and 1972. Until just before the agreement of February 1975, all dealings had been confined to contact with officials from the Second European Department of the Foreign Ministry, whose title is a little misleading, for it rather charmingly rivets the whole of its attention on the white countries of the old British Empire.

It doesn't make much difference who the British diplomat wishes to deal with in Moscow: all procedures are invariable from one Soviet department to another. Whatever it is that he wants to say to his opposite number he must write down on paper and, having said it, he must leave the paper behind so that it can be filed and subsequently used, if need be, as proof of the words he uttered. The diplomats are never quite sure whether this requirement arises from Russian suspicion of foreigners or a specifically Soviet desire for precision in all things; whichever it may be, it is uncommonly tedious to more casual souls from farther West. Nothing whatsoever, apart from making an appointment, may be transmitted in any other way, the very idea of picking up a telephone to discuss business being regarded in Moscow as a bit of a liberty, and a very baffling one at that. So gingerly do both sides feel they must tread even at the best of times, that in their official encounters they normally talk to each other through an interpreter (who is always a Russian), even when they speak each other's language well. That goes for a First Secretary from the embassy, trying to clarify a delivery date at Tilbury Docks with a quite lowly figure from Sovexport, whom he may visit every other day for weeks; it goes for the Ambassador himself, during his interview once or twice a fortnight with the Head of the Second European Department, or when he is closeted with Mr Gromyko four or five times a year.

Normal contact can be tedious and set negotiations are always exhausting. This is where the formality of Moscow reaches a height unsurpassed anywhere, equalled only by other Eastern

European countries, and attractive to no one but those nations which are developing politically similar frames of mind. They, too, have acquired a taste for the issue of formal public documents on the most ordinary diplomatic occasion, and the long and weary work that goes into their composition. There are meetings between the British and Russians four times a year on current documents, which means that preparatory discussions are almost continuous. It is these that take the stuffing out of all but the most robust men, and diplomacy in this part of the world may be rather less a matter of guile than it is of sheer physical stamina. The most effective diplomatic weapon the Soviet representatives use is endless repetition, which can wear the opposition down. Frequently the same argument will be repeated for months until, the figures across the table visibly wilting, it will be switched to something rather different, which had been meticulously planned as the final position right from the beginning. When Western nations tussle among themselves, it is customary for bargains to be made at the table by diplomats with sufficient authority to strike them impromptu if they judge this worthwhile. Nothing could be more alien to the methods used in Moscow. If there is to be the smallest concession from the hosts, it will have been thoroughly debated by 'the leadership' first, before any hint of it is allowed to reach the opposition.

Neither the British nor anyone else, however, are helpless before this diplomatic juggernaut. Getting in the first draft gives you a certain initial advantage, say the diplomats, for it places you in the driving seat for the first lap. You put up some suggestions that are quite dispensable, so that you will eventually have appeared to give generous ground when you have not retreated at all. You take care not to have an agenda too fixed, which only plays into the hands of the heavy mob at the expense of those who are lighter on their feet. You bear in mind the fact that, although the Russians can be as devious as anyone on earth, they are no more liars than you are and they will never undertake to do anything unless they are sure they can deliver.

When a major political visitation is afoot, like that of Harold Wilson and his supporting cast to Moscow in February 1975, a taste for small drama and useful public relations ordains that the agreement signed by the politicians shall seem to have sprung out of the visit itself. Nothing, of course, could be more far-fetched; the diplomats on both sides had been working on the Anglo-Soviet agreement for months beforehand. Hundreds of man-hours had been spent on shaping just one paragraph, whose final form was this:

> 27 The two sides reviewed the possibilities of extending their contacts into other fields. In this connection they reached agreement on an exchange of visits between representatives of the Armed Forces.

The main object of the journey by the Prime Minister and other members of his government was to seal certain commercial and economic understandings between the two countries; henceforth, unless there is some shockingly bad weather, they will swap textile equipment for hydrofoil ships among many other things, and may even get round to the joint design of civil aircraft engines in due course. But the final agreement sprawled across a number of other issues, including the one referred to with such difficulty in Paragraph 27. Not all of them had been quite resolved by the time the British leaders reached Moscow, and during the five days of the official visit, the diplomats were still trying to agree on the expression of Paragraph 24, which was to do with cultural links. This contained just eighty words. The British wanted more specific language used as the deadline approached, the Russians preferred to keep things vague. In the end, the final working party spent three full hours debating the weight of a solitary word. This by then had assumed such transcending importance that when the Russian and British secretaries were given the final draft agreement in two languages to type out for signature by Mr Wilson and Mr Brezhnev, they were instructed to leave a blank space for Paragraph 24, so that it could be popped in at the very last minute. The communiqué signalling the end of the official talks had itself been hammered out sentence by sentence in the course of three consecutive nights, which started at some time between 6 p.m. and 7 p.m. and never ended before 2.30 a.m. Not at all strange, maybe, to men accustomed to late sittings in the House of Commons, though they passed up most of this one and got on with 'useful conversations'. Their big moment came when the diplomats abandoned their strategic positions in the Ministry of Foreign Affairs and a commandeered hotel, and moved in for the climactic moment at the Kremlin. And there, in a chamber where the Czars used to meet the Knights of St George, while the flashbulbs flared and the diplomats looked drained, the two leaders signed their agreement and smiled upon the world amidst many a bilateral cry of 'Peace and Friendship'.

Parleying in other places can be as wearying as any long passage of diplomatic arms in Moscow, and some of the most intricate negotiations have left participants feeling that they have been far removed from reality for a very long time. It took twenty-five years of intermittent haggling for the United Nations to reach an agreed definition of 'aggression'. Even when a long-sought object has been achieved through negotiation, diplomats do not wallow too long in a sense of their own success, for experience has taught them that every triumph on earth is likely to be accompanied by certain unwelcome consequences. It was jolly nice in 1974 to have stage-managed for Massey-Ferguson & Perkins a deal with the Polish Government worth £150 million to the British. It would have been even nicer if it hadn't carried a high probability that the next ten years would bristle with complaints by the Poles about British technicians spying out there, and complaints by the British about Polish treatment of Her Majesty's loyal subjects.

There are certain ground rules to negotiation everywhere. It is essential to understand the other man's case and position, where his weaknesses and his strengths lie, and where he can make his concessions. Unless both sides can be content with their agreement it is unlikely to last for long. You need everlasting patience and, although controlled indignation can be a useful lever, sarcasm is the last thing that will help a diplomat's cause. Ernie Bevin drummed it into a rising generation of Foreign Office men that they should always resist the temptation to score points, and the advice has not been forgotten. It is helpful to create as much time as possible in which to think out your next move and it is for this reason as much as any other that, in set pieces, interpreters are the rule rather than the exception. The squad provided by the United Nations are excellent and, of the rest, the Russians and the Chinese are reckoned to be the best-trained, and utterly reliable. There is no one to beat the British in Arabic, French interpreters are a mixture of the brilliant and the comic, while the polyglot Americans can usually produce someone to cope perfectly well with any language spoken. Even the most highly-skilled diplomat is sometimes glad of the pause these experts provide while he re-musters his wits for the next tack. But if one thing distinguishes the brilliant negotiator from the merely adequate, it is his own sense of timing his moves. This, in itself, demands a most sensitive feel for the way things are going, an appreciation that flexibility will pay because a favourable settlement will thereby be coated with goodwill, or that obstinacy is the thing, in order to cut impending losses as much as possible.

This sense of timing, say British diplomats, is a distinctive Foreign Office contribution to all those international meetings in which the government is mostly represented by specialists from other parts of Whitehall staffed by the Home Civil Service. It is no longer an exclusive FCO skill in such circles, for many Home men are now highly experienced in the negotiating jungle of the Common Market. But a man from the Department of Trade, an expert on aviation at a conference on hi-jacking, is still rather more likely to come in on the wrong beat than the diplomatic maestro playing second fiddle to him at the next desk. He will be an exceptionally well-informed civil servant if he has a diplomatic grasp of all the potential repercussions abroad of any position he may wish to adopt for purely special-ist reasons. At a telecommunications conference some years ago, diplomats were attached to a squad of Post Office experts, to steer them through the bewilderments of pan-European and transatlantic compromise. The Postmen came to the conference with a strong conviction, based on technical grounds alone, that British methods and equipment should henceforth tally with those of the United States; and the Americans, naturally, sought the same alliance. The experts seemed quite unaware that if Britain took this line it would be interpreted by the other European delegates, the French in particular, as a political stance; and that this might have a disastrous effect on Britain's chances of entering the Common Market, which at that time mattered more to the Foreign Office than any other issue in the world. The diplomats in the delegation therefore started the week's operation by getting to work on their own Postmen, per-suading them that a purely technical decision would be folly for the nation. 'In the end,' said one of the diplomats later, 'we didn't get quite what we wanted, the Yanks didn't get quite what they wanted, the Europeans didn't get quite what they wanted. But the thing has worked tolerably well since and relationships have been maintained.'

Diplomats have long been fond of stories illustrating the ineptitude of Home civil servants in faraway places, and the taste for them has only recently shown signs of waning. Some from the dimmer past are hair-raising, none more so than one dating back to 1944, when a conference on civil aviation was held in Chicago. This had gathered, in effect, to carve up the aircraft production cake that was obviously waiting to be devoured as soon as peace was declared. The Americans were in an overwhelmingly strong position before the first session began. Not only had they developed a wartime capacity which could satisfy demands for civil aircraft throughout the world; alone, among all competitors, their industry had not suffered by so much as one war-damaged brick. From the outset they were intent on a free-for-all in peacetime aircraft production. The British and the French, conscious that they were heavily handicapped in this race, wanted controlled post-war expansion. The British delegation was led by Lord Swinton, a politician, whose chief advisers were Sir Arthur Street, Permanent Secretary at the Ministry of Aviation, and Mr George Cribbett, the leading expert on international air transport. On arrival in Chicago, these two men announced that they would be too busy to attend the delegation meetings, which meant that the diplomats in the team were severely underbriefed when they took to the conference floor. 'If Lord Swinton had had more international conference experience, or if I had had more rank at the time,' writes Lord Gore-Booth, who was in the Foreign Office team, 'this nonsense would have been stopped. As it was, the delegation met from day to day in the absence of the top aviation policy experts.'[1] The Americans ran rings round the British in Chicago; and Boeing subsequently took off with an unchallengeable lead in civil aviation.

Lord Gore-Booth tells another story which sheds a tiny beam upon the covert ways by which diplomats sometimes arrive at compromise. As a rising man, he was involved in Anglo-German talks on the matter of military upkeep costs in post-war Germany. He got on well with the chief German negotiator, Dr A. H. van Scherpenberg, and together they arrived at a figure that was

---

[1] Gore-Booth, p. 131.

acceptable to both sides. This still left the date for a final payment by the Germans subject to argument by the two governments. 'Scherpie passed me a note: "I can't suggest May 15th,
but I might get it accepted if you propose it." After a few
minutes on some formal points, I said that, at peril to my reputation, I would be prepared to suggest May 15th.'[1] Thus the
matter was settled, though the anecdote doesn't make it crystal
clear which government came nearest to achieving its un-
compromised objective.

Compromise being the very essence of negotiation, the most
extraordinarily laborious steps are taken to reach it at international meetings. Which languages official utterances shall be
made in, how precisely the seating of delegates shall be arranged,
who shall act as chairman at which sessions – all such matters
are carefully contrived to reduce the risks of inflammation in
hypersensitive quarters, which might imperil compromise before
the opening speech has even been spoken. A classic example of
this extreme care was the Geneva Conference in 1954, which
met from April 26th to July 21st that year, in an attempt to
sort out some peaceful solution to hostilities in Korea and
Indo-China (see Figure 2). In Korea there was stalemate,
following the armistice at Panmunjom, signed the year before.
In Indo-China, the French garrison at Dien Bien Phu fell to
Viet Minh forces while the Geneva Conference was actually in
progress. A highly diplomatic procedure, in fact, was to hold
two consecutive conferences in the Palais des Nations under the
one title, the first to consider Korea, the second Indo-China.
This required a great deal of ingenuity. For twenty-three
delegations had gathered in Switzerland, and some of them
were from governments which did not recognize the existence
of others. Many of those that did maintain embassies in each
other's capitals were distinctly hostile. To avoid what the
diplomats regarded as 'embarrassing proximities', two different
seating plans were devised for the delegates. One, used for the
Korean phase of the conference, placed them in a semi-circle
in English alphabetical order; the other, for the debates on
Indo-China, had them in an oval or a hollow square according
to the French alphabetical order. Similar thought was given
to the languages which should be used. It was decided that the

---

[1] Gore-Booth, p. 235.

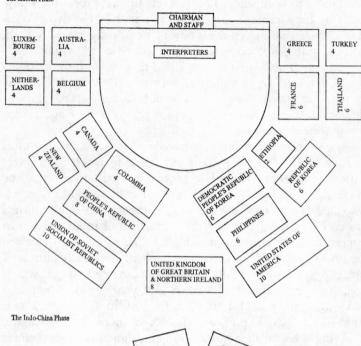

The Korean Phase

CHAIRMAN AND STAFF

INTERPRETERS

LUXEMBOURG 4

AUSTRALIA 4

NETHERLANDS 4

BELGIUM 4

GREECE 4

TURKEY 4

FRANCE 6

THAILAND 6

CANADA 4

NEW ZEALAND 4

COLOMBIA 4

PEOPLE'S REPUBLIC OF CHINA 8

UNION OF SOVIET SOCIALIST REPUBLICS 10

UNITED KINGDOM OF GREAT BRITAIN & NORTHERN IRELAND 8

ETHIOPIA 2

DEMOCRATIC PEOPLE'S REPUBLIC OF KOREA 6

REPUBLIC OF KOREA 6

PHILIPPINES 6

UNITED STATES OF AMERICA 10

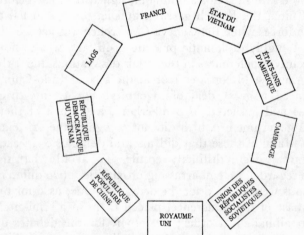

The Indo-China Phase

FRANCE

ÉTAT DU VIETNAM

LAOS

ÉTATS-UNIS D'AMÉRIQUE

RÉPUBLIQUE DÉMOCRATIQUE DU VIETNAM

CAMBODGE

RÉPUBLIQUE POPULAIRE DE CHINE

UNION DES RÉPUBLIQUES SOCIALISTES SOVIÉTIQUES

ROYAUME-UNI

FIGURE 2 *Delegation Plan for the Geneva Conference, 1954*
The different seating plans for the two phases of the conference. The figures show the number of seats allotted to each delegation.

(*Source*: Satow, p. 321.)

official tongues of the conference would be French, Russian, English, Chinese and Korean, each used for a day at a time in that order: all speeches were interpreted into the language of the day on the conference floor, with simultaneous translations into the other four provided through headsets. The chair of the conference was carefully rotated from one session to the next, too. On Korean topics it was occupied in turn by three foreign ministers – Prince Wan of Thailand, Mr Molotov and Sir Anthony Eden. For Indo-China, first the Englishman and then the Russian sat in the top seat. 'The pattern of the Geneva Conference', according to the patriarchal Satow, 'was reminiscent of many conferences of the eighteenth and nineteenth centuries. It had a character and dignity of its own, which, except during the final week, were unruffled by the pressure of drafting treaty texts and voting on numerous clauses and amendments which is typical of conferences in recent times.'[1] The conference may have had a fine old-fashioned flavour, but it did lack something. It failed to break the deadlock in Korea, and it produced no political stability in what we were shortly to call Vietnam.

What diplomatic gatherings at that level are always driving towards is the treaty. Even the diplomats themselves use this word rather loosely these days to cover a number of circumstances that are more properly identified as conventions, declarations, agreements, protocols, or even simple exchanges of Notes. A purist will insist that a real treaty is a formal instrument by which states establish a relationship under international law; which is a comparatively rare condition. It is still significant enough, however, for the men on the Quai D'Orsay to go very cannily when they put their signatures to such pieces of paper. There is an article in the United Nations Charter stipulating that all treaties are to be registered with the UN. This is something the French regularly neglect, unless the document is heavily to the advantage of Paris, so that the treaty cannot be invoked at the International Court at The Hague in anybody's dispute with France.

The oldest abiding treaty maintained by the British is that much quoted parchment of 1373 swearing to Peace, Friendship and Alliance with Portugal. Its negotiators – 'we, William Lord

[1] Satow, p. 321.

Latimer, of the Army, Baron and Royal Chamberlain, and Thomas Youngman, Officer of the Court of Canterbury ... ' on the one hand, and 'Fidalgo John Ferdinand de Andeiro, of the Army, and the Venerable and Discreet Senhor Velasco Domingo, Precentor of the Cathedral of Braga ... ' on the other – were following procedures which have not changed all that much across six centuries. It is the number of treaties concluded now, compared with their days, which has altered beyond all recognition. In 1973, the Foreign Office had a hand in 130 treaties, though well over three-quarters of them were exchanges of Notes. Even so, ten years earlier the figure would have been somewhere between 90 and 100. The increase was ascribed to the number of new states which had been created in that time, all panting to make their mark in the diplomatic world. Not every stripling ministry of foreign affairs is instantly equipped with the studied techniques of drafting a treaty, but there is a camaraderie among all diplomats which is meant to surmount such obstacles. A young country in the Third World thus felt quite able to approach the local British embassy not so long ago to say that it would be taken kindly if the British, in preparing their own version of the treaty about to be signed between the two parties, would just run off a variation of it at the same time, composed from the alternative point of view. Treaty-making is frequently much more tiresome than that between long-established allies. The men in the Nationality and Treaty Department at the Foreign Office sigh heavily and turn to their legal adviser the moment they hear that some negotiation with the Americans is coming to a harmonious end; for, in many cases, the Federal government in Washington cannot vouch alone for the USA, and the document has to be touted round some proportion of the fifty state capitals. But all treaty-making is a laborious business. Drafting the Treaty of Accession, by which Britain entered the Common Market in 1972, took a team of diplomats three full months, during which they worked every day from 10 a.m. to midnight, with the exception of just two Sundays.

This is where protocol flourishes at its thickest, where it must be observed most carefully if trouble is to be avoided later on. No government Minister from Britain may make a treaty without express permission, which only the Foreign Secretary can give him. An Ambassador may sign a treaty, but only if he, too, has been given special powers which make him a Plenipotentiary as well as an Excellency. It is vital to get the termination clause right, and not to forget what the time limit is. Britain once had an extradition treaty with Brazil but it was abrogated in 1913 and, like many an author with his copyright, no one had bothered to renew it. Sixty years later a confident hand reached for the document and discovered that the Metropolitan Police had no power at all to retrieve the Great Train Robber Ronald Biggs from Rio de Janeiro.

There are, however, no rules about where a full-blown purist's treaty shall be signed. It usually depends upon which capital the next Ministerial cavalcade visits, so that the result of so much diplomatic spadework, ponderous with seals and handsomely bound in red, shall be properly saluted with maximum ceremony. The instrument of ratification (bound in blue with the royal arms embossed) is signed later in the opposite camp with much less fuss and bother. When this event happens in London, it is relegated to a Foreign Office by-way near the St James's Park tube station, where the visitors are thoughtfully given a glass of sherry, so that they will not dwell too much on the austerity of their surroundings and may feel that their journey has been really necessary after all. And if only, say the diplomats, if only that were the end of our labour ... But it isn't. Diplomacy involves so many things today that were not even necromantic conjectures in 1373. Parts of it might make Sir Harold Nicolson wonder whether his definitions were still adequate. The wise diplomat in some quarters can almost expect the barometer to tell him how busy he will be this day, for if the monsoon should fail over Bangladesh, who knows what things will have to be settled in the chanceries of Dacca, New Delhi and Islamabad? And how on earth *do* you present the National Enterprise Board overseas to foreign investors with a paralysing fear of nationaliza-tion?

U

12 Bread and Butter Business

It is not always possible to guess what manner of mission you have come to from a quick look round the reception area in the chancery building. The visitor to Moscow might suppose that he had wandered into an affiliation of the Travellers' Club, or conceivably a stray ancestral home of the Landseers. In Cairo the lobby suggests postal sorting or driving licences, some form of provincial civil service anyway, all pastel distemper and utility metal window frames. A few posts, quite lacking good old-fashioned style, yet manage to hint that there may be some grandeur within, and Washington is one of them. Most of the entrance hall there is merely an updated version of what Cairo has, with a security notice about WINDOW CLEANING TODAY parked under the stairs and a great deal of plate glass to worry about when the day comes. There is also a marble wall alongside the lift shaft, with a deeply incised list of all the British Ambassadors to the United States gleaming in gold upon it, from '1791 George Hammond' to '1971 The Earl of Cromer'. No place makes the newcomer blink more than the British Embassy in Teheran; so much so, that many must have continued to revolve in the doors and left again in the belief that they had come to the wrong address. For, standing in the middle of the floor, is a display frame with great blown-up photographs exhibited on four sides under the title 'The British Poultry Industry'. According to the caption beneath one perky-looking bird, 'The Babcock B300 white-egg laying hen averages 265–280 large eggs each year and is consistently successful in comprehensive laying tests.' This is not quite what you'd expect of a place where Churchill, Roosevelt and Stalin met to settle Eastern Europe's hash, where the Englishman presented the Sword of Stalingrad to his gallant Soviet ally. But times do change and diplomacy sometimes adjusts. A reflective glance at the Babcock B300 might suggest that the British Embassy in Teheran thinks rather more of bread and butter, rather less of grand political alliances, today. And that is no less than the truth.

Outside the Ambassador's office a row of portraits hangs upon the wall. You find similar photographs in every embassy, but in few places do they subtly tell you more about transformed international relationships than these. The first is of Sir Percy Loraine, taken in 1922, and it is followed by one of Sir Reginald Hoare, presenting his credentials in 1931. Then comes Sir Hughe Knatchbull-Hugessen, who was here between 1934 and 1936. Those were the days when Great Britain ruled a lot of the world and put many distant potentates firmly in their place. Even so lustrous a figure as the Shah of Iran did not merit a full British Ambassador in London's eyes. Sir Percy, Sir Reginald and Sir Hughe were merely His Majesty's Ministers in Teheran, men of secondary importance at the Foreign Office in an age when knighthoods came along with the diplomatic rations to most people in charge of a British mission. By the time Sir Reader Bullard reached the embassy in 1944, however, Iran had risen in our estimation; possibly because she had not contested Allied occupation during the war, maybe because her oil was already something more than the coming thing, conceivably because this was ground over which old allies might swiftly fall out. So Sir Reader came as British Ambassador: and there he is outside his successor's office, surrounded by rather rigid fellows in diplomatic full dress, and a winsome young lady clad in academic gown and mortar board, who these days prefers tweeds and is known in London University and much farther afield as Professor A. K. S. Lambton, the world's chief authority on the subject of Persian land reform.

Ambassadors do not always share the same skills, and a country's interests abroad can change enough for a mission to be led through one term of diplomatic duty by a man with a rather different talent from his predecessor's. When Sir Peter Ramsbotham became Ambassador in Teheran in 1971, Britain was withdrawing her military forces from the Persian Gulf, a power vacuum was created in the area, and the Foreign Office needed close to the Shah a man whose nose twitched at the smell of high politics and Defence; and Ramsbotham, just tested by a couple of years on the political tightrope in Nicosia,

with twelve months at the Institute for Strategic Studies beforehand seemed the man for the job. By the time he left for
Washington two and a half years later, things in Teheran had
changed. The Shah was in confirmed alliance with Britain and
America, and had built up his armed forces beyond the risk of
challenge by threatening neighbours. He had also started to
capitalize on his country's strength as an oil producer, leading
the rush to raise prices after the October War in the Middle
East. From where London was rather faintly sitting by then, a
somewhat different manner of Ambassador in Teheran was
called for; a man who might have been marginally less effective
than Sir Peter Ramsbotham, faced with the instructions of 1971,
but who had a greater zest for economic diplomacy. The Foreign
Office now wanted someone who would get into the most
profitable commerce with the Shah, and they asked Sir Anthony
Parsons to take the post. He was an Arabist who had just spent
three years in London as an Assistant Under Secretary. The
first thing he told his new staff was that he didn't want to read
a lot of elegant reports from them about social conditions in
Iranian villages. He saw this as one of the few places where an
embassy could do something positive about British interests,
rather than merely reacting to other people's pressures.

The Ambassador's arrival coincided with a boom time in
Teheran which has been compared to Dawson City's sensational
years during the Klondike gold rush at the end of the nineteenth
century. A country of relatively modest influence and fairly
primitive structure had suddenly become a paymaster of the
Western world, with grandiose plans for its own improvement
which attracted the official entrepreneur and the private
carpetbagger from every industrialized land which needed to
sell more frantically than ever before in the face of soaring bills
from the oil producers. Some cool diplomatic customers in 1974
were taking the view that by 1977–8 Iran would itself be
borrowing money again, that it would be 'a proper country
then, instead of Father Christmas'. Meanwhile, it has represented a jackpot to be shared by anyone who can make the right
bids, or is merely willing to accept certain personal hazards.
Americans teaching Iranians to fly Bell helicopters are paid 10
per cent danger money to compensate for the risk of assassina-
tion which not even Savak (the state security police) can obviate.

The Shah's attitude to the British is one of surprising benevolence, from one who has deeply resented imperial history. This is a very complex ruler who wants to create an Aryan Japan out of a traditionally Muslim peasant society, who has a lofty contempt for the democratic rot he observes in Western Europe, who has a lurking admiration for the refined old discipline of the English public school. He despises the permissive society tolerated by London, yet he has no desire to see Great Britain's total collapse. His loan of £1 billion in 1974 may be thought of as an autocrat's whim to obtain pleasure from the sight of old patrons sunk sadly in debt and gratitude, but it was at least as generous as the American Lend-Lease Act of 1941, and not nearly so long in coming to relieve a time of need. The extent of London's dependence on the Shah could be gauged in the mid-1970s by anyone who tried to cross a main road in Teheran, an act which demands the nerve and reflexes of the bullfighter; for most of the cars in that minatory rush of traffic are Peykans, which should be translated as British Hillmans built under licence. It is widely believed in Westminster that the government was finally moved to spend £162·5 million to rescue the Chrysler motor company's operation in Britain because, just before a crucial Cabinet decision, a telegram landed on the table from Sir Anthony Parsons: it is said to have pointed out that if Chrysler, which had a large contract with Iran, were allowed to collapse, the whole future of Anglo-Iranian trade would be in jeopardy.

The Teheran embassy is almost totally geared to the trading relationship. Even matters which might seem to originate in considerations of politics or Defence are more carefully totted up now for the financial credit they maintain at this supermarket of the Near East. A contract for 800 Chieftain tanks, signed in 1971, may have then seemed above all a means of promoting stability in a notoriously volatile part of the world, but by the time the contract was due to be completed, in the summer of 1976, the most gratifying thing to the British was the fact that it represented 800 × £125,000. By then, another welcome contract had opened another cash flow in the right direction. The British had developed a superior appliance for soldiers called a Training Theatre, which is exactly what its name suggests: a military auditorium which, by the manipulation of various controls and the shifting of scenery as in any other pantomime, will simulate battle conditions of any kind with wondrous realism. The theatres cost £854,000 apiece and the Shah ordered twenty-three at one go – which is probably more than we have ourselves.

The organization of a medium-sized embassy is shown in Figure 3. By tradition, the chancery in any embassy is pre-occupied with politics. Commercial activities, consular work, cultural matters and other forms of diplomacy have historically been thought of as subordinate parts of the mission. The Head of Chancery (usually a First Secretary, though in large posts a Counsellor) is in immediate charge of the political assessments and reports made by the post when he isn't discharging his other function, which is to oversee the general effectiveness of the mission: playing First Lieutenant to his Ambassador's Captain. In Teheran this political role has not been thrown out of the chancery window, but the demands of commerce are now a first charge on everybody's time. All the analytical reporting of economic matters is done by the chancery team, instead of being left to some hard-pressed fellows down the corridor who would feel, and be, out of the mainstream of the mission's activity. As the day's diplomacy is plotted around the table at morning prayers, the Head of Chancery in Teheran prompts his men with phrases that may be heard in every British embassy on earth: 'London ought to know about that ... HE should be advised by tomorrow at the latest ... ' But the background of his directions has a flavour much less familiar in comparable meetings elsewhere. This group of First, Second and Third Secretaries is concentrated on cold-storage problems in Iran, a projected visit of beekeepers to Britain, the sale of some advanced technology in which we still have a useful international lead. By 1975 Iran had become Britain's fastest growing market, and not for one minute was anyone in the embassy there allowed to forget it.

The Ambassador was up to his shirt-sleeves in commerce as much as anyone. Every day, some five or six pretty heavyweight figures from Britain, straight off the plane from Heathrow, would obtain audience and be given a rapid run-down on prospects in their fields, or a summary of just where some delicate negotiation involving Her Majesty's Government as well as their own companies had got to. Smaller men were received by descending ranks of diplomats, with or without appointment, and given at least basic information on the way commerce is

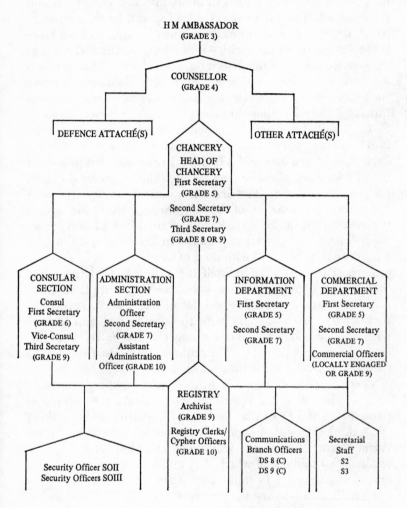

FIGURE 3 *Organization of a Medium-sized Embassy*
(*Source*: FCO.)

run in the land of the Shah. This has enough very local rules and customs for people from a country with no great traditional experience in these parts to be at a disadvantage. The Danes have made enormous efforts to break into the market without great success. The Japanese do not do as well for themselves as usual, because their customary commercial approach – a large trade delegation to start with – is not very effective where personal whim counts as much as it does in Teheran. This, as much as anything, is the soundest advice British diplomats can give their compatriots, with relevant names and telephone numbers furnished when it is thought these might have a beneficial effect on the national balance of payments, rather than profit to some purely private purse. Not every entrepreneur with an impeccable English manner and a faultless British passport gets what he is looking for when he goes through the revolving doors on the Avenue Ferdowsi. The first few questions the diplomats put to persons who come out of the blue are designed to distinguish the men rooted in the West Riding or the Black Country from the fellows operating out of premises in London, controlled by a headquarters in Paris, with most of its capital lodged mysteriously in Panama. This in itself taxes diplomatic energy and time in an embassy which has been receiving more than 4,000 business visitors a year. The volume of such calls has grown at such a pace since the boom came to Teheran that staff to cope with commercial work and nothing else has lately been increased every six months. The Ambassador himself reckons to spend 80 per cent of his time on such matters.

There is probably no other British embassy where the workload is so intensively weighted in favour of commerce. But it is estimated at the FCO that between one-quarter and one-third of all the Diplomatic Service's resources are now deployed on various forms of economic work. The FCO budget for 1973–4 totalled £73 million, of which £53 million was spent overseas; and of that figure, £13 million was spent on export trade promotion. Half a century ago, every British Ambassador would have been horrified had he been required to concern himself with such work to the extent now expected of most heads of mission. It would have been the same as asking him to serve in a shop. True, a Commercial Department had been created in the Foreign Office as long ago as 1866, but it had been regarded as a departmental dustbin, and the Commercial Attaché at an embassy was not quite the sort of fellow to engage His Excellency's attention. By 1919 a certain status was given to this tradesman's role by the formation of the Commercial Diplomatic Service, which one diplomat of the 1970s described as 'the unloved bastard of a socially startling union between the Foreign Office and the Board of Trade'. Even in the 1920s, Commercial Attachés were 'not asked to dine at the embassy'.[1] Although the union ended in divorce at the conclusion of the Second World War, with the commercial men achieving at least nominal parity with other diplomats by being morganatically incorporated into the reorganized Foreign Service, they were still among the dogsbodies of the service until the 1960s. Then their work suddenly became a thing for rising young Administrative officers to have experienced.

Ardent careerists had once before, in the post-war years, found themselves specializing in a hitherto unfashionable field in response to a lead handed down from above. After the Drogheda Committee in 1954 reported on British propaganda abroad, there was a great rush to expand all the information work of British missions and enthusiasm in this direction lasted for several years. Any man who fancied his future as a well-rounded figure who might one day have his own embassy, would drop the hint to Personnel that he would not be displeased if he were asked to do one stint as an Information Officer, even though the work itself scarcely carried the glamour of high policy-making. By the mid-1960s, however, commercial work had taken the place of information duties in the career stakes. Lord Plowden's Committee had spoken now:[2]

We cannot emphasise too strongly the importance of the commercial work to the new Diplomatic Service. The country cannot afford to entrust commercial work to any but the best. The custom is growing of ensuring that promising officers get experience of commercial work in the early and formative stages of their careers. This custom should become the rule. We look forward to the day, in the not too distant future, when every Ambassador and High Commissioner will have served in a commercial capacity

[1] Steiner, p. 184.
[2] Plowden, p. 63.

and have acquired at first hand a detailed knowledge of export promotion and what it entails. Each Ambassador and High Commissioner must regard commercial work as a prime function of his Mission and its subordinate posts.

Without being so tactless as to imply Diplomatic Service superiority in a field which also concerned a lot of Home civil servants working in what was then the Board of Trade, the Duncan Committee heavily endorsed Plowden's view when it reported in 1969. With British entry into Europe clearly in mind, it spent a lot of time arguing a general thesis that 'in modern diplomacy economics is often the very stuff of politics'. By far the longest chapter in the report was the one on commercial work as a Diplomatic Service function. 'The urgency of that task', it said,[1]

is beyond question ... The commercial work of the Diplomatic Service cannot have absolute priority, since the preservation of peace and security must clearly be an overriding aim. But in our present circumstances it seems right that it should absorb more of the Service's resources than any other function.

Duncan made it quite clear that the chief responsibility for increasing the nation's earnings abroad belonged to British industry; diplomats and other civil servants could play nothing more than a supporting role. But it took the view that, five years after Plowden, this role was still not properly understood even by the men who were most willing to fulfil it if they could. Members of the Committee had visited a number of British missions and come away with the feeling that there was no general grasp of how much more effort was required if national insolvency was to be relieved. Specifically, they had found no evidence of a plan to exploit British industry's cost advantages following the devaluation of sterling in November 1967. This was not the fault of the men in the diplomatic posts, who seemed to be doing their best with inadequate information, so much as a failure in dialogue on export strategy between the embassies and Whitehall. It perhaps had something to do with Duncan's suspicion that

[1] Duncan, p. 68.

there was 'still some hang-over from the period when commercial work was at arm's length from important matters of policy
such as concern those likely to reach the higher ranks of the
Service'.[1] But there was a feeling that commercial staffs at the
embassies didn't talk the businessmen's language; that, while a
great deal of initiative was shown by diplomats in the arrangement of trade missions and trade fairs, they were a pretty lame
lot when it came to nosing out specific export opportunities that
could be put to specific British firms; that they needed a lot
more training than they received before being posted to a
commercial job overseas.

A standard form of commercial training was introduced by
the FCO's Export Promotion Department in 1968, while the
Duncan Committee was collecting its evidence. It consisted of
a four-week course on the mechanics and techniques of export-
ing, marketing and market research, with talks given by people
from industry and commerce and by representatives of the
Board of Trade and other departments in Whitehall. The idea
was that every diplomat would be given this course just before
leaving for a commercial post. There was another course, lasting three weeks, covering high-level economic, financial and
commercial policy matters, marketing strategy, development
problems and certain specific subjects like insurance and financial guarantees: this one was for the benefit of senior diplomats
who would never have been given the opportunity of taking the
longer instruction. The members of the Duncan Committee had
no chance to see these courses in action, but they thought that
such training ought to be expanded in some way, that this could
'readily be extended to three months' duration'.[2] At about the
same time as the Committee produced its report, the Diplomatic Services Association was conducting its own survey among
the under-forties on a number of professional matters; and 60
per cent of the people who answered its questionnaire thought
FCO training courses in commerce inadequate.

Duncan was not attracted to the idea of simply emulating
diplomatic practice in other countries. In Sweden, for example,
it is not at all unusual for a man to divide his career between
business and diplomacy; for a businessman to spend some years

[1] Duncan, p. 81.
[2] Duncan, p. 80.

with the Diplomatic Service, and for some years in business to be a recognized part of a diplomatic career. While conceding that cross-fertilization of that order was desirable, Duncan doubted that it could be applied in Britain, where 'efforts to second people between industry and the Diplomatic Service have not been very successful in the past'.[1] It had to be accepted that other countries had worked out different ways of approaching the whole subject of export trade and the involvement in it of diplomats. German industrial associations play a major part in export promotion, but they are far stronger than equivalent bodies in the United Kingdom. The export power of big trading companies in Japan is likewise something that has produced a form of promotion inimitable in British conditions. Duncan believed that, while certain practices elsewhere might be worth following, the best bet for this country would be the adaptation of existing methods rather than a complete change to alien ones. This would certainly include greater know-how by diplomats. And yet, astonishingly, seven years after Duncan reported, no real effort had been made by the FCO to achieve this object. By 1976, the three-week advanced commercial course for senior diplomats had been abandoned 'because', someone said, 'there was not enough call for it'. The basic course of four weeks remained a basic course of four weeks, just as it was invented in 1968. The Chief Clerk had told MPs on the Expenditure Committee in 1971, two years after Duncan, 'At the moment we do have a very substantial programme of training for our commercial officers',[2] without specifying what it was apart from the tour every commercial Counsellor makes, before going abroad, of British firms with interests in his destination; and men of that rank are relatively few in the full muster of commercial diplomats. Things are ordered rather differently in other diplomatic services. A Belgian has to pass three commercial examinations before he can be appointed an Ambassador.

As Duncan suggested, our diplomats have never failed to put maximum effort into the great set-piece promotions of British trade. They usually go about these things with the will displayed during the British Week held in Amsterdam in 1965. The object was to attract Dutch shoppers to a wide range of goods manu-

---

[1] Duncan, p. 81.
[2] *Fifth Report from the Expenditure Committee; Session 1971-2*, p. 30.

factured in the United Kingdom and specially displayed for the occasion in most of the city's department stores. The bait to focus local attention on this commerce was of a scale and nature that could only have been managed with the co-operation of two or three government departments (not to mention Buckingham Palace) and a thoroughly diplomatic instinct for representational effect. Princess Margaret and Lord Snowdon cruised into town aboard *Britannia*. There was a proper naval visit besides, and a military tattoo. There were operas from Sadler's Wells, trips by Hovercraft, the inevitable London Transport bus, and a complete English pub imported lock, stock and beer barrel. This was not a unique show. In Tokyo, a few years later, a similar event was laid on at a cost of £1 million. In 1971, 5,200 British firms were officially supported at 270 trade fairs in 38 different countries, 2 British Weeks, 3 British Shopping Weeks and 37 store promotions abroad. Most of the government energy on all these projects was expended by men from the Departments of Trade and Industry; but the diplomats played their part as well. No other country gives its private enterprise official backing on that scale. Some do not provide a comparable service in the embassies either. In Nairobi, where the British High Commission runs to a First and Second Secretary (Commercial), together with their supporting staff, the German embassy has a solitary official to help anyone come to Kenya in search of trade. The Americans are amply staffed, but they demand payment for any information supplied.

It is in these more direct relationships, involving unspectacular graft, that both businessmen and diplomats have generally found each other wanting. A fairly typical story told by diplomats to illustrate commercial crassness concerns the manufacturer of men's braces, who sought the help of the British Embassy in Kabul to open a market in Afghanistan. It was explained to him that there was no future out there for his product, however superior it might be to any rival's, because Afghan males kept their trousers up by means of drawcords. He persisted in his demands, getting the same reply to a stream of letters, until he ended with an angry note to the Ambassador, telling him it was the embassy's *job* to open a market; that was what he paid his taxes for. In every British mission, the commercial section can tell comparable tales illustrating the failure of British businessmen to do their homework before seeking diplomatic help. The

African posts can also tell of massive miscalculations in the boardroom which have actually lost markets once dominated by the British. It is a depressing fact, observed by every visitor to East or West Africa, that the majority of vehicles in sight are French Peugeots or Japanese Toyotas, where they are not American Dodges. In both areas twenty-odd years ago, most of the private cars at least were British Austins and Morrises. The diplomats insist that two failures by British manufacturers were responsible for this reversal. For one thing, British cars were always made for British conditions. Far from incorporating special gadgets designed for hot countries, like air-conditioning, these did not even have suspension systems adapted to the rougher demands of backcountry dirt tracks. As long as something resembling imperial preference remained, however, sales could still be struck in Commonwealth countries. Much more crucial was the decision made at the top of the car industry when American corporations began to turn British companies into transatlantic subsidiaries. This was to concentrate the sales force on what seemed an easy, domestic market (which in the event turned into one of the toughest and most competitive) and to abandon the relatively small African market as not worth the long-distance effort involved.

For every such gibe from the diplomats, the businessmen can generally be relied on to produce two of their own. They will complain that the information they are given about companies abroad is not always up to date; that commercial staffs at embassies do not stay long enough at a post to develop any great local expertise; that information, when it is forthcoming and useful, is not passed home fast enough. Frequently they reckon that the very best people they encounter in the embassies are locally engaged staff, who are not given enough status or responsibility by their home-based superiors to be as effective as they might be. There is a great deal of antagonism on both sides, latent and ready to be released the moment diplomats and businessmen have to deal with each other. It is significant that on the last morning of the FCO's commercial training course, a prescribed exercise is for each student in turn to act like an irate businessman letting rip at another student playing First Secretary (Commercial), who must counter with every diplomatic bromide he can muster.

In the autumn of 1974, a British trade mission went on a

three-week tour of the Far East, sixteen businessmen with various interests having been invited to undertake the trip by the Departments of Trade and Industry. It was hoped, before they left England, that they might obtain orders worth £1 million; in the event they came back with business amounting to £1·5 million. So it was a successful venture. Although it was arranged in the first place by the DTI, and would have got nowhere without the skill of people who made and sold products, its success depended to a large extent on the co-operation of British diplomatic posts in the target area. The report made by one of the businessmen to his trade association afterwards tells a great deal about the mission's relationship with diplomats, about the performance of diplomats, and about the attitudes and expectations of the businessmen themselves. There is no reason to suppose that it is untypical, in what it reveals, of most missions of its kind; and it should be assumed that when the author of the report uses the word 'mission' he is referring to businessmen and not diplomats.

The object of the journey was to drum up trade in Japan, Hong Kong and Singapore, but the party stopped for a weekend in Bangkok on the way out:

Having arrived in Thailand late on the Friday night, I telephoned the Embassy on Saturday morning on no less than seven or eight occasions, but received no reply. The telephone numbers had been changed but I likewise tried the new numbers but to no avail. I then went to the Embassy by myself by taxi, to be greeted by a Guard smoking a cigarette at the open gate, where I asked if there was anyone available I could speak to. He directed me to a small office, where there was another Guard sitting ... [and] what did disturb me was the fact that there were some 100 or more letters (including registered) all lying loose on top of the desk, and which I can assure you I could have collected and walked out with, without any questions being asked. On the Monday morning I telephoned the Embassy and asked if I could have an appointment with the Ambassador, and also if I could have help with transport to the hospital, for unfortunately I had been bitten by a mosquito which had set up poison through my body. I was told that the Ambassador would see me at four o'clock, but regretfully there was no transport, as all cars were being used to take and collect couriers from the airport ...

The party first got down to business in Tokyo, where a briefing session took place in the embassy at 9.30 a.m. 'It is the opinion of many members of the mission, and my own, that such briefing sessions are a waste of time.' The author thought that background material on the economics and statistics of foreign trade could be provided much more effectively in writing before trade missions left England. In spite of this qualification,

The Embassy itself was most helpful. Furthermore, arrangements had been made for HM Ambassador to receive the mission at his residence, which certainly boosted the morale. I was informed by at least six members of the mission who had been on trade missions before, that they had never met any of HM Ambassadors, High Commissioners or otherwise, on any previous trade missions, not only in the Far East, but to other countries. It was obvious that the Embassy in Tokyo, and in particular the First Secretary had done a tremendous amount of spade work to assist members of the mission. A cocktail party was held in the evening which was jointly hosted by the Minister Commercial and members of the mission. The cost of this cocktail party to members of the mission was some £500 and the drinks were paid for by the Embassy.

The time in Hong Kong was even more gratifying:

I cannot speak highly enough of the abundance and amount of excellent work, organization and help, received at the office of this British Commission. Senior officials met the mission at the airport and escorted them to their hotel. TV and radio interviews and press conferences were arranged etc. Members of the mission were helped in every way possible, even to transport. The Cocktail party ... was the most advantageous and helpful of the whole trade mission. This obviously was brought about by the vetting of the guest list by the Embassy commercial men to see that

the right people were there to meet members of the mission
for business to be done ...

Singapore, alas, fell below par for the course:

I was utterly appalled at the little help the mission received
from this particular Embassy ... The reception received at
the airport from these gentlemen was more one of duty than
pleasure. On looking through an envelope of documents the
following morning which had been left by Mr X, I found
... that five names which I had personally listed to be invited to the cocktail part that evening had not been invited ... X had completely ignored the list of names which
I had given them – chairmen of banks etc. – to be sent personal invitations. The mission had received hardly any
publicity whatever and a press release had not even been
given to the press until the day before we were due to leave.
Mr X or his deputy had duplicated a list of customers to
two people in the mission both selling similar commodities,
and I might add that both members of the mission were
disgusted. At a cocktail party no name tabs had been prepared for the mission members or people attending the
cocktail party, or members of the High Commission, which
could identify anyone. At previous cocktail parties in Tokyo
and Hong Kong the Embassies had gone to a lot of trouble
to prepare name tabs of different colours, in order that one
would know who one was meeting and speaking to.

The author of the report made a number of suggestions, apart
from the one about proper briefing before leaving home, that
he thought might improve matters for future trade missions.
Publicity for a visit should be started some time before the
tradesmen actually arrived at any place where they were
hoping to do business. The businessmen should, as part of the
English briefing, be given information about the cost of living
wherever they intended to stop, and particularly the excess
baggage charges at the different airports on their route: at
Singapore this particular party had found them so high (£6·22
per kilo) that one man threw away all the samples he had
collected in the previous three weeks. The group also deplored
the fact that, at Tokyo and Singapore, the diplomats had in-

2A

vited to the trade receptions a number of local people who
were of no potential use to the visiting tradesmen. In Singapore
there were representatives of Ben Line Containers, but none
from a competing company, OCI, which was partly owned by
the British government.

The Far East is a circuit well trodden by British businessmen
with order books at the ready, though many others (like the
man who left his samples at Singapore airport) are on the look-
out for things to buy as well as sell. There are many other parts
of the world which regularly see British trade missions and not
all of them are in what the Foreign Office has regarded as the
'dynamic markets' of North America, Western Europe, the
countries of the Communist block, Japan and China. Oil-
producing countries other than Iran have become a prime target
of exporters in the past few years – Kuwait, for example, seeing
no fewer than ten missions come and go in 1974. In that particular place the British parties have included men whose stock
in trade was Scotch whisky, which is a rather strange thing to
be trying to sell in officially non-alcoholic territory. 'The DTI',
said a diplomat cryptically, 'doesn't take the advice of the embassies too seriously sometimes.' Sceptics may hear that as yet
another defensive diplomatic noise, when it may not be.

The Duncan Committee pointed out how blurred was the
division of responsibility for export promotion between the
DTI's forerunner (the Board of Trade) and the Foreign Office.
The Committee was told that, broadly speaking, the FCO took
the lead in matters with a strong political content, like negotiations with the EEC; and the Board of Trade led in everything
else. A diagram attached to the Duncan Report (see Figure 4)
showed what a misleading simplification that was. The Committee's comment on it was, 'We suspect that the FCO and the
Board of Trade have never really applied themselves to the
principles underlying the distinctions given in the charts and
that the result, so far as commercial policy and economic work
is concerned, is a certain waste of effort and duplication of
activity in London.'[1] It recommended that the Export Department of the Board of Trade should be strengthened by, among
other things, a transfer of relevant staff from the FCO to the
Board. In other words, that the FCO should no longer run a

[1] Duncan, p. 66.

headquarters department of its own with an interest in such matters. That was another recommendation unadopted seven years after Duncan. The only detectable change made between 1969 and 1976 was a translation of the FCO's Export Promotion Department into its Trade Relations and Export Department.

The Board of Trade had changed its name, too, in that time, but there is no reason to suppose that the twinned Departments of Trade and Industry's export experts (under whatever subsectional name they may go) are in a less complicated relationship with the diplomats than they were when Duncan reported. In such a mishmash of uncertain responsibilities, it is perhaps not surprising that a man should be dispatched from London with high hopes of selling Scotch whisky in one of the world's few areas of prohibition. There are other examples of British commercial failure abroad, outside the private sector of industry, where the responsibility does not rest with the British diplomatic apparatus in the countries concerned. In the Middle East, a substantial contract to pave an airport and its surroundings was lost by a remarkable case of myopia in Whitehall. The embassy had obtained what amounted to a promise of the contract going to Britain, and the first step was for a government consultant to fly from London to see what work was to be done before an estimate of costs was made. The airport authorities were prepared to accommodate the man free of charge while he investigated, but assumed that the British would fly him out. The British wouldn't and, in spite of frantic messages from the Ambassador, refused to budge from what Whitehall declared was a matter of principle. The contract went to the Yugoslavs.

Sometimes responsibility for such monumental failures lies in quarters even more difficult to establish than when faults appear to issue from somewhere within a government department. In the early 1970s, a diplomat with a commercial assignment in the United States was seized with the idea that the Advanced Passenger Train, then being developed at an experimental stage by British Rail, could make a lot of money for us in North America; possibly by being manufactured there under licence. The idea was put up to BR's chairman, Richard Marsh, who was almost as enthusiastic as the man who had first thought of it. It foundered for the given reason that an Act of Parliament would be necessary for such a transaction to take place; and

none was forthcoming. 'But, my God,' said the diplomat concerned, much later, 'it would have been a different story if the
position had been reversed and Congress had got a glint of the
dollars they might have made out of it.'

It is true that at one stage in the 1960s, bright and ambitious
young Administrative officers – like that one – took care to obtain commercial experience with an eye to higher things; truer
still that in more recent years the potential Ambassadors of the
future have been directed into such posts. You hear of them
making five-day trips into the wilds of Macedonia, touting for
British business in chemicals, steel mills and machinery. In the
Brussels embassy in 1975, the First Secretary (Commercial) was
an experienced Arabist who now spent a couple of days a week
away from his desk, visiting up to 200 Belgian businessmen a
year, one by-product of such exertions being the reliance Marks
& Spencer placed on embassy advice for two and a half years
before opening a store in the city. But it would be mistaken for
anyone to suppose that Britain's exports, so far as the Foreign
Office has anything to do with them, are now solely in the hands
of the fastest rising diplomats. What the FCO calls its 'teeth
staff' in this field are the people who do most of the actual leg-
work abroad. In 1975, the 'teeth staff' consisted of 375 diplomats working on export promotion alone who came mainly from
the Executive Grades, plus 340 people locally engaged to
perform the same function, plus 1,000 clerical and secretarial
workers, also recruited on the spot. Political work is apportioned
rather differently.

It is also true that, whatever grading diplomats engaged in
commercial work have, they generally accept the propositions
of both Plowden and Duncan about the necessity of British
exports to national survival. But there can be some highly individual interpretations of what this means in terms of diplomatic
activity, and even doubts about its basic validity. At one post
in the Levant, a Commercial Counsellor, a fugitive from
British business, which he had forsaken in favour of diplomacy,
offered the opinion that the Eastern Mediterranean scared
potential trade off more than it should, because of fears about
its stability. He saw his own function as much more one of in-
ducing local business people to try their luck in London, than
of enticing British businessmen into the market place out there.
This would have sounded more plausible had he not started by

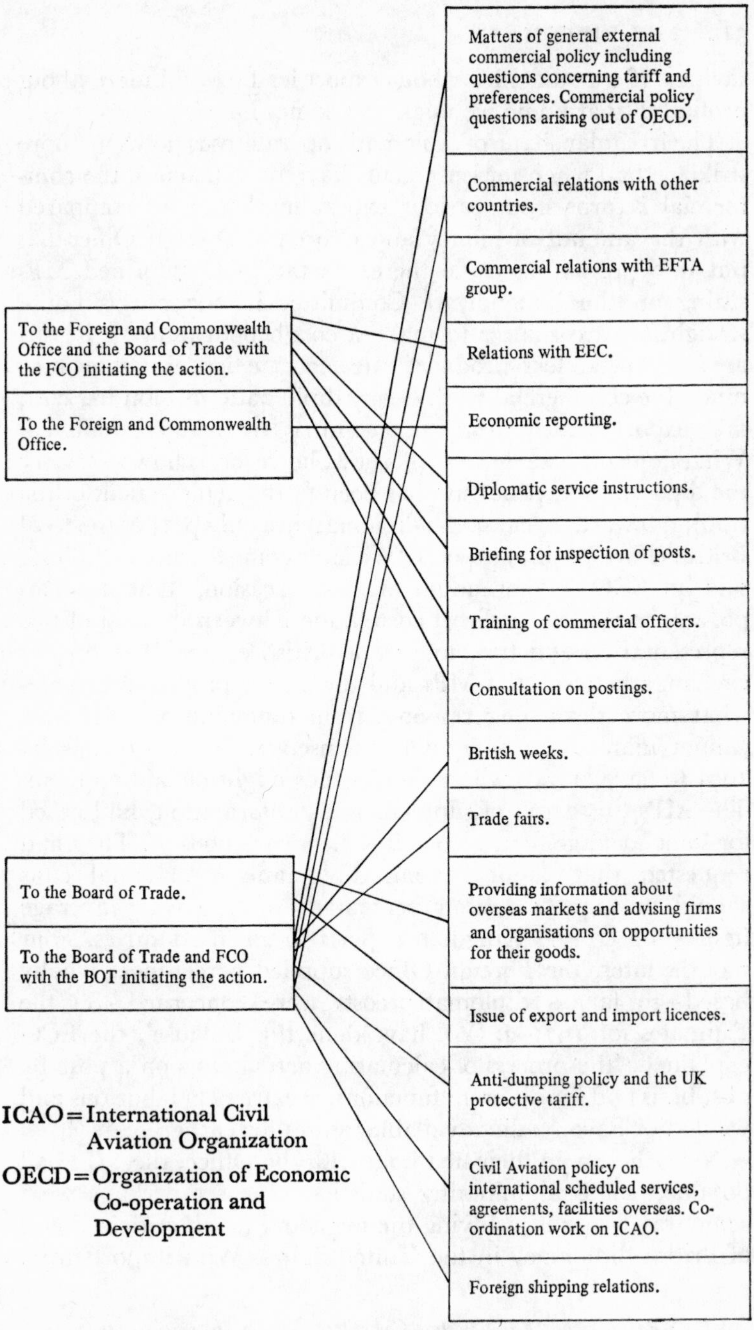

Matters of general external commercial policy including questions concerning tariff and preferences. Commercial policy questions arising out of OECD.

Commercial relations with other countries.

Commercial relations with EFTA group.

Relations with EEC.

Economic reporting.

Diplomatic service instructions.

Briefing for inspection of posts.

Training of commercial officers.

Consultation on postings.

British weeks.

Trade fairs.

Providing information about overseas markets and advising firms and organisations on opportunities for their goods.

Issue of export and import licences.

Anti-dumping policy and the UK protective tariff.

Civil Aviation policy on international scheduled services, agreements, facilities overseas. Co-ordination work on ICAO.

Foreign shipping relations.

To the Foreign and Commonwealth Office and the Board of Trade with the FCO initiating the action.

To the Foreign and Commonwealth Office.

To the Board of Trade.

To the Board of Trade and FCO with the BOT initiating the action.

ICAO = International Civil Aviation Organization

OECD = Organization of Economic Co-operation and Development

FIGURE 4 *Britain's Foreign Trade — the Responsibility in Whitehall*
(*Source*: Report of the Duncan Committee, 1969, p. 65.)

saying, 'If we talked less about export leading and more about profitability at home we might get somewhere.'

The irregular shape of diplomatic operations is nowhere more striking than when measurements have been taken of the commercial returns from various export markets, and compared with the amount of money and effort the Foreign Office has put into promoting trade there. As the FCO informed MPs sitting on the Expenditure Committee in 1971, it is not a straightforward matter to make a cost/benefit analysis in this area. It is possible to produce quite accurate figures to show how much the commercial work of any diplomatic mission has cost, and export returns from any country are easily calculated. What none of these figures will show, however, is how necessary the diplomatic expenditure has been in the achievement of the trading reward, because the diplomats are only part of the total British effort put into exports. 'We have come to the conclusion', said an FCO memorandum on that occasion, 'that it is impossible to make any direct correlation between the cost of this representation and the amount of British exports.'[1] A further exchange between the MPs and the Office produced a somewhat more disturbing response from diplomats who, if they cannot manipulate computers themselves, ought perhaps by 1971 to have known where other hands might be laid on them. The MPs, in search of supplementary information, had asked for some average figures covering the years 1968–70. They had requested that, among them, diplomatic commercial costs should be expressed as a percentage of three-year average figures for United Kingdom exports to given countries. Four months later, the Foreign Office supplied percentages wholly based – so far as diplomatic costs were concerned – on the Estimates for 1971–2. 'We have done this because', the FCO explained, 'the process of calculating actual costs on a post by post basis and for different functions, is extremely laborious and we do not have readily available figures for earlier years.'[2]

Nevertheless, in their first bout with the Office, the MPs had obtained some illuminating statistics. One set perhaps went some way towards justifying the huge and much criticized cost of British diplomacy in the United States. With imports from

[1] *Fifth Report from the Expenditure Committee; Session 1971–2*, p. 26.
[2] Ibid., p. 83.

Great Britain in 1970 standing at £932·7 million, the USA was outstandingly the best British export market, worth some £430 million more to us than our second-best customer, West Germany. The total diplomatic staff in the United States (stationed at twenty-odd posts throughout the country, as well as at the embassy in Washington) was given as 163, with locally engaged staff amounting to another 567. Included in those figures were 48 British diplomats devoted to commercial work, and 149 locally engaged staff with the same function. The total cost of the entire diplomatic operation was put at £4·731 million and, of this sum, £1·599 million had been spent on commercial activity. In short, the diplomatic effort in promoting those colossal British exports was responsible for 34 per cent of all diplomatic expenditure. If those figures were 'quite accurate', as the Foreign Office told the MPs such figures could be in July 1971, and not merely estimates because accuracy involved too much hard work (as they maintained in November 1971), then they would appear to take some of the wind from the sails of parsimonious critics.

The MPs were much more interested in what the figures seemed to tell about diplomatic effort in other countries. How was it, they asked, that the diplomatic posts in India, our twenty-sixth best customer, contained four times as many commercial staff as were employed by the Foreign Office in Ireland, our third largest customer? That one was fairly easy to answer. Ireland is almost an extension of the British trading area and commerce continues without much official effort being required. But what about the case of France, where British diplomacy costs more than anywhere else except in the United States and Germany, but which stands at No 7 in the export league? Or Italy, sixth most expensive country, twelfth most rewarding? The MPs were led to believe that the high cost of diplomacy in France was caused as much as anything by the need to keep many consular posts going for the protection of British holiday-makers; commercial costs, indeed, were ignored by the Chief Clerk making these explanations. Italy wasn't even mentioned in the verbal exchanges.

The patterns made by the arrangement of such figures have not changed very much in the years since the Expenditure Committee examined them. As the diplomats said at that time, it is very difficult to provide straight answers to some of the questions the figures suggest. The cost of commercial diplomacy in the countries of Eastern Europe is pretty high and the returns have been no more than moderately good so far. But the fact is that, with trade in those countries (except in Yugoslavia) completely in the hands of state trading corporations, British exporters would get nowhere at all were it not for the efforts of the diplomats. On the other hand, in 1974 the Netherlands was taking 5½ per cent of Britain's total exports, and this required only 3½ per cent of all the Foreign Office's commercial activity. Excluding the highly controlled Communist markets, it is almost wholly a matter of guesswork what would happen to British trade if diplomatic help were withdrawn tomorrow and businessmen had to fend completely for themselves. Would they be able to manage at all if they were suddenly deprived not only of the official contacts available to them overseas but also of the information regularly Telexed from the embassies to the DTI's export intelligence computer in London? It is true that Syria was taking £10 million-worth of British goods a year by 1967, when diplomatic relations were broken off, and that the figure had declined to £7·2 million by 1969. But to what extent was that due to an absence of commercial officers in Damascus? How much of it resulted from sudden political coolness? Or other factors having nothing to do with politics or diplomacy? No research which might produce answers to such questions has been done by the FCO or any other institution; and would, indeed, be very laborious, even if it were possible.

Certain discouraging trends have become apparent to the export watchers in the FCO, however. Latin America, so heavily dominated by North American business, has scarcely seemed to justify the attention we have paid it; absorbing just 8 per cent of our diplomatic commercial efforts, it has returned only 2 per cent of the British export trade. This has not been the only part of the world where a scattering of seed has fallen upon fairly stony ground. At the end of 1974 a commercial diplomat confessed that 'We've tried to cover too many countries in the past. We're now doing a rethink to redeploy staff into the most promising countries.' This was but a short form of Duncan's message, delivered in 1969. It was possibly more representative of our diplomatic approach to many things, besides commerce, than that perky Babcock B300 in the reception area at Teheran, and all the other sterling work in the embassy there. And the diplomatic approach itself may be seen as no more than a characteristic of the nation as a whole. Slow to acknowledge and respond to much writing on the wall, as well as in the pages of official reports.

13   Consuls and Attachés

The generalist tradition of British diplomacy has always had its limits. At all but the smallest embassies there has ever been a sprinkling of names on the *Diplomatic List* suggesting specialized talents and, sometimes, an allegiance divided between the Foreign Office and other headquarters. Clearly recognizable are the Honorary Chaplains, who in sundry places minister to the diplomatic spirit in exchange for duty-free petrol and other temporal privileges. In 1975 no fewer than 26 British embassies enjoyed the services of 22 parsons. The discrepancy was accounted for by two of the chaplains each serving more than one embassy, the more remarkable missionary zeal being that of the reverend doctor based in Helsinki, whence he came periodically to Moscow and Ulan Bator.

British entry into the EEC meant a considerable transfusion of Home civil servants into the bloodstream of Brussels, but long before that a number of Whitehall departments had sent men on attachment to British missions abroad. The old Ministry of Labour began placing officials overseas back in the 1940s (R. H. Tawney was the first Labour Attaché at the Washington embassy) and the habit was maintained through all its changes of title. Today, over a quarter of all civilian Attachés are posted from the Department of Employment throughout Europe and in places like the West Indies, where industrial relations and factory conditions are of more than passing interest to us. Tawney's successor in the American capital today is frequently found dashing off to labour conventions when he isn't reporting to Whitehall on the President's new pension reform scheme, or notifying the British Factory Inspectorate of new American standards on PVC. The Ministry of Agriculture has for several years had a couple of veterinary surgeons at the embassy in Buenos Aires, to keep a sharp eye on the quality of Argentine beef destined for the British market, and a small handful of their colleagues are to be found elsewhere. The Department of Education and Science is responsible for highly qualified experts in the embassies at Washington, Paris, Moscow and Tokyo, who keep track of things that not even the most versatile Arabist would easily understand.[1] The DSc posted to Moscow, for instance, in his dealings with the Academy of Science there has gone deep into tribology which, being the study of friction and wear, is of anxious and mutual concern to Great Britain and the Soviet Union. There is a civil aviation expert from the Department of Trade in Beirut, and a regional police adviser from the Home Office in Bridgetown. Men from the Treasury are to be found in one or two well-loaded places abroad. The British Embassy in Washington may very well contain a representative of every government bureau, with the conceivable exception of the one devoted to ancient monuments and historic buildings.

And then there are the men from Overseas Aid, mostly based in developing countries of the Commonwealth, but sometimes in other places, too. Amongst other things, they staff the five development divisions attached to the British diplomatic missions in Bangkok, Beirut, Blantyre, Bridgetown and Nairobi. The purpose of the divisions is to identify local priorities, to supervise British aid projects and to evaluate the results, and that over a very wide area. The East African Development Division of seven men attached to the British High Commission in Nairobi, for example, covers the East African Community, Burundi, Ethiopia, Kenya, Madagascar, Mauritius, Rwanda, Seychelles, Somalia, Tanzania and Uganda. Between them, the divisions are at the spending end of Britain's overseas aid budget, which is somewhere in the region of nearly £500 million a year. A proportion of this, however, is actually deployed by other hands. A growing amount, as we shall see in the next chapter, has become the business of the British Council. And many officers working on aid abroad are simply FCO diplomats who, in subsequent postings, turn their attention to other matters, as usual.

The professional aid men belong to an organization which has an uneasy sibling relationship with the Foreign Office. Origin-

---

[1] The Scientific Counsellor in Bonn, however, is thoroughbred FCO.

ating in 1961 as the Department of Technical Co-operation, within a few years becoming the Overseas Development Administration, then the Ministry *for* Overseas Development, this was always seen as the biddable child of diplomacy until the Labour party returned to power in 1974 and put a strong-minded woman, Judith Hart, in political control; up to a point. ODM at once became the Ministry *of* Overseas Development, a prepositional change which was thought to give it a more in-dependent sound. Being physically separated from the FCO by the long length of Victoria Street, it even had an independent look. But Mrs Hart never had a Cabinet seat, which meant that her policies at that level were in the hands of the Foreign Secretary, just as they were partially shaped at ODM head-quarters in Eland House by a hierarchy of senior officials which included an Assistant Under Secretary from the Foreign Office, when he wasn't attending to the departments under his direction at the FCO. As for the execution of policy, in spite of the advisory role of the development divisions, that was effec-tively in the control of FCO Ambassadors and High Commis-sioners, who had the personal authority to decide on what pro-jects a high proportion of any local allotment should be spent. Until Mrs Hart left office some eighteen months after assuming it, following a disagreement with the Prime Minister on party philosophy, there was a tension throbbing through the distri-bution of British aid that had been unnoticeable before. At her going, it was announced that ODM, while keeping its physical independence, had been restored to the Foreign Secretary's general supervision although it was given a political foreman, Reg Prentice, who was allowed to retain the Cabinet seat he had occupied as Secretary of State for Education and Science. Such are the quaint party compromises of Parliamentary democracy.

The Hart period clearly demonstrated a moral attitude to-wards aid. It would not be fair to the diplomats to conclude that their own views were devoid of morality, but it certainly never matched that of Mrs Hart. To her, quite simply, the relatively rich countries of the world were under an obligation to the comparatively poor ones and aid was a means of dis-charging it, the poorest countries to be served first, with the biggest helpings. It was a source of perpetual and public exas-peration to her (as it was, privately and in another sense, to her political colleagues) that Britain went only half-way towards meeting the United Nations target figure for aid – o·7 per cent of the gross national product.[1] The tussles between Mrs Hart and the diplomats were much more frequent than the moments of union. Generally, she accused them of using aid as a white knight to secure a position on the chessboard of international affairs. More often than not they believed her to be ridiculously naive or tediously high-minded or a mixture of both. It is possible that only once did they work together with a real will – when the diplomats grafted on her behalf among their European colleagues in Brussels so that, with some EEC acquiescence in her brief case, she could offer at least part of what the Africans and others sought at the Lomé Convention in 1974.

Certainly the Foreign Office has never seen aid in the simple terms proposed by Mrs Hart; and, generally, the Foreign Office view prevailed. 'Everyone here', said one man in the FCO, 'would think of aid in our long-term interests.' Another diplomat put it more bluntly: 'We're not in the charity business. There are occasions when we tell ODM to do it differently because of British commercial interests involved.' That happened when Mrs Hart wanted to reduce aid to Indonesia, as soon as it became apparent that the discovery of oil there was likely to turn the country into the Brazil of South-East Asia. The diplomats took one look at Britain's growing trade with Jakarta and decided that aid should continue as a favour which might produce much greater rewards in the long run. Aid has also been used to gain advantages other than commercial ones. The Foreign Office advocated it for Cyprus virtually as a means of buying our sovereign bases there. At the time of decision the Treasury was saying, 'Quantify what we shall get in return for this expenditure from Cyprus', and ODM was arguing that Cyprus was not poverty-stricken enough to qualify for aid. The diplomats won the argument. Their view has also shaped the considerable help given to Kenya, by no means the poorest country in the Third World. Money has been spent handsomely there with a very thoughtful eye on repercussions. As the diplomats see it, had British funds not been made available for buying out white farmers, the transfer of political power would

[1] Some rich countries are much more off target than we are. The Soviet Union takes the superior view that the Third World was impoverished by colonialism and that it is therefore up to the old colonizing nations alone to provide aid.

have been much less orderly than it was. That would have produced instability, with heaven knows what results. At the very least, it would have reduced the likelihood of Kenya's becoming a useful trading partner as soon as she did. When it was announced that Asians holding British passports were to be expelled from the country in the direction of the United Kingdom, the diplomatic response was to offer a lot more cash under the aid programme, and Nairobi's demands were modererated at once, allowing the British to organize a carefully controlled transfer of passport holders on a voucher system, instead of having to open floodgates at Gatwick which would have had Enoch Powell and the London dockers on the warpath again within hours.

The men from ODM in British missions abroad tend to stand somewhere between the positions adopted by their old mistress and their perpetual foster-parents. They are quick to deny that they see themselves as moral ambassadors; as though, in the company they are keeping, this were something only a sneaky fellow would admit to. But they can be very subjective in their attitudes to the job. 'I find it easier on my conscience', said one, 'sitting administering aid out here than working for the Ministry of Defence.' They sense that the initial response of the diplomats is to 'look upon aid as a rather wet and soggy thing'. The diplomats, of course, would never be so crude as to say any such thing, whatever they might think, though they can make very cutting remarks about politicians. 'The Judith Hart view of the Third World', said one Counsellor in the FCO, 'was essentially one of Nanny knows best.' ODM officials reckon that an Ambassador or High Commissioner with a development division attached to his mission 'will tend to think of it as a fifth wheel on the coach'. But they usually add that no such head of mission would put forward a project on purely commercial or political grounds. They see the ODM working best within the diplomatic atmosphere when it is not encouraging divisions between the political and the moral attitude to aid, when it is helping to form judgments that are balanced between the two.

Most are not diplomats by nature, though in the field they have to pick up many diplomatic techniques fast, like anyone else on attachment to a mission. Some of them drifted into Overseas Aid as a logical transfer of career when the old Colonial Office folded up. Many more have backgrounds in anything from the Home Office to the Nature Conservancy. Or else they have come straight in from their education. The difference between them and the diplomats doing aid work is sometimes quite striking. The men from ODM seem to have a grip on what they are doing; above all, they are interested. Except in the missions with development divisions attached, where the aid programme is so intensive and so consequential that it probably involves everyone to some extent, from the head of mission downwards, this is not always the case among the diplomats. Aid is something that tends to be tossed out of chancery in the direction of some Executive dogsbody; or else it is found in the hands of some Administrative First Secretary, rising fifty and no more promotion in sight. It is possible to hear the first of these say – of some British technician working up-country on the aid programme, for whom he is locally responsible – 'I honestly don't know what he's doing.' The second is unlikely to make any such admission; instead, he will probably adopt a knowing air and bluff his way around his ignorance. A man from ODM will be caught in neither position. The cast of mind which the brightest young diplomats frequently bring to bear on aid shows most clearly these days when Administrative recruits to the Foreign Office attend the introductory course to their new careers. One of the lectures is given by an old Foreign Office hand who for a dozen years has been working in ODM. At the end of the talk, all moral assumptions behind aid are challenged quite fiercely by the entrants. No other lecturer during the fortnight's course is subjected to such a vigorous interrogation; and ten years ago, it is said, the ODM thesis would not have come under such fire. 'They are', says a witness, 'a very hard-nosed lot these days':

We used to assume we had a responsibility for the poor and the weak, we didn't need anyone to tell us that. Maybe it was a leftover from the paternal side of imperialism. But they've come up differently, this past few years. They know it's a tough and competitive world they live in, and they want value for money.

It was in a Nairobi tranquillized by the aid programme and with arrangements for Asian British passport-holders working smoothly, that a man from the Foreign Office stood up one day in a Sikh temple, with his shoes at the door and his handkerchief knotted politely round his head, while he explained to 600 people the complexities of the voucher system that was of such paramount importance to their lives. Some time before, he had been up in the Highlands milking a cow on an African farm, which he regularly visited because he was a friend of the man who owned it and always dropped in during his periodic excursions among the remaining white settlers in the district. At morning prayers in the high commission later that month, while rendering an account of another day's work, he cheerfully informed the other diplomats round the table ' ... and then I finished up at the Salvation Army tea party'. This would have been startling intelligence at a similar gathering in the Paris embassy, say. Nor would the average First Secretary in his thirties, a flyer with a brilliant future in diplomacy almost promised him by his contacts in the Personnel Department of the FCO, expect to take tea anywhere with the Salvation Army, let alone milk a cow for a farmer in the course of his duties. The official in Nairobi who had done both these things was the Consul, however, and that marks a striking difference between one sort of diplomat and another. Again, it is not a clear-cut one, and any number of exceptions may be found on either side of the boundary. The High Commissioner in Nairobi at that time, Sir Antony Duff, was a man liable to put himself in all the situations his Consul had been in. But it is an historic fact, not yet substantially altered, that Consuls have played the part of Martha in British diplomacy, to the Marys whose lives have been exalted in the chanceries.

The Consul's antecedents are as long as anyone's, traceable in the British service to Florence in 1456. It is from the time of the eighteenth-century reforms that their distinctly separate status from that of Foreign Office clerks and diplomats becomes pointedly apparent. Until well into the twentieth century they spent their lives abroad, like the diplomats; but, unlike the diplomats, they were never considered suitable for transfer into the policy-making society of the Foreign Office. They were organized into a separate Consular Service, with compartments of its own which segregated them even further — the General, the Levant, the Far Eastern and so on. Like the old Oriental Secretaries (many of whom belonged to the Levant Consular Service) all Consuls became specialists with great local knowledge, which was exploited to an incalculable degree in the construction of the British Empire. The Macdonnell Committee in 1914 complained that the calibre of men in the General Consular Service was inadequate, but this could never have been said of the men in the Levant Service, where entry qualifications were at least as high as those for the superior Diplomatic Service. Knowledge of French and German was taken for granted and Arabic was always added to it; sometimes Persian and Turkish as well. For these skills and much hard work, the Consuls were paid so deplorably that few men could afford to marry before their thirties unless they had some other source of income. Things did not change very much until a few years before the Second World War and, more especially, until the Eden–Bevin reforms which immediately followed it. In 1935, the regional consular services were united, and from the 1943 White Paper onwards Consuls, like commercial diplomats, were considered part of the integrated Foreign Service. By then, the calibre of Consuls had evidently improved; or perhaps it was simply that in the post-war reorganization, quality that had always been there was recognized for the first time. At any rate, three men who had joined the Consular Service together in 1938 were on their way to the highest ranks of British diplomacy. Sir Thomas Brimelow, Permanent Under Secretary from 1973 to 1975, started his career as Vice-Consul in Danzig. Sir Terence Garvey, Ambassador in Moscow from 1973 to 1975, began as Vice-Consul in San Francisco. Sir Edward Peck, Ambassador to NATO from 1970 to 1975, first worked as Vice-Consul in Barcelona.

Almost certainly, that hat trick will never be equalled. It is not unknown for a man who has come into the Foreign Office as an Administrative entrant from university to be given a posting as a Consul at some stage before the middle reaches of his career; and a coming man may serve as a Consul-General once before promotion to Grade 3 Ambassador abroad or Assistant Under Secretary at home. But the vast majority of consular officials are men who have been recruited into the Executive class and who will not expect to rise higher than Grade 4 in the Diplomatic Service. A great number of them are among the 'teeth staff' of our commercial diplomacy, because beating a drum for British trade is seen as an important function of many consular posts. A typical British consulate in 1975 was the one in Puerto Rico, with three officials on the Diplomatic List, supported by a non-diplomatic staff of typists and other aides. The Consul there was a First Secretary in his late fifties, almost ready to retire. The Vice-Consul was nearing thirty, with two other foreign postings already behind him, and still at Grade 9. The Pro-Consul was locally engaged, with no other future in British diplomacy. The Consulate-General in Marseilles at the same time had five officers on the Diplomatic List. Two Vice-Consuls and the Pro-Consul were locally engaged. Above them came two FCO career men – the Consul-General, who was at Grade 4 and fifty-eight years old, and the Consul (Commercial), who was Grade 5 and forty-seven years old. 'I have never known a flyer become a Consul,' said a man in Africa, 'as the Plowden Committee recommended.' On rare occasions a flyer has; but from a look at most Diplomatic Lists, it is easy to see what the man meant.

These are not, then, the most highly rewarded of diplomats. Ambassadors may expect to be decorated with mounting distinctions in the Order of St Michael and St George. Consuls have to be content with the OBE or the MBE, though a man who has slogged upward in this speciality may finish as a Consul-General with the MVO. They do not even enjoy, as a rule, the same degree of exemption from customs duties and local taxations as the diplomats in the embassies, though that is a matter of international protocol and is not the responsibility of the FCO. The same rule book stipulates the degree of public respect befitting a Consul. Except when he is posted to an embassy or high commission he is, of course, his country's official representative in whatever town or city he is based in. As such, British Consuls may fly a flag on the bonnet of their cars, just like an Ambassador, except that their small Union Jack has a Tudor rose in the middle instead of the royal arms. If their consulate is a maritime one, they are entitled to a seven-gun salute when visiting a warship in the harbour, a thirteen-gun salute in the case of Consuls-General. But these cannonades are severely rationed in ways that the nineteen-gun salutes for Ambassadors are not. Consuls and Consuls-General may be saluted 'only once within twelve months, and by one ship only on the same day'.[1] An Ambassador, in theory, may satisfy his

[1] Satow, p. 49.

sense of theatre by coming aboard and ashore again continuously, from dawn to dusk every day of the week, and the saluting guns will be obliged to keep firing until their blank cartridges run out.

Yet the existence of the consulates, together with the pressing needs of British subjects, is swiftly mentioned by the hierarchy of the Foreign Office whenever MPs begin to put leading questions about economies and a reduction of British diplomacy to a level more in keeping with our international stature. It is sometimes mentioned in such a way as to imply that this is where a very large proportion of diplomatic resources are spent. And, generally speaking, when an axe has been taken to British diplomacy it has fallen on consulates instead of on embassies where (as diplomats themselves concede privately) the same savings could usually be made merely by chipping out superfluous manpower. An illustration of the way the consulates are used as a stalking-horse was provided at a session of the Expenditure Committee in 1971. The MPs had remarked on the contrast between the cost of British representation in some countries – specifically Australia, Ireland and the Netherlands – and the disproportionate returns by way of exports. They noted that the cost of the missions in Holland amounted to £350,000, with exports there worth £377·8 million. The cost in Australia was £977,000, with exports worth £31 million less. 'It is an astonishing difference, really,' said the questioning MP, 'when we are dealing with quite big figures.' The Chief Clerk of the Foreign Office replied:[1]

> There is a difference, certainly, but to take, for example, France, we have to put out a very substantial consular effort in France because it happens to be one of the countries where British subjects like to go for their holidays and need consular protection. We have a good number of consular posts in France.

This was not only sliding away from the point at issue, but it was obliquely hinting at something not obviously supported by facts. According to figures supplied by the FCO to the Duncan Committee, the total annual cost of independent consular posts (that is, excluding the consular sections of embassies and high

[1] *Fifth Report from the Expenditure Committee; Session 1971–2*, p. 14.

commissions) was running at £6·9 million a year in 1969. The Diplomatic Service Vote was then £47 million. As Duncan indicated, British tourists in Western Europe can very well be catered for by honorary consular posts, staffed by retired career officers or by British businessmen resident abroad. They are relatively cheap to run because an Honorary Consul's remuneration is normally a percentage of the consular fees he collects for the supply of new passports, visas and other documents to his benighted customers.

The professional Consuls – the ones who change posts but never jobs when they are abroad – are different in style from the wandering stars of the chanceries. They tend to be blunter, less mannered, more open, and they are rarely pretentious. They are for ever at close quarters with every sort of Her Majesty's subjects, as well as other people's, and this shows. The artful ploys of negotiation and the studied formalities of representation are not unknown to them, but they are uncommon enough not to have become addictive. Consuls seem, in many ways, more realistic. There is sometimes something terribly vulnerable about the precious young men destined for the top of the diplomatic profession, which all their sophistication cannot hide. Vulnerability is just about the last thing a Consul conveys, and this is not wholly to be accounted for by the difference in age. It is difficult to imagine a time when the average Consul was not aware of a world unsheltered by diplomatic privilege and immunity, when he was not growing more toughly practised in its gregariously unsettling ways. When you question Consuls about their work and what it demands, they often compare themselves to priests and doctors. And the three jobs do have much in common.

There is a humdrum side to the consular section of every embassy, or any consulate, and the worst of it consists in issuing visas and passports, a bread and butter business which can sometimes produce a tidy little income to the Crown – in Athens recently, £12,000 in one year. Maritime Consuls until 1973 spent a great deal of their time down at the docks, because they alone could sign on and off British shipping crews, authorize a change of Master and authenticate the articles of discipline; even today, a Master can only dismiss a member of his crew in a foreign port with the permission of the nearest Consul. But what occupies a lot of an average Consul's time are the personal affairs of the shorebound. Some of them are empowered to conduct marriages, and occasionally find themselves acting as marriage guidance counsellors later on. All of them, sooner or later, are involved in every imaginable kind of trouble a Briton can get himself into abroad.

There is a story, carefully preserved in consular lore, about a travelling circus that once went bankrupt in France. Indigent Britons are frequent visitors to Her Majesty's consulates and there is a standard procedure for dealing with them. Their family resources at home are carefully ascertained, liability is firmly settled where it belongs, the vagabond is provided with a ticket for the cheapest conveyance home, and the immigration officers in England confiscate the passport until such time as the bill has been paid. The clowns, the acrobats and the ringmaster of the travelling circus were all handled easily according to this procedure. Then they insisted on their elephant being repatriated, too. As they produced a certificate proving its birth in a British zoo, and as the Consul could find nothing in *Diplomatic Procedures* offering him a loophole large enough to take the beast in any other direction, it was finally put on the cross-Channel ferry with its owners; officially listed as 'Distressed naturalized British elephant'.

Repatriations are not often funny. The most distressing cases in the itinerant post-war years have involved the many young people who have taken the swinging trail to India and Nepal and come to grief at their destination or somewhere en route. Every official between Calais and Calcutta has seen youngsters come stumbling in, sick with hepatitis or dysentery, having neither the strength nor the money to go a step further. Some have just about made it as far as British sanctuary and then collapsed on the consulate floor. There are places in the Middle East where the Consuls have had to rescue adolescents exhausted and penniless even after they have sold their blood at the local market price of 10 dinars per pint. There are times when some hysterical girl has fled to the embassy or the consulate from an employer who, according to the agency in England, was prepared to pay good money to a first-class secretary or nanny, but who turned out to be looking for a concubine instead. None of these kids is ever shown the door by the Consuls. The sick ones are decently doctored, the hysterical ones are probably taken home for the night to be comforted by the Consul's wife. And then, after the procedures have been carefully followed, they are put on the way home. It is said that only the Danes do better than the British in such cases: they simply give their people a ticket to Copenhagen and don't ask for the money back. The Americans tend to make a bigger fuss than anyone else when something goes amiss for a US citizen. When the Colonels' regime was on its last legs in Greece and it looked as if there was to be a headlong collision with Turkey over Cyprus, crisis was so strongly in the air that a certain amount of evacuation took place; the US Embassy in Athens received thirteen letters of complaint about the way this had been conducted, and a Congressional sub-committee flew pronto from Washington to investigate.

The Consuls are also used to helping Britons who have got on the wrong side of the law abroad. For a couple of months in one place, half the consulate's customers were lorry drivers working for unscrupulous operators who had provided them with forged permits, which the local authorities had detected. Two of the men had been imprisoned in a distant town for swearing at a judge on top of their original offence. 'There was a spongy cloud between us and the authorities,' the Consul said later, 'with all the telephone lines said to be down or blocked; we had all hands working on that case for two weeks.' Much more agonizing are the cases that have regularly occurred in Istanbul, in Ankara, in Teheran and at other points on the road home from Afghanistan and places farther East, where young people have been caught smuggling drugs. The penalties in all these places are invariably heavy. In Iran the standard sentence is two years in prison, plus a massive fine for every gramme of drug carried – and one lad was caught with 248 kilos in his truck. There is nothing the Consuls can do in those parts to bail offenders out. They can only arrange for lawyers to defend the culprits, contact the families in England, and pay visits to the prison for a long time afterwards. There are few places in the world where more than that can be done, but Los Angeles has been one of them. A British Consul there had to cope with no fewer than ten murder trials involving Her Majesty's subjects during the term of his posting, and these followed all due processes of the local law. But much more often, it was handsomely waived when British youngsters were caught in possession of drugs. Almost always, State officials and British Consul would discreetly arrange between them for the offenders to be deported on the next plane to London – often at the American taxpayer's expense. Listening to the reminiscences of Consuls can restore a lot of faith in human nature and diplomacy.

In Mediterranean towns, the Consul will sometimes hear of an ancient lady, Maltese in origin but essentially a relic of the British Empire, destitute in a shack with nothing much between the tin roof and the concrete floor. Valletta doesn't want her any more than London does, so the Consul unearths some fund that will provide a pittance to keep her alive where she is. Anywhere at all he is likely to be at the burial of British dead in the course of a year. In a non-Christian country he is probably secretary of the Protestant cemetery committee and one such official found, when he totted up his annual accounts, that 2 or 3 of the 14 deaths on his books had ended up in the local graveyard. Apart from the deaths, 17 car crashes had come his way, 13 people in hospital, 30 in prison, 18 marriages and 64 persons in various forms of distress which justified official repatriation. The people represented by such figures are, in every sense, a mixed bunch. The penniless youngsters who have caused so much trouble generally turn up trumps in the end: the relieved parents are very good at paying the debt when they are safely home and the kids themselves usually write rather touching letters of gratitude for the help they've been given – 'though one little bitch took £4 from me and it was worth it to get rid of her'. Some people come in and thump the desk and demand their Britannic rights, and later write unpleasantly to the newspapers because they have been given a dusty reply. Some seem to regard the consulate as a more reliable poste restante than anything the locals can provide. One woman who, it was discovered, had lived on social security for years, had managed to save enough for a single fare to the Mediterranean and a fortnight's holiday there. When it was over she marched into the consulate for her return ticket and got it; but grudgingly. Patiently and impatiently, the Consuls sort out all these customers. From time to time, though, something happens to upset them rather badly: the three girls whose bodies had to be sent home after an air crash, the boy whose parents never dreamt that he might be travelling back with 10 lb of hash in his bags ...

It is all rather different in that part of the embassy, usually some distance from the consular section, where the Defence, Military, Naval and Air Attachés are to be found. Not that every British mission runs to four individuals, each wearing a hat with one of those labels. Only the biggest posts have more than one soldier, one sailor and one airman on the staff; supported, naturally, by a squad of other ranks. Plenty have only a couple of officers from the armed services. Even more have only one, who must manage as best he can to cover three disciplines with his solitary commission. But only the smallest British missions have no Servicemen at all, to advise His Excellency, to keep a weather eye lifted for the local hardware – by invitation to the military manoeuvres and otherwise – to do his bit for the balance of payments, and to smarten up all official occasions with his own turnout of sword and tassels. There is neither rhyme nor reason to the deployment of the Attachés; none that the Ministry of Defence would want us to know, anyway. The views of the Ambassador are said to be 'material' to the final choice. Surprisingly, that doesn't even depend on how many Service Attachés of its own the host country may have sent to London. We just decide how many men we want in a particular place and pack them off, after getting permission to do so first. The Service Attaché is the one person, other than the head of mission himself, whose name must be cleared by the host country before his appointment can be confirmed.

Diplomats can be a bit patronizing about them. Sir Douglas Busk even went so far as to imply that they were not the very best men going, on the grounds that no officer is obliged to accept a posting to an embassy and that the most ambitious men would probably dodge such an invitation because it would remove them for some years from the mainstream of their profession. A great number of those serving nowadays (ten years after Busk was writing) seem to be men on their last assignment before retiring: but then you come across a clipped and blooming major, who has just taken up post after commanding infantry in Ulster and manoeuvring tanks in Germany ... Young diplomats are mostly apt to mock the excessive self-consciousness of the Attachés when they are dealing with anything that might be remotely construed as intelligence work. At one embassy, a First Secretary was reading a volume of topography, well illustrated with photographs, which he had picked up in a local bookshop. In walked the Naval Attaché, who whipped a miniature camera from his pocket and took a quick conspiratorial snapshot of one of the pictures. 'You didn't see me do that,' he muttered, as he slipped the camera into his pocket again and left the room. First Secretaries enjoy telling yarns like that.

The Attachés don't patronize the diplomats, but they can be quite breezy about the embassy way of life. 'Being an Attaché', said an airman, 'is a holiday compared with commanding a V force.' They reckon that they form judgments and take decisions faster than any of the civilians who surround them. They are usually very critical indeed of diplomatic administration, leaving the impression sometimes that a bit of the old one-two-one-two might go a long way to straightening it out. 'I often think that what this place really needs', said the colonel at a Grade 1 embassy, 'is a retired sergeant-major permanently on the staff.' Another Military Attaché arrived at his mission – as diplomats themselves generally do – ahead of his household effects, which had been shipped from England. At weekly intervals he inquired of the embassy administrators whether there was any news of these things down at the docks. Each time, heads were shaken sympathetically. In due course a warehouse on the wharf was destroyed by fire, and he learned that all his possessions had been sitting there for three months, waiting for someone to come and collect them. He blamed his loss, basically, on an excess of diplomatic paperwork, which jammed too many of the diplomatic works. Another military complaint is that junior diplomats today suffer from a peculiar helplessness that their predecessors a generation ago, who knew National Service, did not share. It seems that they are not very good at acting as extra eyes for the Attaché and his other ranks, because they simply don't know what a military objective looks like. Even when they show willing and try, it is usually a waste of time because 'these young lads don't know the difference between a division and a battalion, and they wouldn't be able to tell you whether what they had seen in the harbour this morning was a visiting missile ship or the local gash barge.'

Whatever pointed little professional rivalries run between them, however, both Foreign Office and Ministry of Defence set a great deal of store by the Service Attachés – much more than any comparable country does. Their numbers and their range, in fact, have been growing over the past few years, when most other things about diplomacy have been contracting. When the Duncan Committee reported in 1969, the French had 119 Attachés posted in 58 countries and the Germans 58 in 28 countries. The British at that time maintained 165 Attachés in 69 countries. That figure included six men at the Washington embassy; they were the Attachés proper, specially accredited, like all Service Attachés, to the government of the host country. By 1975, totally excluding all personnel in Washington, we had 164 Attachés based in 71 countries – and 41 of them were accredited as non-resident Attachés to a further 23 countries, which they visited periodically from the neighbouring embassies and high commissions where they were based.

The full muster of the British Defence Staff in Washington when Duncan reported was 67 Service officers and 131 men from the Ministry of Defence, with a similar mixture of another 99 people skirmishing elsewhere round the United States. The figures for the British Defence Staff in the American capital have declined since then: at the end of 1974 they were unofficially said to stand at about 40 Service officers and a grand Defence Staff total of 123. But this remains a unique assembly of soldiers, sailors and airmen from one country in one building in a foreign land. There are moments, on the upper floors of the embassy, when the outsider feels so much as if he may have wandered into the headquarters of the old wartime Combined Operations, that he would not be in the least surprised to see Lord Louis Mountbatten heaving to in the midst of all that plate glass. The Chief of the Defence Staff in Washington is, indeed, a sailor from time to time, a vice-admiral who three years later gives way to a general, who hands over in turn to an air marshal.

They make out a persuasive case for such defensive topweight, with the most effective kind of sales talk. It does not sound exaggerated even when it quite palpably ignores the most critical questions: like, why do we need so much more of all this than the Germans, who are also solid partners in NATO. 'Here,' says an enthusiast, 'we have access to an $80 billion military machine. We know just what the Americans have tried and discarded in hardware, and what they've proved effective. We're utterly persuaded that we get value for money in this access ... ' But do the Americans really tell us everything? Well, that, of course, is why the BDS is so big; because it requires a lot of men spending a lot of time trying to persuade the Americans to release all the information the British want. ' ... And we do get a great deal more from them than they get from us. There isn't total openness, but it's there to a very large degree. Sometimes they're cagey about the potential commercial threat to them in supplying information to us, and there are times when they think we've short-changed them. Can't think of a reverse example, to tell you the truth.' One gets an odd feeling, talking to the men in the BDS, that perhaps this whole operation is to do with commerce more than defence; that, fundamentally, it is concerned with amassing dollars on the one hand and trying to restore sterling on the other; that far less than we like to think is it all about preserving democratic freedoms. But no, that's not fair. ' ... And we maintain close personal links with their officers, which helps when we set up commands, in NATO etc. Since the US pulled out of Vietnam, the relationship has been fairly dynamic. But I can conceive of our lacking the will to do our part, and therefore endangering the alliance. The Yanks are mercurial, you know; they can cut off their noses to spite their faces.' His Excellency downstairs is privy to all this, of course. All messages sent by the vice-admiral or the general or the air marshal to the Chief of the Defence Staff in London, are copied for the British Ambassador's benefit. They discuss anything at all they're up to with 'the Defence elements in chancery'.

Service Attachés, known tactfully as 'Advisers' in Commonwealth posts, work closely with their Ambassadors at all British missions although, if it comes to the pinch, they can insist on any report of theirs with which the Ambassador might disagree, going direct to the Ministry of Defence in London. What goes into their reports depends, in a general as well as a particular way, on which part of the world they are stationed in. Very simply, if the country is by long tradition friendly or in reliable alliance with us, the Attaché's function, beyond that of decoration on ceremonial occasions, is to keep the alliance in good repair by exchanging military information, to do what can be done to sell military equipment of British manufacture, to act as the immediate go-between in strategical planning. In a neutral environment, salesmanship may be equally balanced with intelligence work. In a potentially adversary relationship not much can be done except to be as friendly as possible and to find out as much as you can about local arrangements and intentions. At one post in the Middle East, the Military Attaché will reckon to spend 60 per cent of his time on intelligence, 30 per cent on Defence sales and 10 per cent on representation. At another, Defence sales may occupy 70 per cent of his time. At a third post in the same quarter of the globe, where the supply of armaments has already been pre-empted by another source, 80 per cent of the Attaché's work will be intelligence, the rest of it merely showing the flag. This is not always to a soldier's taste, in spite of the popular image. 'The trouble with all these formal cocktail parties', said one long-suffering soul, 'is that you have to turn up in uniform, which ruins the rest of the evening for you. Well, I mean, you can hardly roll on afterwards to a down-town restaurant togged up like that; you'd look a proper Charlie.'

In Nairobi, the Defence Adviser spends a lot of his time on liaison work with the Kenyan Army. This means arranging courses for Kenyans at Sandhurst and other establishments in Britain, and preparing for British troops training in Kenya – two full infantry battalion exercises and an Engineers' exercise every year. In Teheran, the two Military Attachés are up to their necks as commercial travellers for Ministry of Defence Sales, as well as advising the Shah's army on the establishment of a Junior Leaders' College on British lines. The Naval Attaché is meanwhile trying to get our oar into whatever contracts may be going when a new naval base is created at Chah Behan on the Persian Gulf. The Air Attaché, from an office decorated with signed photographs of Prince Philip and Prince Charles in RAF uniform, supervises the six Vulcan bombers which are occasionally based at Shiraz and the four Canberras at Meshad as CENTO's main reconnaissance force, and the other two machines which come to Iran once a fortnight for low-flying practice. The Attaché fervently hopes that in the course of these operations some idiot doesn't get his flight plan so confused that he zooms in over the Shah's palace rooftop, which is usually interpreted as an undiplomatic gesture. In Belgrade, the Colonel of Dragoons at the British Embassy coaches a Yugoslav four-in-hand team for an appearance at the Windsor Horse Show and goes off to see yet another Partisan battlefield, one more wartime headquarters of President Tito, of which he will probably, by the end of his posting, have had much more experience than the average Yugoslav. And this is not a waste of time. It is part of the subtle, tedious and – to outsiders – usually incomprehensible business basic to all forms of diplomacy, which is to hold countries as closely to each other as their independent interests will allow. Every British ex-Serviceman who fought with the Yugoslav Partisans during the Second World War still has the right, under local law, to buy a house there and live in it if he wishes. That law might have been repealed at any time during the past thirty years, given the political differences of Europe. Diplomacy is why it has stayed put.

It is outside the competence of this book to say anything about intelligence that has not already been published elsewhere. It is a foggier subject than anyone who has not worked at its uppermost levels can ever, one supposes, pretend to suggest. There really wouldn't be much point to it otherwise. Diplomats who have nothing to do with intelligence work say that it is all redundant anyway – for anyone in alliance with the Russians or the Americans – since the advent of satellite photography, which can keep track of any military objective on earth. But that hasn't discouraged spying on the ground yet. The Foreign Secretary himself, it may be assumed, does not know all that goes on partly in his name. He is, it is true, required not only to swear himself to secrecy on assuming office, but on relinquishing it he has to take another oath that he will at once forget every secret he has ever been told as a Minister; which, as more than one man in this position has told those before whom he has sworn most solemnly, is a pretty ludicrous thing to expect of any human being. But something more than the conventional secrecy of regular diplomacy is involved here. Foreign Office men can be as thoroughly pickled in intelligence work as anyone camouflaged by the Ministry of Defence. And politicians prefer not to know about international state secrets unless absolutely necessary. They can stain a reputation indelibly, even when it takes thirty years for the truth to be revealed.

There are two main operative bodies, the Secret Intelligence Service and the Security Service, and both are represented on the co-ordinating intelligence body of the British government, the Defence Intelligence Committee. Between the two of them

it is said that 'Co-operation is usually, but not invariably, close'.[1]
The Security Service deals with counter-intelligence, with stop-
ping foreigners from learning our secrets. The Secret
Intelligence Service is busy trying to find out other people's
secrets. All those cryptic little bureaux we fantasize so much are
farmed by one or other of these units. Thus, DI 5, which organizes counter-intelligence officers, belongs to the SS; DI 6, which
runs to spies, comes under the SIS. Readers of John Le Carré's
books probably know as much as there is to be known about the
ways they all work. As David Cornwell, Le Carré was himself
a diplomat for five years in the 1960s before turning to his typewriter, and the Foreign Office is said to be not yet wholly
reconciled to the disclosures he has cleverly made in a stream
of bestsellers since. The Foreign Office involvement in this intriguing network of spies and counter-spies is considerable. Two
of the FCO's departments, Defence and Permanent Under
Secretary's, work in close liaison with the Defence Intelligence
Committee; and the Committee's chairman is usually someone
from diplomacy rather than from the military world. Moreover,
the head of the Secret Intelligence Service is always a Deputy
Under Secretary in the Foreign Office. Until 1973 he was Sir
John Rennie who, as he rose in the diplomatic ranks, had occupied a number of commercial posts in embassies as far apart as
Warsaw and Buenos Aires, had never been an Ambassador and,
as SIS chief, was officially listed as the Superintending Under
Secretary of the Planning, the Research, and the Library and
Records Departments. It has been claimed that a subsequent
'Head of MI 5 and MI 6' was Sir Maurice Oldfield,[2] whose
career details in the *Diplomatic Service List* end rather abruptly
at 1964 when, as a forty-eight-year-old Counsellor, he moved
from the Washington embassy to the FCO, decorated with the
CMG (he acquired the KCMG which made him 'Sir Maurice'
in 1975). Whatever he had been up to after that, therefore, he
was due for retirement in 1976 from diplomacy and any kindred
fun and games.

There is no telling who, in any embassy, is a straightforward
diplomat and who has been specially charged with work for
SIS; or who, indeed, may be a soldier disguised as a diplomat

[1] McDermott, p. 136.
[2] *Evening Standard*, November 18th, 1975.

because he would be *persona non grata* as an Attaché. The Russian KGB, notoriously, is apt to station its most powerful agents in the guise of the Twenty-Fifth Trade Secretary's bat-man-cum chauffeur; and the American CIA's real bossman in London could very well be – in spite of all the heady revelations early in 1976 – that determined-looking lady who has just handled your visa inquiry in the consular section of Grosvenor Square. Military Attachés, from whatever branch of the Armed Forces they have come, are merely the overt and licensed operators in this trade, according to the unwritten rule book accepted by all countries. The main rule is not to be caught doing what the host country would prefer you not to be doing, which is to be taking note of things that have been carefully concealed; but your hosts would think you most splendidly negligent if you didn't even try to satisfy your curiosity to some extent – provided, of course, this didn't involve the subversion of their own nationals. When that happens, everyone gets rather angry, as though spying were a shockingly alien thing, and you are promptly declared *persona non grata*. But it is on the basis of these rules that the Attaché who is resident in Country A, with a non-resident accreditation to Country B, periodically decides to drive from A to B, instead of flying, so that he may pass a new installation he has heard about, whose details will be quite clear to the scrutineers in London (or Moscow, or Washington, or Paris), provided he has remembered to fit the right lens to his camera, and so long as no one sees him taking snapshots of the landscape.

When they are not thus occupied, however, the Military Attachés of two countries whose governments are not on the best of terms usually enjoy quite a jovial relationship. Next year they may be dropping H-bombs on each other, but for the time being they are all rather matey. One may read of the dinner dance of Quad A (the Association of Assistant Army Attachés in London) which was held at the Columbia Club, where Lt-Colonel G. D. Yakovlev, Soviet Assistant Military Attaché, was dancing with 'the lovely Camille Hudman', who is wife of the United States Assistant Army Attaché, Lt-Colonel George Hudman.[1] This form of operation doubtless takes a bit of getting used to by a very new Military Attaché, recently arrived from

---

[1] *The Diplomatist*, March 1974.

the firing line in Ulster, or even from tactical simulations with Chieftain tanks on Lüneburg Heath. He is ready for the two Russian colonels who keep trying to pump him for information whenever he meets them at cocktail parties, and he is not so naive as to be astonished when his wife informs him that their wives are perfectly nice, really, after they have coincided at hen parties in the neutral capital: but there are limits, surely, to how close you can get to these people? Presently, however, he may find himself approaching life like one of our Attachés in Southern Europe. 'Oh, I see quite a bit of the Russkie Colonel one way or another, and we get on perfectly well together. Whenever I have to go over to his place, first thing I say is "Now then, Vassili, you old dog, where've you put the tape recorder today ... " ' And, by the time one of these officers has to leave his embassy, to return to being a proper soldier, sailor or airman, his potential adversary will, like all the other Attachés in town, gladly subscribe towards a piece of silver plate, to remind him in times to come of the tolerably civilized days when they observed each other closely over their half-open sights.

It is sometimes easy to forget what a very serious business it is that the Military Attachés are about. But then, one day in Washington, a member of the British Defence Staff distracts himself from his thoughts on the Anglo-American alliance, and generalizes about the state of the nation at home and its awareness of the world it lives in. 'They've got to be warned,' he declares. 'We mustn't allow them to be surprised.' He is referring to the British people, and military threats to them from abroad, and he means it very passionately indeed. These are not men sent to lie abroad for the sake of diplomatic effect alone; they are warriors by profession and occasionally they let it slip quite chillingly. An Attaché was discussing the relative merits of two armies, one belonging to the country in which he was situated, the other its immediate neighbour's. In equipment, obtained from a variety of sources, the two forces appeared to be evenly matched. They had not been in combat, but this was always a lurking possibility. 'It would be interesting,' said the detached Attaché, 'if there were a scrap, to see who came off better.'

Yet few men can spend three years in a strange environment and come away from it completely untouched. A colonel who was about to return to the stiffer disciplines of his regiment after the comparatively languid ways of the embassy, admitted that he was not quite the same fellow who had arrived. 'There's one thing the diplomats have taught me,' he said. 'Shake hands with everyone on principle.'

14 Cultural Diplomacy

When British officials utter the words 'cultural diplomacy' they usually have the French in mind. The reference is to what undiplomatic souls might crudely call brainwashing, and anyone professionally involved in the subject will readily illustrate what he means at the lift of an eyebrow. It means that books extolling the French heritage travel to South America fast and free of charge by courtesy of Air France, whereas comparable English texts are transported slowly and expensively by the next available tramp steamer. It means that the Quai D'Orsay will cheerfully take sixty students from Cairo to Paris for a long vacation entirely at its own expense to teach them nothing but the merits of France, while the British struggle to produce the funds for a brace of scholarships in ophthalmology or some similarly untendentious subject. It means, in the long run, that if you go to Algiers today and talk to the most fervent nationalist, he will frequently struggle to express himself in Arabic and in the end have to fall back on French, which has been much more his native tongue. This, truly, is not a mark the British ever left on India, for all the bilinguality on the sub-continent. 'Cultural diplomacy' is to some extent the expression of an ancient rivalry between the British and the French. What it really boils down to is that when both were colonial powers, the French extended their influence with the aid of their own literature rather more than by relying on The Book; that they conducted themselves in far-flung outposts to the strains of Offenbach as much as 'La Marseillaise', instead of being tone-deaf to almost every sound but the thump of 'The British Grenadiers' and the tinkle of the cash register. There is much British jealousy of the way the French still go about these things, as though it were a very dubious form of one-upmanship. But the British—in the past, at any rate—are not the only people to have felt like that. In 1929 the German Reichstag was invited by the Foreign Minister, Gustav Stresemann, to purvey its *Kultur* abroad more assiduously. 'Look at the French Republic,' he cried. 'She has never spared funds for this: she knows exactly how she has won over the Orient intellectually, with her French schools, with her French influence.'[1] Almost a decade before that, Lord Curzon had been coming to the same conclusion, cranking up the handle of the Foreign Office machine that would eventually produce a British response. He set up an FO committee in 1920, to see whether it seemed desirable to encourage British propaganda in foreign countries, and in 1934 the machinery at last coughed up 'The British Council for relations with other countries'.

Over the years since then, the most consistently effective propaganda has probably been provided less by the British Council than by the External Broadcasting Services of the BBC, particularly since the war, when the whole corporation gained its international reputation for telling the truth – as much as possible. Apologists for the BBC are apt to overlook the fact that during the war it was subject to censorship like every newspaper but, as such reputations go, it is almost certainly better deserved than any rival's. Of no area will this be truer than the External Services, which evolved from the BBC's old Empire Service, started in 1932. The External programmes are disseminated from Bush House in the Strand, which is a good two miles away from the BBC radio headquarters in Broadcasting House, and which points up an essential difference of substance if not philosophy between the two branches. For while what goes on in Broadcasting House is based upon an income derived from our radio and television licence fees, what comes out of Bush House is almost completely subsidized by the Foreign Office, which spends over 10 per cent of the total costs of overseas representation in this way. It is the Foreign Office connection that makes men from Bush House excessively sensitive to the use of the word propaganda in their hearing; they jump at the sound, as though someone had shouted 'Dr Goebbels!' That association of ideas is ridiculously remote, but the fact is that propaganda is their business, in the very best traditions of the BBC. This does not only consist in broadcasting the news in English and thirty-odd

[1] White, p. 2.

other tongues, from Hausa to Thai, from Russian to Spanish; Bush House also puts out talks and summaries expressing British attitudes and the British way of life. I myself have sat in a studio there and gone on about the election of a new Salvation Army leader in London, and about how an Englishman rides a camel in the Sahara Desert. Which just goes to show what a subtle brainwashing these people are capable of, when they stick to the austere precepts of Lord Reith.

What the Foreign Office gets in return for its money is much more in the nature of a gentleman's agreement than anything else. The terms of the BBC Charter quite distinctly leave editorial control of External programmes completely in BBC hands. At the same time, the FCO has the power to order Bush House to stop transmitting any service. This, it is said, has never happened yet. The FCO can also shape External broadcasting by 'advising' how many hours each week should be spent transmitting programmes to a given part of the world, and has done so constantly since the services began. It can achieve certain diplomatic objectives by 'suggesting' that a new service should be opened in some direction or other, and that has happened more than once. Most recently, the diplomats were keen for Bush House to start a new service beamed at Korea. This is an area in which they have developed an intense interest in the mid-1970s, since it looked as if it might have the trade potential of Hong Kong and for much the same reasons, of cheap labour and rapid industrial expansion. The request to Bush House came at a bad time. The broadcasters replied that they would be happy to start talking Korean if the FCO produced the extra money needed for the new service. As the Treasury had just invited the FCO to cut its BBC grant by £500,000 this hasn't been forthcoming so far.

Beyond orders that have never been issued, and persuasion that is not always successful, the Guidance and Information Department of the FCO has regular dealings with Bush House. It doesn't usually monitor the broadcasts, but it did ask for transcripts of everything that went out in Arabic during the Middle East wars with Israel. If someone in Bush House describes the Persian Gulf as the Arabian Gulf on the wrong wavelength, the Shah's teeth are immediately set on edge and that means that while the FCO's Middle East Department has to make soothing noises in Teheran, the Guidance Department has to rap knuckles half-way across London. Occasionally, British Ambassadors in any part of the world will anticipate the sensitivities of their hosts and lodge their own complaints, and at such times Guidance very often tells them not to be so daft. All possible precautions are taken to prevent the broadcasters from unwittingly creating a diplomatic incident. Every day the top brass in Bush House (as well as the BBC's Diplomatic Correspondent) are supplied with the FCO's latest intake of telegrams from abroad, including classified material that is otherwise seen in only the most secure parts of Whitehall. Occasionally, as during the Cyprus crisis of 1974, these can pass beyond the merely 'confidential' to the 'secret'. This is a very sore subject with MPs, who are even more sensitive about other people's exclusive privileges than they are about their own. But the relationship between the Foreign Office and Bush House is a rather special one, and some slips are worth risking to be sure that others will never occur. 'It's in the vital interests of both the BBC and FCO to support each other,' said one diplomat. 'We each have clear areas of authority, but neither exercises it in full.'

The most blatant British propaganda is provided by the Foreign Office itself through diplomats posted to embassies as Information Officers. This is no longer the growth industry it was after the Drogheda Committee in 1954 said that information services should be directed at the influential few and, through them, at the many. The Cold War was at its chilly peak then and Britain was still playing the role of a first-class world power; and under this misapprehension the Foreign Office needed only Drogheda's blessing to elevate the previously inferior status of the Information Officer to a vaulting horse for likely flyers. The illusion of power began to fade not long afterwards, though enthusiasm for information work took somewhat longer to abate. By the time Duncan came along, attention was being drawn to the fact that in many posts – particularly in India – the information sections were far too large for the job that had to be done. They have subsequently been trimmed, but the bigger embassies still carry one diplomat who peddles handouts provided by the Central Office of Information, and keeps on drinking terms with the local journalists, so that he can amiably try to divert them when the headlines become too unfriendly. In two places, however, information is still a major operation. One is in Brussels. The other is in New York; and there, on Third Avenue, seven or eight British diplomats apply themselves to the business of propaganda on a thoroughly American scale.

The amount of material they produce by way of chatty news-sheets, condensations of British press opinion, highlights of political speeches in London, carefully-captioned photographs of 'Revolutionary Liquid Oxygen Apparatus for Mine Rescue' and suchlike, is heartbreaking to anyone who knows how much of this material usually goes straight into any journalist's wastepaper basket after a cursory glance. The men on Third Avenue, however, are not aiming only at journalists. Their *British Record*, a news-sheet that would not disgrace the *Young Observer* section of that paper's Sunday colour magazine, is sent to 7,000 'opinion moulders' (including people from 'the higher reaches of the academic world') by mail. Nor are they concerned only with the written word and the captioned photograph. They offer short films for use on television, on subjects like a British gadget to help handicapped people in the home, and the Transport and Road Research Laboratory's work on accident prevention. Their greatest excitement comes when they manage to get a British VIP interviewed (preferably by mettlesome Ms Barbara Walters) on the all-American *Today* show, which United States citizens do not often fail to watch, even though many of them must go quite cross-eyed with concentrating on their breakfasts at the same time.[1] Occasionally, visiting VIPs are less than helpful to either the diplomats or the United Kingdom. When our men on Third Avenue heard that the Duke of Edinburgh was to visit New York in October 1974, they asked Buckingham Palace if he would please find time to appear on NBC television in the city, at the prospect of which even Ms Walters (who has her weaknesses) would doubtless have drooled. The request was refused on the grounds that 'they [NBC] had us last time'. As, indeed, they had; some years previously.

The British Council is on a significantly different plane from either the BBC or the official information services, even though it was the Foreign Office's own first thought in the direction of propaganda, and today embodies elements built into each of

[1] In November 1976, Ms Walters went from NBC to the rival ABC network, for a multi-million dollar contract.

the other two operations. The most striking thing about it is that it straddles so many different objectives, being at one and the same time a purveyor of information about the British way of life, an impresario of the arts, an agent of academic education, a means of dispensing aid to the developing countries and – most recent addition to this ungainly mixture – yet another way of trying to save us from insolvency. A voice from within the Council remarked, a decade before the new carpetbagging role was conceived, that the Foreign Office 'has seemed at some stages to change its priorities for Council work too often for the Council's good'.[1] That is the trouble with patrons who pay the piper, particularly when they are not at all sure what tune they want to hear. Some 32 per cent of the British Council's revenue comes from the Foreign Office, another 60 per cent being allotted by ODM (though well over half that allotment, amounting to £13·6 million in 1974/5, is money which the council simply administers as the Department's agent). Consistently, from year to year, two-thirds of the British Council's own income is provided by the Foreign Office. And it is perfectly true that, from one decade to the next, the British Council has never been quite sure what its chief paymaster has expected of it. This means that the politicians behind the diplomats haven't had much of a clue, either.

> Whereas it has been represented to us by our Principal Secretary of State for Foreign Affairs that for the purpose of promoting a wider knowledge of our United Kingdom of Great Britain and Northern Ireland and the English Language abroad and developing closer cultural relations between our United Kingdom of Great Britain and Northern Ireland and other countries ...

Thus begins the royal charter the Council acquired in 1940, with an unpunctuated preamble which states the essence of what had already been done in the first six years. At the end of 1936, for example, the year's work included: provision of funds for British institutes and societies for English studies in 4 European and 3 South American countries; financial support for English schools in Egypt and 2 European countries; English

<hr>

[1] White, p. 65.

libraries in 36 countries; bursaries enabling 55 student-teachers of English from 13 European countries to take a term at British universities alongside 15 lads from Malta, Cyprus and West Africa, and another 14 from South America; chairs and readerships of English established in 5 European countries; tours by British musicians in 12 European countries; exhibitions of British watercolours in Vienna and Prague, of British contemporary art in Johannesburg. This was typical British Council activity of the pre-war years. What was left of the Council after the war was conducted on the same lines; but now everything it did was drastically reduced because funds were short and there was even, at one stage, a government hint that the organization might be abolished altogether. It was in this period that the newspapers owned by Lord Beaverbrook began a long campaign of derision at the Council's expense, fairly wetting themselves with mirth at the idea of 'Morris dancers for Mexico' and other images that were sometimes of their own invention. No one is at all clear why the campaign started, unless it was because the Council made an easy target for the bully boy of Fleet Street. Conceivably, it was inspired by politicians anxious that this vehicle of culture should seem dispensable to the public. It marked the British Council more than even Beaverbrook might have hoped. People there today say that a lot of its uncertainties since that time, many of its failures to be its own boss (to the degree that the men at Bush House are their own boss) are traceable to the collective psychological damage done by that campaign when the Council was already sinking to its knees. The BBC resisted Foreign Office influence to start a new Korean service, on the grounds that its available resources would be overstretched. The British Council didn't, and opened a new outpost in Seoul in 1973.

There *was* something dilettante about the Council in the Beaverbrook years, and it has not yet vanished. There are still quite a lot of people about who sigh for the days when dear old Edwin Muir would put in a couple of years as a Council officer, until he had saved enough money to go off and concentrate on his poetry again, knowing that when the cash and/or the inspiration ran out, the Council would indulgently find him another post. There are ladies in the British Council headquarters, who are so jolly proud to be daughters of figures in the Council's pantheon that it is almost the first thing they tell a new acquaintance. There are still Council representatives abroad who, so far as one can detect, are there because they had a lifelong ambition to live in that spot, not so much to brainwash the natives with the best of British culture as to wallow in the local form of civilization and deliver erudite lectures on it. But changes began soon after Lord Drogheda reported. This coincided with two new appointments at the top of the British Council, which were followed some time later by another one related to it outside. Sir David Kelly, lately British Ambassador in Moscow, became chairman in 1955. The year before, a new director-general had started a fourteen-year stint, which is so far easily the longest in the Council's history. He was Sir Paul Sinker, a Classics lecturer at Cambridge before making a wartime reputation at the Admiralty and serving just after the war in the Treasury, after which he became the First Civil Service Commissioner. The related appointment outside the Council came in 1961, when the Department for Technical Co-operation was created, the forerunner of the ODM, and its first Permanent Secretary was Sir Andrew Cohen who, as Governor of Uganda, had exiled the Kabaka in 1952.

The changes that overtook the British Council now were one of policy and one of character. The prescription of the Drogheda Committee was for a contraction of work in Europe and an expansion of work elsewhere. The first of these was to be pretty severe. British institutes and Council centres, in Drogheda's view, should be self-supporting or they should close down, and scholarships should be very exceptional awards. Most severe of all the proposed changes, British Council offices should be closed and, instead, Cultural Attachés should be appointed to the nearest British embassies. Beyond this, Drogheda saw an enormous new field of work for the Council, especially in the teaching of English in India, Pakistan, the Far East generally and the Middle East. The Kelly–Sinker combination was tough enough to resist most of the European proposals, which would have reduced the Council's work even below the level of the post-war retrenchment. In the end, things there were left more or less as they had been before Drogheda reported. In Asia and the Middle East, however, expansion began as soon as the government had accepted the report and released through the Foreign Office the money needed to carry out its proposals. By 1959 the Council's income was twice what it had been in

1954, its activities had spread to seventy countries, and four-fifths of its resources were being spent in Asia and Africa. At the same time, it was organizing the flood of students that came to Britain from these places: by 1956 there were 30,000 young people from overseas in Britain, and a third of them came from colonial territories. Old Council hands who were around at the time say that the air of confidence generated by this expansion also derived to some extent from a more professional approach that Sinker had brought into the organization:

> In the early days, people had the idea that foreigners wanted to know about Britain as though the BC was a bloody travel agency. We used to give lectures on Windsor Castle to ladies in hats, who were either experts themselves or just old and devoted anglophiles. Paul Sinker began to put a stop to that sort of thing.

But the same voices maintain that Sinker was no match for Cohen when the ex-Colonial Governor came along in 1961 and looked to the British Council as a tool for his new trade. These are not always the purists (and there are plenty of *them* still about, too, usually the ones who direct an outsider's attention to the preamble of the charter) who regret the passing of the days when the British Council stood for not much more than the promotion of an English language that had not yet been muddied with words like 'parameter' and 'interface' in the conversations of Whitehall. Some, who say they were quite ready for the Council to move on to completely new ground without abandoning the old, argue that the director-general should have made sure that if the British Council was now to go into technical co-operation, as well as culture and English teaching, it should be given more money to cover the more complex administration required of it in future, instead of being limited to extra funds for use only in the field. They imply that this is where the Council's administration began to get itself into knots which have not yet been completely untied, in spite of the Duncan Committee's concern in 1969 about 'the danger of over-lap and duplication between the British Council and Diplomatic Service staff overseas in relation to aid administration'.[1]

---

[1] Duncan, p. 93.

The biggest additional burden that Cohen and his successors in the Ministry of Overseas Development placed on the back of the British Council was the administration of educational aid overseas – and few things expanded more than that as a British conscience about the Third World developed in the 1960s. The work, familiar in its essentials from the Council's foundation, was not now to be confined to teaching English, though that has remained the biggest part of it. Technical education was also involved henceforth, and the strain imposed upon the Council machinery has been evident at times ever since. Not so long ago, a couple of Somalis were sent to London at the British expense, to take a course in air-traffic control which they would then usefully apply to their work at Mogadishu airport. On the way back from England, however, they simply got off the aircraft at Abu Dhabi where, as they well knew, they could get much better paid jobs than Mogadishu would ever provide. Someone who watched all this happening at close quarters, and claimed that similar wastage occurred with about 20 per cent of Somalis taking British aid courses, was of the opinion that 'The British Council's lousy administration was responsible. They just hand out tickets to these people instead of attaching strings that would tie the students up until they were safely back where they were supposed to be.'

The Council went through a bad patch when Sir Paul Sinker left it in 1968 to become chairman of the Council for Small Industries in Rural Areas, and its administrative weaknesses were one of the causes. There was another reason, however, and that was petty jealousies at the top. It is a hard thing for any man to succeed to a command after someone else has held it for fourteen years, hardest of all when the successor is an outsider. The new director-general was Sir John Henniker-Major, and he came in from the Foreign Office against the expectations and hopes of several Council careerists who – professionals now – thought one of them should have had the job. The next four years at headquarters were not particularly edifying and, given the situation that awaited him at the British Council, Henniker-Major was almost the last man who should have been appointed, for all the diplomacy he brought to bear on rebellious seniors. He had been British Ambassador to both Jordan and Denmark, as well as an Assistant Under Secretary at the FCO, but in none of these posts had his reputation exceeded the one he had made earlier as chief of the Foreign Office's Personnel Department. He was in that job far longer than normal because he had proved to be an outstanding organizer of a complicated business. He was a born administrator, who would cut rather sharply through waffle to get things moving. He was very professional indeed, and he was now invited to lead an institution which retained quite a lot of its old (and often endearing) amateur ways. One of the things he did was to bring in two officials from the Civil Service Department, a Mr Moore and a Mr McCosh, to investigate the working of the London operation. The Moore–McCosh report is said to have been highly uncomplimentary to the administration; critical enough, anyway, for it to be regarded as an uncomfortably Top Secret document, from the very mention of which senior British Council men, years later, still shy away like nervous young colts.

The induction of a diplomat at the top of the Council starkly caricatured the tug-of-war that is a permanent feature of the relationship with the Foreign Office. This is not to say that combat between the two is the dominant characteristic, because that is far from being so; in most ways the Council is an accomplice of the diplomats. The Permanent Under Secretary of the FCO always sits on its executive committee. As an institution in its own right it is structurally modelled on the Foreign Office, and it even calls its filing system the registry. People working for the British Council are graded like diplomats, but instead of moving up from Grade 10 to Grade 1, they climb from Grade J to Grade A. The Council runs its own selection boards, for it is no part of the civil service, and is very proud indeed of the quality it attracts. 'The FCO', says a recruiting officer, 'is a depressed profession, as diplomacy's great days are over, but in our case things are on the up and up.' Most men who look to a career in the Council come in at about twenty-eight years old, and this is deliberate policy. Such people have by then reached their age of decision, and there is little wastage in the long run. At present, about fifteen graduates join the Council each year and what they certainly can't look forward to at the end of the day are the commercial directorships that drop into the laps of ex-Ambassadors like apples off a tree. But by the time they are forty-five or so, they can expect to be running their own shows abroad as British Council Representatives somewhere. The posts are graded for nominal importance, like the British embassies, and the top forty-one in 1975 were classified as follows:

Grade A: India.
Grade B: Brazil, France, Germany, Indonesia, Iran, Italy, Japan, Nigeria, Pakistan, Spain and Egypt.
Grade C: Argentina, Australia, Bangladesh, Bahrein, Belgium, Canada, Ethiopia, Ghana, Greece, Iraq, Kenya, Malawi, Malaysia, Mexico, Poland, South Africa, Sri Lanka, Sudan, Thailand, Turkey, USA, Yugoslavia, Zambia; together with six subsidiary posts in India.

The extent to which these Representatives *are* running their own shows depends on a number of things. The Foreign Office in London has a certain amount of control, quite beyond finance and broad lines of policy. It determines, for example, which countries shall see large exhibitions of British paintings, though the organization is then left to the Council. Thus, although the Council might be aching to mount a Turner exhibition in, say, Turkey, it would get nowhere with it if the FCO decided that British diplomacy's purposes would be better served at the time in Germany. When the Queen visited Japan a few years ago, it was what the diplomats call 'an initiative' from the Foreign Office that led to the British Council's labours in getting the Royal Ballet to perform in Tokyo at the same time. But it is out in the field that most of the contests take place to decide whether the British Council Representative or the British Ambassador is really in charge of Britain's cultural diplomacy. Some Ambassadors, more than others, take a great deal of interest in what the Council can arrange by way of gorgeous cultural spectaculars, for which the local populace will tend to give much more credit to His Excellency seated in the royal box than to the British Council Representative stationed in the wings. Some Ambassadors write griping dispatches to the FCO when they feel they are being left behind in competition with their diplomatic colleagues from other nations, to the effect that 'We hardly ever seem to be able to compete on equal terms. Why, for example, can the French mount here in Erewhon a staggering great exhibition of world-beating Impressionists whilst we are feebly proffering a tatty little show of "British graphic arts", dog-eared and shop-soiled from Ruritania, where I saw it three years ago?' Ambassadors sometimes make arrangements of their own which the British Council then has to support, even though it might have chosen otherwise itself. When Sir Robin Hooper was Ambassador to Greece, Lord Bessborough came to lecture on the achievements of British industry, which wasn't quite what the Council Representative would have picked as a likely topic in Athens; but he had to stage-manage it. Ambassadors find the Council's manpower useful in all sorts of ways unmentioned in the royal charter. In Iran, Council officers based in Shiraz, Isfahan and other provincial cities, are expected to show visiting British businessmen the local ropes on the embassy's behalf; and also to organize a Queen's Birthday Party when June 11th comes round.

Ambassadors with a taste for private empire very often attempt to seduce the British Council Representative into accepting the title of Cultural Attaché, and the closer supervision that goes with it; an embassy staff list thus embellished looks more impressive than before to the rival Ambassadors in town and to the most influential hosts His Excellency has to deal with. In only one capital is the Cultural Attaché not a British Council employee. In Moscow he is a Foreign Office man for very good political reasons. Anglo-Soviet cultural agreements are much more sensitive matters than comparable arrangements in other countries; they include oceanography and agriculture in the same package as ballet and music; and their contents are generally the first pieces to be swept off the board when the political chess match gets bad-tempered. There is a strict limit to what can be done there at the best of times. By some mysterious diplomacy of his own, the impresario Victor Hochhauser has a monopoly of negotiating with the Bolshoi and Kirov ballet companies for visits to London. Art exhibitions are complicated by the refusal of the Russians to accept one more British canvas than we will show of theirs – and the number of British galleries that are wild about People's Realism is still fairly restricted. Beyond manoeuvring for a greater interchange in the arts generally – and music is much easier to handle than either painting or literature, because it is less contentious ideologically – the Attaché and his staff are busier than for a long time in the past because student exchanges are now happening on a bigger scale; but under very careful controls. The latest agreement says that the Russians will stipulate beforehand what materials a scholar may consult when he arrives from London, which should reduce the number of wasted journeys that have occurred in the past.

Not every British Council Representative has needed much seduction to become the Ambassador's Cultural Attaché. Some have inherited the role and found it impossible to become detached. Those who serve as less than enthusiastic Attachés say that it is essentially a schizophrenic position, for while the Council wants them to feel independent of the Ambassador's judgments, the Ambassador makes it quite clear that he believes them to be part of his personal entourage. At the same time, a social distance is maintained between the diplomats and the Council staff, which can be even greater when they have less to do with each other. Council officers very often say that 'The Ambassador recognizes us, after a fashion, at the dentist's'. Or 'A Third Secretary will use a tone of voice denoting superiority even when he is talking to someone in a higher grade from the Council.' Comments like that, of course, may demonstrate nothing more than a hypersensitive soul with imagination: the significant thing is that they are made. It is, however, proper to add that at one post the British Council Representative said of His Excellency, whose Cultural Attaché he was not, 'I'd die for that man'. So the relationship can be a good one, with both sides (presumably) feeling that whatever job has to be done is being done in the best way possible.

This, though, does not seem to be a majority view among British Council officers overseas. The majority are very anxious that the Council's operational autonomy shall be safeguarded as much as possible, and they believe it to be compromised far too often. The measure of its independence is, as one man put it, that 'we don't need to justify the antics of our government to the locals'; which is literally true, without revealing all the truth. In practical terms the Council's peculiar status has meant that sometimes, when diplomatic relations have been broken off and the British embassy has closed down, the British Council premises have remained open and its staff have stayed put to get on with their work. This in itself is of diplomatic advantage in the long run, it being far easier for governments to start talking again when their nationals have kept up some sort of communication. Over the past thirty years, however, the Council has drifted into an equivocal position even where it is seen to be physically detached from a British embassy, as it is more often than not. This is something apart from the careful watch the Foreign Office maintains over any independent spirit it may show. The Council is known to be a quasi-official body, which works on behalf of the British government in many fields of education and other forms of aid. The Goethe Institutes run by the Germans overseas are only approximate equivalents to the British Council, for they purvey pure culture and have nothing to do with German aid programmes or German scholarships. This gives them a real independence that their British colleagues lack. During the regime of the Greek Colonels, the Goethe Institute in Athens was putting on programmes with a high political content, almost overtly courting the intellectual opposition to the regime. Eventually they were told to stop it, and they did. But the British Council would never have dared try. Our planned participation in the Athens Festival one year, to which the Council was heavily committed, only failed to materialize because both Equity and the Musicians Union blacked it in London. When the Byron Centenary was celebrated in 1974 'we put in a lot of money doing things that couldn't possibly offend either side'.

It is when Council officers become exasperated at the restrictions placed on them by the Council's equivocal position that they say things like 'I think it's time we decided whether we're a BBC-type operation or a diplomatic operation'. Those who have served longest in the field are liable to add 'The British Council is totally pusillanimous when it comes to a pushing match with the Foreign Office'. The mildest officers say, 'We still suffer from the same old story of the Council: it says yes to everything proposed and then struggles to find ways of doing it.' From this dissident chorus comes the view that the Council's shift of headquarters from just off Oxford Street to a new building near Admiralty Arch a few years ago, was symbolic of an increasing drift towards the Foreign Office.

Nothing that has happened lately suggests that the view might be mistaken. True, it was the Duncan Committee which thought there was a strong case for altering the whole balance of Council activities towards Western Europe: but so many of Duncan's recommendations have been quietly ignored that this one could have foundered alongside others, had the Foreign Office not wanted to throw everything available into the struggle for Europe, and had not a new Prime Minister arrived at the right moment to back the diplomats all the way. Under Edward Heath's government, therefore, the British Council was committed to organizing £6 million-worth of what a diplomat called 'British cultural noises preceding entry into Europe'. This was the Rippon package, known as such after Mr Geoffrey Rippon, the Minister for Europe who supervised it at the start. The money was spread over four and a half years, perhaps not quite in the way Sir Val Duncan and his colleagues would have distributed it had they been directing the operation. There was a flurry of youth exchanges to begin with, and a certain amount of increased British cultural activity in Brussels towards the end of the package period, but a lot of the money had by then been spent on a piece of propaganda called Fanfare for Europe, which the British Council was obliged to trundle around Great Britain on behalf of the worried Marketeers.

The Rippon package was but half-emptied when there was a change of management at the Council. It acquired a new director-general in Sir John Llewellyn, a benign crystallographer from Gloucestershire who went to a chair of chemistry in New Zealand shortly after the war and, in the course of the next twenty years, became the Dominion's most experienced administrator, from university Vice-Chancellor to member of the New Zealand Atomic Energy Committee. Llewellyn came to the British Council at the same time as a new chairman, Lord Ballantrae, who is still better known to a lot of people as the Brigadier Bernard Fergusson who used to have spare monocles parachuted to him in the Burmese jungle, where he fought with Wingate's Chindits during the war. Long after that, Fergusson was an extremely popular Governor-General of New Zealand, by which time Llewellyn was chairman of the NZ Broadcasting Corporation. The British Council was thus endowed, at a stroke, with a new double act which probably stood a better chance than any other in its history of presenting a common front to all-comers, standing up to unwelcome pressures, and smothering those jealousies which could damage the efficiency of headquarters. There were signs of these things happening after Ballantrae and Llewellyn arrived in 1972 and it is conceivable that the Council would have ceased to be everybody's batman by now, had the country not taken such a desperate economic dive when it did. But the dive happened and any experienced Council officer could have predicted what came next.

'It's a whole new different ball game now!' Twice in the same day I heard that phrase on the lips of senior British Council officers at the beginning of 1975 (heaven knows what the Council's chartists, with their tender regard for the English Language, would have made of it). The officials concerned were indicating that the Council was now under orders, unheard of before, to come down from its cultural mountaintop and other unprofitable areas it had known over the years, and get stuck into the market place with the rest of the tribe. It had suddenly dawned on someone in the national hour of need, that a great deal of what the Council had been offering the world for a smile and a song was a commodity, like oil, which could be sold for a price to people who would pay and perhaps wonder why they had never been asked to do so before. The oil producers (as it happened) wanted education and teachers and programmes and university buildings – and a lot of other things that Franklin Roosevelt might have intoned had he ever been sitting where the British were sitting now. Then they would be given education and teachers and programmes and university buildings – and the British would get a bit of their own back under a new deal. What this has meant at a flourishing Council post like the one in Teheran, for instance, is that money is now changing hands for services which, until quite recently, were given freely. The Iranians have started spending £10 million a year on having students trained in England. English-language work of various kinds has been conducted in Teheran for years. The Council runs training courses for Iranians who teach English in their own schools, and it examines the Iranian students who seek further education in Britain. There is a test of aptitude in English which every student coming to Britain must pass. That now costs money. About 600 people come to the British Council offices every week, simply to inquire about their chances of education in Britain. London suggested that each of these calls should cost money, too, but the Council staff in Teheran – who are a strong-minded crowd with a taste for ethics as well as hard work – told London to get lost. They do their best to slip aside when the embassy up the road begins to lean too heavily for comfort.

Those forms of income represent only the chickenfeed in what the Council now refers to as Paid Educational Services. Spring Gardens contains a number of young-ish men whose dynamic approach to this subject is about as far removed from the old Beaverbrook cartoons of the British Council as it could be. As they survey a Middle East suddenly hungry for the most sophisticated educational appliances, and with a great deal if not most of the money in the world at its disposal, these heirs of Edwin Muir eagerly discuss the new poetry of very high finance. Their talk is of 'recycling oil money through education' and of £1,000 million being 'up for grabs' out there over the next few years. There is a School of Nautical Studies to be created from scratch in Iran, and a fabulous university development project in Saudi Arabia, and so on. Already they are frantic with the work of co-ordinating the University Grants Committee, the Inter-University Council, the Committee of Vice-Chancellors, the construction companies and various other people who will together make a great British bid to supply a phased and integrated system for higher teaching, learning and research from start to finish and even (who knows?) to provide its buildings as well ... So they go on, impatient with the Ministry of Overseas Development now, which is for ever wasting time in committees. They themselves can see the goal clearly, are intent on sweeping towards it swiftly, and are just a little bit in danger of blowing themselves up with a great combustion of their own energy. Nevertheless, where there was such wild enthusiasm as this at the start of 1975, there was six months later a signed contract with Saudi Arabia worth £1 million; and a hint that dozens of others like it were in somebody's pipeline. The British Council's first major essay in Paid Educational Services was for the teaching of English in the engineering and medical departments of King Abdul Aziz University at Jeddah. It would recruit the lecturers, the administrators and the back-up staff, provide all the audio-visual equipment necessary for the new departments, package the whole lot off, and enjoy the effect of it all on our balance of payments.

The enthusiasm of the Paid Educational Services organizers is not shared by everyone in the British Council. There are still some fundamentalists around who prefer not to be posted to places where the educational content of the work (paid or un-

paid) is high, whose bent is towards culture at its most glorious-
ly vague. There are many who regard the education of the
underprivileged as a privilege in itself, and who feel a little
soiled by talk of millions being up for grabs. There are even
more who are standing back to see whether Paid Educational
Services are just one more passing fancy which others have incorporated into the Council's patchwork history. The new device
has not really changed anything the Council was already doing
before it was invented; it has merely added to the load, complicated the administrative processes yet again, left the future as
hazy as ever.

In London things go on as always. Home Division are billet-
ing and shepherding and making every imaginable arrangement for the thousands of foreign students who come through
the front door every year. Books Division prepares for next
year's Frankfurt Fair, at which it will doubtless once again
have a much bigger display of texts than any British publisher.
It dispatches new publications from the commercial houses to
its panel of 1,500 reviewers and in due course sends overseas
another edition of *British Book News* full of their thumbnail
criticisms. Six more *Writers and Their Work* are given the full
critical treatment this year by the heavyweight men of letters.
The Low-priced Books Department (cast off by the Central
Office of Information in 1973) sends to developing countries
volumes costing less than a quarter of their market price in
Britain – and hopes that pirates at the end of the line do not
swindle the locals and enrage forbearing British publishers, who
have agreed to lose an outlet in the name of international
morality. Arts Division is meanwhile plotting numerous courses
across oceans of music, painting and drama. The trick here, as
much as anything, is to make sure that the foreign audiences
are going to be offered what they want, which is not a straightforward matter. In Greece they will take experiment and in-
novation in the theatre, but anything permissive goes right
against the local grain. Chamber music gets the deaf ear in
Africa, but Julian Bream or the Allegri Quartet go down a treat
in India – and in Korea they will accept almost anything but
the Tokyo Symphony Orchestra. So where shall the Philip
Jones Brass Ensemble tour next, with the statutory item by a
British composer in its programme? And how about this proposal for the New Shakespeare Company to do the *Dream* by

moonlight right under the Sphinx? Must get the ticket prices right, though; that was an awful mess at Ibadan, when scarcely a university student turned up for the contemporary English play because someone had overestimated their spending power.

They plod on, too, in the outposts. In Cairo, where there is a Ceri Richards hanging on one man's wall and a fly-blown copy of 'If' framed on another's ('Reproduced', it says, 'by special request for ESB listeners in view of the lines quoted from it by the PM, Mr Winston Churchill, in his world broadcast on Sunday, May 29'). The telephone rings with an Egyptian complaint that the projectionist failed to turn up for the film show last night, which meant that they all went home again after waiting a long time for nothing to happen. 'Oh, Christ!' mutters one of the British Embassy's Assistant Cultural Attachés, apologizing, offering to do the show again and hoping, dear God, for the best next time. His Council colleague down the corridor, a PhD in cosmic ray physics, is arranging for British scientists to come out, to take advantage of the unusually clear atmosphere over the Nile for some important astronomical observations.

In Belgrade, too, they are busy with scientific exchanges. A doctor from the local Mother and Child Institute is to study the problems of adolescent gynaecology for three months at King's College Medical School in London, and an electrical engineer from Lanchester Polytechnic is to visit the Pupin Institute to see what they can tell him about the automatic control of robots and industrial manipulators. All such two-way exchanges require preparation by the British Council at both ends. That travel-weary British graphic arts exhibition is by now up-country in Ljubljana and, in due course, a show of Bosnian Folk Embroidery and Jewellery will go to the Horniman Museum in London and then to Coventry. Down in the big city here, in the library, people are borrowing books by British authors at the rate of 25,000 a year and poring over thickets of journals and magazines. The most frequent borrowings are in fiction, after that Eng Lit, after that Eng Lang. The most popular periodicals are the medical journals, which the British Council supplies from its own funds. The Central Office of Information provides *Honey*, *Vogue*, *Country Life* and, inscrutably, *Radio Times*.

In Teheran they are busier than people should be for too long at a stretch. They organize cultural manifestations there, too: the New London Ballet went out in 1975. They run a library and they bring out experts in many disciplines to have their brains picked by the locals. But most of all they teach, endlessly and repetitively. A woman whose patience is still quite incredibly intact after long hours of grappling with semi-comprehension, looks as if she needs the weekend break that will take her to the Valley of the Assassins in the hope of spotting a squacco heron or a leaping golden carp, which will refresh her for yet another bout with these eager, hungry people. And a Scots girl is doggedly handling the frustrations of trying to set up a television programme that will help teacher-training to another giant step forward.

It is much the same in any of the eighty countries where the British Council is now to be found. An emphasis is different here, a project is specifically devised for there, but all over the place a dialogue is going on between people. This adds up, more than anything else, to a pervasive warmth, a very genuine thing that is sometimes missing from other forms of diplomacy. It is possible for someone under obedience to the British Council to do something outstandingly silly that would not be conceivable in a Foreign Office employee: like the lad recruited to teach in Egypt, who somehow managed to get to Israel for a week's holiday just to satisfy his curiosity, and wondered what on earth the rumpus was all about when he got back to Cairo. British Council officers can be sentimental, a weakness that is rare in diplomats. They tend not so much to calculate the effect they are having on other people; or, when they do, to be much more obvious about it. But, above all, they are part of the world they inhabit to a degree achieved by few diplomats other than Consuls. They do not always let the embassy know what the locals have told them, because they believe they are in a very special position of trust.

'Our first response', says one of them, 'must be to the country where we are; we need people with a beating heart and a sense of compassion.' If that is a totally undiplomatic statement (and it is) it will be because it is such an unsophisticated one. It is human, even before it is humane. The same man, asked what he thinks the British Council and all its works is up to, replies 'If you peel away the layers of sophistry and self-defence, you've got the statement that you're doing it all because you believe

Britain has something worthwhile to offer. There are many less worthy things in life.' If there is such a thing as a beating heart of diplomacy then that statement will lie close to it, though sophistication will not usually allow it to be spoken except in the most impersonal circumstances. An official report may dare to express itself in those terms, even an Ambassador's speech at an official luncheon. But a First Secretary would think it more than his reputation for cool was worth. Not everyone is so clear in his own mind, however, about the purpose of this much-used institution, this sometimes old-fashioned, hugely overworked, maddeningly inefficient but always hopeful thing of fits and starts. The new and thrusting imperatives of Paid Educational Services have only added to the confusion of some. It was never like this when Father worked for the Council. 'I really don't know', said a son of the manse, 'what the British Council is on about in the long term.'

The French, alas, appear to know exactly what they are on about. Not only do they spend four times as much as the British on their cultural diplomacy (and the Germans spend nearly twice as much as we do), but they control every franc of it from the Quai D'Orsay, without an intermediary agent like the British Council. The French Foreign Ministry is divided into five directorates and, of these, the General Directorate for Cultural, Scientific and Technical Affairs is regarded as quite the most important after the Political Directorate, by the French government as well as on the Quai. 'As one French observer has suggested, given that the age of gunboat diplomacy is over, this is the next best way of influencing people. In 1971, 47 per cent of the Foreign Ministry's budget was earmarked for this directorate alone.'[1] In foreign cities it is therefore always a diplomat at the French embassy who organizes the interchange of scientists and other experts; it is he who supervises the activities of the local Centre Culturel Français. And when pure propaganda is to be purveyed, the French diplomats thus engaged usually manage to leave their British counterparts standing some way behind. In New York, for example, they furnish inquisitive students and schoolchildren with special kits complete with maps, all carefully graded for different age levels, as well as separate aids for teaching. The British Information Services

[1] Tint, p. 218.

office in the city, as a matter of policy, has nothing to do with schoolchildren at all. Cultural programmes, too, are organized as British events rarely are. Manifestations of one kind or another run in series, instead of in isolation, and they are often crowned with genius himself. A week of Jean Renoir films is screened for the benefit of Greeks and, on the last night, Renoir is there in person, aged, not entirely audible beyond the front rows of the stalls, but very, very presentable. The British, again, do not compete with this. But they do envy it. 'We really do suffer from envy of the French,' says a man in the British Council. 'We tend to say to ourselves "Ah, if only we had their resources, what couldn't we do ... " '

This envy is perhaps the most old-fashioned thing about the British as a whole, understandable in the ambitious just after the Norman Conquest, but a bit out of place in the middle of the twentieth century. For what the Quai D'Orsay is first of all trying to do in its cultural diplomacy, in its wishful thinking to civilize the world, is to turn French into Everyman's second language where it cannot, unhappily, be his first. In this, the French are butting hopelessly against an historic tide in communication. The matter was settled 200 years ago, when James Wolfe took Quebec from Louis Joseph de Montcalm, and a vast continent of colossal natural wealth – two great nations in the end – was bound to the speech of Shakespeare rather than to a patois derived from the Gauls. The most satisfying thing to francophobes must be the fact that the British Council has been asked by the Algerians to supply 400 or 500 teachers of English in a year.

15 'The Great Game of the Twentieth Century'

In one respect, diplomacy has changed out of all recognition inside a single generation. The traditional ways of nation speaking unto nation were fairly simple and straightforward, a matter of representing their patriotic interests to each other in twosomes and in terms that any decently educated man might understand. To be sure, there were ever alliances of nations working in concert to frustrate other alliances, with their Congresses and their Peaces cluttering history to the despair of any student with a bad head for dates. But there has never been anything to match the new fashion for conducting diplomacy as in a bazaar, wherein alliances will change quite acceptably as different items come up on an agenda, or even as the clock gives a different time of day; and wherein some diplomats do not even represent their own countries any more, being loaned by their foreign ministries to the management of the bazaar. Afflicted with the name of multilateral diplomacy, the new fashion has obliged its participants to understand matters which were once thought to be the exclusive province of aliens like bankers, economists, mathematicians and domestic civil servants, certainly no business of honest envoys. Indeed, it has both widened the trade of the diplomats and admitted the aliens to diplomacy. 'I feel,' said a British Ambassador who was about to retire from a distinguished career which had been thoroughly bilateral from start to finish, 'I feel like a handloom weaver nowadays.'

The old League of Nations between the two world wars was never really part of this fashion, being but half-hearted in everything it did, whereas multilateral diplomacy is nothing if not a full-blooded commitment to its own devious ways. These were formed for the first time by the League's residuary legatee, and they have gradually evolved as the United Nations itself has evolved from a circus conducted by victorious powers to something more closely resembling a deliberative assembly of the world. To some extent the United Nations cannot shake off its origins because its greatest collective judgments can only be enacted by kind permission of the Security Council, whose composition cannot be changed except by an alteration to the United Nations Charter, which cannot itself be done without the approval of the Security Council's permanent members – Nationalist China (Taiwan), France, Great Britain, the Soviet Union and the United States. Notwithstanding this security lock, however, an emphasis has demonstrably shifted since the General Assembly's first meeting at Central Hall, Westminster, in 1946, and its subsequent location on the banks of New York's East River. There are now alliances of countries – each one unheard of or thought puny at the United Nations' inception – which exert considerable collective power in the world outside the General Assembly. They have caused a United States delegate to rant at them like a helpless bully, while his old pals from London have thrown cold water over him in public. Such has been the measure of change.

It is a popular cliché that the United Nations is little more than a stage upon which international rhetoricians simply bore everyone else stiff. Conservative governments in Britain have tended to this view whereas Labour governments have always hoped for better things to come out of it. There are plenty of people in the Foreign Office who take it into account chiefly because their work does not allow them to ignore it all the time, but they do not include the men and women who have had something to do with the United Nations at first hand. These can be as pained as a Daniel Moynihan or a Transport House idealist at the observed fact that, when India blew its atom bomb, there wasn't a squeak of disapproval from the Third World delegates in New York. They can agree that in many ways the UN is a mockery of all the lofty notions which impregnated its charter. But they do not accept for a moment that it is a useless waste of time. Nor do they justify its existence merely by reference to the many United Nations agencies of one sort or another which, by and large, have fulfilled the hopes placed in them by their founders. What they say is that if the United Nations were to disappear, it would be necessary to replace it with yet another international forum, because it is still safer for nations to posture and rage at each other in front of a knowing audience, which can closely observe just who is most ready to throw down the gauntlet of war. Our people at the United Nations can enumerate the institution's failings more completely than any outsider, but when they have done so they always say the same thing in the end: 'Just remember, the UN *did* keep the peace for years in the Middle East, in Kashmir, in Cyprus – and it will do so again in other hot spots.'

Outsiders are sometimes surprised to discover that the United Nations delegations function throughout the year, and not just when the General Assembly sits from September until Christmas. In a way, that is when they are least usefully employed, for that is when they are busiest making speeches designed more than anything for domestic consumption. At any time in the year, the British delegation is liable to find itself sitting in the Trusteeship Council or some other arena, with the West Germans, the Guyanese and the Indians on the row in front, the Russians and the Americans to left and to right, and an open invitation to a false move in the shape of three buttons on the delegation leader's desk – a green one at the top marked 'oui', a red one below it marked 'non', a yellow one at the bottom marked 'abstention' (now there's French cultural diplomacy for you). Yet the bulk of a delegation's work is not conducted in any formal situation. It goes on from day to day in the endless lobbying for influence, at one babbling party after another, or in quiet and acoustically perfect corners of the building. Trendy jet-setters from Latin America are to be found in urgent colloquies with the astute new men of Arabic diplomacy. Buoyant Africans are dawdling with the Chinese, who have a weakness for speeches about the old political divisions (when all that matters at present is economics), who are utterly straightforward, but who switch their friendships on and off like a light. Indians move in and out of almost every huddle, though they hardly ever give parties of their own. The Americans are distant, because the United Nations isn't really their scene. Their greatest adversary is also a bit downstage, once more led by the remarkably durable Jacob Malik, operating just as he did in the darkest days of Korea, when he would denounce the United States representative as a fascist beast in this building and, a few hours later, sup Bourbon with an understanding host in the library of the Dulles residence on East 91st Street. But the majority talk with anyone, because these days anyone may be able to do them a bit of good. It is essentially as practical as that. 'It is not part of your job', says one of the FCO team in New York, 'to take a high moral tone with the Indians when you're aghast at their nuclear bomb, feeling betrayed and all that. It's your job to get them on your side on another subject.' More often than not, the lobbying results in nothing to shake anybody's world. A British delegate persuades an Egyptian to switch his vote in a secret ballot on rationalizing procedures, because the man has received no instructions from Cairo and the Briton is, well, persuasive. But sometimes something precious results from this affable and in many ways over-indulged pattern of behaviour. It is conceivable that because the Greek and the Turk here are civilized men who personally find no fault in each other, the Turks held their armoured hand in 1974 on the perimeter of Nicosia airport, when a lot of frightened refugees were ready for the worst.

From time to time, the United Nations presses the nations towards the resolution of something extraordinarily important to all of them. It has a committee, which may sit from now till Doomsday, negotiating a treaty on outer space, but which has at least arrived at a definition of space as something which cannot be territorially owned by anyone. It has also, since 1958, been responsible for five episodes of a periodic conference to thrash out a new Law of the Sea – a topic whose importance the world in general did not begin to appreciate until the 1970s were well under way. There is a small unit in the Foreign Office perpetually in training for the next bout on the Law of the Sea. It collects assessments and briefs from the Ministry of Defence, the Ministry of Agriculture, Food and Fisheries, the Department of Energy and the Department of Trade, all of whom have particular interests in what lies upon and under the sea bed, what swims over it, and what could in certain places poke above the surface of the waves to the benefit of Her Majesty's subjects. The FCO's job is to point out to the other men of Whitehall what is negotiable and what is not, to prepare positions and to make sure of home ground, ready for the next episode of international argument. When that comes round, the diplomats collect the rest of the crew from Whitehall, press-gang a mineralogist here, a marine biologist there, and set sail in a task force to do battle for the high and low seas, with many others similarly equipped to arrive at some sort of tolerance by multilateral diplomacy. At the last conference, held in New York in 1976, some 5,000 delegates from 150 countries thrashed around these international waters for eight full weeks, without coming to a sight of landfall.

There was a time when our delegations to the United Nations in New York and Geneva could get on with their multilateral juggling acts in the British interest alone, so long as they remembered to make a dutiful bob at the start and finish of every performance in the general direction of the North Atlantic alliance. That time ended when Britain committed itself to Europe and complicated life on the East River. 'The amount of time now spent on co-ordination among the Nine', said one of the UN team, 'is horrendous, bloody inefficient'. Co-ordination is a key word in the new diplomatic fashion, and in the name of European solidarity it has become an important responsibility of every British mission throughout the world. Every week, in every capital city, a First Secretary from chancery sits down with his opposite numbers from the embassies of other countries in the European Economic Community, to discuss what joint positions they are to adopt in the next seven days. Once a month, their Ambassadors do likewise. This happens even where the Nine are not Nine at all, but some smaller number because Two or Three have individually decided that they can't run to representation in that particular quarter of the globe. At one place there is thus a monthly meeting of Ambassadors from the Four. The German arrives with his latest instructions from Bonn so thick that he's still trying to digest the front half while his colleagues are asking him questions about the back half; the Frenchman is so full of his own importance that his allies refer to him as M. L'Embraceadeur behind his back; the Italian is 'a mere fonctionnaire from Brussels'; and the astringent Englishman may just have a reputation for patronizing all three. Co-ordination can be a self-satisfying thing, but it is now practised in the name of European community from the diplomatic cradle to the grave. A year or so before Britain's future was settled by referendum, the Foreign Office mustered fledglings of its own and seven other countries, packed them off to Windsor Great Park for a week, and asked them to cudgel their brains with 'Europe – the Way Ahead'. There was no question mark attached to the title of the seminar.

People sometimes talk as if the Foreign Office has been vigorously pro-European ever since the Schuman Plan was launched in 1950. Those who do not see the EEC as a blessing, tend to suggest that our diplomats have from the beginning led a rush to national dissolution out of a misguided professional desire to lord it over a continent in place of their lost empire. And some diplomats, who like to take as much credit for a national benison after the event as anyone else who might be in the running, try to make out that the Foreign Office alone was a voice crying in a wilderness of unconcern for donkey's years. We shall not know the precise truth until the relevant state papers begin to fetch up in the Public Record Office towards the end of the next decade. But it seems likely that Foreign Office commitment was somewhat later, and rather less wholehearted at first, than is generally assumed. Certainly there was no thought of a pan-European future in its collective mind until the consequences of Suez had properly sunk in. At that stage the diplomatic hierarchy did consist of men who had been reared in the traditions of British Empire and who were still living in high hopes of British Commonwealth; and however horrified they might have been at Eden's reaction to Nasser, they could scarcely be expected to identify Suez as the watershed it was while still numbed by the humiliation of it. It is the recollection of a senior man today that there was no great enthusiasm for Europe until a long time afterwards. It was entirely missing when European Foreign Ministers met at Messina to prepare the EEC's birth certificate, the Treaty of Rome, which was signed in 1957. The diplomats were still lukewarm about anything but a transatlantic alliance even as they were signing Britain into the European Free Trade Association, the alternative to the EEC, in 1959. 'In those early days of the EEC, too many men here said don't let's join, let's wait and see, we can always pick up the pieces later on.'

There seems little doubt that the first inclination towards Europe, and the only one for some time, came from the politicians, from Harold Macmillan in particular. And the first powerful thrust in Whitehall certainly came not from the Foreign Office, but from next door at the Treasury. In 1960 it acquired a new joint Permanent Secretary in the person of Sir Frank Lee, a pre-war Colonial District Officer who eventually served in the Board of Trade, where he had helped to draft the

EFTA constitution. By the time he moved to the Treasury, however, Sir Frank had thought again and persuaded Macmillan (emotionally a European already, though still not sure which brand of European) that the EEC was the horse to back. That same year, Macmillan put Edward Heath into the sphere of diplomacy as Lord Privy Seal with special responsibility for European affairs. There is no indication that even then the diplomats did more than scrupulously execute political orders to the best of their ability; and these were perhaps less than wholeheartedly European with a Foreign Secretary, Lord Home, who was himself no great enthusiast. Nevertheless, in mid-1961, when a political decision had been taken to negotiate with the EEC in Brussels, a strong-looking team was chosen with a multilateral whiff to it, including Sir Eric Roll from the Ministry of Agriculture. The Foreign Office might have seemed more determined, however, if it had chosen one of its top men from London to lead the delegation. Instead, Sir Pierson Dixon was simply asked to head the main party as an excursion from his embassy in Paris.

A turning point came in 1962, when much writing appeared on the Berlin Wall and certain noises were made on the banks of the Potomac, neither of whose implications the diplomats could ignore any longer. For it suddenly became clear to them that the old special relationship between London and Washington was in danger of being replaced by a new one between Washington and Bonn – even if President Kennedy did need some hours of coaching to get '*Ich bin ein Berliner*' right when he praised the fortitude of Willy Brandt's townsfolk in the shadow of the wall. In July that year, the President openly said that he looked forward to a partnership between the USA and a United Europe; and at the end of December the hint was dropped even more heavily at West Point, when Dean Acheson said:

> Great Britain has lost an empire and has not yet found a role. The attempt to play a separate power role, that is, a role apart from Europe, a role based on a special relationship with the United States, a role based on being head of a 'commonwealth' ... this role is about played out.

The following June, Sir Con O'Neill returned to London after only two years as British Ambassador to Finland, a significantly shorter term than is usual in the Helsinki post. It is from about this time, mid-1963, that senior people in the Foreign Office began to take Europe very seriously indeed.

Sir Con's is one of several names that from now on were to be inseparable from British attempts to get into Europe with the Six (as they were at the time) and stay there. He should be remembered for it rather more than for the extraordinary pattern of his career, with three resignations from the Diplomatic Service and three returns to it after tasting other professions. On his return from Helsinki he was appointed Ambassador to the European Community in Brussels, to make what he could of the situation after General de Gaulle had firmly rebuffed the first British application to join. By 1965, O'Neill was back in London as Deputy Under Secretary in charge of the European operation, urging an uncertain Michael Stewart, the Labour Foreign Secretary, that Britain must make another application to join as soon as possible. Stewart's successor, George Brown, needed no such pressure; he was himself committed enough to set up a European Economic Integration Department at the Foreign Office. But when the Wilson government's own application to join the Common Market in 1967 was again put down by de Gaulle, Sir Con decided that he'd had enough of headlong confrontation for the time being. Brown wanted him to return to Brussels, to start up the negotiating machinery there all over again, but Sir Con was hankering after Bonn by then and resigned for the third time when the post was refused him. In 1969, however, George Brown being out of the way, he rejoined the Service, went to Brussels as leader of the British negotiating team and stayed until the Heath government's application was accepted in 1972. Then he abandoned diplomacy once and for all: but not his developed passion for Britain in Europe. No sooner had the Wilson government of 1974 let it be known that the terms of entry were to be renegotiated, that the whole issue of Europe was to be reopened and decided by a national referendum, than Sir Con O'Neill popped up like a jack-in-the-box again, this time as the private director of the pro-Marketeers' campaign to collect the vital votes from people of all political allegiances.

By the time the Common Market battle had been conclusively won, in June 1975, a number of other Foreign Office men had staked and established their careers on its progress to and fro.

One was John Robinson, a First Secretary in the original negotiating team led by Sir Pierson Dixon, who stayed in Brussels
for five years and came home to head George Brown's new
European department. He went back to Brussels in 1970 as
O'Neill's special assistant, but in 1971 returned to London as
an Assistant Under Secretary, charged with the crucial whipping job along Whitehall. It was well understood in the Foreign
Office by then that if Britain did get into the Market, she would
have to be represented by a combined operation of diplomats
and Home civil servants on an unprecedented scale. And Whitehall was still dithering almost as much as the country at large.
The Treasury and the Departments of Trade and Industry were
as firmly convinced about Europe as the Foreign Office; the
Department of the Environment and the Department of Energy
were not, while the Ministry of Agriculture was as nearly hostile
as a government office could still be at that stage. Robinson's
task was to use all the diplomatic persuasion he could to get
everybody into line. But it is a measure of the reluctance he
faced in some quarters that in 1973, with Britain inside the
Market, Edward Heath felt it necessary to create a European
unit inside the Cabinet Office, to keep an eye on co-ordination
between the Foreign Office and the rest of Whitehall in
London, and between the whole bag of tricks there and its
companion in Brussels. At this point, after ten years' hard labour
in Europe, Robinson was rewarded with a foreign mission of
his own, as British Ambassador in Algiers.

Michael Palliser did even better. He was marked as a flyer
shortly after coming to diplomacy from his war in the Cold-
stream Guards. After only one stint abroad, in Athens, he began
to develop a flair for the diplomacy of Whitehall, first as Private
Secretary to the Permanent Under Secretary, Sir Ivone Kirkpatrick, before Suez, later as Harold Wilson's Private Secretary
at No 10 Downing Street. He was thus right on the inside of the
decision-making process when Britain's first thoroughly organized approach to Europe was being prepared; he was the vital
linkman between the Prime Minister and the Foreign Office.
He also spoke French as well as he spoke English, acting as interpreter when Wilson met de Gaulle and, later, when Heath
met President Pompidou. His spell at No 10 over by 1969, he
went as Minister to Paris and it was there, in 1971, that he was
part of a secret meeting with the French to prepare for the

2E

Heath–Pompidou summit talks which unlocked the door barring Britain's entry. In London, the only people who knew about the meeting were Heath, Douglas-Home, Geoffrey Rippon (Minister for Europe), the PUS (Sir Denis Greenhill), O'Neill (over from Brussels for the occasion) and Robinson. In Paris, besides Palliser, the Britons involved were the Ambassador, Sir Christopher Soames, and John Galsworthy, another of the Foreign Office's early converts to Europe. He had been a Counsellor in the Dixon team, had later gone to Bonn as an economic specialist, and was by now the Paris embassy's Minister for European Economic Affairs, a post that had been created after de Gaulle's second veto, when it became plain that Paris held the key to Brussels. Soon he, too, was to be rewarded with his own embassy, in Mexico City. Palliser, however, was to spend another four years in the deepest waters of European diplomacy. Between 1971 and the end of 1972 he worked in tandem with O'Neill as head of the United Kingdom delegation to the European Communities; from the beginning of 1973 he was British Ambassador and UK Permanent Representative to the EEC in Brussels, leading the operation there through all the cliff-hanging months of renegotiation. And then, when all was safely gathered in, he came back to London at the end of 1975, to be the new Permanent Under Secretary of the FCO and Head of the British Diplomatic Service.

Sir Christopher Soames is one of two men who became diplomats by invitation rather than profession and played important parts on the road to Europe; the other was Sir David Ormsby-Gore, later Lord Harlech. Of the two, Soames has made the more lasting impression in Europe, for when he ceased to be a British Ambassador he became an EEC Commissioner, thus joining the most select group of civil servants in the European Community. Son-in-law of Churchill and sometime Minister of Agriculture, Soames was sent to our Paris embassy in 1968 when Anglo-French relations were as bad as they have ever been since Trafalgar and Waterloo. De Gaulle, at the height of his French renaissance, had imperiously booted aside the British petition to enter Europe the year before and Soames, a devoted francophile, was recruited by Harold Wilson to pacify the President as best he could. Instead, he will for ever be remembered in the annals of Anglo-French diplomacy for the incident memorialized as *L'Affaire Soames*. He had been in Paris only a few months when, promisingly, he got the French Foreign Minister, Michel Debré, to persuade de Gaulle to see him. After meeting the President, Soames did something which was common in nineteenth-century diplomacy, but which nowadays is almost confined to dealings with the Russians. After sending his account of the meeting to the Foreign Office by telegram, he presented the Elysée Palace with a copy of it, a prudent move to establish the authenticity of the account. This was accepted and, when he met Soames a couple of days later, Debré did not complain of its inaccuracy. But shortly afterwards a violent anti-French campaign was loosed in the newspapers of continental Europe, attacking de Gaulle and his Ministers for secretly working towards a new European concept, with a four-power political leadership and nothing more than a subsidiary free-trade role for other countries. This campaign, the French were to say, resulted from a Byzantine manoeuvre by the Foreign Office, which had leaked a distorted version of the Soames telegram to other European capitals. De Gaulle died before he could give his own account of the crucial meeting in his memoirs. Sir Christopher has not yet published his. The nearest thing to an official British account is the Prime Minister's own disclosure that he was presented with the Soames report a week after it had reached the Foreign Office. In his memoirs, Mr Wilson described how he was about to leave for Bonn and had one day in which to make up his mind whether or not he would confide the content of the report to the German government. He thus had no opportunity to consult his Cabinet colleagues on the matter, and had to rely for guidance entirely on British diplomatic advice. One day, state papers will doubtless tell the full British version of *L'Affaire*.

Sir David Ormsby-Gore was never associated with anything so dramatic, but he was as responsible as anyone for swinging the Foreign Office into the European camp in the first place, and he remained a principal fighter for Europe until the position was secured. His first brush with diplomacy came when, as an MP in the early 1950s, he was Selwyn Lloyd's Parliamentary Private Secretary when Lloyd was Minister of State at the Foreign Office, a post Ormsby-Gore himself held within a few years. When he became British Ambassador in Washington, in October 1961, he took some mighty impressive credentials across the Atlantic. Not only was he the son of a former Colonial

Secretary, but he was related by marriage to his Prime Minister (Harold Macmillan) and – distantly – to the President of the United States; he and Jack Kennedy, in fact, were old friends. No British Ambassador in Washington (or anywhere else for that matter) has ever occupied a more influential position than Ormsby-Gore did, at least until Kennedy was assassinated. His greatest influence was upon the Foreign Office in London, which he convinced that Kennedy meant exactly what he and Dean Acheson said in public; and that the failure of the Skybolt missile programme on top of London's growing complacency about its position in life, meant that Britain's only salvation lay with Europe – and with getting into Europe as fast as possible. She was by no means there by the time Ormsby-Gore returned to England in 1965; but at least the Foreign Office was no longer in any doubt of where it stood in the matter. After a decent respite to attend to his lands in Shropshire and to prepare for a new career as a television impresario, Lord Harlech (as he had become on his father's death in 1964) committed himself to the new alliance as a freelance. In 1967 he became chairman of Britain in Europe, one of the pressure groups that Sir Con O'Neill was later to co-ordinate in his own private capacity. The connection between this organization and the Foreign Office was already a close one. It had an income of £7,000 a year, mostly provided by corporate subscribers. But the figure included an annual 'travel grant' of £2,500 from the Foreign Office, which in 1968 was increased to £7,500 on the authority of Lord Chalfont, the Labour Minister of State at the FCO. The diplomats themselves were sparing nothing by then in their anxious concern for Europe.

The focal point of all this hustling, all this bustling along, is Rond-point Robert Schuman, a hazardous traffic roundabout in uptown Brussels. It is dominated by that stylish building we catch glimpses of behind the reporter's head when television brings us another opaque bulletin from the Common Market. That is the Berlaimont Palace (named after a mayor of the city), within whose curving glass walls the European Commission seethes and bubbles in a perpetual ferment of calculation, negotiation, and plain old-fashioned horse-trading that will subsequently affect everyone living between Loch Eriboll and Isola di Correnti. Just across the road is the Charlemagne Palace, not at all stylish but even more important; for this enshrines the

Council of Ministers who adjudicate on the Commission's proposals, and the Committee of Permanent Representatives (the Ambassadors' team, known as Coreper for short) which plots and schemes the council meetings. Directly opposite the Berlaimont, across the roundabout, stands the headquarters of the British delegation, code-named UKREP at home. It is very easy to miss its entrance and to walk into the Red Lion pub next door instead, for both are in a shabby little block that has seen much better days, not at all what anyone would associate with treaty-making; and, certainly, no other British Ambassador in the world has ever found himself so close to a metricated pint of tap-room bitter. What goes on all round the Rond-point Robert Schuman, however, is itself a great and overwhelming intoxication of Eurocrats. It looks and feels as if it deserves to be called multilateral diplomacy, though a British official had an even more memorable phrase for it. He was working for the Commission itself, on loan to Europe from the Foreign Office, and he had just been explaining how Ted Heath had made it clear to Personnel that anyone thus seconded to help the dream along must be sure of a good job when he returned to the FCO. For the time being, however, this diplomat of undoubted talent was more than content to be where he was. 'It is', he said, 'the great fascinating game of the twentieth century.'

There are quite a lot of rising young British diplomats, posted to less palpitating spots, who would give a great deal to be in the middle of all this. Someone based on the backside of Europe said, 'I'd much rather be in the nitty gritty of Brussels than be Chief Boy Scout in Paraguay.' For Brussels at present is what the United Nations must have been like a generation ago; a place of high hopes and exhausting activity and a minimum of the fussier bits and pieces of diplomacy. There used to be quite a lot of Prussian ceremony here in the 1960s, when Professor Hallstein dominated the Commission, but it irritated de Gaulle and so withered away. New Ambassadors present their credentials to the court of the Common Market in lounge suits, not frock coats. It is, moreover, bracingly European. Treaties are drawn up in six languages at once. The normal working language is supposed to be French, but English has displaced German as second choice since 1972 and is fast overtaking French itself in general use: the Italians stick to French, the Dutch and the Germans prefer English, and some people make compromises to suit themselves, like the French and the Irish, who speak to each other in their own tongues and get along fine. There is, in fact, a collegiate feeling among the men of Brussels, as well there might be when they are so intensely thrown together. They lobby one another, and they intrigue against one another, but at bottom they understand one another and make allowances for one another to a degree that the parochial citizens back home might find rather alarming, surely baffling, if they could sit and watch. A group of nine senior men, representing quite conflicting interests, sit round a table in the Berlaimont one morning, and one of them starts the day's ball rolling. 'Well,' he announces, 'we've got bloody stupid instructions from London today ... '

They are in profound alliance now. They have discovered each other's strengths and weaknesses to a degree that perhaps all their bilateral diplomacy before had not revealed. The British reckon that the finest performances come from the Dutch, with not a dud official among them, brilliant committee workers to a man. The Germans, everyone else says, are overloaded with paperwork, even more so than the British, which sometimes prevents them from seeing the wood for the trees. The British, say the French, have still not mastered the techniques of community negotiation, they are far too ready to go for the quick compromise. But the Eurocrats make these observations with sympathy. It is only when one of their political masters breaks away from alliance that this fails. In Europe now, you are expected to clear things with your colleagues before you go it alone. The trick is to devise ways of doing some things independently without breaking the new European law, to exploit the Rome Treaty to get what you want out of Europe, knowing the inevitability of having more and more to defer to Europe. The French infuriated the rest when they voted to seat the Palestine Liberation Organization in the General Assembly of the United Nations in 1974, because they had not consulted their colleagues beforehand. The British upset everybody when they manoeuvred for an independent say in the Paris energy conference in 1975, because they were defying all the collegiate rules. 'But there are times', said an Englishman in Brussels, 'when it all comes together: French logic, Italian allure, Dutch robustness ... and it's marvellous then.'

For that hope of something marvellous, the Foreign Office

and quite a lot of other people in Whitehall were prepared to commit everything but treason to see Britain still in Europe after its 1975 referendum. Some diplomats concede that the terms of British entry in 1972 were unsatisfactory, that a re-adjustment of the European budget would have been sought by London even if Mr Wilson's government had not succeeded Mr Heath's in 1974: but in that event the process would not have been termed 'renegotiation'; it would have been blandly styled 'the ongoing work of the Community'. It was the referendum that had the Foreign Office scared stiff, even after someone had overheard Wilson confidently telling an Italian not to worry about Britain's future in the Market because 'in six weeks before the referendum I can persuade the people that our interests lie in staying in'. The FCO was by no means so confident. The corridors of Gilbert Scott's palazzo heard frequent mutters about impending national disaster, and in Brussels they talked of an awful collapse of diplomatic morale should the vote go the wrong way. In both places, they did their damndest to make sure that neither of these things occurred.

There was by then a fair degree of unanimity along White-hall, though the fervour for Europe was nowhere as complete and as intense as it was among the combined operators in Brussels. Several government departments in London had for some time been working under two Permanent Secretaries each, the second chieftain having been created to supervise his department's European connections. All were represented in the European unit of the Cabinet Office under the direction of Patrick Nairne, who had come to the job from the Ministry of Defence, and was to leave it when the battle was won to be Permanent Secretary at Health and Social Security. The Foreign Office had never been totally reconciled to this arrangement of Edward Heath's, although some revolutionary young diplomats early in 1975 were saying that more of the work done in the FCO's European Integration Departments could profit-ably be shifted to Nairne's unit. Much interdepartmental jealousy, however, had evaporated in the heat of common cause. It was accepted that the Foreign Office might tell another department that some notion ought to be dropped because it didn't square with broad policy towards the EEC; but the diplomats themselves accepted that the days had gone when they could loftily declare that 'Foreign policy dictates ... ', an

approach which would now have them laughed to scorn. Even
the conventional struggle with the people next door had been
abandoned for Europe's sake. 'One thing about the Brussels
operation,' somebody said, 'we've never had to fight the
Treasury for money. If we want a photocopying machine there,
the Treasury doesn't quibble and say "Use a quill pen" ... '
None of this amity along Whitehall was false; but, then, neither
was the Foreign Office's assurance that it held the trump
card. It controlled the lines of communication with Europe.
All in-coming and outgoing telegrams passed through the
palazzo. 'This gives us our last chance of seeing that they
accord with our view of things. In the last resort we could
block other departments by appealing to Callaghan, who'd
have to fight it out in Cabinet. But a block hasn't occurred
yet.'

The diplomats made it as certain as possible that in any
Cabinet battle, the Foreign Secretary would be through the
barbed wire before any opponent had even struggled out of his
trench. An Assistant Under Secretary, Michael Butler, who had
come to the European campaign after a sabbatical year at
Harvard and a short stretch in the Washington embassy, was
given the task of mustering everything the European Integration Departments and Brussels could provide to ensure that
James Callaghan was more meticulously briefed than anyone
else in the British government. In the early days of their association, Butler's job had been to make certain that the Foreign
Secretary knew in which direction he was supposed to be
marching. By the end of 1974, Callaghan was in no further
need of a compass; and although he had accepted the ministerial implications of the European unit bequeathed by Edward
Heath, he had made it perfectly clear that he alone was going
to renegotiate with Europe, that he had no intention of merely
being the sergeant of a political platoon. It was vital to the
Foreign Office by the start of 1975, however, that he should be
properly equipped for any skirmishes within the Parliamentary
Labour party. Even more, that he should be skilfully armed
for the cut and thrust in Cabinet when faced with the fixed
bayonets of the anti-Marketeers there, particularly Peter Shore
and Anthony Wedgwood Benn, who headed the two ministries
which mattered more than most in Europe, Trade and
Industry. All this was Butler's province. Meanwhile, the Deputy

PUS at the Foreign Office, Oliver Wright,[1] took charge of the diplomatic co-ordination with Nairne's unit, to be sure that none of the allies in Whitehall ran out of ammunition at an embarrassing moment, or got shot in the back – by accident or otherwise.

In Brussels by this time, these allies had done something that, not so many years earlier, Whitehall could never have thought to see. Michael Palliser was commanding a thoroughly capable operation, a team of experts which had trained to a high degree of efficiency. Second in command to the career diplomat, whose cultural roots lay in public school, Oxford and Guards Club, was a Deputy Secretary from the Department of Trade, Bob Goldsmith, who would still have passed as a recognizable product of the local grammar school in his native Huddersfield after a long time in the London corridors of power. No 3 was a senior man from the Ministry of Agriculture, Jon Dixon. There were others from Trade and from Agriculture in the delegation, as well as men from Industry, Environment, Employment, the Treasury, Health and Social Security, Customs and Excise, the Inland Revenue, the Northern Ireland Office, and the Bank of England. There were also, of course, a lot of diplomats besides Palliser. But they were outnumbered by the rest, 21 to 16.

'You begin to realize', said one of the Home civil servants, who had never worked abroad before in his life, 'that the similarities with other countries are much greater than the differences.' The same dawning had occurred within the delegation. It was a general opinion of the diplomats – usually offered with an air of discovery – that the Ministry of Agriculture was one of the best outfits in Whitehall. There was plenty of opportunity for the diplomats to arrive at this conclusion for, by then, men from that Ministry were coming over in droves to supplement their colleagues in the delegation and conduct most of Britain's agricultural policy in Brussels. Mandarin noises were still audible from the direction of the Berlaimont or the Charlemagne buildings, where British diplomats were dug into the Eurocracy proper, on attachment to the Commission or the Council of Ministers. These were quite capable of vowing that

___

[1] Later Sir Oliver Wright and, since October 1975, British Ambassador in Bonn.

there was nothing a good Foreign Office man couldn't do, and thanking God that linguistic fluency still settled the leadership of multilateral delegations. But such noises were conspicuously missing from the rented accommodation above the Red Lion.

For their own part, the Home civil servants had a few reservations about the diplomatic approach and the diplomatic contribution. They didn't much care for the habit of people flying out from the Foreign Office for secret meetings inside the Commission. Some thought that the only essential diplomatic role was one of communication. 'There's no reason to run this outfit from the FCO at all,' said one. 'It's more a matter of convenience than anything.' In the early days together, the Home men became irritated by many FCO habits they were required to adopt. 'At one stage we played the silly game of staggering up three flights of stairs twice a day, arms full of classified material which had to be dumped in the Secure Area. But classified material here is of such low security value that we pressed for proper safes in our rooms, and got them in the end.' They also regarded diplomatic devotion to paperwork as a nuisance – 'you know, you must never write anything to so and so without copying it to so and so and so and so.' The delegation's Head of Chancery, an FCO man, came to agree with them, and the habit was severely curtailed. Gradually the team shook down together, compromising on different ways of doing things, its members identifying much more with the delegation and its work than with their parentage at home. By the time the crunch of the referendum approached, Home men were thinking like Foreign Office men. 'There's no room for pique in international relations,' said one. 'My Permanent Secretary comes over from London and wades crudely into a negotiation – and that requires a great deal of tact in reporting,' said another. Somebody thought they'd all learnt a hell of a lot from Palliser.

They had acquired the *esprit de corps* of any group that is driven hard, reckons that all hands can rely on the next man, and believes it knows what it is doing. No one was driven harder than Palliser himself who, every Wednesday, before the Thursday Coreper meeting, would take the first plane out of Brussels at 7.40 a.m., tackle a heavy day in London, and fly back on the last plane to land, just after 10.30 p.m. In Brussels he worked much the same hours as everybody else, and these were insane.

People would regularly be at their desks or at a meeting in the commission by 9 o'clock in the morning and not call it a day until twelve hours later. It was not unusual for someone to be going until midnight or even after that. No one cracked up under the strain, though some thought that there would have been casualties had it not been for the almost academic holidays of the Common Market – a month in summer, a fortnight at Christmas and another at Easter. A man from one of the Home departments said, 'You simply can't control your hours and you're often asked to work unreasonable hours – but you're never asked to do anything stupid or unnecessary. People are very proud of belonging to this crack unit. There's a great contempt here for Whitehall clockwatchers.' The only people in the delegation who seemed to be less than exhilarated by it all were the poor Foreign Office secretaries, who regularly complained to their London supervisors that they couldn't understand the reams of dense material they had to type every day, and so lacked the usual diplomatic job satisfaction. It needed a blank kind of doggedness to churn out interminable papers from UKREP to FCO about 'Admission to the occupation of road haulage operator for national and international transport operations', or 'Proposal for a directive on the quality of surface water intended for the abstraction of drinking water in the member states'. It would have required a sharp sense of history and a penetrating imagination, as well as total indifference to fatigue, to realize that all those dull words spoke of creation, the simplest foundations of a new social order.

There was absolute commitment to the work in hand, complete devotion to standing fast in the Market. The renegotiation of terms, quite obviously, would have failed without them. The result of the referendum might easily have gone the other way, too. There is a percentage of any national vote which expresses a gut reaction of many people who are beyond the immediate influence of evidence and argument; the crucial voters are those who can be swayed this way or that by the tides of political presentation right up to the moment of ballot. It would be difficult to overestimate the influence on that floating vote of the civil service alliance in Whitehall combined with the activity of the British delegation in Brussels. For, however strongly the politicians felt about the issues of the Common Market, one way or the other, however clearly they believed they saw its implications for Britain, they were almost entirely dependent on the alliance and the delegation for their information. Government politicians in particular, whether working in Home or Foreign affairs, could not give the Common Market their undivided attention. When they came to Brussels to participate in negotiation, they were tail-enders in an event which, for sheer technical complexity, surpasses anything that has happened before in a congress of nations. A brilliant man in one of the FCO's European departments in London said at this time that he reckoned it took a full year of total concentration to understand properly how the Common Market works. Ministers rushing off to Brussels, feverish from their latest bout with the British trade unions, or anxious about an imminent round of international disarmament talks, could not avoid being steered through the next innings at the Charlemagne Palace by officials who alone knew precisely how the pitch was playing that day, and whether or not the ball was beginning to swing through the air. The progress of an EEC negotiation is quite as intricate and subtle as a game of cricket.

Those Ministers who wanted Britain out of the Market were at an even greater disadvantage. For they were in the hands of officials who, without being cynical, saw it as their duty to execute government policy to the best of their ability; and declared government policy was to remain in the Market as long as new terms could be negotiated to satisfy the national interest. Any healthy man will interpret such a declaration as an unmistakable political ambiguity. Officials, however, do not have much option but to read it literally and follow its purported drift. In Brussels, this meant that they saw it as legitimate and perfectly honourable practice to throw all their weight behind the emphasis on remaining in the Market, and to frustrate any attempts to turn the emphasis in the opposite direction. The codes of civil service say that at all times you support your own Minister in any conflict with another branch of government. That rule went overboard in Brussels. As one of the Home men put it, 'In conflict here, you would fix your eye on the collective government decision, and you'd try to blunt the impact of any Minister if you thought he was opposed to that decision.' As another said, 'What upsets us is when P. Shore comes out and buggers up the national interest as an anti-Marketeer. Do you know' – genuine astonishment in the voice here – 'in a speech

here last summer he more or less told the Market to get stuffed!'
So some of the Home civil servants in the delegation from time
to time quite deliberately kept their own departments in
London ignorant of what was going on in Brussels for a delicately balanced day or two, or even for a few vital hours. This
was not a betrayal of colleagues in Whitehall; it simply meant
that what Whitehall did not know, Whitehall could not pass on.
Even the men least enamoured of Foreign Office ways and
means, had occasion to give thanks for its grip on communications, for the times when a telegram from UKREP lingered in
the palazzo before the government messenger took it by hand
to its final destination.

They were all very relieved when the referendum was over.
And in many a corner of the Foreign Office, they decided they
deserved champagne that day.

One of the most ardent Europeans in the Office had said, a
few months before the vote, 'People who've been involved in the
European thing may not like it – there's a hell of a lot wrong
with it – but it's here and we've got to be part of it.' That man
was critical of the balance between the European Parliament
in Strasbourg, its secretariat in Luxembourg, the Council
machinery and the Commission in Brussels, and all the national
governments. He thought the degree of genuine expertise in the
Commission, as distinct from bureaucratic accomplishments,
was inadequate to deal with that in the governments. This exposed it to the endless procedural wrangles provoked by governments seeking to justify diplomatic activities of their own which
were not community-minded. The chief British apostle of
Europe, Sir Con O'Neill, has complained that the Community's
decisions are made far too slowly and elaborately except when
events, usually agricultural or monetary, cause them to be
accelerated. And when a proposal goes for a final decision and
enactment to the Council of Ministers 'the veil of confidentiality
falls; and I cannot deny that the ensuing process resembles
that of an inter-governmental conference. Its secrecy is, however, mercifully punctured, as a rule, by continual and exhaus-
tive leaks to the Press.'[1] Other critics have complained that the
thickest secrecy cloaks the Ambassadors in Coreper, the real
heart of Common Market decisions, which in nine cases out of

[1] O'Neill, p. 15.

ten are merely hallmarked by the superior Council of Ministers. But these voices are most scathing when they contemplate the composition of the Brussels Commission, arguing that its low calibre is chiefly responsible for the creation of scandalous Common Market food surpluses at enormous cost. 'Too many governments', according to one commentator, 'have found Brussels a convenient dumping ground for pensioned-off politicians or public figures. No more than a third of its thirteen members would reach a remotely exalted position in the affairs of their own countries.'[1]

Many British diplomats will privately admit all these things. Yet you would have to search very hard to find one who did not believe in Europe as the way ahead for Britain. This belief originally sprang from an immediate fear that, outside Europe, Britain would have been lost in a tight little corner of its own, without the power to negotiate anything worth having, without the resources to buy all that it needed. But beyond that fear, the diplomats have a concept of grand alliance which includes the integration of all things national. The economic fusion will be followed by the financial, and then the political. They do not doubt this for a moment: they see it as their job to help the process along. Sir Con O'Neill has seen something else, besides that: 'As a member of the Community, we shall recover some of the influence we have lost.'[2] Before too long, all Europeans will bear the same passport, bound within the limp covers that Lord Home of The Hirsel would defy unto death. This will be the symbol of the thing to come, the united Europe that can act as a real force in world affairs, as a body whose parts are not to be played off against each other any more. In their strenuous pursuit of this concept, the diplomats were soon to be confronted with the very hazard that the sardonic anti-Marketeers had warned the nation about. Less than six months after the referendum had sealed British membership, it became apparent what a hindrance multilateral commitments could be.

The renewed cod war with Iceland dramatically illustrated Britain's confusion about where she should – or could – stand in the matter of a 200-mile economic maritime zone, when she had to consider the claims of an alliance as well as her own.

[1] John Palmer, *Guardian*, March 29th, 1976.
[2] O'Neill, p. 21.

In the dispute with Reykjavik, London was hampered by the dragging weight of NATO – in essence, by that of Washington, whose own strategic needs were at stake. But the cod war was only the tip of an iceberg, by which the ship of state could be badly holed. Some time before the New York session of the Law of the Sea conference had convened in 1976, to adjudicate on territorial waters, economic zones, continental shelves and all relevant matters, many countries were fixing things to their own advantage in the good old-fashioned way of treating with each other in twosomes. The Americans, the Canadians, the Spanish, the Russians and the Poles were all involved in deals which would protect the waters 200 miles off their shores, and the Norwegians were of the same mind, too. But the British, a coastal people with maritime needs as vital as Iceland's, were anchored firmly to the fisheries policy of the EEC; and this had not yet been conclusively agreed. The British cynic could make his own choice of the reason why not. Was it because delay was to the benefit of Continentals, who could continue to plunder the island waters until the United Nations at some distant date forbade this? Or was it simply another symptom of a malaise prevalent in Brussels, where Transport Ministers, after a year of deliberation, had not even been able to agree about the standard size of juggernaut lorries rolling around the EEC roads?

Valedictory

Farewell to the Diplomatic Service?

The vision of Europe has transcended all anxieties about the future of British diplomacy, but now it incorporates them. At one time, all such anxieties were sheltered by a huge bulk of Empire, visible on every horizon. They continued during the illusionary moment of Commonwealth and they were perhaps at their sharpest when the nation was in no-man's-land. Today, they go on before the beckoning future of Europe. They are inseparable from the nation's ups and downs in whatever world it inhabits. They tend to be focused on 'the Foreign Office' without a proper discrimination between their true and their supposed source. The mythology of British institutions, one of the most powerful things in our collective folk memory, has seen to that. So has the secrecy attending diplomatic activity, which has kept every British citizen – from MPs downwards – in a state of deep ignorance about diplomatic performance, and generally incompetent to form reasoned judgments of it.

Even with the gift of hindsight, any summary of British foreign policy failures is bound, to some extent, to be arbitrary. Issues are rarely as clear-cut as the Suez disaster in 1956. A recent commentator, as informed as anyone can be outside the government itself, or the higher reaches of professional diplomacy, has enumerated seven distinct areas where British diplomacy has been found wanting since the Second World War: (1) a failure to interpret correctly developments in the Middle East before Suez; (2) acceptance, after 1950, in NATO rearmament negotiations, of a British contribution too great for us to bear; (3) the lack of a safeguard clause in the 1955 Bonn Agreements on the cost of maintaining British troops in Germany; (4) the failure between 1956 and 1958 to appreciate how committed were Continental governments to European integration; (5) short-sightedness in developing major bases in

Kenya and Aden in the early 1960s; (6) over-emphasis by successive governments on the relationship with the Commonwealth and the USA; (7) the failure to expect and to plan for Rhodesia's UDI.[1]

It would be unfair and unrealistic for anyone accepting that summary to lay the blame for the failures squarely on 'the Foreign Office'. The academic who drew up the list above went on to remark:[2]

One cannot escape the impression that successive Ministers have blamed their civil servants for lack of foresight and strategic thinking in foreign policy in the same way as bad workmen blame their tools; that it has been their reluctance to consider the possibility of choice, or to demand and decide upon clear alternatives, which has been the fundamental failure in British foreign policy over the last twenty years.

Given the structure of British government, and the power that ultimately resides in the hands of the politicians, it is difficult to quibble with that assessment. And yet it excludes so many factors which have been the topic of this book and which tend to modify in varying degree and in different circumstances, the power the politicians really have in the decision-making process. The very most this book can have hoped to achieve is a rough outline of what those factors can be. They do not all apply at any one time, and until state papers are examined there is no way of telling beyond shrewd assumption which ones have pressed any particular decision this way or that; leakage of information from either politicians or civil servants does not always – conceivably never – provide a wholly accurate account of anything. One fairly consistent factor in the making of British foreign policy since the war has been described by another outsider as 'the adoption of the line of least intellectual resistance ... geared, essentially, to the handling of problems as they arise, rather than to the definitions of goals and objectives in terms of which such problems as arise are to be dealt with'.[3] Excessive pragmatism is something which senior British diplomats freely

[1] Wallace, pp. 76–7.
[2] Wallace, p. 82.
[3] Vital, pp. 109–10.

concede about the formation of our foreign policy. What they never make clear is whence it springs.

Whatever is the true balance between the two, there is a responsibility belonging to the politicians alone for foreign policy, and another one which rests with the civil servants working in the sphere of diplomacy. Twenty years ago the civil servants' responsibility was almost entirely confined within the Foreign Office, the Commonwealth Relations Office and the Colonial Office. Now it is more vaguely located at a number of points along Whitehall, besides the Foreign and Commonwealth Office. The re-shaping of the world outside the UK, the increasing sophistication of mankind, has helped to fashion this shift of responsibility. Home civil servants have increasingly been drafted into our diplomacy because the expertise of the Diplomatic Service has been inadequate to compete with that of foreign officials negotiating specialized non-political matters with the British. Most conspicuous of all has been the accretion of responsibility (and the power that goes with it) by the Cabinet Office, and a number of things have contributed to this. British Prime Ministers, responding to a growing international taste for summitry, have come to regard it as their most useful all-purpose service station. Successive Cabinet Secretaries have been quite happy to enlarge their personal areas of influence. Officials from the State Department in Washington have, over the past few years, preferred more and more to confer with their 'opposite numbers' at the centre of things, instead of invariably dealing as tradition insisted with men in Gilbert Scott's palazzo, who might subsequently be overruled by an indistinct authority up the street. In all these ways has the pattern of civil service responsibility for foreign policy been changing over recent years.

'Such a development must call into question the separate existence of the Diplomatic Service.'[1] The question has been put in various quarters more than once in the past decade, but not until 1976 did it issue in black and white from a source as close to the Foreign Office as Chatham House. It was formed with some hesitation because, as the author well knew, few things in British life would be likely to produce more sales resistance than a government proposal for the integration of Home

---

[1] Wallace, p. 273.

civil servants and professional diplomats. As someone else has remarked, 'the very ferocity with which the proposal is so often resisted shows how near the bone it reaches'.[1] In spite of the changes wrought in the Foreign Office appliance since the war there is still built into the profession of diplomacy an elitist attitude that, among its British exponents, will not easily yield the manifest seal on its traditional primacy. The Foreign Office can still be caught harking back to its great old days with some nostalgic gesture, and the Chief Clerk's title, revived in 1970, was an example of this. It was a charming idea. But why did it happen? The Office can also be found in defensive postures when something more positive might serve its independent future better. Its response to increasing Home Civil Service involvement in foreign affairs has been to expand its functional departments in order to keep its end up in Whitehall; rather than to recruit the specialists who might have made Home men unnecessary to our diplomacy.

There is much more realism in the Diplomatic Service about the world it inhabits, at home and overseas, than is usually acknowledged in public. Its best men and women are mindful of the need for change, of one kind or another. Lord Trevelyan has written that 'Its members must adapt themselves to the new order of things, or they will find themselves engaged in little more than opening doors for the experts and acting as dispensers of government hospitality abroad ... '[2] Since becoming Head of the Diplomatic Service at the end of 1975, Sir Michael Palliser has let it be known along Whitehall that in his view it is extremely important for recruits to the Home Civil Service to be more adept in foreign languages, especially French, than has been the case so far. There are few people in the Foreign Office who do not concede that the appliance they serve is now too large for its purposes. This does not mean that they will applaud any outside attempt to enforce pronounced change in the Diplomatic Service. It remains to be seen, at the time of writing, whether the investigations of the Cabinet Office's 'think tank' eventually lead to a large reorganization of the Foreign Office. If the diplomats are obliged to dismantle some of its pieces, or to prepare for integration with the Home

[1] Brittan, p. 26.
[2] Trevelyan, p. 53.

Service, they will make just as much fuss as miners facing a pit closure; and for the same reason. Neither colliers nor diplomats may take kindly to being seen in some ways as equals. Yet the Queen's Commission flourished by one is no more a symbol of pride than the lodge banner borne by the other. Exemption from Customs duties may quite properly be weighed in the same scales as an allotment of free coal. And the Diplomatic Service Association pursues just the same aim as the National Union of Mineworkers.

Bibliography

The literature of British diplomacy is colossal and I cannot pretend to have read more than a small part of it. I could list sixty-odd books and official reports which I have read, basically to establish bearings before starting research on what is, essentially, a contemporary report on the FCO and British diplomacy. Two or three sentences in Chapter Eleven might not have been the same had I not reread a couple of chapters from *Orientations* by Sir Ronald Storrs (Nicholson & Watson, 1939); and the brief reference to *L'Affaire Soames* in Chapter Fifteen was mostly derived from the much lengthier account given by Uwe Kitzinger in his excellent *Diplomacy and Persuasion* (Thames & Hudson, 1973). I have, however, taken the view that it would be pretentious (as well as arbitrary) to run a reading list which includes many volumes that have little or no direct bearing on my own piece of work. The book list below is confined to publications from which I have quoted.

Boardman, R., and Groom, A. J. R., eds: *The Management of Britain's External Relations* (Macmillan, 1973).

Brittan, Sam: *Steering the Economy* (Penguin, 1970).

Brown, Lord George-: *In My Way* (Gollancz, 1970).

Busk, Sir Douglas: *The Craft of Diplomacy* (Pall Mall, 1967).

Cadogan, Sir Alexander: *The Diaries 1938–45*, ed. David Dilks (Cassell, 1971).

Clark, Eric: *Corps Diplomatique* (Allen Lane, 1973).

Duncan, Sir Val: *Report of the Review Committee on Overseas Representation 1968–1969* [The Duncan Report] (HMSO, 1969).

Gore-Booth, Lord: *With Great Truth and Respect* (Constable, 1974).

Kelly, Sir David: *The Ruling Few* (Hollis & Carter, 1952).

2F

Kirkpatrick, Sir Ivone: *The Inner Circle* (Macmillan, 1959).

McDermott, Geoffrey: *The New Diplomacy* (Plume Press, 1973).

O'Neill, Sir Con: *Our European Future* (London University Press, 1972).

Plowden, Lord: *Report of the Committee on Representational Services Overseas* [The Plowden Report] (HMSO, 1964).

Rumbold, Sir Horace: *Recollections of a Diplomatist* (Sampson-Low, 1902).

Satow, Sir Ernest: *Guide to Diplomatic Practice*, 4th edn, revised by Sir Nevile Bland (Longmans, 1957).

Steiner, Zara S.: *The Foreign Office and Foreign Policy 1898–1914* (Cambridge University Press, 1969).

Strang, Lord: *The Foreign Office* (Allen & Unwin, 1955).

Tint, Herbert: *French Foreign Policy Since the Second World War* (Weidenfeld, 1972).

Trevelyan, Humphrey: *Diplomatic Channels* (Macmillan 1973).

Vital, David: *The Making of British Foreign Policy* (Allen & Unwin, 1968).

Wallace, William: *The Foreign Policy Process in Britain* (Institute of International Affairs, 1975).

White, A. J. S.: *The British Council: the First 25 Years* (British Council, 1965).

Sixth Report from the Select Committee on Estimates; Session 1957–8 (HC 232, HMSO, 1958).

Fifth Report from the Expenditure Committee; Session 1971–2 – Diplomatic Staff and Overseas Accommodation (HC 344, HMSO, 1972).

Eighth Report from the Expenditure Committee; Session 1974–5 – Diplomatic Manpower and Property Overseas (HC 473, HMSO, 1975).

Index